P9-AFX-650

# CURRENT TOPICS IN LANGUAGE

## Introductory Readings

NANCY AINSWORTH JOHNSON
*Michigan State University*

WINTHROP PUBLISHERS, INC.
*Cambridge, Massachusetts*

**Library of Congress Cataloging in Publication Data**

Main entry under title:

Current topics in language: introductory readings.

Includes bibliographies.
1. Language and languages—Addresses, essays,
lectures. 2. Linguistics—Addresses, essays, lectures.
I. Johnson, Nancy Ainsworth
P106.C8     410     75-45304
ISBN 0-87626-169-1

© *1976 by Winthrop Publishers, Inc.*
17 Dunster Street, Cambridge, Massachusetts 02138

*All rights reserved.* No part of this book may be reproduced in
any form or by any means without permission in writing from
the publisher. Printed in the United States of America.

10   9   8   7   6   5   4

P106
C8

*For my family*

# Contents

# Foreword

During my twenty-five years in professional education, I have had the opportunity to see many innovations, concerns, and focuses in education come and go. As a profession we have sometimes become concerned with one aspect of education such as the way the child learns. Then money and effort are focused on the gifted for a period of time, or the slow learner or the culturally deprived or the dyslexic or the hyperactive or the learning disabled. When we get tired of one term we seem to develop a new term which often has the same definitions or characteristics that the old term had. At other times, method has been our concern and we have examined lecture, discovery, programmed learning, or other approaches to helping children learn. Still in other periods of time we have worried about how to organize the school or the classroom or the instructional materials center and we have concentrated on improving learning with self-contained rooms, departmentalized organizations, open corridors, or learning centers. Occasionally when academic people have been concerned with the results of twelve years of schooling we have concentrated on what we teach in our classrooms and have focused on special programs in math, linguistics, anthropology, or science.

We have seldom examined how all these concerns (for the learner, for the method, for organizing the learning environment, and for the content of what is to be learned) support learning as they interrelate and interact with each other as an educational dynamic.

When I was a young teacher I believed that someone who knew how to teach could teach anything to anybody. During the same period of time I often heard my friends who were going into academic fields proclaim in their put-down of professional education, "those who can, do; those who can't, teach." I still believe that knowing the art and science of teaching is basic to good teaching but my lack of concern for understanding the knowledge and structure of the discipline to be taught was as naive as the statement from my academic friends.

The separation of subject matter areas in education for the purpose of advanced study may be necessary to solve specific problems. But to separate them and then apply principles generated by studies conducted in carefully controlled, antiseptic, isolated laboratories, libraries, or university seminars to a dynamic vibrant classroom filled with complex human beings is fallacious and may be one reason for the little progress we seem to be making in professional education.

No matter how open a classroom can be, no matter how involved the student is in selecting his or her own learning experiences, no matter how positive the teacher in her or his approach, if the teacher does not understand the significance of the content to be taught, the learner will be deprived of a rich and full educational experience.

Not only have we focused on narrow aspects within the study of education but those fields of study that have something to say about language and learning—so basic to understanding the dynamics of the educational process—have often gone their separate ways and tried to give educators advice about how to teach from their own particular vantage points. I remember listening to a lecture given by Roman Jakobson about ten years ago when he said that the individual fields of study (psychology, sociology, anthropology, and linguistics) that examine language can go no further in their knowledge and understanding without working and studying together. I latched on to that statement, added teachers and teacher educators to his list and have advocated that approach ever since. In the years since that statement we have made some progress. There is new language to take care of some of our mutual concerns. There are psycholinguists and sociolinguists. Texts in the teaching of reading, English, and special education refer to scientists such as Charles Fries, Roger Brown, and Basil Bernstein. But we have a long way to go before we develop a concept of an interdisciplinary field one might call educanthrobiolopsycholosociolinguistics. It will take effort and commitment to learn to work together, to respect each other and to trust each other and our purposes. Educators are not always sure what linguists mean when they discuss syntax; psychologists and linguists argue about the definition or the existence of competence. Few of the academic groups are clear what the teacher educator means when he or she talks about "the language experience approach."

Nancy Johnson has done all of us a service. We are in desperate need of the kind of multilog presented in this book.

She has found articles written by sociolinguists, biologists, psychologists, linguists, psycholinguists, and educators who explore issues or present theoretical positions relating to language acquisition, language variation, grammar, and the reading process. Related to each area of concern there are also articles that discuss the merit and feasibility of applying the theoretical principles to the classroom. This book will be useful to those in applied fields of study concerned with language and learning. It will be especially useful to pre-service and inservice teachers.

YETTA GOODMAN

# Preface

My major aim in this book is to provide readings about language that form a coherent whole, so that a student can easily understand the relationships among the readings; a general introduction, four part introductions, article prefaces, and four summary articles all are designed to point out those interrelationships. Secondly, I've tried to relate these readings to teaching, in both general and specific ways—this is one of the major functions of the four summary articles. Finally, the book attempts to promote a critical, questioning approach to the large body of literature about language. I realize, of course, that these are ambitious aims, and I would not claim to have fully accomplished them. It seems to me, however, that the book is at present unique in taking these three directions.

The stands I have taken in my summary articles may seem unduly conservative or unduly radical, realistic or idealistic, and so on, depending upon the reader's own views. In any case, they should provide a point of departure for classroom discussion, discussion which can help develop the critical approach mentioned above.

Since the book does attempt to form a coherent whole from the many articles it contains, it can be used as a basic text. But I have also tried to make each article and section self-contained, reiterating major points and defining basic terms, so that the user can choose a starting point at any of a number of places.

My thanks go to Dotty Carringi, for generously giving me the benefit of her sound editorial judgment; to Elda Austin, for patiently producing page after page of beautifully typewritten manuscript, only to see it cut to ribbons and given back to be retyped; to the students whose lively minds and difficult questions pushed me to formulate many of the tentative answers given here —Dayna Reynolds, Paula Block, Yvonne McLravy, Barbi Mott, Curt Martin, and George Keeler, among others; to Yetta Goodman, David DeCamp, and Paul O'Connell for their advice and encouragement; and finally, to Beth and David Johnson and to Marion Ainsworth for their invaluable moral support, affection— and insistence that authors should also be human beings.

NANCY AINSWORTH JOHNSON

# Acknowledgments

Abrahams, Roger D., "Black Views of Language Use: Rules of Decorum, Conflict, and Men-of-Words." Reprinted from Roger D. Abrahams, *Positively Black*, © 1970. Reprinted by permission of Prentice-Hall, Inc., Englewood Cliffs, New Jersey.

Bailey, Mildred Hart, "The Utility of Phonic Generalizations in Grades One Through Six." Reprinted from *Reading Teacher*, February 1967. Reprinted with permission of the author and the International Reading Association.

Baratz, Joan C., "Reading and Black Dialect: A Review of the Literature." Reprinted from James L. Laffey and Roger Shuy, editors, *Language Differences: Do They Interfere?* Copyright © 1973 by the International Reading Association. Reprinted by permission of the author and the International Reading Association.

Bloom, Lois, "Why Not Pivot Grammar?" Excerpted from "Why Not Pivot Grammar?" *Journal of Speech and Hearing Disorders*, February, 1970. Reprinted by permission of the publisher and the author.

Dale, Philip S., "Dialect Differences and Black English." From *Language Development: Structure and Function*, by Philip S. Dale. Copyright © 1972 by The Dryden Press. Reprinted by permission of The Dryden Press.

Fader, Daniel N., and McNeil, Elton B., "Leeway in Matching Books and Children." Excerpted from *Hooked on Books* by Daniel N. Fader and Elton B. McNeil. Copyright © 1966 by Daniel N. Fader. Copyright 1968 by Daniel N. Fader and Elton B. McNeil. Reprinted by permission of Berkley Publishing Corporation, New York.

Fries, Charles C., "Language and Change." Excerpted from Charles C. Fries, "Implications of Modern Linguistic Science," *College English*, March, 1947. Reprinted by permission of the publishers and Mrs. Charles C. Fries.

Fries, Charles C., "Lexical and Structural Meaning." Excerpted from "Grammar from the Point of View of Structural Linguistics," mimeographed. Reprinted by permission of Mrs. Charles C. Fries.

Fromkin, Victoria, and Rodman, Robert, "Generative Phonology: Phonemes, Phonological Rules," and "Generative Syntax: Grammaticality, Phrase-Structure Rules." From *An Introduction to Language*, by Victoria Fromkin and Robert Rodman. Copyright © 1974 by Holt, Rinehart and Winston, Inc. Reprinted by permission of Holt, Rinehart and Winston.

Goodman, Kenneth, "Reading: A Psycholinguistic Guessing Game." Reprinted from *Journal of the Reading Specialist*, 1967, Vol. 4. Reprinted by permission.

Goodman, Kenneth S., and Buck, Catherine, "Dialect Barriers to Reading Comprehension Revisited." Reprinted from *Reading Teacher*, October 1973. Copyright 1973 by the International Reading Association. Reprinted by permission of the authors and the International Reading Association.

Goodman, Yetta, "Reading Comprehension: A Redundant Phrase." Reprinted from the *Michigan Reading Journal*, Spring 1975. Reprinted by permission.

Gough, Philip B., "The Limitations of Imitation." Reprinted from *New Directions in Elementary English*. Copyright © 1967 by the National Council of Teachers of English. Reprinted by permission of the publisher.

Gumperz, John J., and Hernández-Chavez, Eduardo, "A Visit to a California Classroom." Reprinted by permission of the publisher from John L. Gumperz and Eduardo Hernández-Chavez, "Bilingualism, Bidialectalism, and Classroom Interaction," in Courtney Cazden et al., eds., *Functions of*

*Language in the Classroom.* New York: Teachers College Press, copyright 1973 by Teachers College, Columbia University, pp. 101–105.

Herndon, Jeanne H., "Two Thousand Years of Language Study." From *A Survey of Modern Grammars,* by Jeanne H. Herndon. Copyright © 1970 by Holt, Rinehart and Winston, Inc. Reprinted by permission of Holt, Rinehart and Winston.

Jakobson, Roman, "Emergence of the Speech Sound." Excerpted from Roman Jakobson, *Child Language, Aphasia, and Phonological Universals,* 1968, Mouton and Co., Publishers, translated by A. Keiler. First published by Almgvist and Wiksell, 1941. Reprinted by permission of the publisher.

Joos, Martin, "The Styles of the Five Clocks." Excerpted from *The Five Clocks,* copyright 1967 by Martin Joos. Reprinted by permission of Harcourt Brace Jovanovich, Inc.

Judy, Stephen N., "Writing for the Here and Now." Reprinted from *English Journal,* January, 1973. Copyright © 1973 by the National Council of Teachers of English. Reprinted by permission of the publisher and the author.

Klima, Edward S., and Bellugi, Ursula, "Acquiring Negation and Questions." Condensed from "Syntactic Regularities in the Speech of Children," by Edward Klima and Ursula Bellugi, published in its original form in Lyons and Wales, editors, *Psycholinguistics Papers,* University of Edinburgh Press, 1966. Reprinted by permission of the authors, the publishers, and Aldine Publishing Company.

Labov, William, "Mitigation and Questioning in a Verbal Repertoire." Reprinted from pp. 51–59 of *The Study of Nonstandard English* by William Labov. Copyright © 1970 by the National Council of Teachers of English. Reprinted with permission.

Labov, William, "The Reflection of Social Processes in Linguistic Structures." Reprinted from Joshua Fishman, editor, *Readings in the Sociology of Language,* 1968, Mouton and Company, Publishers. Reprinted by permission of the author and the publisher.

Laird, Charlton. "Phonemes, Morphemes, and Meaning." From *Thinking About Language,* by Charlton Laird. Copyright © 1959 by Charlton Laird. Reprinted by permission of Holt, Rinehart and Winston.

Lambert, Wallace E., "The Advantage of Being Bilingual." Excerpted from Wallace E. Lambert, "A Social Psychology of Bilingualism," *Journal of Social Issues,* Vol. 23, No. 2 (1967). Copyright 1967 by the Society for the Psychological Study of Social Issues. Reprinted by permission of the publisher and the author.

Lenneberg, Eric H., "Language and General Intelligence." Reprinted from *New Directions in the Study of Language,* edited by Eric Lenneberg by permission of the M.I.T. Press, Cambridge, Massachusetts. © 1964 by the Massachusetts Institute of Technology.

Liles, Bruce L., "Generative Syntax: Transformational Rules—Negation, Questions." Reprinted from *An Introductory Transformational Grammar* by Bruce Liles. © 1971 by Prentice-Hall, Inc. Reprinted by permission.

Lindberg, Margaret, and Smith, Laura A., "Teaching Vocabulary as an Introduction to New Material: Is It Worthwhile?" Printed here for the first time by permission of Margaret Lindberg and Laura A. Smith.

Link, Terry, "22,000 'Retarded Children' Face Second Chance." Excerpted from *National Catholic Reporter,* February 4, 1970. Reprinted by permission of the National Catholic Reporter and the author.

Lyons, John, "Chomsky and the Creativity of Language." Reprinted with minor changes from *Noam Chomsky* by John Lyons. Copyright © 1970 by John Lyons. Reprinted by permission of The Viking Press, Inc., and the author.

Malmstrom, Jean, and Weaver, Constance, " 'Syntactic Maturity' and Syntactic Appropriateness in Teaching Writing." From *Transgrammar* by Jean Malmstrom and Constance Weaver. Copyright © 1973 by Scott, Foresman and Company. Reprinted by permission of the publisher.

McDavid, Raven I., Jr., "Language and Prestige: 'Standard English.' " Excerpted from Raven I. McDavid, "Go Slow in Ethnic Attributions: Geographic Mobility and Dialect Prejudices," in Richard W. Bailey and Jay L. Robinson, editors, *Varieties of Present-Day English*, 1973, The Macmillan Company. Reprinted by permission of the author.

McNeill, David, "The Pattern of Early Speech." Abridged from pp. 20–28 in *The Acquisition of Language* by David McNeill. Copyright © 1970 by David McNeill. By permission of Harper & Row, Publishers, Inc.

Miller, Wilma H., "The Language-Experience Approach to Reading." Excerpted from Wilma H. Miller, "A Critical Appraisal of the Language-Experience Approach to Reading." Retitled and reprinted by permission of the Wisconsin State Reading Association and the author.

Modiano, Nancy, "Juanito's Reading Problems: Foreign Language Interference and Reading Skill Acquisition." Reprinted from James L. Laffey and Roger Shuy, editors, *Language Differences: Do They Interfere?* Copyright © 1973 by the International Reading Association. Reprinted by permission of the International Reading Association.

Penfield, Wilder, "Language Learning and the Brain." Excerpted from Wilder Penfield, "Conditioning the Uncommitted Cortex for Language Learning," *Brain*, November, 1965. Reprinted by permission.

Rigg, A. G., editor, "The Facts of Linguistic Change: Old, Middle, Early Modern, and Modern English Versions of One Text." From A. G. Rigg, editor, *The English Language: A Historical Reader*, © 1968. Reprinted by permission of Prentice-Hall, Inc., Englewood Cliffs, New Jersey.

Rigg, Pat, "Reading for Speakers of English as a Second Language." This paper was presented at the International Reading Association convention, May, 1974. It appears here in published form for the first time, by permission of the author.

Saville, Muriel R., "First-Language Influences on Ethnic Dialects: Spanish and Navajo." Reprinted and retitled by permission of Harcourt Brace Jovanovich, Inc., from "Language and the Disadvantaged" by Muriel Saville in *Reading for the Disadvantaged: Problems of Linguistically Different Learners*, edited by Thomas D. Horn, © 1970 by Harcourt Brace Jovanovich, Inc.

Shuy, Roger W., "Discovering Regional Dialects." From *Discovering American Dialects* by Roger W. Shuy. Copyright © 1967 by the National Council of Teachers of English. Reprinted by permission of the publisher and the author.

Sledd, James, "Doublespeak: Dialectology in the Service of Big Brother." Reprinted from College English, January 1972. Copyright © 1972 by the National Council of Teachers of English. Reprinted by permission of the publisher and the author.

Slobin, Dan I., "They Learn the Same Way All Around the World." Reprinted from *Psychology Today* Magazine, July 1972. Copyright © 1972. Ziff-Davis Publishing Company. All rights reserved.

Stalker, James C., "Syntactic Ambiguity in the Poetic Dialect." Abridged from "The Poetic Dialect: Syntactic Ambiguity," mimeographed. Michigan State University, 1973. Reprinted by permission of the author.

Troike, Rudolph C., "Receptive Bidialectalism: Implications for Second-Dialect Teaching." From Roger D. Abrahams and Rudolph C. Troike, editors, *Language and Cultural Diversity in American Education*. Copyright © 1972 by Prentice-Hall, Inc. Reprinted by permission of the publisher.

Williamson, Juanita V., "Selected Features of Speech: Black and White." Reprinted from *CLA Journal*, June, 1970, by permission of the College Language Association and the author.

# QUESTIONS, INTERRELATIONS, AND APPLICATIONS: A General Introduction

## THE QUESTIONING PROCESS

Three ten-year-old girls were sitting on the floor discussing a comic book story entitled something like "Wonder Woman Battles Super Lizards"; it seems that the island home of Wonder Woman and her sister goddesses was under attack.

"Why does Wonder Woman live on an island?" questioned one child.

Child Number Two: "Because it's a paradise."

"Unh-uh!" objected the third girl. "It's not no paradise, with super lizards on it."

The year before this incident, one of these girls—my daughter, then about nine years old—had come home from school unhappy with her long skirt. Pants were her usual outfit. That morning at recess she had tripped on the skirt while chasing a boy in her class. The skirt was torn, her nose was scraped, and "I'm never going to wear no stinky dresses no more."

A prominent Greek-American in the Nixon administration had just been forced to resign his office, and an elderly Greek-American man in Detroit was asked by a television reporter to express his opinion. "I don't like nobody in the [Nixon] White House. All pigs got the same nose."

Why did I take special notice of these comments? Because they illustrate a conflict between my early beliefs about language and my later beliefs about language. Many of us grew up accepting without question a number of interrelated beliefs about truth, goodness, and beauty in relation to language:

> Children learn language by imitating their parents' speech. Unfortunately, many parents don't know how to talk. If only our schools would give children a good dose of grammar, their writing and their speaking both would clear up. The logical way to speak (called Standard English) is used by our community leaders; this form of language allows people to make themselves clear, and it is necessary for getting and keeping a job. Children need to learn this type of speech in order to understand what they read. Of course, if they aren't taught to sound out the letters of words, they won't learn to read anyway.

Among the details of this set of beliefs is the rule "Never use the double negative, for it is illogical and confusing; two negatives added together make one positive." This old view that "double negatives" are illogical, unclear, and fumbling is in direct conflict with my newer appreciation for the clarity, forcefulness, and relevance of the three comments—"It's not no paradise, with super lizards on it"; "I'm never going to wear no stinky dresses no more"; and "I don't like nobody in the White House. All pigs got the same nose."

"Double negatives" and "standard" negation are simply different ways of expressing the same thought; "double negatives" *are* the standard way of expressing negation in many languages, including French, Spanish, and some early forms of English itself. Even a brief acquaintance with the study of language will make that point quite clearly. This fact calls into question other common assumptions about language; if one belief is so wrong, all should be reviewed carefully.

We cannot simply dismiss all popular beliefs about language as unscientific; there may be elements of truth in these beliefs. After all, they have survived for quite a while, and that survival may be due to some basic strengths.

What if we poll our current authorities on language, asking for lists of worthless and worthwhile views about language? This would be an easy way out, and if it were feasible the following articles would be fewer and each would be briefer. The problem with this approach is that even if we find widespread agreement among our authorities, a list we make today will not take care of new claims that appear tomorrow.

Language study is always in flux; views of language are constantly being revised. In order to evaluate both old and new claims about language, we need to acquire critical approaches—tools for thinking critically about language, not answers prefabricated to meet the specific challenges that face us at present. We must acquire a *questioning process* rather than a list of questions and their answers. "How do small children acquire language?" is a question. "By imitation of their parents' speech," is an answer. But the *questioning process* goes further: "What proof do you have that children learn to speak by imitation? What evidence? What logical arguments?" An answer has to stand on its own evidence; the fact that some authority gave that answer is not enough.

Our problem is to compare the evidence for one answer with the evidence for another answer, and this is not easy. The task is complicated by answers that appear to be partly right and partly wrong, forcing us to sift out the good from the bad. Going through this questioning process may not be easy, but it has an exhilaration that simple answer-absorption does not; and it is the one approach that does not go out of style.

Probably the best way to develop our own critical tools is to vicariously experience other people's use of evidence. In the articles that follow, authors question all the common-sense beliefs we have mentioned. These articles center on four topics: the way language is acquired; reasons for variation in the way people speak; modern ways of describing language; and new views of what is happening when people read. Within each topic several controversial subtopics are treated:

| | |
|---|---|
| *Language acquisition:* | Is language partly controlled by biological processes? |
| | Do children learn language through imitation? |
| | Are "pivot-open" descriptions of early sentence structure accurate? |
| | What sociolinguistic abilities do children lack? |
| *Language variation:* | Does "Black English" exist? |
| | Are some children "verbally deprived," with their cognition affected by language? |

|                       | What problems in English are experienced by Mexican-American children whose home language is Spanish? |
| *Modern grammars:*    | What kinds of linguistic change are common? |
|                       | What are prescriptive versus descriptive grammars? |
|                       | What does a generative-transformational grammar include? |
| *The reading process:* | What—speaking generally—happens in the mind of a reader? |
|                       | Is phonics important in reading? |
|                       | Do "nonstandard" dialects interfere with reading? |

These are not all the questions covered, and, of course, not all sides of each question could be represented. But the views you will read are supported; these authors give reasons and evidence for the stands they take, and they give reasons for rejecting alternate positions. They realize that we can never have absolute perfection; any answer will have some weaknesses. But they also realize that some answers are far better than others. The most valuable experience a beginning student of language can have is that of following an author through the questioning process as the author explains the weaknesses and strengths of the alternate answers.

## INTERRELATIONS AND APPLICATIONS

Interrelations among the selections are the major focus of introductions and prefaces in this book, and these relationships receive a great deal of attention in the summary articles at the end of each section. The summary articles give equal attention to applications that the other articles have to teaching. Applications are not by any means confined to the summary articles, however; it is not always easy to separate theory from application, and a great many of the articles suggest applications as a natural outcome of their theoretical positions.

In fact, all the articles were chosen with applications in mind. Since theory and method are intimately related, this requirement did not prevent including important statements of theory; if anything, the requirement of applicability demanded the inclusion of major breakthroughs in understanding language and its use.

At the end of each section, two or three articles that focus on specific applications are provided, as well as my summary article that discusses the specific interrelations and applications of the earlier articles. Here again an attempt was made to include some current controversies that are subject to the questioning process. These topics include:

| | |
|---|---|
| *In language acquisition:* | How can writing become part of the natural language-learning process? |
| | Can children acquire two dialects at once? |
| *In language variation:* | What are the consequences of the "verbal deprivation" theory? |
| | Should users of nonstandard dialects be required to acquire "Standard English"? |
| *In modern grammars:* | Can transformational grammar be used to improve writing? |
| | Are linguistic analysis and poetry related? |
| *In the reading process:* | Are all reading "mistakes" equally important? |
| | Is teaching reading separate from teaching literature? |

## OVERVIEW OF LANGUAGE

Language consists of subsystems working together to produce a whole. In a sense it is artificial to deal with these subsystems separately, for language is a product of their interaction rather than of their addition. But these subsystems do have a degree of independent existence; we can discuss them separately. Thinking and talking about language in terms of these subsystems is much easier than trying to deal with all the forms and content of language under that one term, *language*. Many an hour has been wasted in arguments over the nature of "language," or "the language" of the ghetto child; we can head these arguments off—and use our time in more fruitful discussion of language in relation to philosophical and social problems—by beginning with questions like "What part of language are we dealing with? Its sounds? Its words? Sentence structure? Social expectations about its use?"

Following are some beginning definitions and descriptions of the parts and processes of language. The articles in the rest of this book will, of course, give more precise definitions and descriptions than can be given here; but novices in the study of 'language need to start with an overview, an introduction that will give them a broad frame of reference into which the following articles can, initially, be fitted. Those articles will in turn revise and refine the broader definitions given here.

## Phonology: Phonemes and Phonological Rules

The phonemes of a language and the rules for combining those phonemes are known as the *phonology* of that language. The description of these phonemes and rules is also called *phonology.*

Most of us are aware that other languages are composed of sets of sounds different from those of our native language. The sounds of a language are known as its *phonemes;* the phonemes of Spanish and the phonemes of English can be contrasted as follows: [1]

| PHONEMES OF ENGLISH | | | | | | PHONEMES OF MEXICAN SPANISH | | | |
|---|---|---|---|---|---|---|---|---|---|
| p | | t | č | k | | p | | t | č | k |
| b | | d | ǰ | g | | b | | d | | g |
| | f θ | s | š | | h | | f | s | | x |
| | v ð | z | ž | | | | | | | |
| m | | n | | ŋ | | m | | n | ñ | |
| w | | l | y | r | | w | | l | y | |
| | | | | | | | | r | | |
| | | | | | | | | r | | |
| iy | | uw | | | | i | | u | | |
| ɪ | | ʊ | | | | | | | | |
| ey | | ow | | | | e | | o | | |
| | ə | | | | | | | | | |
| ɛ | | ɔ | | | | | | | | |
| æ a | | | | | | | | a | | |

A complete definition of *phoneme* is given in Part 3 by Fromkin and Rodman. Laird, in Part 3, also gives a definition of the term.

---

[1] From Rudolph C. Troike, "English and the Bilingual Child," in *Contemporary English: Change and Variation,* ed. David L. Shores (Philadelphia: Lippincott, 1972), p. 310.

Fromkin and Rodman's discussion of phonemes is the more modern of the two; their article points out two dimensions of a phoneme's existence, the spoken representation and the underlying form, whereas Laird's earlier view deals only with the spoken representation.

Most of us are aware, also, that other languages allow phonemes to be combined in ways that English does not allow. In English a word can end with the combination [ts] [2], as in "pan*ts*"; but English does not allow a word to begin with that combination of sounds. If I develop a new product, I am not likely to call it a [tsIb]. Russian, on the other hand, does allow this combination of sounds at the beginning of a word, as in *Tsanoff*, the name of a Russian philosopher. These restrictions on the sound combinations that can build a word make up one kind of *phonological rule.*

Another kind of *phonological rule,* more important in describing language in actual use, creates the difference between the underlying form of a phoneme and its surface representation (the sound uttered by a speaker); Fromkin and Rodman, in Part 3, describe in detail the action of this type of rule. This second kind of phonological rule relates a phoneme to the phonemes that precede and follow it—its phonological environment. Perhaps the best known example is the rule, appearing in English dialects such as that of New York City, that deletes an /r/ when that /r/ is immediately followed by a consonant phoneme. In the underlying form of the word we spell "bird," there are four phonemes: the consonant /b/, a vowel, the consonant /r/, and the consonant /d/. But before the word is uttered, phonological rules are applied to its underlying form. One of these rules is the "*r*-dropping rule" we have just discussed. Since the /r/ in this word is followed by a consonant phoneme, it is deleted before the word is uttered. In the word we spell "bread," however, the underlying /r/ will not be deleted; it will be represented in the surface pronunciation by the [r], because it is followed by a vowel in this word.

A final point to make about phonological rules is that these rules can be variable. Syntactic rules, also, can be variable; but linguists have studied variable phonological rules much more closely than syntactic ones. A *variable* rule may or may not be applied to the underlying forms of a speaker's words and phrases;

[2] For explanations of brackets, slashes, and phonetic symbols, see the Appendix.

it is not categorically present or categorically absent. For instance, in New York City the "*r*-dropping rule" just discussed
is variable; it is applied to some percentage of /r/ phonemes
followed by consonants, not to all /r/ phonemes followed by consonants. The lower socioeconomic groups in the city use this "*r*-
dropping rule" more frequently than do the higher socioeconomic
groups. And all socioeconomic groups use the "*r*-dropping rule"
more frequently in casual speech than in formal situations. Labov,
in Part 2, gives details about these facts. In Part 4 this variability is related to oral reading; the presence or absence of a
language feature in oral reading can no longer be seen as a
simple yes-or-no indication of the presence of that feature in the
reader's language system as a whole. The possibility that this
feature is variable must be considered.

### Syntax: Morphemes, Syntactic Rules, and Semantics

The morphemes of a language and the rules for combining
those morphemes into sentences are known as the *syntax* of that
language. A *morpheme* is the smallest unit of meaning in a
word; examples include stem words, prefixes, and endings such
as the sounds [d] or [t],[3] written "-ed," that signal past tense.
One word can have more than one morpheme in it: the word
[lʌvd], spelled "loved," has two morphemes—the verb [lʌv],
"love," and the past tense morpheme, [d].

Just as the combining of phonemes is controlled by phonological rules, the combining of morphemes into sentences is controlled by *syntactic rules*. Two major approaches to the study
of syntactic rules have been used within the past several decades
in America. The structural approach was dominant from about
1930 until about 1960; out of one branch of structuralism grew
the transformational approach, which has been dominant since
about 1960.

Before contrasting these two major approaches, we should
briefly discuss their underlying *descriptive* goals. Both of these
approaches are *descriptive* rather than *prescriptive;* they attempt to describe language as it is rather than attempting to
enforce some set of views about the way language should be.
This descriptive approach has been much misinterpreted. People
who have not fully understood the descriptive approach have

---

[3] Whether this ending is represented by a [d] or a [t] depends on its
phonological environment.

often claimed that linguists oppose all standards for judging language.

This claim rests on use of the term *language* with no qualifications: if we take one meaning for the word, the claim is valid, but if we take another meaning for *language* the claim is not valid. A linguist thinks of language as a code, having phonological and syntactic rules. From this viewpoint, one linguistic code is not inherently better or worse than another. But no linguist would claim that social standards for the use of language are so trivial that they may be completely ignored; linguists abide by social standards in their own writing and speaking. The linguist using a descriptive approach does, however, insist that social standards for language use are arbitrary; such standards are based on social attitudes toward some type of language, not on any inherent flaw in the phonological and syntactic rules of that language. In Part 3, Herndon gives a brief account of the emergence of descriptive approaches to language study.

Of the two major descriptive approaches used today, *structural* linguistics was the first; Laird and Fries, in Part 3, state the structural emphasis on scientific observation of language, and they both say that structuralists avoid including meaning in their descriptions. Fries, however, makes it clear that structuralists did not completely ignore the need to consider meaning when describing language.

Not dealing with meaning limited structuralists' descriptions of language severely. In the late 1950s a second major kind of language study arose; *transformational* linguists suggested that the meaning of a sentence must be considered in describing sentence structure. For instance:

(1) John is easy to please.
(2) John is eager to please.

To a structuralist, these sentences are quite similar. To a transformationalist, they are quite different. The transformationalist considers the underlying meaning; in (1), John is being pleased; but in (2), John is pleasing someone else. The relationship between *John* and *please* in sentence (1) is not at all the same as the relationship between *John* and *please* in sentence (2).

Transformationalists want to capture the differing structures of the two sentences above in their description of syntactic rules. So they attempt to show how a sentence may be created, beginning with its basic meaning and then showing how the basic, underlying meaning is transformed into the final, or surface, sentence structure. Two kinds of syntactic rules make up this process of construction of a sentence: sentence-creating rules and sentence-transforming rules. The first kind is used by a speaker to create a simple, basic sentence, such as "John hit George"; the second kind transforms that basic sentence into variations such as the question "Did John hit George?" and the negative "John did not hit George." These two kinds of sentence-structure rules are called *phrase-structure* rules (used to construct basic phrases in the sentence) and *transformations*, or transformational rules.

In the articles that follow, these two kinds of syntactic rules are often important: in Part 1, we see that children first acquire the first kind of rule and then begin acquiring the second. In Part 2, we find that two dialects may use the same phrase-structure rules to create a basic sentence, but use slightly different transformations to form the final, surface structure; for instance, "It's not no paradise, with super lizards on it," differs from "It's not any paradise, with super lizards on it" only in a detail of one transforming rule—a detail that substitutes *no* in the sentence instead of *any*. In Part 4, several articles suggest that the dialect differences we saw in Part 2 may cause a reader to produce in oral reading some differences from the written text without losing any of the meaning of the text. Readers simply use some of their own sentence-transforming rules when uttering the sentence, rules that differ slightly from those used by the writer of the text.

The idea that language has an underlying level as well as a surface level ties together many of the following articles. Children have to acquire both levels; language variation is more common at the surface level than at the underlying level; modern grammars try to describe both levels; and reading involves finding the underlying meaning—exact reproduction of the surface structure may not be necessary to get that basic meaning.

The work collected here is interrelated in other ways, as well. True, the psycholinguistic study of language acquisition and of reading focuses on what is happening within one person's head; sociolinguists studying language variation focus on communication among people in groups; and modern grammars describe the abstract knowledge underlying language use, as far as this is possible. But in each of these fields awareness is growing that the three fields can never be entirely separated. In reality, language always occurs in the head of an individual who is communicating with others in a group, by means of shared knowledge of linguistic rules; and it is the purpose of this book to provide an integrated view of language, an understanding of the interrelationships among language acquisition, language variation, modern grammars, and reading.

Looking at these topics can give a coherent picture of language and the way it is studied. Applying the questioning process to the topics discussed here should build a fruitful approach to claims and counterclaims about language, no matter what the details of those claims may be. And the inclusion of applications and consequences of such claims should clarify the importance of acquiring both that overview and that questioning approach; for a native Spanish-speaking child placed in classes for the retarded, and a tenth-grade boy who has been told for ten years that he cannot read, are people in our society whose problems result from our own general, societal lack of information about language and how it is used.

# 1

# LANGUAGE
# ACQUISITION

## Introduction

Beth, 7, and her brother David, 5, walked just ahead of me into the living room of a new friend's apartment. Confronting us was a large poster from *Easy Rider*, showing Dennis Hopper sitting on a motorcycle, lounging back on the seat and presenting to the world a classic obscene gesture made by raising one finger. My children and I stared. I was transfixed; I assumed that my children would go home and insult their friends with this new gesture, bringing angry neighborhood women to my door.

David spoke first: "Why is he trying to hitchhike? He's got a motorcycle."

Beth was disdainful. "Stupid. He's out of gas."

The moral of this story is that children do not interpret adult symbols the way adults do; they have their own communication systems, which are often substantially different from those of adults. In recent years psychologists and linguists have tried to approach these systems without assuming, as I did, that adults and children are using the same system. I expected my children to notice which finger was raised, and to link this gesture with the defiance in the motorcyclist's expression. But they—sheltered middle-class children that they were—interpreted what they saw using their own previously established set of categories. At this point, they had only one category into which they placed all raised fingers: *hitchhiker*. Later they would learn that adults make distinctions between one raised finger and another.

The intense study of children's language acquisition which began around 1960 has uncovered some surprising and very interesting facts. First, there are universal characteristics of language acquisition. Second, it seems highly unlikely that language is acquired through imitation. Third, biological factors appear to play an important role in the acquisition of language. And finally, we can find stages in the acquisition of language—in the acquisition of the sound system, the sentence structure, the semantic system, and the sociolinguistic abilities of children.

Part 1 considers in order the list of ideas just given, applying the questioning process to each claim and ending with suggestions for applying these ideas to teaching.

## EVALUATING LANGUAGE ACQUISITION RESEARCH

There are special problems for researchers studying language acquisition. The broad-scale investigation of children's language systems has been taking place for a comparatively short time, giving researchers less to build upon than is available in other fields. In attempts to isolate stages of development, it is difficult to find subjects who can be studied over a long period of time. And collecting language data is a staggering task; children, like adults, utter enormous numbers of words in short periods of time. However, they may or may not utter the particular language structures you are studying, and trying to get them to utter these structures is far more difficult than questioning and testing adults.

Finally, the study of child language acquisition is a special kind of project; it resembles study of a completely new language. Of course child language can be analyzed in terms of adult language to some extent, and Bloom points out that it is important to see relationships between the two. But researchers hope to avoid preconceived categories in listening to children. They are interested in the child's grammar, or set of language rules, not in repeating adult grammars. If you were studying a completely new language, in order to discover its new grammar you would find it more profitable to follow one speaker around all day than to listen to twenty speakers for fifteen minutes each. For these several reasons, then, many studies of child language involve only a few children. Over all, a great many children have been studied; and child language researchers try to incorporate information from these other studies into each small-scale project they report.

## STAGES OF LANGUAGE ACQUISITION

A brief overview of the stages of language acquisition is appropriate, to help put in perspective the details of the following articles.

### Phonology

The first speech sounds most children make are a consonant made far in the front of the mouth and a contrasting vowel made far in the back of the mouth. Children seem to perceive gross contrasts first, and then break these down into subtler contrasts.

Front consonants made with the lips (as far front as the child can get) are /b/, /p/, and /m/. The vowel that is farthest back is /a/. Combinations of these produce the nursery words in many of the world's languages, as Jakobson points out.

Usually a child will acquire sounds in classes; first a *stop* consonant, then a *nasal* consonant, and then a *continuant* (meaning: a consonant made by completely stopping the flow of air through the mouth, like /p/; one made by vibrating air in the nasal passages, like /n/; and one made with a continuous flow of air through the mouth, like /s/, respectively). The child will then proceed to break down the category into kinds of stops, kinds of nasals, and so on.

The sound /r/ and the two sounds spelled in English with "th" are acquired late, as are consonant clusters.

### Syntax

Children have two main kinds of syntactic abilities to acquire: sentence-creating abilities and sentence-transforming abilities; beginning definitions of these abilities are given in the general introduction's overview of language, and the two abilities are explained in detail in Part 3 by Fromkin and Rodman and by Liles. Sentence-creating abilities allow a child to create a simple, basic sentence such as *Mary hit John*. The second, sentence-transforming set of abilities allows the child to transform that simple sentence into some variation on the basic sentence pattern, such as a question—*Did Mary hit John?*—or a negative sentence, *Mary didn't hit John.*

These two kinds of syntactic abilities are acquired in four general stages. The first of these is the *holophrastic* stage, in which the child is limited to uttering one morpheme at a time. This one morpheme, however, appears to stand for a complete sentence when the context of the utterance is considered. Examples: the child points to a round streetlight and says, "Moom!" ("There's a moon!") ; the child finishes eating a bowl of cereal and begins banging the highchair with a spoon and yelling, "Moey!" ("Give me more!").

Next comes the *telegraphic* stage, in which the child can utter more than one morpheme at a time but leaves out inflections (such as the past-tense signal spelled -*ed* in "loved") and function words (*the, of, with*, etc.). At first in the telegraphic stage the child can utter only two morphemes at a time; but he manages to convey a number of differing phrase structures and sentence structures with these two words. Examples:

> Noun phrases consisting of a modifier (M) plus a noun (N) :
> $M + N$
> Two sock
> Big boot
> My mommy
>
> Verb phrases consisting of a verb (V) plus a noun (N) :
> $V + N$
> See truck
> Put truck
>
> Nouns as subject and object of a sentence, verb omitted:
> $N + N \; (= N + V + N)$
> Eve lunch (= Eve is eating lunch)

Examples of three-word telegraphic sentences uttered by children:

> Kim go bye-bye
> That a horse
> Put truck window
> There go one
> No fall down
> Here big truck

The third stage of acquisition of syntax is one without the major limits on the length of sentences seen in the previous two stages, and with the inflections and function words that were missing in the telegraphic stage. But these inflections and endings may be used in ways no adult would use them. Example: "Why did Joe fighting me?"

The last stage of acquiring syntactic abilities is, of course, the stage of full control of adult syntax.

# Modes of Language Learning: Rule-forming Versus Imitation

## They Learn the Same Way All Around the World

DAN I. SLOBIN

Slobin explains that children everywhere go through the same general stages of language acquisition, in the same order. The existence of these universals in children's language suggests two things; first, language is not learned through imitation; if it were, children in two different cultures would acquire language in different ways. Second, there are biological limits on acquiring language. Like walking—another universal human attribute— talking apparently is based in physical, biological structures in the brain, structures which develop progressively greater abilities as the child's overall physical growth takes place.

In the subsequent selections, Philip Gough and Wilder Penfield discuss the roles of imitation and biology, respectively, in acquiring language. Then several authors give details (as far as they are known) of the stages in which sounds, sentence structures, and sociolinguistic abilities are acquired.

According to the account of linguistic history set forth in the book of Genesis, all men spoke the same language until they dared to unite to build the Tower of Babel. So that men could not cooperate to build a tower that would reach into heaven, God acted to "confound the language of all the earth" to insure that groups of men "may not understand one another's speech."

What was the original universal language of mankind? This is the question that Psammetichus, ruler of Egypt in the seventh century B.C., asked in the first controlled psychological experiment in recorded history—an experiment in developmental psycholinguistics reported by Herodotus:

"Psammetichus . . . took at random, from an ordinary family, two newly born infants and gave them to a shepherd to be brought up amongst his flocks, under strict orders that no one should utter a word in their presence. They were to be kept by themselves in a lonely cottage. . . ."

Psammetichus wanted to know whether isolated children would speak Egyptian words spontaneously—thus proving, on the premise that ontogeny recapitulates phylogeny, that Egyptians were the original race of mankind.

In two years, the children spoke their first word: *becos,* which turned out to be the Phrygian word for bread. The Egyptians withdrew their claim that they were the world's most ancient people and admitted the greater antiquity of the Phrygians.

SAME. We no longer believe, of course, that Phrygian was the original language of all the earth (nor that it was Hebrew, as King James VII of Scotland thought). No one knows which of the thousands of languages is the oldest—perhaps we will never know. But recent work in developmental psycholinguistics indicates that the languages of the earth are not as confounded as we once believed. Children in all nations seem to learn their native languages in much the same way. Despite the diversity of tongues, there are linguistic universals that seem to rest upon the developmental universals of the human mind. Every language is learnable by children of preschool-age, and it is becoming apparent that little children have some definite ideas about how a language is structured and what it can be used for:

*Mmm, I want to eat maize.*
What?
*Where is the maize?*
There is no more maize.
*Mmm.*
Mmm.
[Child seizes an ear of corn]:

*What's this?*
It's not our maize.
*Whose is it?*
It belongs to grandmother.
*Who harvested it?*
They harvested it.
*Where did they harvest it?*
They harvested it down over there.
*Way down over there?*
Mmm. [yes]
*Let's look for some too.*
You look for some.
*Fine.*
Mmm.
[Child begins to hum]

The dialogue is between a mother and a two-and-a-half-year-old girl. Anthropologist Brian Stross of the University of Texas recorded it in a thatched hut in an isolated Mayan village in Chiapas, Mexico. Except for the fact that the topic was maize and the language was Tzeltal, the conversation could have taken place anywhere, as any parent will recognize. The child uses short, simple sentences, and her mother answers in kind. The girl expresses her needs and seeks information about such things as location, possession, past action, and so on. She does not ask about time, remote possibilities, contingencies, and the like—such things don't readily occur to the two-year-old in any culture, or in any language.

Our research team at the University of California at Berkeley has been studying the way children learn languages in several countries and cultures. We have been aided by similar research at Harvard and at several other American universities, and by the work of foreign colleagues. We have gathered reasonably firm data on the acquisition of 18 languages, and have suggestive findings on 12 others. Although the data are still scanty for many of these languages, a common picture of human-language development is beginning to emerge.

In all cultures the child's first word generally is a noun or proper name, identifying some object, animal, or person he sees every day. At about two years—give or take a few months—a child begins to put two words together to form rudimentary sentences. The two-word stage seems to be universal.

To get his meaning across, a child at the two-word stage relies heavily on gesture, tone and context. Lois Bloom, professor of speech, Teachers College, Columbia University, reported a little American girl who said *Mommy sock* on two distinct occasions: on finding her mother's sock and on being dressed by her mother. Thus the same phrase expressed possession in one context (*Mommy's sock*) and an agent-object relationship in another (*Mommy is putting on the sock*).

But even with a two-word horizon, children can get a wealth of meanings across:

IDENTIFICATION: *See doggie.*
LOCATION: *Book there.*
REPETITION: *More milk.*
NONEXISTENCE: *Allgone thing.*
NEGATION: *Not wolf.*
POSSESSION: *My candy.*
ATTRIBUTION: *Big car.*
AGENT-ACTION: *Mama walk.*
AGENT-OBJECT: *Mama book* (meaning, "Mama read book").
ACTION-LOCATION: *Sit chair.*
ACTION-DIRECT OBJECT: *Hit you.*
ACTION-INDIRECT OBJECT: *Give papa.*
ACTION-INSTRUMENT: *Cut knife.*
QUESTION: *Where ball?*

The striking thing about this list is its universality. The examples are drawn from child talk in English, German, Russian, Finnish, Turkish, Samoan and Luo, but the entire list could probably be made up of examples from two-year-old speech in any language.

WORD. A child easily figures out that the speech he hears around him contains discrete, meaningful elements, and that these elements can be combined. And children make the combinations themselves—many of their meaningful phrases would never be heard in adult speech. For example, Martin Braine studied a child who said things like *allgone outside* when he returned home and shut the door, *more page* when he didn't want a story to end, *other fix* when he wanted something repaired, and so on. These clearly are expressions created by the child, not mimicry of his parents. The matter is especially clear in the Russian language, in which noun endings vary with the role the noun plays in a sentence. As a rule, Russian children first use only the nominative ending in all combinations, even when it is grammatically incorrect. What is important to children is the *word*, not the ending; the *meaning*, not the grammar.

At first, the two-word limit is quite severe. A child may be able to say *daddy throw*, *throw ball*, and *daddy ball*—indicating that he understands the full proposition, *daddy throw ball*—yet be unable to produce all three words in one stretch. Again, though the data are limited, this seems to be a universal fact about children's speech.

TOOLS. Later a child develops a rudimentary grammar within the two-word format. These first grammatical devices are the most basic formal tools of human language: intonation, word order, and inflection.

A child uses intonation to distinguish meanings even at the one-word stage, as when he indicates a request by a rising tone, or a demand with a loud, insistent tone. But at the two-word stage another device, a contrastive stress, becomes available. An English-speaking child might say BABY *chair* to indicate possession, and *baby* CHAIR to indicate location or destination.

English sentences typically follow a subject-verb-object sequence, and children learn the rules early. In the example presented earlier, *daddy throw ball*, children use some two-word combinations (*daddy throw, throw ball, daddy ball*) but not others (*ball daddy, ball throw, throw daddy*). Samoan children follow the standard order of possessed-possessor. A child may be sensitive to word order even if his native language does not stress it. Russian children will sometimes adhere strictly to one word order, even when other orders would be equally acceptable.

Some languages provide different word-endings (inflections) to express various meanings, and children who learn these languages are quick to acquire the word-endings that express direct objects, indirect objects and locations. The direct-object inflection is one of the first endings that children pick up in such languages as Russian, Serbo-Croatian, Latvian, Hungarian, Finnish and Turkish. Children learning English, an Indo-European language, usually take a long time to learn locative prepositions such as *on, in, under*, etc. But in Hungary, Finland, or Turkey, where the languages express location with case-endings on the nouns, children learn how to express locative distinctions quite early.

PLACE. Children seem to be attuned to the ends of words. German children learn the inflection system relatively late, probably because it is attached to articles (*der, die, das*, etc.) that appear before the nouns. The Slavic, Hungarian, Finnish and Turkish inflectional systems, based on noun suffixes, seem relatively easy to learn. And it is not just a matter of articles being difficult to learn, because Bulgarian articles which are noun suffixes are learned very early. The relevant factor seems to be the position of the grammatical marker relative to a main content word.

By the time he reaches the end of the two-word stage, the child has much of the basic grammatical machinery he needs to acquire any particular native language: words that can be combined in order and modified by intonation and inflection. These rules occur, in varying degrees, in all languages, so that all languages are about equally easy for children to learn.

GAP. When a child first uses three words in one phrase, the third word usually fills in the part that was implicit in his two-word statements. Again, this seems to be a universal pattern of development. It is dramatically explicit when the child expands his own communication as he repeats it: *Want that . . . Andrew want that.*

Just as the two-word structure resulted in idiosyncratic pairings, the three-word stage imposes its own limits. When an English-speaking child wishes to add an adjective to the subject-verb-object form, something must go. He can say *Mama drink coffee* or *Drink hot coffee,* but not *Mama drink hot coffee.* This developmental limitation on sentence span seems to be universal: the child's mental ability to express ideas grows faster than his ability to formulate the ideas in complete sentences. As the child learns to construct longer sentences, he uses more complex grammatical operations. He attaches new elements to old sentences (*Where I can sleep?*) before he learns how to order the elements correctly (*Where can I sleep?*). When the child learns to combine two sentences he first compresses them end-to-end (*the boy fell down that was running*) then finally he embeds one within the other (*the boy that was running fell down*).

ACROSS. These are the basic operations of grammar, and to the extent of our present knowledge, they all are acquired by about age four, regardless of native language or social setting. The underlying principles emerge so regularly and so uniformly across diverse languages that they seem to make up an essential part of the child's basic means of information processing. They seem to be comparable to the principles of object constancy and depth perception. Once the child develops these guidelines he spends most of his years of language acquisition learning the specific details and applications of these principles to his particular native language.

*Work Done*

| Indo-European Family | Other Families |
|---|---|
| *Romance Branch:*<br>Italian, Spanish, French, Romanian | *Semitic Family*<br>Hebrew, Arabic |
| *Germanic Branch:*<br>English, Dutch, German, Danish, Swedish, Norwegian | *Uralic Family*<br>Finnish, Hungarian |
| *Slavic Branch:*<br>Russian, Polish, Czech, Slovenian, Serbo-Croatian, Bulgarian | *Turkish Family*<br>Turkish |
| *Baltic Branch:*<br>Latvian | *South Caucasian Family*<br>Georgian (spoken in Georgian Soviet Socialist Republic) |
|  | *Eastern Sudanic Family*<br>Luo (spoken in Kenya) |
|  | *Korean Family*<br>Korean |
|  | *Japanese-Ryukyuan Family*<br>Japanese |
|  | *Han Chinese Family*<br>Mandarin |
|  | *Bodo-Naga-Kachin Family*<br>Garo (spoken in Assam, India) |
|  | *Austronesian Family*<br>Samoan |
|  | *Mayan Family*<br>Tzeltal (spoken in Yucatan) |

The available material varies greatly, from detailed observational and experimental studies to brief and anecdotal reports. We have reasonably firm data on about 18 of these languages. In addition, I am aware of ongoing research on the acquisition of the following native languages: Kurdish, Persian, Armenian, Albanian, Ukranian, Swahili, Koya, Tagalog and Quechua. The language classification in this table comes from the University of Indiana language archives (C. F. Voegelin and F. M. Voegelin). —Dan Slobin

LAPSE. Inflection systems are splendid examples of the sort of linguistic detail that children must master. English-speaking children must learn the great irregularities of some of our most frequently used words. Many common verbs have irregular past tenses: *came, fell, broke.* The young child may speak these irregular forms correctly the first time—apparently by memorizing a separate past tense form for each verb—only to lapse into immature talk (*comed, falled, breaked*) once he begins to recognize regularities in the way most verbs are conjugated. These over-regularized forms persist for years, often well into elementary school. Apparently regularity heavily outranks previous practice, reinforcement, and imitation of adult forms in influence on children. The child seeks regularity and is deaf to exceptions.

The power of apparent regularities has been noted repeatedly in the children's speech of every language we have studied. When a Russian noun appears as the object of a sentence (*he liked the story*), the speaker must add an accusative suffix to the noun—one of several possible accusative suffixes, and the decision depends on the gender and the phonological form of the particular noun (and if the noun is masculine, he must make a further distinction on whether it refers to a human being). When the same noun appears in the possessive form (*the story's ending surprised him*) he must pick from a whole set of possessive suffixes, and so on, through six grammatical cases, for every Russian noun and adjective.

GRASP. The Russian child, of course, does not learn all of this at once, and his gradual, unfolding grasp of the language is instructive. He first learns at the two-word stage that different cases are expressed with different noun-endings. His strategy is to choose one of the accusative inflections and use it in all sentences with direct objects regardless of the peculiarities of individual nouns. He does the same for each of the six grammatical cases. His choice of inflection is always correct within the broad category—that is, the prepositional is always expressed by *some* prepositional inflection, and dative by *some* dative inflection, and so on, just as an English-speaking child always expresses the past tense by a past-tense inflection, and not by some other sort of inflection.

The Russian child does not go from a single suffix for each case to full mastery of the system. Rather, he continues to reorganize his system in successive sweeps of over-regularizations. He may at first use the feminine ending with all accusative nouns, then use the masculine form exclusively for a time, and only much later sort out the appropriate inflections for all genders. These details, after all, have nothing to do with meaning, and it is meaning that children pay most attention to.

BIT. Once a child can distinguish the various semantic notions, he begins to unravel the arbitrary details, bit by bit. The process apparently goes on below the level of consciousness. A Soviet psychologist, D. N. Bogoyavlenskiy, showed five- and six-year-old Russian children a series of nonsense words equipped with Russian suffixes, each word attached to a picture of an object or animal that the word supposedly represented. The children had no difficulty realizing that words ending in augmentative suffixes were related to large objects, and that those ending in diminutives went with small objects. But they could not explain the formal differences aloud. Bogoyavlenskiy would say, "Yes, you were right about the difference between the animals—one is little and the other is big; now pay attention to the words themselves as I say them: *lar-laryonok*. What's the difference between them?" None of the children could give any sort of answer. Yet they easily understood the semantic implications of the suffixes.

TALK. When we began our cross-cultural studies at Berkeley, we wrote a manual for our field researchers so that they could record samples of mother-child interaction in other cultures with the same systematic measures we had used to study language development in middle-class American children. But most of our field workers returned to tell us that, by and large, mothers in other cultures do not speak to children very much—children hear speech mainly from other children. The isolated American middle-class home, in which a mother spends long periods alone with her children, may be a relatively rare social situation in the world. The only similar patterns we observed were in some European countries and in a Mayan village.

This raised an important question: Does it matter—for purposes of grammatical development—whether the main interlocutor for a small child is his mother?

The evidence suggests that it does not. First of all, the rate and course of grammatical development seem to be strikingly similar in all of the cultures we have studied. Further, nowhere does a mother devote great effort to correcting a child's grammar. Most of her corrections are directed at speech etiquette and communication, and, as Roger Brown has noted, reinforcement tends to focus on the truth of a child's utterance rather than on the correctness of his grammar.

GHETTO. In this country, Harvard anthropologist Claudia Mitchell-Kernan has studied language development in black children in an urban ghetto. There, as in foreign countries, children got most of their speech input from older children rather than from their mothers. These children learned English rules as quickly as did the middle-class white children that Roger Brown studied, and in the same order. Further, mother-to-child English is simple—very much like child-to-child English. I expect that our cross-cultural studies will find a similar picture in other countries.

How. A child is set to learn a language—any language—as long as it occurs in a direct and active context. In these conditions, every normal child masters his particular native tongue, and learns basic principles in a universal order common to all children, resulting in our adult Babel of linguistic diversity. And he does all this without being able to say how. The Soviet scholar Kornei Ivanovich Chukovsky emphasized this unconscious aspect of linguistic discovery in his famous book on child language, *From Two to Five:*

"It is frightening to think what an enormous number of grammatical forms are poured over the poor head of the young child. And he, as if it were nothing at all, adjusts to all this chaos, constantly sorting out into rubrics the disorderly elements of the words he hears, without noticing as he does this, his gigantic effort. If an adult had to master so many grammatical rules within so short a time, his head would surely burst. . . . In truth, the young child is the hardest mental toiler on our planet. Fortunately, he does not even suspect this."

## The Limitations of Imitation

PHILIP B. GOUGH

There are some major objections to the idea that a child learns language through simple imitation, and there are reasons to think instead that the child learns language by first noticing a pattern, or rule, that governs the language he hears, and then internalizing that rule. This process cannot be called imitation because these patterns are abstract, contrasting to something concrete like a sound. A sound can be echoed, or imitated, but an abstract pattern cannot.

A child may notice that past tense is shown by attaching an ending to verbs: "I walked," as opposed to "I walk." At first the child will use this ending for all verbs: "I falled down and hurted myself." Then imitation does come into play, as he notices exceptions to the rule and imitates these exceptions *(fell, saw, had).* In both cases—rule-forming and imitation—the child learns primarily from being exposed to language in context, not from explicit instruction by an adult.

Gough relies on examples of sentence structure to support his view, but the way children acquire speech sounds also supports his stand. Later in Part 1 Roman Jakobson describes universals in acquiring these sounds, universals that could not exist if language were acquired by simple imitation.

The child must be taught many things in school, but before he gets there he has learned something without which he could scarcely be taught anything at all; he has learned his native language. This fact is so commonplace that it has failed to excite our wonder, in part because we have thought we understood if not in detail, at least in outline, the way in which language is acquired. But recent work in psycholinguistics suggests that language is not learned in the way we have supposed, that the child's feat is far more wonderful than we have imagined.

In this paper, I hope to illustrate this work by showing how it casts doubt on what I take to be the traditional and prevailing view of language acquisition, that language is learned largely through imitation. In this view, the child tries to mimic his parents' speech. If he is successful, he is reinforced; if he errs, he is corrected. Once he has mastered certain forms, he will generalize what he has learned to create novel utterances, he will extend what he knows by analogy.

If one means by *imitation* simply that the child learns the language of his parents, then we cannot doubt that the child learns through imitation, for that is a fact. If they speak English, then so will he. But *imitation* is typically not used simply to describe this fact; it is used to explain it, to describe a process by which the child comes to speak like his parents. In this usage, the meaning of imitation is vague, but it clearly suggests a humble, mechanical process, one devoid of complex mental or intellectual activity, so that, in the extreme, the child is seen to resemble a parrot, or a kind of biological tape recorder, storing parental utterances for use at an appropriate moment.

It is this latter view of imitation I wish to challenge, for I hope to show that whatever the process of language acquisition, its accomplishment demands a high order of cognitive activity on the part of the child.

There are two ways to evaluate an hypothesis about the way something is learned. One is to observe how the learning develops, to see if it proceeds as it should; the other is to examine the final achievement, the product of learning, to see if it could have been learned in that way. Both of these tests can be applied to imitation as an hypothesis about language learning. Let us begin by examining the course of language learning.[1]

## THE COURSE OF LANGUAGE LEARNING

Sometime around his second birthday, a child begins to sound like a man. Prior to this, he has mastered, to a reasonable degree of approximation, the phonology of his language, and he has acquired a workable vocabulary. But he has been limited to single-word utterances. Now he takes an important step toward linguistic adulthood; he begins to utter sentences.

The child's earliest sentences are not adult sentences. When we hear "Ride horsie" or "Want apple" or "White sweater on," we know that we are not listening to an adult. We should also recognize that we are not listening to an accurate imitation of adult speech, for these sentences are not good English. If the small child is a tape recorder, he is a faulty one, for he seldom produces a faithful reproduction of an adult sentence.

The metaphor of a faulty tape recorder holds, however. The child's productions do not appear to be random combinations of words; they look like recordings of adult sentences in which some words and word endings have been skipped, for we can add a word or affix here and there to the child's utterances and get good sentences like "I want to ride a horsie" and "I want an apple." We have little trouble in understanding the child's sentences, and we might conceive of the child as producing economical imitations of adult sentences, leaving out redundant and uninformative elements. In fact, Brown and Fraser (1964) have observed that childish sentences are similar to those produced by an adult when words cost him money; they are telegraphic. Thus we might maintain that the child's telegraphic productions are simply imitations with omission.

---

[1] The author's research is supported by a grant from the U. S. Public Health Service (MH11869 01).

If this is the case, then it behooves us to explain his omissions. One possibility is that they are simply failures of memory. When we use the term *imitation,* we use it loosely, for the child seldom echoes adult speech. His imitations, if they are such, are usually not immediate; they are delayed. It seems reasonable to suppose that he simply forgets parts of the utterance he is reproducing, and the result is "telegraphese."

If the child's telegraphic sentences are poorly remembered imitations, we would expect his direct and immediate imitations to be accurate. The child occasionally does produce immediate imitations, and, in fact, we can ask him to. Brown and Fraser (1964) have asked two- and three-year-old children to repeat sentences like "I showed you the book" and "I will not do that again." The children reply with sentences like "I show book" and "Do again." The accuracy increases with age, but at any age, these solicited and direct imitations do not significantly differ, in length or complexity, from the child's spontaneous utterances.

Evidently the child's reductions of adult sentences cannot be blamed on failures of memory, for the child similarly reduces sentences he has just heard. If they are imitations, they are limited imitations. Those limitations decrease with age. But the decrease is not achieved through imitation, for the child's imitations do not seem to differ from his spontaneous productions (Ervin, 1964). We must look for another explanation of the increasing length and complexity of childish utterances, and this is a first reason for doubting the adequacy of imitation.

No one supposes that the child is purely imitative, for we are certain that he creates novel utterances. If many of the child's utterances seem to be telegraphic versions of adult sentences, many do not. When the child says "All gone outside" or "more page" or "three high," it is hard to imagine adult models for his utterances. Moreover, when the offspring of college graduates uses word forms like "comed" and "breaked" and "foots" and "sheeps" (those familiar errors commonly attributed to "regularization" of irregular nouns and verbs), it is not likely that he is repeating forms he has heard.

The usual explanation of such productions is that they are generalizations, extensions by analogy. This is a vague and unsatisfactory explanation, for there are any number of analogies which might be extended but are not, any number of generalizations the child might make but does not; and it would seem that an adequate explanation would predict which analogies or generalizations would occur, and why. But we might ignore this problem and assume that novel utterances are produced by generalization, to see where this assumption leads us.

The notion that novel utterances of this sort are generalizations implies that the child has a basis for generalizations; the idea of extension by analogy requires that the child know something to extend. In the case of the regularization of word endings for example, as in the plural of nouns or the past tense of verbs, we should expect to find the child forming regular plurals (boy-boys) and past tenses (walk-walked) before he extends these endings to the irregular nouns and verbs.

Ervin (1964) has found that the development of the plural noun proceeds in just this way. The appearance of regular plurals in the child's speech precedes by some weeks the first appearance of a regularized irregular; the child says "blocks" and "toys" and "dogs" considerably before he says "foots" or "sheeps" or "mans."

But Ervin has also found that the development of the past tense does not proceed in this way. Instead, the first past tenses used are the correct forms of the irregular verbs, forms like "came" and "went" and "broke." This is probably not surprising, for these are among the most frequently used forms in adult speech, and we might well expect the child to imitate them correctly. But the interesting and important fact is that when the child first learns to use the past tense of a very few regular forms, like "walked" and "watched," the correct irregulars disappear, to be replaced by incorrect over-generalizations. That is, despite the fact that the child has correctly imitated and practiced the correct past tense of these forms, and has presumably been reinforced for his usage, the forms disappear with the appearance of the regular tense system.

## GENERALIZATION AND EXTENSION
## AS BASIC PROCESSES

This fact is intriguing, for it suggests that when the child produces novel utterances, novel forms, he is not generalizing or extending some pattern which has been gradually accumulating in mechanically imitated forms. It suggests that extension by analogy and generalization are not secondary processes, operating on a basis of practiced and reinforced imitations. It suggests instead that generalization and extension are themselves basic, that the child does not record particular adult utterances but registers their pattern.

In fact, we should have reached this conclusion earlier. The assumption that the child produces some utterances through imitation and others through generalization leaves us in an uncomfortable position, for ultimately we must be forced to distinguish between them. We must assume that some of his utterances like "comed" and "foots" are generalizations, and not imitations, for we are confident that he has not heard these forms. But this should surely make us wonder whether many of his correct productions, like "walked" and "boys," are not generalization, too. And if any of the child's utterances might be generalizations, we might even wonder if they all are. Instead of assuming that the child says familiar things in imitation, and novel things through imitation and generalization, we might speculate that the child creates all that he says through a kind of "generalization"; that he internalizes the pattern, the rules, of his language, and uses that pattern or those rules to create each of his utterances.

Thus a second reason for doubting the adequacy of the imitation hypothesis is that it does not correctly predict the appearance of novel utterances in the course of development; moreover, it forces us to impose what seems to be an arbitrary classification on the productions of a child.

So far we have been looking at what the child says. We have tacitly assumed that the acquisition of language is the acquisition of language production. But there is a familiar observation which shows that this is a false assumption. The child not only learns to speak; he also learns to listen. And most observers (cf. McCarthy, 1954) claim that the child learns to listen before he learns to speak, that comprehension precedes production.

We all know many more words than we use, and we hear more sentences than we utter. (We must, for we hear all those we utter, but not vice versa.) The same is true of children; moreover, most of us believe that they comprehend before they produce. A recent experiment by Fraser, Bellugi, and Brown (1963) has confirmed our beliefs.

These investigators compared three-and-a-half-year-old children's comprehension and production of ten grammatical contrasts, like the difference between the singular and plural forms of *be* (*is* vs. *are*), the singular and plural in the third person possessive pronoun (*his* or *her* vs. *their*), and the present progressive and past tenses of the verb (*is spilling* vs. *spilled*). They wrote a pair of sentences exemplifying each contrast (e.g., "The sheep are jumping" and "The sheep is jumping"), and drew a picture corresponding to each sentence (e.g., a picture of two sheep jumping over a stile and a picture of one sheep jumping while another watches).

Each child heard both sentences and saw both pictures. Then his comprehension of the contrast was measured by reading him one of the sentences and asking him to point to the correct picture; his production of the contrast was measured by pointing to one of the pictures and asking him to name it. With each contrast, comprehension exceeded production; more children pointed to the correct picture, given a sentence, than produced the contrast, given the picture.

(Of course, it might be objected that pointing at a picture is easier than uttering a sentence; this is surely true, but it does not explain the relative difficulty of the production task, for the children were able to utter the sentences, in an imitation task, more accurately than they could comprehend them.)

This result is not novel, but it does provide experimental confirmation of our casual observation that comprehension precedes production. Some children comprehended contrasts they could not produce, but no child was able to produce a contrast which he could not comprehend. Whatever the child needs to comprehend a sentence is necessary for his production of it; the child must learn how to comprehend a sentence before he can produce it. But this fact is crucial in evaluating the imitation hypothesis, for, while the child may imitate sentences, he could not possibly imitate the comprehension of them. There are many things a parent might do to indicate that he understood a sentence, and the child could observe these things. But he cannot see or hear or feel the comprehension itself, and surely one cannot imitate something one cannot even sense. Hence a third and seemingly insurmountable difficulty for the imitation hypothesis is that it demands that the child imitate something he cannot observe.

From studies of language development we can draw, then, at least three cogent arguments against the hypothesis that language is learned through imitation. We can draw as many from studies of the product of language learning, the linguistic competence of the adult.

## STUDIES OF LINGUISTIC COMPETENCE

A person who knows a language knows many things that someone who does not know that language does not. For one, he can recognize the sentences of his language; he can distinguish strings of words, like "The boys will erase the blackboard," which are clearly grammatical, from strings of words, like "Blackboard erase the will boys," which are not. This is an obvious fact, but it is remarkable, for there is an infinite number of English sentences.

To see this, consider the sentence "The boys will erase the blackboard." Obviously, we may insert a phrase like "who chased the dog" after boys, and the result will be an English sentence; we might then introduce the phrase "who lived on Elm Street" after dog, and still have an English sentence. Since this process could be continued indefinitely, we must conclude that there is no longest English sentence—given any sentence whatever, we can produce a longer one by inserting another phrase. If there is no longest sentence, then there is no limit on the number of sentences, and so there is an infinity of sentences.

This is an important point, for it forces us to reject a notion closely related to the imitation hypothesis, the notion that a man recognizes sentences as grammatical because he has heard them before. This conclusion is incontrovertible from a logical point of view, but it may not seem psychologically real. We can make the same point somewhat more concrete by considering the number of sentences of some limited length.

Consider the number of English sentences exactly 15 words long. It seems reasonable to suppose that any such sentence could start with at least 1000 different words; in fact, this estimate is highly conservative. Having begun with any of these words, it seems fair to suppose that the sentence could continue with any of 1000 different words. Then 15-word sentences can begin with any of 1000 (1000) $= 1000^2$ different pairs of words, and if we extend this argument to each subsequent word in the sentence, we reach the conclusion that there are $1000^{15} = 10^{45}$ English sentences of exactly 15 words (Miller, Galanter, and Pribram, 1960). The magnitude of this number becomes apparent when we realize that the number of seconds in a century is on the order of $3.15 \times 10^9$, a tiny fraction of $10^{45}$.

The situation is not noticeably improved by considering the number of permissible sequences of word classes or parts of speech, for by similar reasoning this can be estimated at $10^9$. Thus for a person to have heard each of these sequences just once, he must hear one per second for about thirty years, without time to sleep or talk or hear sentences of other lengths. Obviously, we must reject the conclusion that the speaker of a language recognizes its sentences because he has heard them all, or even all of their patterns. We cannot assume that the speaker of a language has memorized the sentence frames or sentence patterns of his language; there are too many of them.

Thus we cannot describe a speaker's knowledge of his language, his competence, as consisting of a list of sentences or sentence patterns. Even if we could, and could use such a list as an explanation of the speaker's ability to recognize the sentences of his language, it would not be enough. A man knows more than just the permissible sequence of words which constitute those sentences; he also knows their structure. A sentence is not just a permissible sequence, of words, a list, but has a kind of hierarchical organization, and the speaker has intuitions about this organization. For example, many speakers of English recognize that "The boys will erase the blackboard" is composed of two parts, two constituents, *The boys* and *will erase the blackboard.* The latter constituent, in turn, is composed of *will erase* and *the blackboard,* and each of the two-word constituents can obviously be subdivided into two more.

Moreover, these various constituents are of various and distinct types, which the grammarian indicates by giving them labels. *The boys* and *the blackboard* are noun phrases (NP's), *will erase the blackboard* a verb phrase (VP), and so forth. We can summarize these facts in a labeled tree diagram like this:

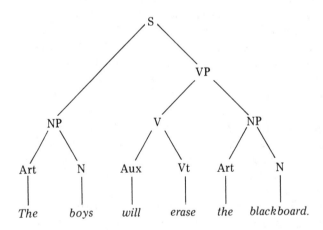

This structure is obvious to any grammarian, to any teacher of English grammar, but the important fact is that it is known to any speaker of English. To be sure, the latter's knowledge is of a different sort; it is implicit and it is often difficult for the teacher to make it, like his own, explicit. But the knowledge is there, as can be shown in several ways. . . .

## TWO LEVELS OF LANGUAGE STRUCTURE KNOWN

. . . Speakers of a language have knowledge of two distinct levels of structure, superficial structure and underlying structure. For notice that while many grammatical relations can be defined in terms of the constituent structure of the sentence, many cannot. For example, in the sentence, "The boy hit the girl," we may define *the boy* as the subject of the sentence (roughly because it is the first NP of the sentence) and *the girl* as the object (roughly because it is a NP which is part of the VP). But notice that in the passive version of this sentence, "The girl was hit by the boy," exactly the opposite relations obtain; *the girl* is the subject and *the boy* the object: Yet any speaker of English knows that, in fact, the relations between *boy* and *girl* and *hit* are the same in both sentences; it is boy who did the hitting and the girl who received the blow.

Another example of this sort is provided by the sentences "John is eager to please" and "John is easy to please." In both sentences, *John* is the subject. This fact is easily characterized in terms of the constituent, superficial structures of these sentences: in both, *John* is the first and only NP. But the speaker's intuition also tells him that the sentences are not alike, for in the first, John seems to be, not only the subject of the sentence, but also the subject of the verb *please*, while in the second he is the object of that verb. That is, the first sentence seems related to a sentence like "John pleases someone," while the second is closer to a sentence like "Someone pleases John."

Evidently speakers have knowledge, not only of the hierarchical organization of the constituents of sentences, their superficial structure, but also have knowledge of another, deeper level of structure underlying this. This knowledge not only enables them to comprehend sentences by providing the basic grammatical relations they express, but also enables them to appreciate relations between sentences. Like the speaker's knowledge of grammaticality, his knowledge of these relations could not be learned as a list, for if there is an infinite number of sentences, there is an infinite number of relations between them, and no one could learn an infinite list in a decidedly finite childhood.

We argue then that the speaker of a language has an enormous stock of knowledge of his language; he knows its sentences, their superficial and deep structures, and their interrelationships.

This knowledge cannot be represented as a list or set of lists, but it can be represented as a finite set of rules, a kind of finite device which will generate or produce an infinite set of sentences and their structures and interrelationships. In fact, the description of the speaker's knowledge in this way is exactly the goal of a current linguistic theory, the theory of transformational generative grammar (Chomsky, 1957, 1965; Katz and Postal, 1964). In this theory, a grammar is not merely a pedagogical device, or a logical description of a language considered as some sort of ideal abstraction, but is instead a description of actual linguistic competence, of the knowledge possessed by speakers of a language which distinguishes them from those who do not speak it.

## BIBLIOGRAPHY

BROWN, R., and C. FRASER. "The Acquisition of Syntax," in U. Bellugi and R. Brown (eds.). *The Acquisition of Language*. Child Development Monographs 29, 1964, 43–78.

CHOMSKY, NOAM. *Syntactic Structures*. The Hague: Mouton, 1957.

──────────. *Aspects of the Theory of Syntax*. Cambridge, Mass.: Massachusetts Institute of Technology Press, 1965.

ERWIN, S. M. "Imitation and Structural Change in Children's Language," in E. Lenneberg (ed.). *New Directions in the Study of Language*. Cambridge, Mass.: Massachusetts Institute of Technology Press, 1964, 163–190.

FRASER, C., U. BELLUGI, and R. BROWN. "Control of Grammar in Imitation, Comprehension, and Production," *Journal of Verbal Learning and Verbal Behavior*, 2(1963), 121–135.

KATZ, J. J., and P. POSTAL. *An Integrated Theory of Linguistic Description*. Cambridge, Mass.: Massachusetts Institute of Technology Press, 1964.

MILLER, G. A. "Some Psychological Studies of Grammar," *American Psychologist*, 17(1962), 748–762.

──────────, E. GALANTER, and K. PRIBRAM. *Plans and the Structure of Behavior*. New York: Holt, Rinehart & Winston, Inc., 1960.

POSTAL, P. "Underlying and Superficial Linguistic Structure," *Harvard Educational Review*, 34(1964), 246–266.

THOMAS, O. *Transformational Grammar and the Teacher of English*. New York: Holt, Rinehart & Winston, Inc., 1965.

VIERTEL, J. "Generative Grammars," *College Composition and Communication*, 15 (May 1964), 65–81.

# Language Learning and the Brain [1]

WILDER PENFIELD

> Penfield is a neurosurgeon who has treated brain damage
> and aphasia (the loss of language abilities). He reports that chil-
> dren under the age of twelve or thirteen have abilities to acquire a
> second language that are far greater than the abilities of people
> past that age. There are some problems with Penfield's specula-
> tions as to the reason for that fact; but the fact itself is very
> important. It confirms the possibility that biological structures
> in the brain exert control over language acquisition, a role implied
> by the findings of Slobin, Gough, and Jakobson in Part 1 of this
> book and Lenneberg in Part 2.
> Penfield's suggested causes for this difference in language-
> learning ability include several that should be viewed with reserva-
> tions: he does not define "switch mechanism"; he does not
> distinguish between receptive language abilities (understanding
> language) and productive abilities (creating sentences); and there
> is no clear evidence that learning a second language involves
> setting up a second speech center, as occurs in children when
> there is brain damage to the first speech center. His suggestions
> about "commitment" blocking language acquisition are spec-
> ulative. But Penfield gives fascinating evidence for the major
> fact that language is controlled by physical structures in the
> brain, structures whose abilities are tied to a biological matura-
> tion process.

The human brain is not a previously programmed calculator.
It is a living, growing, changing organ. It can even carry out its
own repairs to some extent. But it is subject to an inexorable
evolution of its functional aptitudes. No one can alter the time
schedule of the human brain, not even a psychiatrist, or an educator. The built-in biological clock tells the passage of learning
aptitudes and the teacher's opportunity. . . .

I have had a remarkable opportunity to study speech mechanisms, language learning and bilingualism. Most of my clinical
career has been passed in Montreal where my patients were, half
of them, French-speaking and half English-speaking. I have seen

---

[1] A part of this communication was published in different form in *The
Atlantic Monthly*, Boston, July 1964, vol. 214, p. 77, entitled *The Uncommitted Cortex*.

children, below the age of 10 or 12, lose the power of speech when the speech convolutions in the left hemisphere of the brain had been destroyed by a head injury or a brain tumour. I have seen them recover after a year of dumbness and aphasia. In time, they spoke as well as ever because the young child's brain is functionally flexible for the start of a language. They began all over again. Occasionally when such children had become epileptic because of the brain injury, we were able to study what had happened, while we were trying to cure them. In every case, we found they had established a speech centre located on the other side of the brain in what is called the non-dominant hemisphere. (In a right-handed person, the left hemisphere is normally dominant for speech. That is, it contains the whole specialized speech mechanism.)

When the major speech centre is severely injured in adult life, the adult cannot do what he might have done as a child. He may improve but he is apt to be using the remaining uninjured cortex on the side of the injury. He can never establish a completely new centre on the non-dominant side, as far as our experience goes. That is not because he is senile. It is because he has, by that time, taken over the initially uncommitted convolutions on the non-dominant side of his brain for other uses.

Grey matter is made up of many millions of living nerve cells that are capable of receiving and sending electrical impulses. The cerebral cortex, which is the thick layer of grey matter covering the outer surface of the brain, has been called "new" since it is found to be more and more voluminous as one ascends the philogenetic scale from fish to man. It covers the convolutions and dips down into the fissures between them. The underlying white matter is made up of the branching connexions of the nerve cells. They are capable of transmitting electric potentials like insulated wires. Some of the connexions pass inward from cortex into the "old" grey matter of the brain-stem (the old brain) ; some unite cortex and brain-stem with the eyes and ears; some pass up and down the spinal cord and along the nerves to the muscles and the skin.

Certain parts of the cerebral cortex are functionally committed from the start. The so-called "sensory cortex" and "motor cortex" can only be used for sensory and motor purposes because these parts seem to have fixed functional connexions from birth onward.

But there is a large area of cortex covering a given, large

part of each of the two temporal lobes that is uncommitted at birth. This uncommitted cortex will in time be used for language and for perception. For language, it will make possible the remembrance and use of words. For perception, it will play a part in the recall of the past and interpretation of present experience. As the child begins to perceive and to speak, electrical currents must be passing in corresponding patterns through this cortex and underlying brain. After each time of passage, it is easier for the passage of later currents along the same trail. This tendency to facilitation of electrical passage results in man's amazingly permanent records of the auditory and visual stream of his conscious life.

Now, if the posterior half of the left uncommitted cortex is used by the child for speech, as it usually is, it becomes the major speech area, or speech cortex.[2] Then the remaining three-quarters is used for interpretation of experience (interpretive cortex). Functional connexions are gradually established by the child and by the time he enters the teens the general uses of the uncommitted areas are apparently fixed for life.

Much of this information about mechanisms of speech and perception has come to us from the well-known work of others. Some has come to us unexpectedly during long operations on conscious alert patients who were kept from pain by local novocain injection into the scalp while a trap door opening was made in the skull. In the attempt to relieve each patient of his attacks of focal epilepsy, a preliminary survey of the brain was made after the exposure was completed.

A gentle electrical stimulus was applied by touching the cortex here and there with an electrode. This served to map the sensory cortex by causing sensation (visual, auditory or bodily, according to which of the different areas was touched) and the motor cortex by producing crude movement of the face or tongue or limb. When an abnormality in a certain area of brain was suspected of being the cause of fits, the electrode might produce by stimulation there the characteristic beginning of the attack from which the patient sought relief. (Surgical excision of areas

---

[2] There are also two secondary speech areas, both of them in the frontal lobe of the dominant hemisphere: Broca's area in the third frontal convolution, and the supplementary speech area in the supplementary motor area. An adult can recover speech after aphasia of varying lengths of time when either one is destroyed. The posterior speech area (Wernicke's), established in the uncommitted temporal cortex, is the major one.

of bad cortex is a worth-while method of treatment in case conservative medical therapy has failed in the hands of experienced
neurologists.)

The most precious and indispensable portion of the adult's
cortex is the major speech area. It might be worth while to forfeit
other areas and so lose other functions in order to gain a cure of
epilepsy, but never the speech area. Thus the need of a method
to map out the exact territory devoted to speech was urgent.

When the electrode was applied to the speech cortex, it did
not cause a man to speak. It seemed at first to have no effect. But
if the patient tried to speak while the electrode was in place, he
discovered to his astonishment (and to ours at first) that he could
not find his words. If shown a pencil, he knew what it was ànd
could make appropriate movements with the hand, but he had
lost the power of speaking. He was aphasic. The gentle electric
current was blocking the action of the speech cortex, with its
underlying connexion, without disturbing the function of the
adjacent areas. When the patient was shown an object and was
asked to name it, he perceived its nature, and he must have dis-
patched electric potentials along the brain's integrating circuits
to the speech mechanism. But, to his surprise, he "drew a blank."

Normally, when the appropriately patterned potentials reach
the speech mechanism, the word, by instant reflex action, is made
available to consciousness—its sound, how to write it, how to
speak it and how to recognize the written word. As long as the
electrode continued to paralyse the action of the speech unit, none
of these was possible. But as the electrode was lifted, the patient,
not knowing what had been done, would exclaim, "Now I can
speak! That was a pencil."

So we had a much-needed method of mapping out the major
speech area exactly (and the minor ones as well). And we could
remove less useful cortex right up to the speech frontier without
fear of losing speech function. We mapped out the cortical area
thus in hundreds of cases and acquired precise knowledge of the
demarcation in each case. This took the place of anatomical
conjecture. But what about the similar area in the non-dominant
hemisphere and the uncommitted temporal cortex farther forward on both sides? So far, neurologists had found no clear indication of function for these areas.

Stimulation in them never produced aphasia. What were
they used for? One day I stumbled on a clue. I applied the electrode to the right temporal cortex (non-dominant). The patient,
a woman of middle age, exclaimed suddenly, "I seem to be the

way I was when I was giving birth to my baby girl." I did not recognize this as a clue. But I could not help feeling that the suddenness of her exclamation was strange and so I made a note of it.

Several years later during a similar operation, the electrode caused a young girl to describe, with considerable emotion, a specific experience she had when running through a meadow. There is no sensation in the cortex and she could not know when I had touched the electrode to her right temporal lobe but, each time I did so, she described the experience again, and stopped when the electrode was removed. Since that day we have been on the alert and have gathered more and more cases which could be studied critically. We have now published all of them in complete summary.[3]

The conclusion is as follows: There is within the adult human brain a remarkable record of the stream of each individual's awareness. It is as though the electrode cuts in, at random, on the record of that stream. The patient sees and hears what he saw and heard in some earlier strip of time and he feels the same accompanying emotions. The stream of consciousness flows for him again, exactly as before, stopping instantly on removal of the electrode. He is aware of those things to which he paid attention in this earlier period, even twenty years ago. He is not aware of the things that were ignored. The experience evidently moves forward at the original pace. This was demonstrated by the fact that when, for example, the music of an orchestra, or song or piano, is heard and the patient is asked to hum in accompaniment, the tempo of his humming is what one would expect. He is still aware of being in the operating room but he can describe this other run of consciousness at the same time.

The patient recognizes the experience as having been his own, although usually he could not have recalled it if he had tried. The complete record of his auditory and visual experience is not subject to conscious recall, but it is evidently used in the subconscious brain-transaction that results in perception. By means of it, a man in normal life compares each succeeding experience with his own past experience. He knows at once whether it is familiar or not. If it is familiar, he interprets the present stream of consciousness in the light of the past.

Careful comparison of all the brain maps we have made shows no overlap of the boundaries that separate speech cortex (which endows a man with memory of words) and the interpre-

[3] W. Penfield and Ph. Perot—*Brain* (1963), 86, 595–696.

tive cortex which gives him access to the memory of past similar experience and thus enables him to understand the present.

Before the child begins to speak and to perceive, the uncommitted cortex is a blank slate on which nothing has been written. In the ensuing years much is written, and the writing is normally never erased. After the age of 10 or 12, the general functional connexions have been established and fixed for the speech cortex. After that the speech centre cannot be transferred to the cortex of the lesser side and set up all over again. This "non-dominant" area that might have been used for speech is now fully occupied with the business of perception.

The brain of the 12 year old, you may say, is prepared for rapid expansion of the vocabulary of the mother tongue and of the other languages he may have heard in the formative period. If he has heard these other languages, he has developed also a remarkable *switch mechanism* that enables him to turn from one language to another without confusion, without translation, without a mother-tongue accent. . . .

There is a good deal of evidence to suggest that when a young child is allowed to hear a second language and learns to use only a few hundred words of that language—he becomes a better potential linguist; his uncommitted cortex is conditioned to further second-language learning. It is difficult or impossible to condition it thus later in life because the functional connexions tend to become fixed.

This would explain the reputed genius of the Swiss, the Poles and the Belgians as linguists. Most of them hear a second language in early childhood in the streets and the playgrounds, if not at home. On the contrary, the average so-called Anglo-Saxon, in Great Britain or the United States, hears only English until possibly he is taught a modern language in his teens at school.

J. B. Conant (former President of Harvard), in his recent studies of American high schools, concluded that in the best schools of today the work is satisfactory, except in one department: the teaching of foreign languages. The classical method, with its grammar and word lists designed to teach dead languages, is the indirect method of the high school. A little child cannot use it. He would only laugh at it, and yet the little child is the genius in our society for starting languages. The brain of the 12 year old is already senescent in that regard. He is ready for vocabulary expansion.

Education, to be scientific, must consider the physiology of a child's brain. When the classical method is used to start a unilingual teenage pupil or adult in the learning of second languages, the procedure is unscientific and not in accordance with the dictates of neurophysiology. With hard work, it may serve the purpose as a second-best method.

The teaching of additional living languages, as intelligent parents have managed it, ever since the society of ancient Ur became bilingual, is in accordance with the modern findings of speech physiology. . . .

It may serve my purpose best to describe a school in Montreal . . . in which the method of *parallel bilingualism* is used by teachers speaking their native tongue (English or French). They are the teaching nuns of Notre Dame de Sion, 4701 Dornal Avenue, Montreal. The procedure is not at all complicated. Their school has two years of kindergarten and one of first grade. In the morning the children, aged 4 to 6, are received by English-speaking teachers and in the afternoon by French-speaking teachers or vice versa. No time is wasted teaching language as such. The children play and sing and study in one language in the morning and the other in the afternoon. They begin to read and write in two languages. If there is any difficulty in spelling, it disappears spontaneously after the manner of vanishing baby-talk. Every evening the children return to their homes to speak the mother tongue and to receive whatever home religious instruction is desired by their parents.

After two years of bilingual kindergarten and one in the first grade, children of this school have started reading and writing. They are ready to carry on in either language smoothly and without accent or confusion in some other elementary school. They could, of course, transfer to a school that used a third language. Vocabulary expansion could be provided for by reading and conversation almost any time in the first and second decades of life. When they enter middle school, high school or university, these children should be able to study the literature of second languages instead of struggling with grammar.

The child is the genius in our society when it comes to acquiring the early set, the units or the patterns of a language. The enlargement of vocabulary is another story. The 10 year old expands vocabulary as he expands his knowledge miraculously in the direction of his interests.

The secret of the child's freedom from confusion lies in the action of a conditioned reflex that works in his brain auto-

matically from the beginning. It is what might be called the
*switch mechanism*. When the English child (or adult) hears a
French word or meets a French person or enters a French school,
he unconsciously switches on his French "network" with its
vocabulary, however meagre it may be. What he proceeds to learn
is then added to the French network. In the brain, French, English and Chinese, if learned, seem to utilize the same general area
of speech cortex without demonstrable separation into different
areas. Every adult who speaks secondary languages is aware of
this subconscious reflex which brings the word *bleistift* to his
mind instead of "pencil" as he turns to a German companion, or
*crayon* as he enters the class conducted in French. . . .

The first stage of language learning is always in the home.
During the first two years of life, imitation of words comes only
after months of hearing them.[4] Baby talk shows that the set of the
brain for language is not established immediately. It takes time,
and the baby's accent and the formal phrasing and organization
of sentences alters gradually to that of the adult (without the
need of lectures on grammar).

In our own home the two younger children heard German in
the nursery from a governess who could speak nothing else.
When she took them to French nursery school (aged 3 and 4) they
switched to French as they entered the door and switched back
again when they found her waiting outside the door at the close
of the school. Our two older children, aged 8 and 9, first heard
German spoken for a few months in Germany. After that they
spoke German to their younger brother and sister and, on occasion, to the governess, but they were never taught the language
formally. In spite of that, both older children had excellent command of the language, one for a year of university work in
Munich, the other for wireless intelligence in the Second World
War.

A unilingual adult, who begins the learning of a second language late, speaks it with a mother-tongue accent and tends to
learn by translation. However, the adult who has previously
learned some other language in childhood is apt to learn a later
third and fourth language faster and probably better than a unilingual adult. It may be suggested that this greater facility of the

[4] According to W. E. Leopold's careful study, there is a lag of two to
seven months after the child first hears a word in the second year of life
before he uses it in a meaningful manner. (Northwestern University Press,
4 vols., 1939–1949.)

bilingual adult is due, at least in part, to the well developed "switch mechanism" which he acquired in childhood. He is able to switch off the mother tongue more easily and, thus, to learn directly.

It follows, for example, that in a school district where the only foreign native-born teachers available are Swedish or Spanish, it would be the part of wisdom to have beginning years taught in Swedish (or on a bilingual basis—Swedish in the mornings and Spanish in the afternoons). Those children who continue their schooling in English and eventually go on to college and into professional schools will be better prepared to learn the Russian and Chinese which intelligent English-speaking adults of the future will want to understand. The bilingual child, prepared for formal education by the mother and the child's nurse, or mother and a second language kindergarten, has undoubted advantage over other children whatever the second languages may have been and whatever the eventual work of the individual may prove to be.

The experience of many parents has, of course, been similar to our own, past and present. It is a common experience that when families immigrate, the children learn the new language by the direct method (without confusion) and unilingual parents learn it less well and more slowly by translation and with a mother-tongue accent. This is the supporting evidence of common sense and common experience. And yet there are those who argue that it is better for a child to establish the mother-tongue well before confusing him by exposure to a second language! The child seems to be protected from confusion by rapidly acquired conditioned reflexes and by the action of the switch mechanism which is a conditioned reflex.

There is other good evidence that even a limited familiarity with additional languages in the first decade endows the normal child with a more efficient and useful brain [5]. . . .

A second study has been carried out in the same department.[6] In this study, an equal number of bilingual university students was compared with a similar selection of unilingual students. The bilingual students scored higher in intelligence tests when those tests were verbal and also when they were non-verbal.

[5] [Ed.'s note: See "The Advantages of Being Bilingual," by Wallace E. Lambert, in the following section.]
[6] Anisfeld, Elizabeth Peel: The Cognitive Aspects of Bilingualism. McGill University, Ph.D. thesis.

In the bilingual society of the Province of Quebec, those who were bilingual before entering university would have heard the second language early.

In conclusion, man (to a far greater extent than other mammals) is endowed with extensive areas of cerebral cortex which, at birth, are not committed to sensory or motor function. Much of the uncommitted areas covering the temporal lobes that are not used as "speech cortex" will, in time, be used as "interpretive cortex" and so play a role in the process of perception. While the mother is teaching the child to understand and to use a few hundred words and teaching the child to perceive the meanings of words and experiences, she is "programming" the brain. Part of the uncommitted cortex is being conditioned or "programmed" for speech, the remaining uncommitted cortex is used as a part of the mechanism of perception. In the second decade of life, functional connexions seem to have become fixed. Vocabulary expansion and multiplication of perceptions then proceed rapidly.

The mother's method of direct language teaching can be used for second languages but this should *begin* before the age of 6 or 8 if possible. When the uncommitted cortex is thus conditioned early, the individual becomes a better linguist; the child is better prepared for the long educational climb. In the years of life that follow, the man or woman will more easily become the "well-educated" adult for which the future calls so urgently. . . .

# Acquiring Phonology, Syntax, and Sociolinguistic Abilities

## Emergence of the Speech Sound

ROMAN JAKOBSON

      The 1941 work from which this excerpt is taken is one of the classics in twentieth-century linguistics. In it Jakobson dramatizes the basic fact that language does not exist apart from meaning. Researchers had previously been unable to see an order in the acquisition of speech sounds because they had failed to make the distinction between babbling—sounds themselves—and speech sounds, those used by the child to convey meaning. Knowledge that language is always meaningful contradicts the common assumption that some varieties of speech are less meaningful than others.

      Jakobson's second major point is that speech sounds are acquired in a nearly universal order; no matter what language the child hears, he or she will typically begin by acquiring a consonant made at the front of the mouth and a vowel made at the back of the mouth, and will proceed to acquire other sounds in a highly predictable order. Of course, if language were acquired by imitation, this order could not exist; children would acquire first whatever sounds they heard most frequently. The implication is that children are actively constructing their own sound systems, rather than passively absorbing the sounds they happen to hear.

. . . The pre-language stages of the child as well as the initial stages of his linguistic development, which are of the utmost importance for the phonological structure of language, have been neglected for a considerable time. . . .

## PRINCIPLE OF LEAST EFFORT AND CESSATION OF BABBLING SOUNDS

The fact that a fixed order must be inherent in language acquisition, and in phonological acquisition in particular, has repeatedly been noticed by observers and has often been explained by appealing to the principle of least effort, . . . [the notion that] those speech sounds which require the least physiological effort for their production are learned first by children (Schultze, p. 27). This questionable hypothesis was indeed often opposed, particularly because of the quite arbitrary nature of the criteria for determining the degree of effort required for the sounds in question.[1] Nevertheless, a remnant of such a conception is still continually found even in the newer works on child language, *e.g.*, in the famous handbook by Stern.[2] But this hypothesis is completely refuted by an essential fact of the child's linguistic development.

The actual beginning stages of language, as is known, are preceded by the so-called babbling period, which brings to light in many children an astonishing quality and diversity of sound productions. A child, during his babbling period, can accumulate articulations which are never found within a single language or even a group of languages—consonants of any place of articulation, palatalized and rounded consonants, sibilants, affricates, clicks, complex vowels, diphthongs, etc. According to the findings of phonetically trained observers and to the summarizing statement of Grégoire ($\beta$ 101), the child at the height of his babbling period "is capable of producing all conceivable sounds."

As all observers acknowledge with great surprise, the child then loses nearly all of his ability to produce sounds in passing over from the pre-language stage to the first acquisition of words,

---

[1] Thus the predominance of labial sounds in children is explained in two different ways. Schultze suggests that there is some special articulatory facility associated with these sounds, while Röttger suggests [the exact opposite,] that "the motor movements of speech are considerably more extensive and require more energy in labial articulation," and therefore take on an "increased importance" psychologically (79).

[2] "The difficult palato-velar sounds are replaced by the easier dental sounds" (337, cf. 333).

*i.e.*, to the first genuine stage of language. It is easy to understand that those articulations which are lacking in the language of the child's environment easily disappear from his inventory. But it is striking that, in addition, many other sounds which are common both to the child's babbling and to the adult language of his environment are in the same way disposed of, in spite of this environmental model that he depends on. Indeed, the child is generally successful in recovering these sounds only after long effort, sometimes only after several years. This is the case, *e.g.*, with palatal consonants, sibilants and liquids. . . .

The one-year-old son of the Serbian linguist Pavlović recognized and distinguished faultlessly the words *tata* and *kaka* when spoken to him, but consistently said *tata* instead of *kaka*, even though he [had] easily produced [k] in his babbling "concerts" (39). There are two varieties of language for the child, one might almost say two styles—one he controls actively, the other, the language of the adult, only passively (cf. the distinction of male and female language in many tribes: every one speaks only one but understands the other). For a time the child cannot, or sometimes will not, cross over this boundary and in fact demands that the adult also adhere to it. According to the well-known description by Passy, a young French girl said *tosson* for both *garçon* ["boy"] and *cochon* ["pig"], but she protested when someone near her called a boy a *cochon*, or a pig a *garçon*. This example is, in principle, similar to that of older children who still babble, but who become angry when an adult also begins to use baby talk for their benefit. . . .

Babbling, on the one hand, and . . . [comprehension without speech] of the child, on the other, prove that he is deficient neither in motor [ability nor in hearing,] but nevertheless most of his sounds are suddenly lost. . . .

## EMERGENCE OF THE SPEECH SOUND

The selection of sounds in the transition from babbling to language can be accounted for solely by this transition itself, *i.e.*, by the newly acquired function of the sound as a speech sound, or, more accurately, by the phonemic value which it comes to have.[3] . . . As soon as sound utterances "are employed for the

[3] This process of phonemic acquisition is exactly observed and recorded in Grégoire's book; cf. also Delacroix $\beta$ and K. von Ettmayer, who correctly observes that it is not a question here of the ability or inability to articulate certain sounds, but of the mastering and retaining "of the system of phonemic oppositions" (*Berl. Beiträge z. Rom. Philol.*, VIII: 1, 1938, 36).

purpose of designation" the actual stage of language formation is launched, as Wundt correctly realized (283).

It is precisely these arbitrary sound distinctions aimed at meaning which require simple, clear and stable phonological oppositions. . . . In place of the phonetic abundance of babbling, the phonemic poverty of the first linguistic stages appears, a kind of deflation which transforms the so-called "wild sounds" of the babbling period into entities of linguistic value. . . .

But once the first stage of actual language is reached, and the selection of speech sounds and the construction of a phonemic system is launched, we observe a succession which is universally valid and is strictly regulated by structural laws. . . .

Again and again a number of constant features in the succession of acquired phonemes are observed, and again and again doubts are raised in the technical literature against the assumption of a regular order of development, so that the inquiry into its laws is in the meantime suspended. But all of these objections rest on the insufficient delimitation of the relevant components of language from pre-linguistic, external, or linguistically irrelevant elements. Thus, *e.g.*, Schultze's correct observation that ø and *y* in child language belong to the latest phonological acquisitions is neither contradicted nor weakened by Preyer's reference to the very early, prelanguage appearance of [these same] rounded palatal vowels during the babbling period (367f.), since the appearance of phonemes in a linguistic system has nothing in common with the ephemeral sound productions of the babbling period, which are destined to disappear. In the language of the older son of Grégoire, the phonemes ø and *y* were lacking until the end of his second year, whereas he produced spontaneously babbling sounds of a similar articulation in the middle of his first year. In Czech infants the vowels in question appear from time to time as babbling sounds, although they are completely foreign to Czech and are extraordinarily difficult for Czechs who are learning French.

As Meumann has already stated (α 23), a short period may sometimes intervene between the stage of spontaneous babbling and that of true language development, in which children are completely mute. For the most part, however, one stage merges unobtrusively into the other, so that the acquisition of vocabulary and the disappearance of the prelanguage inventory occur concurrently.[4] First of all, then, the "permanent" speech sounds,

---

[4] Cf. Ronjat 41, Cohen 110.

as Gutzmann calls them ($\alpha$ 17), are to be carefully distinguished from the disappearing babbling sounds—the child's embryo-words from the prelanguage residue. The persistence of the sound, the intention to express meaning by the formation in which it occurs, and the social setting of the utterance are fundamental criteria for distinguishing speech sounds from babbling sounds. As the child develops, the social factor becomes daily more important, while babbling is restricted to the leisure of solitary play and of waking and of going to sleep (cf. Grégoire $\beta$ 138), and is later relegated to dreams.

Secondly, as we have already pointed out, as far as the phonemic inventory is concerned, language in the narrow sense of the word (*i.e.*, language as a system of arbitrary signs) must not be confused with sound gestures [*i.e.*, imitations of birds, train sounds, etc.,] whose phonological form is motivated.

Finally, one must rigorously separate what is significant from what is irrelevant to the distinction of words. Some pairs of sounds that are used [in adult speech] to distinguish the meanings of words (and hence are phonemic distinctions) are for the child initially variants of the same phoneme, regardless of the considerable range of variation. The choice between these variants may be determined by the adjoining sounds. I have observed, *e.g.*, that *i* and *u* represent for a one-year-old Czech girl a single high vowel phoneme, and similarly *e* and *o* a single mid vowel phoneme. . . .

# REFERENCES

COHEN, M., "Sur les langages successifs de l'enfant," *Mélanges Vendryes* (Paris, 1925).

DELACROIX, H., $\alpha$) Le langage et la pensée (Paris, 1924).

———, $\beta$) L'enfant et le langage (Paris, 1934).

GRÉGOIRE, A., $\alpha$) "L'apprentissage de la parole pendant les deux premières années de l'enfance," *Journ. de Psychol.*, XXX (1933).

———, $\beta$) *"L'apprentissage du langage* (= *Bibliothèque de la Fac. de Philos. et Lettres de l'Univ. de Liège*, LXXIII, 1937).

GUTZMANN, H., *Des Kindes Sprache und Sprachfehler* (Leipzig, 1894).

MEUMANN, E., *Die Sprache des Kindes* (= *Abhandlungen herausgegeben v. d. Ges. f. deutsche Sprache in Zürich*, VIII, 1903).

PASSY, P., "yn kɛstɲ äbarasä:t," *Le Maître Phonétique*, No. 58 (1937).

PAVLOVIĆ (PAVLOVITCH), M., *Le langage enfantin* (Paris, 1920).

PREYER, W., *Die Seele des Kindes* (Leipzig, 1895).

RONJAT, J., *Le développement du langage observé chez un enfant bilingue* (Paris, 1913).

RÖTTGER, FRITAZ, *Phonetische Gestaltbildung bei jungen Kindern* (= *Arbeiten a.z. Entwicklungspsychol.*, Munich, X, 1931).

SCHULTZE, F., *Die Sprache des Kindes* (Leipzig, 1880).

STERN, C. and W., *Die Kindersprache* (Leipzig, 1928).

WUNDT, W., *Volkerpsychologie* (Stuttgart, 1912).

# The Pattern of Early Speech

DAVID McNEILL

When children first begin to speak, they are limited to utterances only one word in length; this is called the *holophrastic* stage of acquiring sentence structure, or syntax. McNeill says that during the holophrastic stage the child learns to use a word in a number of different ways—it may be the subject of an implied sentence, the object of an implied sentence, and so on. We can usually tell from the context of the remark what the remark means; e.g., the child may point to a truck and say, "Truck!" meaning, "Give me the truck!" By the time the child goes into the next stage of acquiring syntax, he or she already knows a great deal about sentence structure without ever having uttered a sentence longer than one word.

The next stage is called *telegraphic* speech. Here the child can create sentences longer than one word but leaves out articles, such as *the;* prepositions, such as *in;* auxiliary verbs, such as *can;* and inflections, such as *-ing*—just as people writing telegrams leave out words like *the* and prepositions. For example, the child may say "Turn TV" meaning "Turn the TV on." McNeill describes telegraphic speech under two headings, "Pivot and Open Classes" and "Early Phrase Structure." These represent two different ways of describing the same speech, except that the pivot-open (P-O) description can apply only to two-word telegraphic speech, while the rules McNeill gives for early phrase structure can apply to both two-word and longer telegraphic sentences. Bloom, in the following article, disagrees sharply with the P-O description.

## TELEGRAPHIC SPEECH

Brown and Fraser (1963) called the patterned speech of very young children "telegraphic." The word aptly captures one characteristic feature of children's first multiple-word utterances. As in telegrams, certain words are systematically eliminated. At 28 months, for example, articles, auxiliary verbs, copular verbs, and inflections of every sort are missing—*put suitcase . . . for?*, *where birdie go?*, *what innere?*, and *yep, it fit.* . . .

## HOLOPHRASTIC SPEECH

It is essential to begin the description of language acquisition even before the period of telegraphic speech. "Holophrastic speech" refers to the possibility that the single word utterances of young children express complex ideas, that *ball* means not simply a spherical object of appropriate size, but that a child wants such an object, for example, or that he believes he has created such an object, or that someone is expected to look at such an object.

Many investigators of children's language (e.g., Stern and Stern, 1907; de Laguna, 1927; Leopold, 1949a; McCarthy, 1954) have said that the single words of holophrastic speech are equivalent to the full sentences of adults. It is true, of course, that adults often require a full sentence to paraphrase the content of children's holophrastic speech, but this is not what is meant by the term "holophrastic." Rather, holophrastic speech means that while children are limited to uttering single words at the beginning of language acquisition, they are capable of conceiving of something like full sentences. Let us look into this possibility, for it is central to understanding the course of events in the later stages of language acquisition.

In what sense do children have in mind the content of a full sentence while uttering a single word? There are several aspects of holophrastic speech to which we will pay attention in considering this question. No one believes that children have detailed and differentiated ideas in the adult manner. As Leopold (1949a) puts it, ". . . the word has at first an ill-defined meaning and an ill-defined value: it refers to a nebulous complex, factually and emotionally; only gradually do its factual and emotional components become clearer, resulting in lexical and syntactic discriminations" (p. 5). A degree of semantic imprecision in holophrastic speech is therefore taken for granted. There remains, however, a question of what it is that children are imprecise about, and several factors seem to be important.

Often children's single-word utterances are closely linked with action. Action and speech appear to be fused. Leopold's daughter, for example, said *walk* as she got out of a cart to walk, *away* as she pushed an object away, and *blow* as she blew her nose (all at 20 months) ; Leopold calls these utterances self-imperatives. In addition there were normal imperatives, utterances directed toward someone else. Leopold observed *mit* from *komm mit*, *ma* from *come on*, and *away* from *put it away*, again all at 20 months. (Leopold's daughter grew up as a German-English bilingual.) It is not clear that the two kinds of imperatives were in any way distinct for the child.

Besides imperatives children's early speech often is imbued with emotion [ ; we can call this expressive speech]. . . .

There is a third characteristic of holophrastic speech. Holophrastic speech [is referential; it] refers to things. It includes the capacity to name. A child expresses his feelings or evokes an action toward some object referred to by his utterance. The utterance [mam: a], for example, meant for Leopold's daughter both "delicious!" and "food." It had both an expressive and referential component. (It did not mean "mama" until six months later.) . . .

De Laguna (1927) viewed the single-word utterances of children as predicates, as comments, made on the situation in which a child finds himself. The holophrastic word is the comment; together with the extra-linguistic context, the topic of the comment, it forms a rudimentary kind of proposition and thus amounts to a full sentence conceptually.

It is worth quoting de Laguna in full on this:

> *It is precisely because the words of the child are so indefinite in meaning, that they can serve such a variety of uses; and it is also —although this sounds paradoxical—for the same reason, that they are fit to function as complete rudimentary sentences. A child's word does not . . . designate an object or a property or an act; rather it signifies loosely and vaguely the object together with its interesting properties and the acts with which it is commonly associated in the life of the child. The emphasis may be now on one, now on another, of these aspects, according to the exigencies of the occasion on which it is used. Just because the terms of the child's language are in themselves so indefinite, it is left to the*

particular setting and context to determine the specific meaning for each occasion. *In order to understand what the baby is saying you must see what the baby is doing.* (1927, pp. 90-91, emphasis in original)

. . . [P]urely referential utterances never occur. The referential function is always used for predication. Children never utter mere labels, while they do utter purely expressive or [imperative] sounds. This is a remarkable fact of human communication, and we shall see its effects at every stage of linguistic development.

## Holophrastic Speech as Grammatical Speech

Leopold's observations cover the beginning of linguistic development. There is already an indication that holophrastic speech is in a limited way grammatical, that is, relational, speech. During the following 6 to 12 months there is a constant emergence of new grammatical relations, even though no utterance is ever longer than one word. Very young children develop a concept of a sentence as a set of grammatical relations before they develop a concept of how these relations are expressed.

P. Greenfield (personal communication) was the first to note this significant phenomenon, so far as I know. She kept a diary of her daughter's speech, from what seemed to be the first meaningful utterances to the beginning of patterned speech, and noted different grammatical relations appearing during the holophrastic period. Of course, seeing a single word in a grammatical relation is a fact we can know for certain only on the part of the observer of the relation; we have to assume the child has the same relation in mind. The reason for making this assumption in the case of Greenfield's observations, is that she found an orderly *progression* of new relations during the holophrastic period. In the early months, therefore, many opportunities were missed for perceiving relations that appeared in later months. There had been some change in the [kind of one-word utterances the child used].

The child first used *dada* at 11 months in the sense of "caretaker." It was applied indiscriminantly to her mother, father, and a third person also living in the house (Greenfield, 1967). The next step was the assertion of properties. At 12 months 20 days (12;20) the child said *ha* when something hot was before her, and at 13;20 she said *ha* to an empty coffee cup and a turned-off stove. By misusing the word the child showed that "hot" was not merely the label of hot objects but was also something said of objects that could be hot. It asserted a property. At 15 months the child used words to indicate the location of objects as well as their properties. Thus, at 14;28 she pointed to the top of the refrigerator, the usual place for finding bananas, and said *nana*. There were no bananas on top of the refrigerator at the time, so *nana* could not have been a label, and at other times the child called bananas not on the refrigerator *nana,* so she was not saying something about the refrigerator. By 15;11 the child began to use words as the objects of verbs (*door*, meaning "close the door"), as the objects of prepositions (*eye*, meaning "water is in my eye"), and as the subjects of sentences (*baby*, meaning "the baby fell down"). In no case was the verb, preposition, or sentence made explicit. With the exception of *bye bye cat* at 15;11 the child combined no words until 17 months. It is of considerable interest that most of the words noted above are "nouns"; those that are not nouns are "adjectives," i.e., attributes of nouns. "Verbs" are completely missing. . . . [T]he syntactic category of nouns is unique in that it alone appears in every grammatical relation. The richness of nouns in holophrastic speech, therefore, possesses an advantage for communication. Because all grammatical relations are implicit, nouns can be used in every available relation without endangering the comprehension of adults. Verbs do not have this property (compare a verb such as *reach* to a noun such as *banana* for conveying the locative relation).

When words are first combined, therefore, a number of grammatical relations already exist. The new development is not the appearance of grammar but the appearance of patterned speech to express grammar. How this takes place is the subject of the following sections. . . .

## [TELEGRAPHIC SPEECH:] PIVOT AND OPEN CLASSES

The terms "pivot" and "open" are taken from Braine (1963a) and refer to the outcome of a distributional analysis of child speech. When these analyses are conducted on speech collected from children of 18 months or so, at the very beginning of patterned speech, at least two classes of words emerge. One contains a small number of words, each frequently used—the "pivot" class. The other contains many more words, each infrequently used—the "open" class. Words from the pivot class almost always appear in combination with words from the open class and never alone or with each other. Words from the open class, however, may appear alone and with each other. The two classes generally have complementary membership and take fixed positions when combined. Pivot classes may appear first or second in sentences, but no word from a single pivot class appears in both places. The open class is quick to take in new vocabulary while the pivot class is slow to do so.

Such are the characteristics of the pivot-open distinction. These characteristics can be summarized by setting down the combinations in which pivot- and open-words appear—the basic facts supporting the distinction in the first place. Using "P" and "O" for "pivot" and "open," the following occur:

$$P + O$$
$$O + P$$
$$O + O$$
$$O$$

The only possibilities that do not exist are pivot-words uttered alone or in combination with each other. Everything else is possible.

Table 1 shows the pivot and open classes of three children studied by Brown and Bellugi (1964), Braine (1963a), and Miller and Ervin (1964), respectively. The table itself is from McNeill (1966a). For want of space, only a portion of each open class is represented, but the pivot classes are included in their entirety.

For the children in Table 1, sentences consisted of a word from the list on the left followed by a word from the list on the right—that is, P + O. Thus, *byebye fan, wet sock* and *that doed* all might have occurred. Not every combination allowed by Table 1 was actually observed, of course, but there are no evident differences between the combinations that did occur and those that did not and it is assumed that the gaps arise from sampling, not grammatical, limitations. . . .

## [TELEGRAPHIC SPEECH:] EARLY PHRASE STRUCTURE

The distinction between P and O classes is one way of describing the beginning stages of patterned speech. A different but closely associated way of describing these same stages is to write

TABLE 1. *Pivot and Open Classes from Three Studies of Child Language (McNeill, 1966a)*

|  | BRAINE | | BROWN | | ERVIN | |
|---|---|---|---|---|---|---|
| | P | O | P | O | P | O |
| | allgone<br>byebye<br>big<br>more<br>pretty<br>my<br>see<br>night-night<br>hi | boy<br>sock<br>boat<br>fan<br>milk<br>plane<br>shoe<br>vitamins<br>hot<br>Mommy<br>Daddy<br>. | my<br>that<br>two<br>a<br>the<br>big<br>green<br>poor<br>wet<br>dirty<br>fresh<br>pretty | Adam<br>Becky<br>boot<br>coat<br>coffee<br>knee<br>man<br>Mommy<br>nut<br>sock<br>stool<br>Tinker<br>Toy<br>.<br>.<br>. | {this that}<br><br>{the a} | arm<br>baby<br>dolly's<br>pretty<br>yellow<br>come<br>doed<br>.<br>.<br>.<br>{other baby dolly's pretty yellow} |
| | | | | | {here there} | arm<br>baby<br>dolly's<br>pretty<br>yellow<br>.<br>. |

the rules children follow in constructing sentences. Brown and his colleagues (Brown and Fraser, 1963; Brown and Bellugi, 1964; Brown, Cazden, and Bellugi, 1968) have pursued the linguistic development of three children, beginning in each case at about two years and continuing in one case until five, describing the children's linguistic competence at different stages in the form of generative grammars.

Not amazingly, grammars written at the earliest stages of development are simple. The following three rules summarize the performance of one child in Brown's study, Adam, at 28 months (based on McNeill, 1966a) [P stands for pivot]:

$$
\begin{array}{lll}
(1) & S \rightarrow & (NP \,\emptyset\, VP) \\
(2) & NP \rightarrow & \left\{ \begin{array}{ll} (P) & N \\ N & N \end{array} \right\} \\
(3) & VP \rightarrow & (V)\ NP
\end{array}
$$

Rules (1), (2), and (3) describe one-, two-, three-, and four-word sentences, depending on the options adopted in each rule. As usual, optional elements are enclosed with parentheses; following Fillmore (1968), linked parentheses (NP $\emptyset$ VP) indicate that at least one element must be chosen (NP and or VP). Rules (1) and (2) apply to such sentences as *ball, that ball,* and *Adam ball.* Rules (1), (2), and (3) apply together in *Adam want ball* and *Adam mommy pencil.* Notice that the last sentence is ambiguous in that *mommy* might originate with Rule (2) or (3)— *Adam mommy* or *mommy pencil.* Notice also that the verb of the VP in this grammar is optional, while the noun of the VP is obligatory. Other children obey the same strange rule (Bloom, 1968).

# REFERENCES

BLOOM, LOIS. Language development: Form and function in emerging grammars. Unpubl. Doctoral Dissertation, Columbia University, 1968.

BRAINE, M. D. S. The ontogeny of English phrase structure: The first phase. *Language,* 1963, **39,** 1–13.

BROWN, ROGER, and BELLUGI, URSULA. Three processes in the child's acquisition of syntax. *Harvard Educ. Rev.,* 1964, **34,** 133–151.

BROWN, ROGER, CAZDEN, COURTNEY, AND BELLUGI, URSULA. The child's grammar from I to III. In J. P. Hill (Ed.), *The 1967 Minnesota symposium on child psychology.* Minneapolis: Univ. Minn. Press, 1968. Pp. 28–73.

BROWN, ROGER, and FRAZER, C. The acquisition of syntax. In C. N. Cofer and Barbara S. Musgrave (Eds.), *Verbal behavior and learning: Problems and processes.* New York: McGraw-Hill, 1963. Pp. 158–197.

GREENFIELD, PATRICIA M. Who is "DADA"? Unpubl. paper, Syracuse University, 1967.

DE LAGUNA, GRACE A. *Speech: Its function and development.* New Haven, Conn.: Yale Univ. Press, 1927.

LEOPOLD, W. F. *Speech development of a bilingual child: A linguist's record.* Vol. 1. *Vocabulary growth in the first two years.* Vol. 2. *Sound learning in the first two years.* Vol. 3. *Grammar and general problems in the first two years.* Vol. 4. *Diary from age 2.* Evanston, Ill.: Northwestern Univ. Press, 1939, 1947, 1949(a), 1949(b).

McCarthy, Dorothea. Language development in children. In L. Carmichael (Ed.), *Manual of child psychology*. New York: Wiley, 1954. Pp. 492–630.

McNeill, D. Developmental psycholinguistics. In F. Smith and G. A. Miller (Eds.), *The genesis of language: A psycholinguistic approach*. Cambridge, Mass.: M. I. T. Press, 1966. Pp. 15–84.

Miller, W., and Ervin, Susan. The development of grammar in child language. In Ursula Bellugi and R. Brown (Eds.), The acquisition of language. *Monogr. Soc. Res. Child Developm.*, 1964, **29** (No. 92). Pp. 9–34.

Stern, Clara and Stern, W. *Die Kindersprache*. Leipzig: Barth, 1907.

# Why Not Pivot Grammar?

LOIS BLOOM

"Pivot-open" grammar is superficial, according to Bloom; it describes only the surface of a child's two-word sentence, not the underlying structure the child is using. Pivot grammar, then, does not describe fully what a child knows about language, and such a description is exactly what a grammar is supposed to be. Suppose a little boy says "Mommy sock" while his mother is putting his socks on, and later says "Mommy sock" while pointing to his mother's sock. The context of the utterances tells us that the first sentence is different from the second, even though they are superficially the same. The first means approximately, "Mommy is putting on my sock," while the second means approximately, "That is Mommy's sock." But a pivot-open (P-O) grammar will describe both in the same way: P-O, where Pivot = "Mommy" and O = "sock." From looking at the description P-O, you cannot.tell that the child actually uttered sentences that have two different underlying structures.

The alternative to pivot grammar is a set of rules that will describe in two different ways the underlying meaning of those two sentences. In the preceding article, McNeill has suggested some of these rules. Try using them to build sentences.

Bloom also points out that many "pivot" words can be and are used alone a great deal, though the definition of "pivot" says the opposite. To check this claim, compare the "pivot" words in Table 1 of McNeill's article with your own experience of small children's utterances.

Recent studies of language development have focused attention on the early stages of emerging syntax—the use of two-word and three-word sentences sometime during the second half of the second year of life. A number of investigators have reported similar distributional phenomena in samples of early child speech. When children begin to use two words in juxtaposition there are often a small number of words that occur frequently, in relatively fixed position, in combination with a large number of other words, each of which occurs less frequently. Braine (1963) named this first group of words "pivots"; children's speech has since been described in the literature as "pivotal," and . . . in terms of "pivot grammar." The apparent convergence on this point in the literature (in particular, Bellugi and Brown, 1964; McNeill, 1966a) has led to its application to programs for language disorders (see, for example, McNeill, 1966b). However, more recent research (Bloom, 1970) and a careful examination of earlier studies, such as the classic diary study of Leopold (1949), indicate that the time is at hand for a reevaluation of the phenomenon. How real is pivot grammar? . . .

## THE ORIGINAL EVIDENCE

The studies of Braine (1963), Miller and Ervin (1964), and Brown and Fraser (1963) were essentially distributional studies. They viewed children's speech as evidence, potentially, of a distinctive language, and for this reason they were admirably motivated to avoid the classes and categories of adult speech in their accounts. As a linguist would approach an exotic language in order to describe its grammar, these investigators looked at large numbers of children's utterances, and described what they saw in terms of classes of words based on their privileges of occurrence [i.e., where the word can be placed in an utterance]. What they found was essentially an orderly arrangement of at least two, possibly three, classes of words. Certain words such as "no," "no more," "all gone," "more," "this," "that," "here," "there," "off," "on," occurred frequently, in fixed position as either the first or second constituent in a two-word utterance, and shared contexts with a larger number of words that occurred relatively less frequently. Braine (1963) referred to the classes as "pivots" and "x-words," Brown and Fraser (1963) referred to "functors" and "contentives," and Miller and Ervin (1964) referred to "operators" and "non-operators."

Only Braine (1963) was discussing a relatively complete [body of] data. . . .

[McNeill's (1970)] account specifies all noun forms as an unmarked class in the child's lexicon—the class of "open" words. All other words are marked forms—marked, in the sense that they are identified as occurring only with nouns—the verbs, modifiers, and determiners which constitute the originally undifferentiated "pivot" class.

At least two critical questions can be raised about the adequacy of the pivot grammar notion as an account of children's early speech. First, how does pivot grammar relate to the grammar of the adult, model language? Large enough samples of adult speech would undoubtedly reveal [that] . . . [c]ertain words such as determiners, pronouns, and other function words or syntactic markers occur more frequently and in more varied linguistic environments in adult speech than do verbs, adjectives, and nouns. However, such rules of grammar as "pivot + open," "open + pivot," or "open + open" have no real analog among the syntactic structures of the adult model. How does the child progress from using pivotal utterances to using utterances that reflect the complex interrelation of rules that is the essence of adult phrase structure? McNeill, in both of the foregoing accounts, attempted to deal with this question. However, his conclusions are based upon certain assumptions—for example, that pivot forms do not occur in isolation, and that two nouns cannot occur together—that simply are not supported in the data.

The second question concerns the adequacy of the pivot grammar account for describing and explaining children's early speech. What does the notion of pivot grammar tell us about what children know about grammar when they begin to use syntax in their speech?

## THE ADEQUACY OF A PIVOT GRAMMAR ACCOUNT

The studies just discussed focused attention on the formal syntax of children's speech—on the arrangements of words in utterances. However, such descriptions of the form of speech [neglect] . . . the child's interaction in a world of objects, events, and relations. The goal of the research discussed here (and reported at length in Bloom, 1970) was to investigate the development of linguistic behavior in relation to aspects of experience related to the speech children use. . . .

To begin with, the data from Kathryn, Eric, and Gia contained utterances that were similar to those reported in the earlier studies and described as pivotal: Kathryn's utterances with "no," "this," "that," "more," and "hi"; Gia's utterances with "more" and "hi"; and Eric's utterances with "no," "another," "there," and "it." The children's use of these forms, in terms of semantic intention, could be described with some confidence. "No" most often signaled the nonexistence of the referent named by the second constituent (as in "no pocket"), where there was some expectation of its existence in the context of the speech event. "More" or "another" was used to comment on or to request the recurrence or another instance of an object or event (as in "more raisin" and "more read") . . . [C]ertain words occur often in children's speech apparently because of the nature of their referential function. Description of such utterances as pivotal is only a superficial description of relative frequency of occurrence and syntactic position.

Moreover, it turned out that the utterances described as pivotal, in the limited sense just indicated, proved to be a small percentage of the total number of utterances that were obtained from Gia and Kathryn. Only Eric's speech—during the period of time under discussion, when mean length of utterance was less than 1.5 morphemes—contained a preponderance of utterances such as have been so far described. The majority of the utterances of Kathryn and Gia presented certain critical problems for a pivot grammar account.

There were certain words in the children's speech that met all the distributional criteria for specification as pivots. The most frequent of these was either "Mommy" or reference to self— either by first name or, in Kathryn's case, "Baby" as well. . . .

One immediate objection to "Mommy" as pivot is that "Mommy" is a form having lexical status as a substantive or content word rather than a function word or syntactic marker. There is something intuitively wrong about classing "Mommy" as a function word, and, indeed, there has been a general inclination to avoid such characterization in the literature (see, for example, the discussion in Smith and Miller, 1966).

However, more important reasons for arguing against the distributional evidence that would class "Mommy" as a pivot or function form had to do with the fact that different utterances with "Mommy" meant different things. For example, in the first sample from Kathryn, the utterance "Mommy sock" occurred twice in two separate contexts:

(1)  Kathryn picking up her mother's sock
(2)  Mommy putting Kathryn's sock on Kathryn

It appeared that the difference in semantic interpretation between the two utterances (1 and 2) corresponded to a structural
difference in grammatical relationship between the constituents
"Mommy" and "sock." In one instance the structure was a genitive relation and in the other the relation between subject and
object. . . .

It is not the case that the words the children used—for example, "no" and "more"—have only one meaning. All of the
children used "no" subsequently to signal rejection, as in "no
dirty soap" (I don't want to use the dirty soap) and, still later,
denial, as in "no truck" (that's not a truck, it's a car). [But pivot
grammar fails to describe this difference.] . . .

Given that children comment on the notions of existence,
nonexistence, and recurrence of objects and events, one might
well wonder why they should talk about anything else—in the
light of what we know to be the achievements of sensory-motor
intelligence. Piaget (1960) has described a major achievement in
the child's development of thought with the realization of the
endurance of objects when removed in space and time. The child
learns that objects and events exist, cease to exist, and recur,
and so he talks about it. The important conclusion about the
development of grammar appears to be that children do not
simply use a relatively uncomplex syntactic frame (such as pivot
+ open); they talk about something, and syntax is learned by
the child in his efforts to code certain conceptual relations. . . .

[T]here is a crucial relationship between linguistic structure and underlying cognitive function. Indeed, it is difficult to
distinguish between cognitive and linguistic categories when ac-
counting for the expressed relations between actors or agents,
actions or states, and objects or goals.

It appears that the notion of pivot grammar describes children's early speech in only the most superficial way. Although
the notion of pivot speech describes certain distributional phenomena in early utterances, it is clear that children know more
about grammar, that is, more about the inherent relationships
between words in syntactic structure, than could possibly be accounted for in terms of pivot and open class analysis. If treatment
for language disorders in children is ultimately to be derived
from a model of normal language development, there is evidence
to indicate that a pivot grammar is not the model of child speech
to use.

## TREATMENT OF LANGUAGE DISORDERS

. . . Whether or not, and how, the normative data on language development in the literature can or should be directly applied to treating children with delayed language development are important questions (see Bloom, 1967). However, certain observations can be made at this time that should provide hypotheses for research directed toward evaluating procedures for treating language disorders.

First, the results of this study confirmed a conclusion that has been reached in every study of language development of children in the earliest stages of acquiring grammar. Children learn the syntax of language—the arrangements of words in sentences —before they learn inflections of noun, verb, and adjective forms. Although there may be alternation of certain forms from the beginning—"block," "blocks," and "sit," "sits"—the different forms of a word do not occur in contrast. For example, in the early samples, "-s" did not signal a meaningful difference, such as marking reference to more than one block as opposed to reference to only one block without expression of "-s." Thus, children learn word sequences (for example, "throw block") before morphological contrasts (as between "block," singular, and "blocks," plural).

Second, Kathryn, Eric, and Gia did not produce constructions that were potentially analyzable as noun phrases as their first (or most productive) syntactic structures. Rather, the most productive structures they produced (after utterances with initial /ə/) were those which, in the adult model, express the basic grammatical relations: subject-object, subject-verb, and verb-object strings. Although the grammars of Kathryn and Gia specified a noun phrase constituent (with attributive adjectives in Kathryn's lexicon only), this structure was far less productive than others which occurred, and Eric did not produce noun phrases at all. Based on these two observations, children appear to learn the expressions "throw block" or "Baby (subject) block (object)" before the expressions "big block," "red block," or "blocks."

Finally, the results of this study indicated that (1) the status of the referent in the context in which an utterance occurs, and (2) the child's relation to the referent in terms of behavior are critically important as influences on language performance. There were four contextual variables which characterized the occurrence of early syntactic utterances: (1) existence of the referent within the context, (2) recurrence of the referent or addition to the referent after its previous existence, (3) action upon the referent, and (4) nonexistence of the referent in the context where its existence was somehow expected.

The manifestation of the referent in the contexts of speech events was most significant. Utterances most often referred to objects or events which the child was able to see, and functioned as comments or directions, where the referent was manifest or imminent in the context of the speech event, as opposed to reports of distant past or future events. All of the children used a relational term, "more" or "another," to signal another instance of the referent or recurrence of the referent after previous occurrence. The productivity of verb-object and subject-object strings reflected the tendency for the children to talk about objects being acted upon. And, finally, as might be expected given the foregoing observations, their first negative sentences signaled the nonexistence of the referent. On the simplest level, children appear to learn to perceive and to discriminate (and, ultimately, to communicate) (1) such aspects of a referent as its existence, recurrence, or nonexistence, and (2) such relational aspects of events as between agent, action, and object before, among other things, such features of objects as relative size, color, or other identifying attributes.

It might be said that children learn to identify particular syntactic structures with the behavior and context with which they are perceived and then progress to reproducing structures in similar, recurring contexts. To use a structure in a new situation, the child needs to be able to perceive critical aspects of the context of the situation. Thus, the sequence in which the child learns syntactic structures may be influenced as much by his ability to differentiate aspects of situational context and to recognize recurrent contexts as by such factors as frequency of exposure to structures or their relative complexity.

Programs for language therapy that present children with linguistic structure (for example, pivot grammar) without attention to content ignore the very nature of language. It appears that learning a linguistic code depends upon the child's learning to distinguish, understand, and express certain conceptual relations. It would follow that children with language disorders need to learn more than simply the permitted cooccurrence of different words in their efforts at the analysis and use of language.

# REFERENCES

BELLUGI, U., and R. BROWN (eds.), *The Acquisition of Language*. Monograph No. 29, Chicago, Ill.: Society for Research in Child Development (1964).

BLOOM, L., A comment on Lee's developmental sentence types: A method for comparing normal and deviant syntactic development, *J. Speech Hearing Dis.*, **32**, 294–296 (1967).

BLOOM, L., *Language Development: Form and Function in Emerging Grammars*. Cambridge, Mass.: MIT Press (1970).

BRAINE, M. D. S., The ontogeny of English phrase structure: The first phase, *Language*, **39**, 1–13 (1963).

BROWN, R., and U. BELLUGI, Three processes in the child's acquisition of syntax, *Harv. Educ. Rev.*, **34**, 133–151 (1964).

BROWN, R., and C. FRAZER, The acquisition of syntax. In Charles N. Cofer and Barbara S. Musgrave (eds.), *Verbal Behavior and Learning*. New York: McGraw-Hill (1963).

LEOPOLD, W. F., *Speech Development of a Bilingual Child*, Vol. III. Evanston, Ill.: Northwestern Univ. (1949).

MCNEILL, D., Developmental psycholinguistics. In Frank Smith and George A. Miller (eds.), *The Genesis of Language*. Cambridge, Mass.: MIT Press, pp. 15–84 (1966a).

MCNEILL, D., The capacity for language acquisition, *Volta Rev.*, reprint no. 852, pp. 5–21 (1966b).

MCNEILL, D., *The Acquisition of Language: The Study of Developmental Psycholinguistics*. New York: Harper (1970).

MILLER, W., and S. ERVIN, The development of grammar in child language. In Ursula Bellugi and Roger Brown (eds.), *The Acquisition of Language*. Monograph No. 29, Chicago, Ill.: Society for Research in Child Development (1964).

PIAGET, J., *The Psychology of Intelligence*. Paterson, N. J.: Atherton (1960).

SCHLESINGER, I. M., Production of utterances and language acquisition. In D. I. Slobin (ed.), *The ontogenesis of grammar: A theoretical symposium*. New York: Academic Press, 1971, pp. 63–101.

SMITH, F., and G. A. MILLER (eds.), *The Genesis of Language*. Cambridge, Mass.: MIT Press (1966).

# Acquiring Negation and Questions

EDWARD S. KLIMA AND URSULA BELLUGI

Babbling and then using speech sounds are the two major stages Jakobson identifies in acquiring phonology; within the second stage are substages in acquiring particular sounds. Holophrastic speech and then telegraphic speech are the major stages McNeill sees in acquiring syntax; within telegraphic speech are substages in acquiring particular sentence types. Two of these sentence types are described here, by Klima and Bellugi: negative sentences and interrogative (questioning) sentences.

In order to discover the stages of acquiring negation and questioning, Klima and Bellugi studied thousands of utterances of small children; this version of their landmark study is shortened and adapted for beginning students. Capturing these stages in rules is not easy, and Klima and Bellugi would not insist that their rules mirror every detail of these children's speech processes. But it is perfectly clear that these sentences have structure; the rules in this article try to spell out that structure. Jakobson showed the structure in children's earliest sound systems; McNeill and Bloom showed the structure in their earliest sentences; now we see the structure in their earliest negatives and questions. These systems illustrate the fact that all children's utterances, in whatever language or dialect, are structured in every detail of sound and sentence. This realization is a powerful antidote to current theories suggesting that some children's speech is less structured and meaningful than that of other children.

## Methods of Collecting Data

We have as data for this research a developmental study of three children whom we have called Adam, Eve, and Sarah in previous reports with Roger Brown and his associates. Tape recordings of mother-child interchanges were made regularly in the children's homes. Each child was followed by a different investigator. The families were totally unacquainted and independent of one another, and each child heard a different set of sentences as "input." The children were beginning to string words together in structured utterances when we began the study. One child was 18 months old, another 26 months, and the third was 27 months old; however, all three were at approximately the same stage of language development.

**70**

For each child, then, there are two to four sessions of the speech of the mother and child per month as data. These sessions were tape recorded and later transcribed together with a written record made at the time of the recording which includes some aspects of the situation which relate to the meaning of the interchange. Here we describe three stages or periods of development defined by the length of the child's utterances.[1]

## NEGATION IN CHILDREN'S SPEECH

It should be understood that when we write rules for the children's grammar it is just a rough attempt to give substance to our feeling about, and general observations demonstrating, the regularity in the syntax of children's speech. We have intentionally allowed ourselves much freedom in the formulation of these rules. We are interested in the basis for particular constructions: notably those that characterize the language of all three children.

Not very much is known about how people understand a particular sentence or what goes into producing one; but something is known about the systematicity of adult language. It has seemed to us that the language of children has its own systematicity, and that the sentences of children are not just an imperfect copy of those of an adult.

In each of the three periods we studied, the children's linguistic systems could be described with abstract rules. We will first present samples of the data from a period, then attempt to write such abstract rules, rules that capture the underlying regularity of the children's speech at that period of linguistic development.

PERIOD 1. The sentences we want to describe from Period 1 are taken from the records of all three children:

*More . . . no.*
*No singing song.*
*No the sun shining.*
*No money.*
*No sit there.*
*No play that.*
*No fall!*
*No heavy.*

---

[1] [Ed.'s note: Length is measured in *morphemes;* see the General Introduction for a beginning definition of *morpheme.*]

*No want stand head.*
*No Mom sharpen it.*
*No Fraser drink all tea.*

Notice there are no negatives within the utterances, nor are there auxiliary verbs. The element which signals negation is *no* or *not*, and this element either precedes or follows the rest of the utterance.

Let us refer to the elements *Mom sharpen it, more, the sun shining,* in the above sentences as the *Nucleus.* The negation system at Period 1 can be considered as follows (everything within the square brackets is one sentence) :

$$(1) \quad \left[ \begin{Bmatrix} \text{no} \\ \text{not} \end{Bmatrix} - \text{Nucleus} \right]_s \text{ or } [\text{Nucleus} - \text{no}]_s$$

At this stage, there is no clear evidence that the child even understands the negative embedded in the auxiliary of adult speech, without at least some reinforcement. During this early period, the mothers often reinforce their negative statements as in *No, you can't have that,* to insure the children's comprehension of the negative impact of the sentence. What is interesting in the speech of the child at this stage is that he employs extremely limited means for negative sentences in his own speech, and the same system is repeated in all three subjects.

The rule for negation that we have given serves many negative functions in the child's speech at Period 1.

Adult : *Get in your high chair with your bib, and I'll give you your cheese.*
Child : *No bibby.*
Adult : *Oh, you don't want your bibby?*

Adult : *Well, is the sun shining?*
Child : *No the sun shining.*
Adult : *Oh, the sun's not shining?*

(An adult leans over to talk to the child. Child looks up and puts up a hand in warning.)
Child : *No fall!*

PERIOD 2. Some of the sentences we want to describe, again from all three children, are as follows :

*I can't catch you.*
*I can't see you.*
*We can't talk.*
*You can't dance.*

*I don't sit on Cromer coffee.*
*I don't want it.*
*I don't like him.*
*I don't know his name.*
*No . . . Rusty hat.*
*Book say no.*
*Touch the snow no.*

*Don't leave me.*
*Don't wait for me . . . come in.*
*Don't wake me up . . . again.*

*That not "O," that blue.*
*That no fish school.*
*That no Mommy.*
*There no squirrels.*

*He no bite you.*
*I no want envelope.*
*I no taste them.*

A characteristic of child language is the residue of elements of previous systems, and the sentences produced might well be described as a coexistence of the rules at Period 1, and a new system.

The major innovation of this new system is use of *Neg* within the nucleus of a sentence. In order to show where *Neg* now occurs, we will need more symbols:

| Symbol | Meaning |
|---|---|
| S | sentence |
| → | is composed of |
| ( ) | optional; may or may not appear |
| NP | noun phrase; for example, *the sun, I, we* |
| VP | verb phrase; for example, *sit there, say* |
| $\left\{ \begin{array}{c} \\ \\ \end{array} \right\}$ | choose only one line within brackets |
| T | tense |

Let us begin with a basic sentence structure in which a sentence is composed of a noun phrase, followed by an optional negative element, followed by a verb phrase:

(2)  S → NP — (Neg) — VP

In these sentences, *Neg* can appear in speech as *can't, don't, not,* or *no.* At this stage *can't* and *don't* are not the same as in adult language; the child apparently sees each as one word, rather than as *can + not* and *do + not.* Our evidence for this suggestion is that neither *can* nor *do* appears alone (apart from *-n't*) in the child's speech. At Period 2, then, *Neg* can be described as follows:

$$(3) \quad \text{Neg} \rightarrow \begin{Bmatrix} no \\ not \\ \text{V}^{neg} \end{Bmatrix}$$

$$(4) \quad \text{V}^{neg} \rightarrow \begin{Bmatrix} can't \\ don't \end{Bmatrix}$$

It is clear that the child understands the negative embedded in the auxiliary of the sentence by this period. For example:

Mother: *Oh, we don't have any bread.*
Child: *We have buy some.*
Mother: *He doesn't have a ball.*
Child: *Why not he have ball?*

There is also evidence that the child uses negatives to contradict a previous proposition either expressed or implied, as in

Mother: *Did you play in the snow?*
Child: *No, play sunshine.*
Mother: *You told me to sit on it.*
Child: *No, you sit **there.***

PERIOD 3. A sample of the sentences to be described, again from all three children:

*Paul can't have one.*
*I can't see it.*
*This can't stick.*
*We can't make another broom.*
*I didn't did it.*
*Because I don't want somebody to wake me up.*
*I don't want cover on it.*
*I don't . . . have some . . . too much.*
*You don't want some supper.*
*You didn't caught me.*
*You didn't eat supper with us.*
*I didn't see something.*
*Paul didn't laugh.*
*I didn't caught it.*

*I gave him some so he won't cry.*
*Cause he won't talk.*
*Donna won't let go.*

*No, I don't have a book.*
*No, it isn't.*
*That was not me.*
*I am not a doctor.*

*This not ice cream.*
*This no good.*
*They not hot.*
*Paul not tired.*
*It's not cold.*

*That not turning.*
*He not taking the walls down.*

*Don't put the two wings on.*
*Don't kick my box.*
*Don't touch the fish.*

*I not hurt him.*
*I not see you anymore.*
*Ask me if I not made mistake.*

In the speech of the children, the auxiliary verbs *do* and *be* now appear in declarative sentences and questions, as well as in negative sentences; so we can now begin with a basic structure like

(5) $S \rightarrow NP - (Aux) - VP$

and suggest some such rules as follow:

(6) $Aux \rightarrow T - V^{aux} - (Neg)$

(7) $V^{aux} \rightarrow \begin{Bmatrix} do \\ can \\ be \\ will \end{Bmatrix}$

In the speech of the children at this period the negative auxiliary verbs are now no longer limited to *don't* and *can't*, and the auxiliary verbs now appear in declarative sentences and questions, so that the auxiliary verbs can be considered as separate from the negative element of the sentence.

Indeterminates now start appearing in the children's speech, in affirmative utterances such as *I want some supper* or *I see something*. The children's negative sentences have the form *I don't want SOME supper* and *I didn't see SOMETHING*, as opposed to the adult form *I don't want ANY supper* and *I didn't see ANYTHING*. This change from *some* to *any*, *something* to *anything*, is called indefinite coloring; examples of indefinite coloring in the children's speech are rare, and do not appear with any regularity until later stages.

### *Rules For Negation In Children's Speech*

PERIOD 1:

(1) $\left[ \left\{ \begin{array}{l} no \\ not \end{array} \right\} - \text{Nucleus} \right]_s$ or $[\text{Nucleus} - no]_s$

PERIOD 2:

(2) $S \rightarrow NP - (\text{Neg}) - VP$

(3) $\text{Neg} \rightarrow \left\{ \begin{array}{l} no \\ not \\ V^{neg} \end{array} \right\}$

(4) $V^{neg} \rightarrow \left\{ \begin{array}{l} can't \\ don't \end{array} \right\}$

PERIOD 3:

(5) $S \rightarrow NP - (\text{Aux}) - VP$

(6) $\text{Aux} \rightarrow T - V^{aux} - (\text{Neg})$

(7) $V^{aux} \rightarrow \left\{ \begin{array}{l} do \\ can \\ be \\ will \end{array} \right\}$

## QUESTIONS IN CHILDREN'S SPEECH

PERIOD 1. The questions to consider, from all three children are

*Fraser water?*
*Mommy eggnog?*
*See hole?*
*I ride train?*
*Have some?*
*Sit chair?*
*No ear?*
*Ball go?*

*Who that?*
*Why?*
*What(s) that?*
*What doing?*
*What cowboy doing?*

*Where Ann pencil?*
*Where Mama boot?*
*Where kitty?*
*Where milk go?*
*Where horse go?*

Again, one can consider the elements *Fraser water, Mommy egg-nog, Ann pencil, milk go,* in the above questions as the nucleus. As with the negative, in Period 1 there is very limited structure to the nucleus, which consists primarily of nouns and verbs without indication of tense and number.

There are two kinds of questions to be considered here: questions that can be answered by *yes* or *no;* and those that contain a question word beginning with *wh,* e.g., *why, what, who.* The questions without a question word can be thought of as $Q^{yes/no}$ — *Nucleus,* where the *yes/no* marker is expressed as rising intonation.

In this first stage of the development of questions we see a structure similar to the first structure of negative sentences. In *yes/no* questions, as in negation, the nucleus of the early sentence is undisturbed:

(8)  $S \rightarrow Q^{yes/no}$ — Nucleus

The *Wh-*questions can be described as a list which includes only a few routines that vary little across the three children. The most common questions are some version of *What's that?* and *Where NP (go)?* and *What NP doing?* Once again, as with *can't* and *don't* in the negation system, it appears that the words in this period are different from adult structure, and much more limited in meaning. One might tentatively suggest a formulation as follows:

(9)  $S \rightarrow Q^{what}$ — NP — *(doing)*
(10)  $S \rightarrow Q^{where}$ — NP — *(go)*

At this period the children are producing *Wh-* questions that are much more limited than those in adult speech. Evidence of this limitation is found in the children's lack of understanding of some adult *Wh-* questions that superficially resemble those the children are producing. At Period 1 the child generally does not respond, or responds inappropriately, to these adult *what* and *where* questions:

Mother: *What did you hit?*
Child:  *Hit.*

Mother: *What did you do?*
Child: *Head.*

PERIOD 2. Some of the questions to consider are

*See my doggie?*
*That black too?*
*Mom pinch finger?*
*You want eat?*
*I have it?*

*Where my mitten?*
*Where baby Sarah rattle?*
*Where me sleep?*

*What book name?*
*What me think?*
*What the dollie have?*
*What soldier marching?*

*Why you smiling?*
*Why you waking me up?*

*Why not he eat?*
*Why not me sleeping?*
*Why not . . . me can't dance?*
*Why not me drink it?*
*You can't fix it?*
*This can't write a flower?*

There is some development in the superficial structure of the sentences since Period 1. Notably, pronouns have developed, articles and modifiers are more often present, some inflections (*-ing* and the plural inflection *-s*) occur, and the verb phrase may include a prepositional phrase. There are no modal auxiliaries, such as *can* and *may*, in affirmative sentences, and only two negative modal forms (*don't* and *can't*). There are few indeterminates or indefinites, such as *some* or *a*.

There seems to be a gradual development of rules and not necessarily the wholesale replacement of one total system by another. In Period 2, there is still no inversion of subject and verb in *yes/no* questions. But some adult *Wh-* questions are developing. By this period there are appropriate answers to many *Wh-* questions:

Mother: *What d'you need?*
Child: *Need some chocolate.*

Mother: *Who are you peeking at?*
Child: *Peeking at Ursula.*

Mother: *What d'you hear?*
Child: *Hear a duck.*

We suggest for Period 2:

$$(11) \quad S \rightarrow \left\{ \begin{matrix} Q^{yes/no} \\ Q^{what} \\ Q^{where} \\ Q^{why} \end{matrix} \right\} Nucleus$$

$$(12) \quad Nucleus \rightarrow NP - V - (NP)$$

PERIOD 3. The questions to consider are

*Does the kitty stand up?*
*Does lions walk?*
*Is Mommy talking to Robin's grandmother?*
*Did I saw that in my book?*
*Oh, did I caught it?*
*Are you going to make it with me?*
*Will you help me?*
*Can I have a piece of paper?*
*Where small trailer he should pull?*
*Where the other Joe will drive?*
*Where I should put it when I make it up?*
*Where's his other eye?*
*Where my spoon goed?*
*What I did yesterday?*
*What he can ride in?*
*What you had?*
*What did you doed?*
*Sue, what you have in you mouth?*
*Why the Christmas tree going?*
*Why he don't know how to pretend?*
*Why kitty can't stand up?*
*Why Paul caught it?*
*Which way they should go?*
*How he can be a doctor?*
*How they can't talk?*
*How that opened?*
*Can't it be a bigger truck?*
*Can't you work this thing?*

Between the previous period and this one many parts of the children's grammar have undergone developments. Some auxiliary verbs now switch places with the subject in certain *yes/no* questions. At this point, the system that has been developed bears striking similarities to the adult pattern. Notice, however, that the auxiliary verbs are not inverted with the subject noun phrase in *Wh-* questions. There are other aspects that set the child's system apart from the adult language; for instance, the children at this stage do not produce any combinations of auxiliary verbs (*will have, may be,* etc.).

We suggest the following basic structure:

(13) S → (Q (Wh)) — NP — Aux — VP

(14) Aux → T — $V^{aux}$

(15) $V^{aux}$ → $\begin{Bmatrix} can \\ do \\ will \\ be \end{Bmatrix}$

We suggest the following transformations[2] ($X$ = all other sentence elements):

    I. *Wh-* questions:
        Q — $X^1$ — Wh-word — $X^2$ ⇒ Wh-word — $X^1$ — $X^2$

    II. *Yes/no* questions:
        Q — NP — Aux — VP ⇒ Aux — NP — VP

### *Rules for Questions in Children's Speech*

PERIOD 1:

    (8) S → $Q^{yes/no}$ — Nucleus

    (9) S → $Q^{what}$ — NP — (*doing*)

    (10) S → $Q^{where}$ — NP — (*go*)

PERIOD 2:

    (11) S → $\begin{Bmatrix} Q^{yes/no} \\ Q^{what} \\ Q^{where} \\ Q^{why} \end{Bmatrix}$ Nucleus

    (12) Nucleus → NP — V — (NP)

PERIOD 3:

    (13) S → (Q(Wh)) — NP — Aux VP

    (14) Aux → T — $V^{aux}$

---

[2] [Ed.'s note: See the General Introduction for a beginning definition of *transformation,* or *sentence-transforming rule.*]

$$(15) \quad V^{aux} \left\{ \begin{array}{l} can \\ do \\ will \\ be \end{array} \right\}$$

Transformations:

    I. *Wh-* questions:
        $Q - X^1 -$ Wh-word $- X^2 \Rightarrow$ Wh-word $- X^1 - X^2$

    II. *Yes/no* questions:
        $Q - NP - Aux - VP \Rightarrow Aux - NP - VP$

## Mitigation and Questioning in a Verbal Repertoire

WILLIAM LABOV

"Junior, do this over."

"I will not!"

Junior has the ability to create a negative sentence—"I will not" as opposed to the affirmative "I will." He also has the ability to create a question: "Isn't that the best I've done so far?" The question is, how does Junior *use* his ability to create negatives and questions?

If Junior is aware that both "I will not" and "Isn't that the best I've done so far?" are refusals, he can choose between the two kinds of refusal. One refusal challenges the other person; the other refusal is much less likely to cause a confrontation. Junior can choose to challenge or not to challenge. But suppose he is not aware that he can refuse in a mitigated way? If Junior has done this work over three times already and is completely sick of it, he may offer the only refusal he knows, and lose his job or be thrown out of class as a result.

Study of language *use* is called sociolinguistics. Sociolinguists point out that each person has a verbal repertoire, a number of ways of using language. But these repertoires differ from one social or ethnic group to another. Children usually acquire them by exposure. If a child is exposed to only one culture, he or she may be misunderstood by people from different social groups. Labov details this possibility in relation to refusals

and questions in school; but his discussion is equally applicable
to other situations. Joos, Abrahams, and Labov go further into
the nature of a verbal repertoire in Part 2.

## MODES OF MITIGATION AND POLITENESS

We are only beginning to describe the rules for the use of
language, but in this area we can observe many differences between nonstandard and standard speakers. The nonstandard
speaker is undoubtedly handicapped in many ways by his lack of
control over mitigating forms which are more highly developed
in middle class and school language. These forms are used to
avoid conflict between individuals who meet in some kind of face-
to-face encounter. The child may not know the mitigating ways
of disagreeing with the teacher which make such disagreement
acceptable in the school situation. It is not uncommon for Negro
children to simply accuse the teacher of lying where middle class
white children might say, "There's another way of looking at it."
Faced with the statement "You a lie!" most teachers find it necessary to react forcefully. After one or two such confrontations,
most students learn to say nothing. But some students continue
to object without learning the means of doing so without conflict.
In the school records of boys we have studied, we find many cases
where they have been reprimanded, even demoted, for their failure to use mitigating forms of politeness. For one fourteen-year-
old named Junior, who can be described as a verbal leader of his
subgroup, we find such entries as the following:

Nov. 63   Frequently comes to school without a tie. . . . He fre-
          quently calls out answer. When told not to call out he
          made an expression of disgust. He then refused to
          accept the rexographed sheet the teacher gave to the
          class.
Nov. 63   When asked to re-write a composition he adamantly re-
          fused. He said, "I will not." He doesn't practice any
          self control.
Dec. 63   Was fighting with another boy in class today . . .
Sept. 66  *F* in citizenship.
May 67    Mother has been in touch with school regarding son's
          truancy.

This record can be interpreted in several ways. Junior may be
unable to compete with the smart kids and finds a way out in being "bad." Or it may be that he does not care at all about school

and is simply expressing his defiance for the system. It is just as hard for us to interpret the school record by itself as it is for the teacher to deal with the student in this formal situation without any knowledge of the vernacular culture.

When we listen to Junior speaking outside of school, we can see that he has a natural command of language and has no difficulty in expressing his ideas. The following quotations are taken from a session with Junior, a black fieldworker, and Ronald, one of Junior's best friends. First of all, it is apparent that Junior does have strong feelings of resentment against the school and white society.

Junior: Like I'ma tell you the truth. They jus' want everythin' taken away from us. . . . Who do we work for? Whities! Who do we go to school for? Whities! Who's our teachers? Whities!

. . . . . . . . . . . . . . . .

Interviewer: If the whitey's not different from you, how come he has everything?

Ronald: They don't have everything.

Junior: Yes they do!

It is important to note here that Junior and Ronald are members of the Jets, a group which is quite indifferent and even hostile to black nationalism and the Muslim religion. Junior has not been taught to be militant; the resentment expressed here is a product of Junior's own thinking—the result of his own experience. Despite his antagonism towards the dominant white society, he has retained a strong sense of realism in his evaluation of it. An argument with Ronald as to whether high school diplomas are necessary:

Ronald: And I'm 'onna tell you; I'm 'onna say *why* what they say you have to have a high school diploma. Some whitey's probably ain't got a high school diploma, and he still go out to work. My father ain't got a high school diploma.

Junior: Your father ain't no whitey, is he?

Ronald: No, but he has no high school diploma, but he go out there and work, right?

Junior: O.K.! . . . But . . . I'ma tell you, you're wrong in a *way*—cause ev'ry whitey—ev'ry whitey, if

> they out o' school, they went through *high* school.
> If they didn't go to college they went through *high*
> school. If the whities didn't go through high
> school, how come they got everything? . . .
> 'Cause they had the *knowledge*.

It seems clear that Junior is a much better speaker than Ronald.
In complex arguments of this sort, Ronald's syntax gets him into
problems like the double *but* clauses or the unsolved labyrinth of
his first sentence quoted above. Junior has no such difficulty expressing his ideas. Furthermore, he has the ability to put one
argument on top of another which is characteristic of those who
win verbal contests.

> Junior:   If you—if you was in a high school—right? Why
>           do people graduate?
>
> Ronald:   'Cause they try hard to grad—'cause they *want*
>           to graduate.
>
> Junior:   'Cause they *learn* . . . 'cause they *learn*. If they
>           didn't learn, and they just stood around, they
>           wouldn't have everything. 'Cause you got to *work*
>           to get to high school, you got to *work* to get from
>           elementary to junior high . . .

In this dialogue, Junior seems to express very well the values of
middle class society. He shows a full cognitive awareness of the
importance of education. It comes as something of a shock then
to learn that at the time of this interview he was in the eighth
grade and his reading score was 4.6—more than three years behind grade. And the disciplinary record cited above indicates that
he is very unlikely to be graduating from high school himself.
Note that the *they* of *they learn* seems at first reading to refer to
a very general *people* who graduate; it seems to be an inclusive
rather than an exclusive *they*. But when Junior says "*they*
wouldn't have everything . . ." it is clear that he is not including himself among the people who graduate.

Is there any internal evidence within this record as to why
Junior is not learning to read—why he is not taking advantage
of the school system to get what he so plainly wants? It is obviously not a question of his verbal intelligence. A reading of disciplinary events shows serious sources of conflict between him
and his teachers which are preventing him from using his intelligence for the acquisition of knowledge. Each of these reported
incidents was the occasion for an interruption in his school work,
a violent confrontation with authority. The teachers report that

he "calls out answers" and "doesn't practice any self control." The kinds of skills which Junior is lacking appear to be those verbal routines of mitigation which would make it possible for him to object and refuse without a major confrontation. Of course the record reflects the teachers' subjective impressions rather than what actually happened, but we can see enough to reconstruct the kinds of events involved and to isolate the problems for further study. Note that Junior's disciplinary record begins in the fifth grade, when he was eleven. The exchange between him and the teacher must have been something like this:

> Teacher: Junior, this is very sloppy work.
> Junior: No it isn't!
> Teacher: Now you take that composition and write it over again!
> Junior: I will not!

The sentence "I will not" was striking enough to be quoted in the teacher's report. It is an elliptical response, short for "I will not write that composition over again," but it is certainly not illogical. We hear a good deal about the faults of nonstandard language, but its strong points certainly include brevity and clarity. The problem with "I will not" is that it is altogether too clear: it lacks the verbal indirection which could have been used to make the objection and perhaps win the argument. Instead, the direct refusal without mitigation led to the end of the verbal exchange ("You go right down to the office . . .").

To show what Junior did not do, it is necessary to analyze the rules for commands, and for refusing commands, which prevail for standard English and the middle class society in which that language is embedded. Commands and refusals are actions; declarations, interrogatives, imperatives are linguistic categories —things that are said, rather than things that are done. The rules we need will show how things are done with words and how one interprets these utterances as actions: in other words, relating what is done to what is said and what is said to what is done. This area of linguistics can be called "discourse analysis"; but it is not well known or developed. Linguistic theory is not yet rich enough to write such rules, for one must take into account such sociological, nonlinguistic categories as roles, rights, and obligations. What small progress has been made in this area is the work of sociologists and philosophers who are investigating informally the Type I rules which lie behind everyday "common sense" behavior.

We have, however, begun work in this field relative to requests and commands, so that it is possible to indicate what Junior might have done besides answering "I will not." Commands or requests for action are essentially instructions from a person A to a person B to carry out some action X at a time T.

$$A \rightarrow B : X\,!/T$$

This is the explicit form of such a command. But there are a number of unstated preconditions which must hold if the receiver B is to hear the command as valid (or a "serious" command). It is necessary that he believe that the originator A believes four things: that, at time T,

  a. X should be done.
  b. B has the obligation to do X.
  c. B has the ability to do X.
  d. A has the right to request that B do X.

These four preconditions are not only part of the process of judging and reacting to a command. They are also used for indirect ways of making the command or request. Either a statement or a question about any of these four preconditions can stand for and be heard as the command itself. Thus the teacher could have said:

  a. This has to be done over. *or*
     Shouldn't this be done over?
  b. You'll have to do this over. *or*
     Don't you have to do neater work than this?
  c. You can do better than this. *or*
     Don't you think you can do neater work than this?
  d. It's my job to get you to do better than this. *or*
     Can I ask you to do this over?

Some of these forms are heard as forceful requests, but many are heard as mitigated and very polite forms, even more than "Would you please . . . ?" Furthermore, not only are these preconditions used in making requests, but they are also utilized for mitigated forms of refusal. Denials of any of these preconditions, or questions about them, will serve the same purpose as "I will not" as far as the activity of refusing is concerned. Thus Junior could have said:

  a. I don't think it's sloppy enough to do over. *or*
     It's not that sloppy, is it?
  b. I'm not supposed to be doing penmanship today. *or*
     If it's right it doesn't have to be pretty, does it?

  c. I sprained my wrist and I can't write good. *or*
    That's the best I've done so far, isn't it?
  d. You have no right to tell me that. *or*
    Are you telling me to do everything twice?

Except for the last two forms, which concern the teacher's rights and are therefore extremely challenging, these kinds of refusals leave the door open for further negotiation. They are heard as partial refusals, in the sense that it is clear Junior will not re-write the composition unless the teacher repeats the command. But most importantly, they are *deniable* refusals. If someone is accused of refusing a command by such forms, he is entitled to say, "I didn't refuse, I was only . . ." Furthermore, if the teacher wants to retreat, he too can say that Junior did not refuse, avoiding the loss of face involved in accepting a refusal. There are thus many adult ways of doing business in this situation. But the form "I will not" stands in contrast to all of these and signals an unwillingness to use the mitigated forms; it thus represents a direct challenge to the authority of the teacher. Perhaps Junior was angry and wanted to precipitate a crisis: the question is, did this eleven-year-old have the skills to avoid that crisis if he wanted to?

It is not suggested that all of these indirect, mitigating forms be taught in school. Much of this unnecessary elaboration may be expendable, just as much of the elaboration of formal syntax may be a matter of ritual style. But differences in the knowledges of such rules must be studied to isolate the areas of conflict which proceed from ignorance on both sides. It is not entirely clear that all of the adjustment must be on the part of the nonstandard language and the vernacular culture.

## ASKING QUESTIONS

One of the most common speech events which occurs in school is the asking of questions. Teachers ask students questions with astonishing frequency—sometimes five or six a minute or in some schools as high as fifteen or twenty a minute. Students occasionally ask teachers questions, though not as often. Sometimes the teacher asks questions to get students to ask questions, or at least to get them to talk as much as possible. In one way or another, teacher questions are often conceived of as ways of getting students to talk.

In sociolinguistic research, we also use questions to obtain speech—as much as possible—and we have therefore given a great deal of attention to the form of questions, their underlying presuppositions, and the kind of question that gets the most results. We observe very different patterns in speakers of different ages and social backgrounds, and different styles of questioning on the part of middle class and working class interviewers. But, on the whole, it appears that questions may not be very good means of getting people to talk. In order to understand why, it may be helpful to compare questions to the requests and commands discussed in the previous section.

A *question* may be used to execute many different kinds of speech acts, including commands, insults, jokes, and challenges. Here we are properly considering *requests for information*. This is a subtype of requests for action, discussed above, but with several different properties. Abstractly, these have the general form that A asks B to perform one particular act—to give him, by speaking or writing, certain information. The time is normally unstated and is understood as "right now."

A → B : tell me X !

It has been noted, particularly by Skinner, that questions have a mandatory force. In answer to a question, one can lie or equivocate, but there is a strong social compulsion to respond; it is indeed very difficult to say nothing when someone asks you the time. Requests for information are harder to refuse than requests for action. In many social situations, including the schoolroom, two of the four conditions are presumed to hold at all times: B believes that A believes that

    d. A has the right to ask B the question.
    b. B has the obligation to answer.

Students may object to questions asked by the teacher on the ground that they are unfair, unclear, or not included in the assignment, but they cannot object that he has no right to ask. Thus (unless the teacher is a substitute, where anything goes), we do not have reports of

    Teacher:   How much is 7 and 9?
    Student:   You have no right to ask me that!

Correspondingly, the student knows that he is under an obligation to answer, if only to say that he does not know. Given these two constants in the situation, the student then must consider whether the other two conditions hold in order to see what is being done—whether the teacher believes that

    a. X needs to be told to A.
    c. B has the ability to answer.

Under normal conditions, this is not a simple problem to resolve. In the schoolroom, the situation is particularly difficult, since there are different options exercised in rapid succession. Sometimes condition *a* holds : the student believes that the teacher really does not know X and wants to know it. If condition *c* also holds—the teacher believes that the student has this information —we are dealing with a genuine request for information.

    Teacher:    Did you find this homework too hard?

But this is not the usual case; in the classroom, condition *a* normally does *not* hold. There are then several possibilities which the student must consider. He may be dealing with

1. A known-answer question. A believes that he knows the answer and that B may not know it.
2. A no-answer question. A believes that there is no correct answer to the question.
3. A rhetorical question. A believes that he knows the answer and that B knows it too.

The first of these is the most typical—the test question. It is not a request for information about X but about B's ability to give X. More generally, it is *a request for proof*. Students generally understand that they are to say the minimum necessary to establish this proof. On various occasions, they have discovered that this is a situation where anything they say may indeed be held against them. One wrong remark added to an acceptable answer may act as a disproof, whereas a short but correct answer may be accepted as evidence of a larger body of correct information. Answers to test questions are therefore usually quite short.

    The second type of no-answer question is essentially a *request for display*. "Tell me everything you can about *this*!" says the educational tester and places a free-form blank in front of a child. The response desired is for the child to begin talking and continue as long as he can. Discussion questions in high school classes are frequently of this type—leading questions designed to "draw out" the student.

    The third type is equally common, but the work done by these rhetorical questions is often difficult to analyze. If the teacher asks "Now how many eyes do I have?" this may be a prelude to a discussion of bilateral symmetry among animals, a preface to a disciplinary rebuke, or an introduction to a discussion of odd and even numbers. The "correct" response is to give the obvious answer so that the teacher can continue with whatever he has in mind. Yet many rhetorical questions of this sort turn out to be forms of entrapment. After a certain number of bad experiences, many students learn not to volunteer answers to riddles, "come-ons," or invitations.

If we now consider the task of deciding which of these various possibilities holds at any given moment and what the consequences of a wrong decision may be, it appears that students are required to develop a very high level of expertise. Our intuitive responses to such situations run far ahead of our ability to analyze them. Even so, the situation may be quite unclear for many students. Consider the intelligence test in which the examiner holds up an orange and says, "What is this?" The child must ask himself: Is this a known-answer question, or a rhetorical question? If the latter, what is it a prelude to? Such "controlled testing" of educational psychologists provides a constant stimulus, but there is no control on the interpretations which intervene between the stimulus and the response. What is the question getting at? What type of question is it? What are the consequences of answering or not answering? The safest port in these storms may appear to be a simple "I don't know." The problem for the examiner is then to interpret the meaning of this "D.K." If he takes it as evidence of B's ability to give the information, it may be seriously misleading. Given the various pressures and uncertainties of the test situation and the fact that it is impossible for the child not to answer, it follows very often that he will utilize "don't know" as his only available means of refusing the request for information. This is the only assertion he can make which cannot be contradicted.

If we are to understand verbal behavior in the schoolroom situation, we must begin to solve the general question posed here. How do students know, in a given situation, what kind of question is being posed, and what is requested of them? When we have the answers to this, we may simultaneously begin to understand some of the reasons for failure, confusion, and rejection in the classroom.

We will also be in a better position to carry out research on the verbal skills and linguistic habits of school children. It is a simple matter to ask a question, but to obtain a meaningful answer is much harder.

# Applications for the Study of Language Acquisition

## Receptive Bidialectalism: Implications for Second-Dialect Teaching

RUDOLPH C. TROIKE

What do you have to know in order to translate from one dialect to another? You must know both dialects. Yet reading aloud in one's own dialect, while looking at a text written in another dialect, is often seen as evidence of *failure* to understand the other dialect.

Children acquiring language always comprehend before becoming able to produce. Adults retain the ability to understand more forms of language than they can produce; the first twenty minutes of a British movie may be less well understood than the rest of the film, while the audience tunes its receptive abilities to the British dialect. Then an efficient translation starts taking place, and the audience hears the content of the speech, paying little attention to its pronunciation.

Children's receptive abilities are crucial in reading language different from that which they produce, as Goodman and Buck suggest in Part 4 of this book. Troike suggests here that the ability to produce a second dialect can be based on the child's receptive ability to understand that dialect.

Troike believes that a child should have the *opportunity* to learn to speak a high-status dialect, if he or she does not already

**91**

speak it. In Part 2, Sledd speaks strongly against *forcing* a child
to speak a dialect other than that spoken at home. These two
papers on bidialectalism are not, then, in conflict, since one
speaks of chosen bidialectalism and one of forced bidialectalism.

It has long been a matter of common knowledge that a person's receptive competence in his language far exceeds his productive competence: one's "passive" or "recognition" vocabulary
is always larger than one's "active" vocabulary. Even from the
time he is first learning to talk, a child understands more than he
can say, and this state of affairs continues throughout his life-
time. Most people, for example, can understand a speaker from
another area even though they might be quite unable to sound
like him. It is this capacity, then, and its relevance for education,
that we will be concerned with in the present discussion.

The usual assumption of the teacher, and the assumption on
which most language testing is based, is that a student's production will adequately reveal his linguistic competence. That is, if
a student consistently uses such forms as *He don't, We done ate,*
or *She come home at five,* it is usually assumed that he *does not
know* the forms *He doesn't, We have eaten* (or *finished eating*)
and *She comes* (or *came*). While this may sometimes be true,
such an assumption, by ignoring the receptive aspect of linguistic
competence, can often lead to serious mistakes in evaluation and
teaching strategy.

A considerable amount of recent work has shown convinc-
ingly that students from the first grade on (and often earlier)
have a well-developed receptive knowledge of dialects other than
the one which they normally speak. (Here it should be noted that
we are using the term *dialect* in the sense employed by most
linguists as referring to any distinguishable variety of a language, either regional or social, of which the so-called "standard"
is but one.) The clearest evidence has come from testing in which
children and adolescents of various ages have been asked to repeat sentences which they hear recorded on tape, or spoken by
an investigator. The following examples represent the responses
of some preschool and first-grade children from Texas and West
Virginia to such a taped oral-repetition test ("N" indicates Negro, "A" indicates Appalachian white) :

| MODEL | RESPONSE |
|---|---|
| Mother helps Gloria. | Mother help Gloria. (N) |
| Gloria has a toothbrush. | Gloria have a toothbrush. (N) |

| | |
|---|---|
| She cleans her teeth with her brush. | Her clean her teeth with her brush. (N) |
| David has a brush for his hair. | David have a brush for he hair. (N) |
| She has soap on her head. | She has soap(t) on hers head. (A) |
| David and Gloria are clean. | David and Gloria is clean. (A) |
| They are on their knees. | They are on theirs knees. (A) |
| The socks are on Gloria's feet. | The socks is on Gloria's feet. (A) |
| The children go to bed. | The children goes to bed. (A) |

William Labov has obtained similar results with Negro teenagers in New York. Some examples follow:

*Model:*        Nobody ever sat at any of those desks, anyhow.
*Response:*     Nobody never sat in none of those desks anyhow.
*Model:*        I asked Alvin if he knows how to play basketball.
*Response:*     I ask Alvin do he know how to play basketball.

In order to explain why the repetitions differ from the model, we must assume that the child does not merely attempt to mimic the sentence as the model says it, but rather he first *decodes* the sentence for its meaning, and then *re-encodes* it in the form he might have used in framing the sentence as an original utterance. Essentially, then, he is *translating* from the dialect of the model into his native dialect. So consistent is this behavior that oral-repetition testing provides both a rapid diagnostic instrument for determining native dialect characteristics and an excellent device for evaluating receptive knowledge of a second dialect.

A necessary conclusion which must be drawn from the preceding examples is that the students certainly understood the sentences which they heard, or else they would not have been able to translate them into their native dialect. In fact, this is the best sort of evidence for the correctness of their understanding, since if they simply repeated the sentences as given by the model, there would be no way of assuring that they actually understood them. In short, we must recognize that in most instances, children are already receptively bidialectal by the time they come to school.

The effects of this phenomenon are not limited to oral repetition, but extend to reading as well. An early but very revealing example is given by Daniel Defoe in 1724 (in a chapter on Somerset in his book *A Tour Through the Whole Island of Great Britain*):

It cannot pass my Observation here, that, when we are come this Length from London, the Dialect of the English Tongue, or the Country-way of expressing themselves, is not easily understood. . . . It is not possible to explain this fully by Writing, because the Difference is not so much in the Orthography, as in the Tone and Accent; their abridging the Speech, *Cham*, for *I am; Chil*, for *I will; Don* for *do on*, and *Doff*, for *do off*, or *put off;* and the like.

I cannot omit a short Story here on this Subject: Coming to a Relation's House, who was a Schoolmaster at Murtock in Somersetshire, I went into his School to beg the Boys, or rather the Master, a Play-day, as is usual in such Cases. I observed one of the lowest Scholars was reading his Lesson to the Usher in a Chapter in the Bible. I sat down by the Master, till the Boy had read it out, and observed the Boy read a little oddly in the Tone of the Country, which made me the more attentive; because, on Inquiry, I found that the Words were the same, and the Orthography the same, as in all our Bibles. I observed also the Boy read it out with his Eyes still on the Book, and his Head, like a mere Boy, moving from Side to Side, as the Lines reached cross the Columns of the Book: His Lesson was in the *Canticles of Solomon;* the Words these:

"I have put off my Coat; how shall I put it on? I have washed my Feet; how shall I defile them?" The Boy read thus, with his Eyes, as I say, full on the Text: "Chav a doffed my Coot; how shall I don't? Chav a washed my Feet; how shall I moil 'em?"

How the dexterous Dunce could form his Mouth to express so readily the Words (which stood right printed in the Book) in his Country Jargon, I could not but admire.

It is interesting to note that in this instance the boy's translation into his native dialect included not just changes in pronunciation and grammar, but in vocabulary as well. The rapidity and unconsciousness with which the translation was carried out leave no doubt that the boy understood the passage he was reading.

Conversely, if a vocabulary item or grammatical construction is not in a child's receptive competence, he will experience great difficulty in attempting to repeat a model sentence, often producing only incoherent fragments. Labov has found that though Negro teenagers will readily convert a question such as *I don't know if he can come* into *I don't know can he come*, they are frequently unable to repeat otherwise identical sentences containing *whether* instead of *if*. Similarly, most first-graders tested cannot repeat a sentence such as *John and Bill both have their shoes on*, seemingly because of the *both* in the sentence. Apparently if the brain does not possess the necessary information to process a sentence as it is heard, the speaker will be unable to re-encode it or even to simply imitate it as said. Thus, repetition testing can also be a useful means of discovering what grammatical or lexical features *are not* in the receptive repertory of speakers at various age levels.

These observations indicate that a teacher engaged in teaching a standard variety of English as a second dialect should not make the mistake of assuming that because students do not use the standard form they do not know it. Rather, their already existing receptive competence in the second dialect should be recognized, and the task of the teacher should be seen as one of building on this knowledge to enable the students to make use of it in their own production (in the appropriate situations, of course). The speaker who says *It is a book on the table,* but understands and recognizes its equivalence to *There is a book on the table,* clearly does not have to be taught the second structure from scratch, but only needs practice and training in using it in his own production.

However, since not all students are bidialectal to the same degree, it is equally important to assess what grammatical structures are not present in a student's receptive competence. It is patently absurd as well as frustrating to the learner to base reading lessons or classroom questions on structures which are absent from his native dialect and which he does not yet understand in the second dialect. Testing for receptive competence should therefore be an integral part of any second-dialect program (or, for that matter, any language arts program).

It has sometimes been suggested that the first-grade child is too innocent of the social world around him to realize the significance of dialect differences, or to be adequately motivated to acquire command of a second dialect. But five- and six-year-olds are far more socially perceptive than most adults give them credit for, and it is only a cultural myth which prevents the recognition of this fact. Several anecdotes will serve to illustrate the point. As is well known, there are two ways in American English of pronouncing the word *creek:* in northern dialects it is pronounced to rhyme with *pick* (even by educated speakers), while elsewhere it rhymes with *peek.* An acquaintance of the writer happens to be a "crick" speaker, while his wife is a "creek" speaker. Several years ago his son, who was then five, said something to his father about the "creek" behind their home, and was promptly reproved by his four-year-old sister with "Don't you know that you're supposed to say 'crick' to Daddy and 'creek' to Mommy?" In another instance, when a father scolded his five-year-old son for saying *crawdad* instead of *crayfish* when playing with a friend, Jimmy, the boy replied, "All right, I'll say *crayfish* when I'm talking to you, but I'll say *crawdad* when I'm playing with Jimmy, because that's what he calls it."

In still another example, a first-grade girl who was being interviewed was asked to make up a story about a picture in a magazine. The girl drew herself up, began "Once upon a time, . . ." , and launched into a very formal narrative which was notable for containing no contractions. At the end of the story, she visibly relaxed, and from there on freely used contractions for the remainder of the interview. The whole subject of the range of styles and dialects in the productive and receptive repertory of children is only just beginning to receive attention, and a great deal yet remains to be learned. Nevertheless, it is clear that even pre-first-graders are far from linguistically naïve and have already learned a great deal about the adaptive significance of linguistic behavior within their own very real social world.[1]

We do not need to wait until the student is a teenager to begin second-dialect instruction, on the grounds that he is insufficiently aware before then of social significance of a standard dialect. Indeed, this would be a grave mistake, for the optimum age for language learning is before eight, after which it declines, dropping radically after puberty. To be most effective, second-dialect teaching should begin as early as possible. Given sufficient opportunity to practice the patterns of the second dialect, children can readily develop unconscious, automatic control over their use. The longer such instruction is delayed, the less effective it will be, and the lower will be the students' chances of developing complete and unconscious control over the forms of the second dialect, to be available to him should he choose to shift into the "standard" dialect on appropriate occasions.

A satisfactory program should recognize and build upon students' existing linguistic strengths, and where their receptive knowledge already encompasses standard forms, students should be given adequate practice in bringing these to the productive level. Recognizing further that receptive ability always exceeds productive ability, greater efficiency and effectiveness in teaching may be attained by the use of materials and techniques specifically designed to expand receptive competence, which in turn can form the basis for expanding productive ability. There is ample evidence available to show that, given the proper materials and teaching techniques (including the use of tape-recorded materials

---

[1] For further evidence on this point, see John L. Fischer, "Social Influences on the Choice of a Linguistic Variant," *Word*, 14 (1958), 47–56.

for repetition practice), even students in the first grade can develop control over the forms of the standard dialect.

All of the discussion to this point has seemed to assume that second-dialect teaching and learning is a one-way process. But it need not be, and indeed probably should not. One of the most common complaints heard from teachers working in integrated schools is that they cannot understand the speech of their Negro pupils. From this it is apparent that the teachers simply lack any receptive competence in their students' dialect (though inasmuch as the students can understand their teacher, *their* receptive competence clearly exceeds that of the teacher). Since a teacher can achieve greater rapport (not to speak of communication) with her students if she can understand them, it might well be desirable to devise materials to help teachers acquire an adequate receptive, if not productive, competence in the dialect of their students. Such an experience might, if nothing else, impart a greater respect for the students' achievement, and an appreciation of the difficulties involved in learning to speak a second dialect.

## Writing for the Here and Now

STEPHEN N. JUDY

"I believe that arguing is good because people have a way to say it without harming some one or hurting a live thing. But you can't always walk away. (You may not understand this because I haven't got the words to say it.)" The thirteen-year-old who wrote this is saying something important to her, and she cares whether her teacher understands her. Where should a teacher start with this paper? Should the teacher circle "it" and write *Unclear pronoun reference* in the margin, thus confirming the girl's fear that she will not be understood? Doesn't this girl need to know the community's usage rules, which say that in this sentence "it" should be clarified?

In learning how to speak a language, children hear and use words in a real, meaningful context: they are talking to other people, or other people are talking to them; they have something

important to say and someone important to say it to. Stephen
Judy shows how to make a schoolroom part of this natural process.
Judy thinks that writing should be done for a real reason, to a
real audience; and teachers should respond, just as occurs in
the natural speech situation. Teachers should also edit writing.
Judy contrasts responding with editing and shows that each has
its place.

    Usage rules are discussed in McDavid's article on "Standard
English" and Sledd's article on bidialectalism and "Standard
English," as well as several other articles, in Part 2 of this book.
The general introduction to Part 2 attempts to give an overview of
these rules.

Evaluating student compositions has been a problem for
teachers of English ever since writing became a regular part of
high school English curriculums in the nineteenth century. In his
textbook, *Aids to English Composition*, published in 1845,
Richard Green Parker was one of the first to comment on ways
of evaluating writing:

> Merits for composition should be predicated on their neatness, cor-
> rectness, length, style, &c.; but the highest merits should be given
> for the production of ideas, and original sentiments and forms of
> expression.

Parker's approach to the problem seems quite contemporary with
its emphasis on rewarding "the production of ideas" and "original sentiments" rather than dealing exclusively with neatness
and mechanical correctness. However, like many present-day
teachers, Parker found it *easier* to comment on mechanical matters than to wrestle with abstract and nebulous things like content and originality, and on the whole, his text showed far more
concern for pointing out "deficiencies" than for rewarding
"merits." For example, a theme grading guide at the end of the
text dealt almost exclusively with the kinds of errors that could
be indicated in the margins of a paper with "shorthand" symbols,
"arbitrary marks" of the kind "used by printers in the correction of proof sheets."

Throughout the twentieth century, teachers have continued
to develop new approaches for evaluating and assessing student
writing. We have tried pointing out errors and allowing students
to discover their own errors; we have hired lay readers to discover errors and offer advice *in absentia;* we have tried blanket
red-pencilling and selective grey-pencilling of errors; we have
emphasized the positive and tried to slip in occasional comments

about the negative; and we have experimented with grading systems: single grades, double grades (solving the form/content dilemma by avoiding the issue), and multiple grades (the idea of the double grade carried to its logical, and quite possibly absurd, conclusion).

Despite these devices and procedures, however, student writing has not seemed to improve in corresponding ways. Research surveys, including the Braddock, Lloyd-Jones, Schoer *Research in Written Composition* (NCTE, 1963) and Stephen Sherwin's *Four Problems in Teaching English* (NCTE, 1969), show that experiments with grading and evaluation systems have never produced significantly positive results. Research techniques in the field are not sophisticated, of course, and it may be that the lack of "results" is a problem for researchers, not teachers. However, common sense and the experience of most teachers indicate that the research is accurate—that our grading and evaluation schemes, old or new, simple or sophisticated, have not led to significant improvement in student writing.

Why hasn't evaluation worked? Obviously no clear answer to that question is available; if it were, we would have tried it and found success. However, I want to suggest that a major reason may be that from Parker's time to the present, approaches to evaluation have always been *future directed* rather than looking at writing as something for the *here and now*. Evaluation has emphasized getting students ready for "next time," instead of helping them find success now.

For example, with his talk of "merits" and "deficiencies," Parker sounds rather like a Puritan preacher trying to prepare his flock for the hereafter. Although we have softened the language to speak of "strengths" and "weaknesses," our attitude has remained much the same. We have operated on the assumption that if a student writes enough themes and receives enough evaluation, he will, sometime in the near or distant future, write *The Perfect Theme* that will be his pass through the compositional Golden Gates.

People write for many reasons: to share experiences, to help themselves understand what is happening, to record information, and to communicate ideas. Few people write simply for the sake of learning to write better "next time." When an evaluation procedure implies that all work is being done simply in preparation for more work in the future, the reality of the writing situation is destroyed. Ironically, future directed evaluation, even when it is done humanely and sensitively, may actually *inhibit* growth in writing. If, instead, the teacher ignores his hopes for future competence on the part of students and concentrates on helping his students find success with their writing here and now, he can expect to make writing a real, important experience for students, one through which both they and their writing will grow.

A friend who is in publishing once pointed out to me that magazine and book editors are not interested in teaching authors how to write better. When a manuscript arrives, an editor looks through it, comments on it, calls for some revisions, makes some changes, and suggests other modifications. All this "instruction" is simply aimed at getting out a successful publication. On the whole, the editor remains indifferent to whether or not the author's writing improves in the process. However, many authors acknowledge that the process does help them write better, and many writers depend quite heavily on their editors for advice. The "moral" here is that by concentrating on the present, the editor helps the writer find success, and when he does, he becomes, almost incidentally, a "teacher of writing," someone who also helps people do it better "next time."

I think we can escape the trap of future directed evaluation by adopting the general kind of attitude an editor takes. An editor, of course, works with adults who are reasonably accomplished writers to begin with. Because the teacher works with young people who are in the process of growing, both as people and as writers, his specific roles will be more complicated. At times the teacher should be an editor, dealing with strengths and weaknesses in papers as publication or public presentation approaches. At other times, however, he must serve in somewhat more sensitive roles; he may be a talent scout, adult respondent, interested human being, friend, or advisor. He needs to find ways of individualizing the kind of response he makes to student papers, rejecting the narrow role of teacher-evaluator and becoming a kind of "manuscript manager," deciding on an individual basis what needs to happen for a piece of writing to bring satisfaction to the student here and now.

I would like to block out an approach I have tried in both high school and college classes with students of a wide range of ability levels. It consists of a series of stages or "checkpoints" where the teacher can pause to consider alternative ways of helping students. In every case, evaluation, commentary, criticism, and response become directed toward the single aim of helping an individual student have a satisfying experience with his writing as quickly and effectively as possible.

## I. LISTENING FOR THE STUDENT'S VOICE

When a paper first comes in, the teacher needs to begin his assessment by trying to discover whether or not the student was involved in the writing activity. Can you hear the student "talking" when you read it? Is it a lively paper that reveals the student's active participation in his work? This quality in student writing is difficult to define but rather easy to detect. Many people call the quality "voice"—meaning that the paper sounds as if a unique person wrote it, not a computer or a bureaucrat. In *Children's Writing* (Cambridge University Press, 1967), David Holbrook describes it as "sincerity" and characterizes it as a feeling of openness, liveliness, and animation. I enjoy Ken Macrorie's characterization of its *opposite* as "Engfish" and the paper written in that style as being "Engfishified" (*Uptaught.* Hayden, 1969).

In essence the teacher asks, "Is there evidence that this has been a productive, reasonably enjoyable writing experience for the student?" If the answer is "yes," it will be revealed in the tone of "aliveness" which one can sense in the language of the paper.

If the answer is negative, the teacher has reached an important decision point in the assessment process. Traditionally, when a teacher receives flat, dull, colorless writing, he blames it on the student: "You're not trying hard enough. Do it over!" I think this blame has been misplaced. No student deliberately creates lifeless writing. Making "Engfish" is dull and boring, and few people outside the Pentagon would choose to write very much of it. In a majority of cases, dull writing probably can be traced back to the teacher, the assignment, or an unfavorable classroom climate. Perhaps the assignment was poor—too complicated, too easy, irrelevant, or just plain silly. Perhaps the student doesn't trust the teacher or his classmates and is unwilling to share his ideas with them. Whatever the cause, I think the teacher needs to turn his attention to finding out what went wrong, looking as much to himself and his teaching as to the student for an explanation. The teacher can then stay awake at night, trying to figure out something else for the student to do. What *will* work for him? What are his interests? What are his skills? Can we find a project that will excite him? How can we persuade him to trust us?

But what does the teacher do with the manuscript? It seems pointless to demand revision or further work on something that was dead to begin with. I think the teacher should, therefore, respond as positively as he can to the paper, commenting on the "good" parts (without faking a response) and return the paper. Often the teacher can say quite directly, "Look, I had the feeling you didn't enjoy doing this. Am I right? Let's see if we can't come up with something else you would rather do."

Here is a paper that illustrates the problem of voice. It was written in a junior high school class in which the students were asked to write a letter of application for a job they would like to have sometime:

> Good morning Sir I would like to apply for a banking clerk. I think I am well qualified to fill the position. I have had three years of dealing with money I know how to handle money quite well. I am a very responsible man and also very dependable. I could be trusted to handle your money without your having any uncertainty about me. And as I said before since I have been handling money.
>
> My schooling is great, I have just graduate from college, and majoring in bookkeeping which deals with a lot of money.
>
> I can tell you how much money you are making or lossing. If you were to hire me you can be certain that I will do my job to the best of my ability. Yes! This is just the kind of bank that I would like to work at.
>
> I feel that it would be a privilege working for your bank.
>
> (H.) Allen Johnson

Except for a few bright spots, this letter seems to me quite lacking in voice, and I doubt that Allen profited much by doing it. Many of the phrases seem forced, unnatural, and excessively formal: "I could . . . handle your money without your having any uncertainty about me." "I feel it would be a privilege working for your bank." Occasionally Allen's real voice comes through. His exclamation, "Yes!", seems to be a victory over both The Business Letter and his own doubts about the banking business. His signature is done in playful parody of "official" looking signatures and adds an original touch. But the remainder is dull and repetitive, sounding much like a junior high school student trying to "make it" in what he imagines to be adult language.

The result is a letter which, by almost any criterion, is unsuccessful: Allen has not learned much about business letters;

his letter *won't* land him a job; and his teacher must be thoroughly frustrated by almost every aspect of his writing.

What went wrong? I suspect that although the assignment seemed "reasonable" and "practical," the realities of job hunting are so far removed from the world of the junior high school student that the assignment became meaningless. Allen is simply not ready to worry about jobs (and there is no reason why he should be), so the assignment drove him into using a false, stuffy voice. In dealing with the paper I would compliment Allen on his enthusiasm and point out that he has done a good job of thinking about what a banker would want to know about a prospective employee. (He has done a skillful job of "surveying his audience," even though the topic and audience were not closely related to his current needs.) I would then turn attention to finding other projects that Allen would enjoy doing. It is conceivable that he might enjoy going to a bank to find out what actually happens there. I think it more likely, however, that the teacher could find interesting writing ideas for Allen in less academic areas, topics more typically for junior high school, writing sports stories or telling tales of the grotesque and macabre.

## II. RESPONDING TO STUDENT WRITING

One hopes that the amount of "voiceless" writing a teacher receives will be small and that early in the school year he can help each student find areas where writing is profitable and interesting. Once the teacher recognizes that a paper *has* voice, it is appropriate that he take time to respond (orally or in writing) to the student before going on to consider matters of revision or proofreading. A student has spent much time writing the paper; he needs response and reaction quickly.

"To respond" to student writing simply means to react to a paper openly and directly, as a "person" rather than as a teacher. It differs from evaluation in being a shared reaction rather than a set of future directed instructions for improvement. In responding the teacher can tell how he reacted to the paper ("I really felt the fear you described when the storm hit.") ; he can share similar experiences ("I remember the fight I had with my parents over taking a job when I was a sophomore.") ; he can indicate his own beliefs and tell about the ways in which he agrees or disagrees ("I can see your point about the way newscasters operate, but I really don't share your view of the President."). Response can move beyond direct reactions to suggest new or related directions for the student to explore ("You obviously enjoyed writing this. Have you ever read any of Edgar Allan Poe's stories?" "Have you ever made a movie? I think it might be interesting for you to try to catch the same idea on film."). It is the honest reaction of an interested, informed, literate adult, not the pedagogically directed instruction of a theme-grader.

In responding, however, the teacher differs from the ordinary reader in a very significant way: the teacher is willing to ignore all kinds of graphic, rhetorical, and syntactic problems that a regular reader might find frustrating or disagreeable. The teacher will *fight* to dig out the meaning of a page. He will puzzle over idiosyncratic spellings, ignore a 250-word run on sentence, forget about the fact that statistics and supporting evidence are missing, and struggle to uncoil long strings of identical loops that pass for handwriting. It is critical—at this point in the assessment process—that the teacher find the meaning of the paper and correspond with the student about it. Other "problems" can be taken care of at a later point in the process.

As David Holbrook has pointed out in *Children's Writing,* looking past problems to "decipher," appreciate, and enjoy student writing without having one's reaction biased by "errors" and "blights" is extremely difficult, more difficult for English teachers than for most people, since we have all our advanced degrees in linguistic flaw-detecting.

Perhaps the best model for this kind of response is the letter one would write in reply to something received from a young relative—a son, daughter, or nephew. For close relatives most of us are willing to decipher and to respond directly to meaning. Few of us would grade or evaluate letters from a relative, and not many parents would take time to question the usage in a sentence like, "I been smoking pot I like it." We would make almost unlimited efforts to find out what our young friends are saying, thinking, feeling, and doing; teachers should adopt the same attitude in responding to student writing.

## III. PUBLIC OR PRIVATE?

When a response has been recorded (or made directly to the student through conversation), the teacher needs to determine what should happen to the paper next. The question becomes, "Should this paper be published?" Should it be made public and given a wider audience than the teacher? Although we want to avoid writing that is "teacher-written," it is important for us to recall that not all writing is meant to be made public. The teacher should consider carefully whether providing an audience will produce a positive experience for the student.

Here is a paper submitted by a high school sophomore girl:

> One day me and this girl went to the store. The girl was from Chicago and she thought she was bad. She kept pointing her umbrella in my face. I told her stop but she kept pushing so I grabbed it out of her hand and stuck her with it. I felt sorry but I said no better for a person like that. Only fools fight. And when you fight you really lose whether you win or not. I believe that arguing is good because people have a way to say it without harming some one or hurting a live thing. But you can't always walk away. (You may not understand this because I haven't got the words to say it.)
>
> —C. S.

It is possible that C.S. would find it helpful to have other students read and discuss this paper, and her classmates might be able to offer some useful or supporting advice. However, this paper seems to fit an audience-category described by James Britton as writing addressed to "the teacher as trusted adult." C.S. is obviously puzzled and concerned about her behavior, and she seems to be less interested in "communicating a message" than exploring her own experience and seeking a response from someone else. She knows—or thinks she believes—that "only fools fight," and she is persuaded that people should settle disputes through argument rather than "harming some one or hurting a live thing." Yet, "You can't always walk away," and in this situation she felt committed to action. As a "trusted adult" (a role which the teacher should accept with pleasure, even if it sometimes puts him in the uncomfortable position of learning about students' problems), the teacher needs to respond directly to C.S., supporting her efforts to sort out her own beliefs and values.

For writing that is private, this point is another good place to end the assessment process. The teacher can respond to C.S. in the way described in the previous section. The paper should then be returned to her without any pedagogical comment. Although there may be some rhetorical problems with the writing, there seems to be no point in asking for revision. C.S. expressed her feelings; the teacher read, understood, and responded. That seems to be enough.

## IV. DETERMINING A FORM OF "PUBLICATION"

If the teacher thinks a paper should be made public, there are many different ways he can provide students with a readership. Some papers are best "published" by having them read aloud to the class, either by the author or the teacher. Some writing should be read to a tape recorder and made part of the class library of recorded literature. Students' work can be posted on the board, submitted to a class newspaper or magazine, sent to the school paper or magazine, run off on ditto for the class, or circulated in manuscript form. Every form of writing and each kind of publication makes particular, specialized demands on the writer.

Students should, of course, have an audience in mind while they are writing, but often the best form of publication will not be apparent until after the writing has been completed. A short, witty poem that might bring a good laugh to the class when read aloud might die when set in print. A paper that began as an essay on student-teacher relationships might merit being sent to the school paper, and if the editors won't publish it, it should be turned over to the underground paper. A play which has absorbed a student's time for several weeks surely deserves presentation, but it may work better as reader's theater or a radio play than as a full stage production. As an expert on writing forms, media, and styles, the teacher can help the students find the most productive forms of publication.

Here Roman Cirillo, an eighth-grader, writes about "How Airplanes Flies," and his paper presents some interesting publication problems:

> Few people know why or how an airplane flies. The explanation is very simple. There no mysterious mechenism or machinery to study. You don't have to take a plane apart or crawl around inside to understand why it stays in the air. You just stand off and look at it. Airplanes flies because of the shapes of its wings. The engine and propellor have very little to do with it. The pilot has nothing to do with making the plane fly. He simply controls the flight. A glider without an engine will fly in the air for hours. The biggest airlines will fly for a certain length of time with all the engine shut off. A plane flies and stay in the air because its wings are supported by the air just as water supports a fellow. Toss a flat piece of tin on a boat. Toss a flat piece of tin on a pond and it will sink at once. If you bend it through the middle and fasten the end together so its is watertight it will float.

There are obviously many rhetorical problems with this essay. It lacks clarity and it often leaves the reader somewhat confused. But, if one looks past the errors and "infelicities," "How Airplanes Flies" is an open, clever explanation of flight. The paper has a strong, clear voice; we can *hear* Roman's patient instruction to someone who is ignorant of the principles of flight: "You don't have to take a plane apart or crawl around inside to understand why it stays in the air. You just stand off and look at it." Roman is a good teacher, and his explanation of how shaping metal enables the plane to fly is skillful (even though incomplete). Roman would, no doubt, fail any test on writing analogies, similes, and metaphors; but he makes excellent use of analogy in relating how things float in an invisible substance—air—to a common phenomenon that is easily observable—a boat on water.

In its present form, however, the paper will probably not find much success with an audience. There are too many problems of clarity and too much drifting and backtracking for a reader (particularly one who *doesn't* understand flight) to stay with it for long.

Because Roman seems to have so much trouble handling the written word (one senses quite a struggle with the writing process behind this paper), I think the teacher might recommend that this project be completed as an oral "publication," particularly since Roman seems to be such a good "talker." Perhaps he can plan a demonstration for those members of the class who are interested. Drawing on his essay, he might bring in a dishpan and some foil to demonstrate the shaping and floating of materials. Perhaps he can bring in some model planes or photographs or drawings to illustrate flight. An oral presentation should be a good experience for him, and significantly enough, it will be an experience that has its origins in writing.

## V. EDITING

Until writing has reached the publishing stage and the teacher and student have settled on a form of publication, there seems to be little point in offering comments about the rhetoric of students' writing. Up to this point, the teacher has been concerned with responding to the student in personal terms and trying to determine the most valuable route toward publication.

When the form of publication has been determined, commentary about writing becomes appropriate, and the teacher and student can begin raising questions about effectiveness, clarity, organization, style, and structure. However, I think it is important to relate this discussion to the *particular form of publication* and the *particular audience* for the paper. Publications and age levels have differing standards, and if editorial advice is to be helpful, it must be valid. Too often we impose blanket, adult, textbookish standards on student writing which will never be read with adult criteria of evaluation in mind.

For example, if a student writes *"Cowhide* is the crummiest show on t.v.," the teacher's initial reaction may be to point out that "crummy" is not a standard critical term, that one cannot simply declare a show crummy without supplying "reasons" and "supporting evidence." However, if the audience for the paper is a class of seventh-graders who watch *Cowhide* regularly, "crummiest" may be *just* the word; the students know what the show is like and will either agree that it is crummy or argue that "it isn't all *that* crummy." In either case, the students don't need "evidence" or "reasons"; they already know the arguments. On the other hand, if the student is writing to the network president to demand that the show be removed from the air, the teacher can be genuinely helpful by pointing out that the word is inappropriate, *not* to teach appropriateness or critical analysis, but to help insure that the student's letter will be read seriously by the president (or his secretary).

Sybil Marshall has suggested in *An Experiment in Education* (Cambridge University Press, 1966) that it is very difficult for the teacher to know what kinds of advice will and will not seem real to the students. Too often, she suggests, teachers try to force adult standards on young people, with the effect that the teacher's advice consistently comes out seeming hollow, academic, authoritarian, or just plain false.

Perhaps the easiest way to avoid this problem is for the teacher to involve the students in the editorial process as much as possible. When the students ask specific questions, the teacher should, of course, respond freely. However, if students share writing with each other and suggest to one another how their papers can be revised to become more effective, the teacher can be reasonably certain that "real" questions will come up. With a little guidance and practice, students can become quite adept at providing constructive commentary for each other, and their advice will be more realistic (if less sophisticated) than the teacher's.

Here is an essay written for publication in a junior high school newspaper:

*Hippies*

Hippies are people with long hair and dress with beads and flowers. They never shave. They are always marching and causing troubles. On one college they threw spikes, black widow spiders, and lead balls at the police. They burned a lot of things.

Hippies take L.S.D. and many other harmful drugs. This probably causes them to act queer.

The police have to hit them to straten them out.

—Bill Lowe

I would use the editorial conference with other students to sponsor a discussion of the paper. It *may* be that the students will debate Bill's assumptions and offer him advice on bringing both sides of the issue into his paper. On the other hand, it is equally possible that because of. similarities of the students' family backgrounds, values, and the like, the editorial conference will *support* Bill's paper, accepting it without reservation. If that happens, the teacher should not dismiss the discussion of papers by students as "not working" but rather should recognize that "real" audiences don't always make the kinds of demands on a writer that the textbooks say they do. When Bill and his friends are a little older, they will be more sophisticated in their ways of analyzing such situations, particularly if the teacher has the confidence (and the patience) to give them the freedom to make their own editorial decisions now. If students are given frequent opportunities for editorial work, they almost invariably become more skilled, and in many respects more demanding, in asking for changes in writing.

## VI. COPY READING

For too long, textbook writers and composition teachers have blurred the distinction between editing (changing content and form) and proofreading (polishing up matters of spelling, mechanics, and usage). In our zeal to make students skillful writers of "standard" English, we have pounced on proofreading errors as early as the first draft, blithely pointing out problems in words and sentences which may well disappear entirely during the revision stage.

We should delay discussion of mechanical and syntactic correctness until the last possible moment in the writing process, leaving the students free to write, discuss, and revise papers without any hesitation because of uncertainty over rules of correctness. Only after the student has edited his writing into a final form that satisfies him should we open the discussion of mechanics and usage.

The debate over whether we should impose standard English on students is a complex one, involving psychology and sociology as much as English and linguistics, and I will not take it up in detail here. I am personally very reluctant to see "standard" *imposed* on kids in any way, be it done overtly or through subtle plans which claim to recognize the validity of a person's dialect while asking him to change it or to maintain alternatives to it.

However, as part of the copy reading process, I think the teacher should help the students who want it put their papers into a form which larger audiences will find acceptable. The teacher can point out to students (if they don't know it already from years of experience) that some audiences are "offended" by unclear handwriting or language that doesn't conform to certain "standards." The teacher might also note that failing to conform to some standards can create communications problems. Most kids see these ideas readily enough, and if "the quest for correctness" has not dominated the entire writing process, they are willing to participate in a polishing session to get their paper into a form that will not cost them readers.

Once again, however, it is important to note that the teacher should consider the proofreading changes which are necessary for *this* paper for *this* audience at *this* time. For instance, if the paper is simply to be read aloud or tape-recorded by the author, any discussion of spelling, punctuation, or capitalizaton is aimless and a waste of time; even if the paper is misspelled, illegibly written, and totally unpunctuated, the author can read it aloud, and discussing "problems" contributes nothing to his success. If, on the other hand, the paper is going to be duplicated, it is quite legitimate for the teacher to work with the student to help get the paper into audience-acceptable form. Even here, however, the teacher needs to be cautious. If "It's me" is the standard form in the spoken dialect of a class, the teacher should not try to present "It's I" as being appropriate. What matters is the audience, not a textbook description of "standard."

During the proofreading stage, the teacher can be quite direct in the instruction he offers. Instead of setting students adrift in handbooks or rule books or letting them "find their own errors," the teacher can work directly—as a proofreader might— showing the students the changes that need to be made. This takes much of the mystery out of the process and does not unduly delay the final publication.

In practice, of course, much of the copy work can be done by the students themselves. In every class there are a few kids who have—one way or another—mastered "the rules." The teacher can let these students share their enviable knowledge by setting them up as proofreading consultants for other members of the class.

## VII. PUBLISHING

The payoff. If the process has worked, the teacher will have the satisfaction of seeing the student's work well received, whether it is read to the class, printed, hung on the board, pasted in a book, or passed around the classroom. If the teacher has been a helpful editor and manuscript manager, the student will find success.

Equally important, I think, is that although this way of assessing student work is *not* future directed, it is nevertheless likely that the process *will* produce long range changes and improvements in the students' writing. When students find success with an audience, they remember the parts of the process that contributed to their success, including the advice and suggestions offered by the teacher and student-editors. In short, concentrating our efforts on present success will probably produce more change and "transfer" than traditional future oriented methods.

As I have described it, this approach to assessment may seem excessively complicated and time consuming—unrealistic for a teacher with five classes and 150 students. However I have found that with both college and high school classes this approach actually speeds up the assessment process and provides more free time for the teacher to take up other roles. It takes less time to write a note of personal response on a paper than to mull through and write out detailed, pedagogically oriented evaluative comments. It is much faster to offer direct editorial advice keyed to specific publishing situations than it is to puzzle over which errors one will selectively attack "this time." In addition, as a class "grows" in the course of a quarter or semester, the students take over more and more of the process. The stages become less distinct because the students become more adept at editing their own work, which is, of course, one of our traditional goals. All this creates more time for the teacher to move around the class working on a one-to-one basis with students who seek his help as a writing consultant.

I have said nothing of theme *grading* in this essay. There are many precedents for grading based on student recommendation, self-assessment, end-of-term conferences, raw quantity of work, and teacher-student contracts. It is important that anyone who wants to try this approach to the assessment of student writing explore alternatives to conventional grading. Only by beating the grading system can we fully use the advantages of having students write for the here and now.

## Language Acquisition and Teaching

The information in Part 1 can be organized into three major suggestions about language acquisition, each of which has important implications for teaching.

**SUGGESTION I:** A child seems to learn language through active rule-forming, rather than through passive imitation.

*Central Article:* Philip Gough, "The Limitations of Imitation"

*Supporting Evidence in Other Articles:*

Slobin, Jakobson, McNeill: Children in all cultures go through highly similar stages in learning language. If language were learned by imitation, the way it is learned would differ from country to country, varying with the language heard and the local ways of interacting with children.

Jakobson: Comprehension of some part of language always precedes production of that sound, word, or sentence structure. Comprehension cannot be imitated. If the first step of learning language is comprehension, then language cannot be learned by imitation.

McNeill; Bloom; Klima and Bellugi: Children say things they could not have heard. Since adults don't say things like "No fall!" and "Why kitty can't stand up," children must have created these sentences without imitating.

## Implications for Teaching

EXPECT VARIATION. First the child is exposed to language, in context; then he perceives a pattern, or linguistic rule, in the language he is exposed to; then he uses his version of this rule to create sentences, in order to communicate with other people. This process leads to differences in speech; each person is forming his or her own linguistic rules, which will vary in details from other people's linguistic rules. Many of my students combine the words *a* and *lot* into one word, *alot.* They have established a linguistic system slightly different from the one I use, in which *a lot* is a two-word phrase. Exposure to different dialects [1] also leads to variation in language; if the language patterns children hear vary, it is natural that children will acquire those varying patterns.

A third cause of variation operates in children from kindergarten age until age ten or eleven: children alternate between old and new forms of speech. A six-year-old may pronounce *very* with a *w*—"vewwy"—until reaching the stage in which he can say [r]. Even then, however, the child may continue to say "vewwy" part of the time, alternating between the two for a while before settling on the pronunciation with [r]. A second-grader will alternate between "He gots three cookies" and "He has three cookies," and this is to be expected; the teacher need not try to completely establish each new form as it is introduced.

THE THREE C'S. Children are exposed to language in *context;* the child learns language in an active, *creative* process; and language is always a means to an end—*communication.* These should be the touchstones of teaching reading, writing, speaking, and listening. Expose students to language in context; let them read newspapers, hear each other talk, read the Sears catalog to price tents and sleeping bags. After exposure, give them something active and creative to do with language. They can telephone city hall to ask the mayor to speak in class on changes in school boundaries, telephone Sears to price toys in stock or discuss toys in the catalog, organize a real or imaginary camping trip, write a story using someone else's voice. Stephen Judy's article describes this process using examples from secondary-school students' writing, but the process is the same for younger students. One seven-year-old liked monster movies on television.

[1] This term is discussed in the introduction to Part 2.

After discussing the fact that *Godzilla vs. the Smog Monster* began as a written story, she wrote:

### Dr. Zoocle and Dr. Boocle

Once there was two marsmen, Dr. Zoocle and Dr. Boocle. One day when they were out walking they met a monster with 199 eyes!, 51 mouths!, 77 arms!, 19 legs!, and 30 ears!. The monster gobbled them up and then it said, "Mmmm! That was a delicious meal."

This student has grasped the basic plot of monster movies—though dispensing with an ethnocentric ending in which the monster is defeated.

It is especially important to teach reading with language in context. First-graders have full control of the sentence structure "The baby is sleeping." They have said thousands of sentences of the pattern "The _____ is _____ -ing." The first words they are asked to read should be in simple sentences like this, not isolated on flash cards. "The" on a flash card means very little; "The" in the context of a sentence is a familiar part of the language they already know. Goodman, in Part 4, deals with this question.

Teaching oral language is neglected in our school system; we seem to think of "language" and "language arts" as being writing and reading, period. But most of us spend far more hours talking than we spend writing and reading combined. Talk is the way we use our language the most.

*Talking* might be distinguished from *speaking*. Speaking, we could say, is done by one person to a group of others; but talking is the usual, more personal interaction in which people take turns at saying something. In our schools, talking is far more neglected than speaking. We seem to believe that learning can take place only when speaking is going on, and we narrow that process down even further—the person speaking is supposed to be the teacher. "Open classrooms" and similar concepts are eroding these old-fashioned views, but the process is slow.

Talking is functional. You may raise a question while someone is talking to you, in order to be sure you understand; this ability to pinpoint the spot at which your understanding breaks down is crucial to success in school. The reverse process allows you to be aware that someone else has lost track of what you are saying. These skills can keep a conversation going, or keep you learning in a class, or simply keep you in touch with others—a very important part of being good at oral language. Of course, listening abilities are part of this ability to keep in touch with a conversation or an explanation. But simply being aware that your listening has suddenly become unproductive is not enough; you have to explain the problem to the person you are listening to.

Labov's article on ways of using language—ways of refusing, ways of making demands—brings up the sociolinguistic part of success in school. Teachers can give students practice in using language by planning projects that call for getting information from other people; using the telephone to find the cheapest equipment for a camping trip is one example. Students should have some time to talk about the problems they had in questioning and persuading others, and to share their ways of solving those problems.

To teach clear, effective speaking, invite your local clubs or businesses to send someone in with a talk or demonstration; talk about the presentation later (you may find some examples of propaganda here). If outsiders are not available, students might record their own talks on cassettes and pass them around, or evaluate them as a group. To teach listening, let students listen with you for particular purposes—to cassettes, records, the radio. First decide what to listen for, then listen, then talk or write about your experience. Television commercials are the old standby here for secondary-school students.

COMPREHENSION PRECEDES PRODUCTION. Jakobson mentions small children's ability to understand language features they cannot yet produce. This lag may occur for older students, as well. Since comprehension normally precedes production, perhaps teachers should allow some absorption time between a student's exposure to a new word, sentence structure, or type of writing and the demand that the student use the language involved. Many of my college students show a similar "absorption syndrome"; they have trouble producing papers and exams that require linguistic terminology they have encountered only recently.

The difference between comprehension and production also shows up in students of all ages as a contrast between receptive and productive language abilities, as indicated in Figure 1. Troike, in Part 1, points out the implications of this fact for teaching bidialectalism. Goodman and Buck, in Part 4 show how this difference affects students reading a dialect they themselves do not speak.

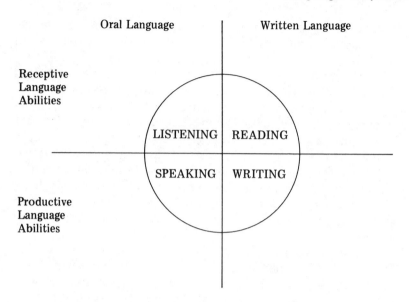

FIGURE 1. *Receptive and Productive Language Abilities*

**SUGGESTION II:** There are physical, biological controls on language and its acquisition; the brain seems to become less able to acquire language as the child gets older, dropping off in this ability dramatically after age twelve or thirteen.

*Central Article:* Wilder Penfield, "Language and the Brain"

*Supporting Evidence in Other Articles:*

Slobin, Jakobson, McNeill: Children in all cultures go through highly similar stages in learning language. The fact that these stages occur at approximately the same ages worldwide suggests that physical maturation of the brain lies behind them.

Lenneberg (Part 2): Language seems to have no direct connection with general intelligence. The wide degree of separation of language and general intelligence suggests that the two are controlled by differing physical structures in the brain.

### Implications for Teaching

BILINGUALISM AND BIDIALECTALISM. It is ironic that most of our public schools begin foreign-language teaching at around age twelve or thirteen—just as the student loses much of his ability to acquire a second language easily. The decision to wait this long is probably made on the grounds that at twelve or thirteen, the student can decide for himself whether he wants to study a second language. But there is no reason parents should not be given the opportunity to place their children in second-language classes at the earliest possible opportunity. Second languages should be part of the elementary-school curriculum beginning as early as possible, since the peak language-learning time is up to age four; but ages four to eight are still high in this ability, and ages eight to twelve are significantly higher than after puberty. These ages are not offered as absolute guidelines, of course. They are approximate, and they vary with the individual. Even after puberty, some people are better at learning additional languages than others.

Bidialectalism, or learning a second dialect, also depends heavily on age, as Troike suggests. In learning a second dialect, there are only a few new linguistic rules to absorb, as opposed to the huge number of rules in an entirely new language. But if students are to acquire native-speaker control over these—especially in phonology (the sound system)—they should be exposed to the second dialect during the elementary grades. Bidialectalism is discussed further in Part 2.

A SPECIAL KIND OF KNOWLEDGE. Language is not the same kind of knowledge as the other subject matter taught in schools. Two-year-old children all over the world do not spontaneously develop algebra or history, but they do spontaneously develop language.

Algebra and history are consciously available to a fourteen-year-old student; a student who has been taught that everyone in the American colonies wanted to separate from England's rule can throw out that "fact" and replace it with the idea that only about one-third of the colonists wanted to rebel. But the same student cannot simply throw out his entire system of negation, acquired during the first few years of life.

I am not suggesting that no change in language is possible after age twelve or thirteen. People do learn second languages and people do change some of their language patterns after that time; but making these changes is immeasurably more difficult for a fourteen-year-old than for a six-year-old. And it is very likely that complete, native-speaker control over the language or dialect will not be acquired, even under the very best conditions. The speaker may be very fluent in the second language but he will probably retain some pronunciation differences that will identify him as a nonnative speaker. Teachers should recognize the fact that bilingual students may not be able to lose this "accent," and that bidialectal students may also be unable to use "standard" phonology at all times.

Lambert, in Part 2, points out psychological factors in this kind of language learning. Even a student who is exposed to a second language or dialect while young enough to learn it most easily needs a particular kind of psychological setting: the student should feel kinship to both language communities, rather than seeing one as alien. Other research in language learning suggests that a child's exposure to a second language or second dialect will not "take" unless the exposure includes conversation with peers or other real, important associates; watching television is not enough.

The distinction between *dialects* and *styles,* discussed·in the introduction to Part 2, may be helpful. Perhaps older students can reasonably be expected to acquire styles, which are probably under somewhat more conscious control than are dialects in general; but these students may not be able to make radical changes in their unconscious control of language. If complete, unconscious control of a second dialect is not feasible, perhaps partial, conscious control of the same patterns can be achieved; the student would then have learned the second dialect as a *style.* Teachers might test the reasonableness of their standards for this sort of learning by trying to acquire a second dialect themselves, or by teaching everyone in the classroom a second dialect. These problems are discussed further in Part 2.

**SUGGESTION III:** Children go through stages in acquiring language; at each stage, the child's language has structure, and this structure signals meaning.

*Central Article:* Dan I. Slobin, "They Learn the Same Way All Around the World"

*Supporting Evidence in Other Articles:*

Jakobson: All children go through a babbling stage, followed by the acquisition of speech sounds. A sound is not a speech sound unless it signals meaning; this means that language does not exist apart from meaning. Speech sounds are structured in that they contrast with one another.

McNeill, Bloom: Children go through holophrastic (one-word) and telegraphic stages in acquiring sentence structure. Even when limited to two-word utterances, they understand and use a wide variety of sentence structures.

Klima and Bellugi: Within the telegraphic stage, there are stages in the acquisition of particular kinds of sentences—negation and questioning.

## Implications for Teaching

LANGUAGE IS MEANINGFUL. Jakobson's article establishes a basic fact: language does not exist apart from meaning. Of course, a speaker can use language in an attempt to evade a question while appearing to answer it; but this is a fact not about linguistic structure itself, but about the way people choose to use it.

All languages and all dialects have meaning, expressed through differing structures. If you hear a language or dialect you don't understand, it is not without meaning; you are without knowledge of its structure and the meanings signaled by its structure. Teachers whose classes include several language backgrounds should try to discover the structure and meaning of dialectal differences and discuss these as a class. Students might translate from one dialect into the other and vice versa; to a limited extent, the same process can be used with entirely different languages—"How do you say it in Spanish?" The entire class (perhaps including the teacher) might learn something about language in general from seeing and hearing a translation; the child who can teach others his or her way of speaking can gain pride and self-confidence. One caution: sensitivity must be used in dealing with dialects in the classroom. If some students' dialect is widely considered to be low-prestige, a teacher might be wise to choose some third dialect not spoken by anyone in the classroom as the one to be translated into orally. An effort to speak another dialect may be laughed at; if that laughter is tinged with ridicule, real psychological damage can be done to students whose native dialect is involved. Study of at least three dialects might avoid this problem. Records of speakers such as John F. Kennedy, from Boston, might provide a noncontroversial model of dialectal differences.

USE WHAT'S THERE ALREADY. Sentence structure is there already; even in the two-word stage of language acquisition, all the child's utterances use sentence structure. The child works best with entire sentences, not with isolated words. What does *the* mean? Are you able to define it? Since children always operate with meaning and with structure when using language, they are much less able to grasp an isolated *the* than to grasp it in a sentence.

In teaching beginners to read, sentences should be simple and complete. This does not mean they should be short; short sentences can be harder to understand than longer ones, depending on their structure:

1. Flashcards: *the, Spot, baby, go*
2. Sentence: The baby is sleeping.
3. Sentence: Go, Spot, go!

Sentence 2 is the easiest one for a six-year-old to work with. It has a structure the child knows: "The _____ is _____ -ing." The words on flashcards have no sentence structure—a child's own words never occur at random like that. The third sentence has a word order of verb-noun-verb; in most of the child's own sentences, major words follow the pattern noun-verb-noun. So sentence 3 has a strange syntactic structure. Both Miller and Goodman, in Part 4, go further into these problems.

Our final suggestion, then, is that teachers recognize and capitalize on the student's linguistic strengths. Of course, a child may lack some sound or complex sentence structure because he or she has not yet reached that stage of acquiring language; a teacher should be aware of this possibility. For instance, many young children do not understand sentences like "Not George but Sally went to town," and the distinction between *ask* and *tell* is often acquired after age seven. But students of all ages do have enormous linguistic strengths; teaching to these strengths will be the easiest and most effective way of teaching.

# 2
# LANGUAGE VARIATION

## Introduction

Language variation is complex and extensive; it must be broken down into categories if it is to be discussed in any useful way. Part 2 describes two major kinds of language variation, their possible effects, and what—if anything—should be done about them.

## DIALECTS AND STYLES

Each of us controls several language varieties, including one or more dialects and, usually, several different styles.[1]

### Dialects

DEFINITION AND CAUSES. A *dialect* is a language variety used by a group of people; the group can be defined by a geo-

---

[1] The word *style* has several meanings; only one of these is intended here. *Style* might refer to changes in language made for rhetorical reasons—improvement of persuasiveness or clarity; for literary reasons—appropriateness to the topic, or other aesthetic considerations; or for social reasons—to conform to audience expectations about appropriate language for differing social occasions, e.g., formal versus informal discussions. Only the last meaning is intended here.

graphic region, or by social factors, or by ethnic background. For instance, all natives of New York City drop the sound /r/ [2] before another consonant (as in words like *beard*) part of the time. This "*r*-dropping" does not occur in my own dialect, which was shaped in New Mexico. These two different ways of speaking, or two *language varieties*, are called *regional* dialects; the group of people living in one of these geographic regions has a dialect that includes "*r*-dropping," but the group living in the other geographic region has a dialect that does not. The physical distance between the two groups of people allows language differences to develop and be maintained. In Part 2, regional dialects are briefly discussed by Roger Shuy.

Social factors come into play within geographic regions. Groups of people within New York City are separated by social space—they seldom talk with people outside their social and ethnic groups, except perhaps in impersonal transactions that have little emotional importance for either speaker. This social distance, like the geographic distance that separates New York from New Mexico, allows language differences to appear.

Dialects caused by social distance are often spoken of collectively as *social dialects*. But a further distinction can be made, a distinction between social dialects and ethnic dialects. The study in Part 2 by William Labov finds dialect groupings related to three characteristics: occupation, education, and income. Groups of people who share similar occupations, education, and income tend to share ways of talking. For example, truckdrivers who have high-school educations and similar incomes probably have language features (pronunciation, vocabulary, and sentence structure) that differ in some ways from the language features of executives who have college educations and similar incomes. In this book, I will use the term *social groups* in referring to groups of people having similar occupations, education, and income; and *social dialects* in referring to the speech of these social groups. Example: "I seen in the paper where there's a lake for sale near Lansing," was said by a mechanic; if this use of *seen* is common among members of his social group, we can say that it is one feature of his social dialect. If IBM executives as a group use a different form of the verb *see* in sentences similar to this, they are using a different social dialect.

Ethnic groups appear within social groups. In Labov's study, blacks use terms (such as "mother-wit") unknown among most

[2] For explanation of slashes, brackets, and phonetic symbols, see the Appendix.

whites. Another example: among truckdrivers in Philadelphia, we may find a group of Irish-Americans who share some language features that do not appear in the speech of truckdrivers with different ethnic backgrounds. It must be remembered, however, that not all Irish-American truckdrivers will have these language features; as we saw in Part 1, a great deal depends on the language the speaker was exposed to as a child, especially the language used by the child's friends. The children in a Chicano family living in a predominantly Anglo neighborhood may show little or no "Chicano dialect." One cannot assume that a person who is black speaks "Black English." Terms like "Chicano dialect" and "Black English" usually refer to a list of language features used by a large percentage of the ethnic group mentioned; there is no guarantee that an individual speaker will have all or even part of those features in his speech. In Part 2, Saville, Williamson, Dale, and Abrahams provide some discussions of ethnic dialects. In each of these articles, any blanket term like "Black English" is carefully defined with a list of particular language features.

DIALECTS AS OVERLAPPING LANGUAGE SYSTEMS. In reading articles about dialects and styles, we need to be aware of some widespread misunderstandings about dialects, misunderstandings that can arise from the way the term is used. First, dialects—standard, nonstandard, regional, or social—are often spoken of as though each were a system separate from the others (see Figure 1). But if dialects were separate systems with nothing in common, they would be separate languages and their speakers would not be able to understand one another. Dialects are forms of the same language. They share a great many linguistic features—words, pronunciations, sentence structures—as shown in Figure 2.

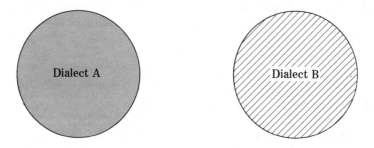

FIGURE 1. *What Dialects Are* Not: *Separate Systems*

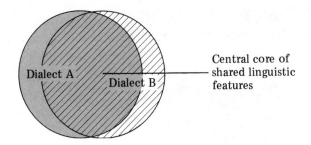

FIGURE 2. *What Dialects Are: Overlapping Systems*

The differences that do appear in dialects of American English are usually superficial rather than fundamentally in conflict. "He ain't home" is only superficially different from "He isn't home"; the meaning is the same, only the word used to represent that meaning differs.

STANDARD AND NONSTANDARD DIALECTS. Most of us have attitudes about our own in-groups; and language, since the use of *shibboleth* in Biblical times, has been one of the tests of "us"-ness and "them"-ness. Using these indicators—like *ain't*—as signs of inclusion in our group has, over the years, turned into claims that some ways of talking are wrong and some are right. Often these claims are simply the result of written records and public rituals being written and conducted by people who use one dialect; the use of that dialect becomes "standard" for formal documents and occasions. McDavid discusses "Standard English" in Part 2, and Sledd discusses the "bidialectalism" controversy that has resulted from recent attempts to teach a "standard" dialect to schoolchildren.

### Styles

Within one speaker's dialect, we find language variation of another kind: *stylistic* variation, changes in language made in response to social expectations. In Part 2, Joos suggests five styles: frozen, formal, consultative, casual, and intimate. He gives examples of vocabulary changes and pronunciation changes that are stylistic. Labov, in Part 2, also uses the term *stylistic variation* to describe the variation in phonology he finds in New York City, variation related to social expectations.

Like the dean in Phil Frank's cartoon, we all use styles; if you are being televised, or your audience is a group of nuns, or your topic is chemistry, you will adjust your speech to fit the

© 1975. Courtesy of College Media Services.

occasion. Society expects a dean to say things like "Henceforth, in terms of all reasonable involvements in aspects of this situation at this point in time . . . ," and Frank's dean is attempting to meet those expectations. He is, however, going overboard in his attempt, so that his elaborate formal style is obscuring his message. Whether this is by accident or by design is uncertain. Perhaps he has no message to send and is deliberately obscuring this fact with a cloud of words.

An example of stylistic variation: in a committee room, eight people are arguing; seven are on one side of the question, one is on the other side. "You're being stubborn," remarks one of the seven. When the eighth person leaves the room to get a cup of coffee, the comment is rephrased: "I didn't realize he was so pig-headed." Another example: in a televised press conference, a presidential press secretary states, "A judgment has not been made as to the appropriate response to your inquiry." You can imagine other settings and audiences that would elicit a less formal style with the same content: "We have not decided what to say in answer to your question," or even, "We haven't figured out what to tell you." If the press conference is not being televised; if the audience is seven people instead of thirty-five; if the topic is an interview with the White House cook, instead of a request to search the White House files—the press secretary may use either the second or third style, instead of the very formal first style.

The term *style* becomes extremely important when the "verbal deprivation" theory is discussed. Labov, in "The Logic of Nonstandard English" (1970), has suggested that the lack of an elaborate formal style is being misunderstood as "verbal deprivation" in recent studies of children in conflict with their schools. Kochman (1969) agrees. In Part 2, my article examines this question at its source—the writings of British sociologist Basil Bernstein, who has suggested that lack of an "elaborated code" is characteristic of lower socioeconomic classes. These lower classes have instead a "restricted code," according to Bernstein. Bernstein has denied that style differences inspired his views; but my article agrees with those of Labov and Kochman in seeing a very high probability that style differences are, in fact, at issue here.

## THE EFFECTS OF LANGUAGE DIFFERENCES

### Language and Thinking

The relationship between language and thinking is not yet well understood, and the articles that touch on this subject are certainly not meant to be definitive; but we can make some helpful statements about the topic, even when what we have to say is negative. An invalid claim is potentially quite harmful in this area, so it is especially important to express criticism of theories about language and thinking.

Lenneberg, Lambert, and I present evidence about language and general intelligence, bilingualism and intellectual capability, and the "verbal deprivation" theory, respectively. In the section on applications, Gumperz and Hernández-Chavez describe some apparent consequences of the "verbal deprivation" theory, and

Link reports the consequences of classifying Chicano school-children on the basis of IQ tests given in English.

### Language and the Breakdown of Communication

The elaborate formal style of the dean in Phil Frank's cartoon can easily interfere with communication, and yet this style is socially approved. It is often seen as prestigious, and it is taught by example on our television sets, in our books, and in some of our college classrooms. But the kind of language variation that *is* commonly attacked as dangerous to our continued understanding of one another is dialectal variation, which is usually perfectly clear in its meanings.

You can judge for yourself whether dialectal variation is truly an obstacle to understanding; we will see in Part 2 examples of dialectal variation and ways of listening for it in our own locales. Most linguists see the differences among dialects of American English as being slight. One basis for this conclusion is that a great many of the differences that do exist are relatively superficial, having to do with pronunciation or with word choice rather than syntax (sentence structure). Of course, there are dialects with syntactic differences, and it is also possible to find understanding hampered by a build-up of small differences, such as those in pronunciation.

Should children with a low-prestige dialect be taught a more prestigious one? Many educators and linguists think the answer is yes. Others, like James Sledd, object strongly to programs like this (known as *bidialectalism* programs). Bidialectalism and the more general question of whether (and if so, how) to set standards for language use are discussed in the summary article at the end of Part 2.

### REFERENCES

Kochman, Thomas. "Social Factors in the Consideration of Teaching Standard English," *Linguistic-Cultural Differences and American Education.* Special issue, *The Florida F-L Reporter,* 7 (1969), 87ff.

Labov, William. "The Logic of Nonstandard English." In Frederick Williams (ed.), *Language and Poverty.* Chicago: Markham Publishing Co., 1970.

# Types of Language Variation: Dialects and Styles

## Discovering Regional Dialects

ROGER W. SHUY

Is it *supposed* to be "crick" or "creek"? "Greecey" or "greezy"? Maybe the answer partly depends on where you live. Shuy talks about listening to the way people from other geographic regions speak. His examples are drawn from pronunciation and vocabulary, but linguists have also found a few syntactic (sentence structure) differences: "My hair needs washed" and "The car needs greased" occur in parts of Ohio and Pennsylvania, and "Throw Papa down the stairs his hat" is attributed to Pennsylvania Deutsch (German) areas.

This last attribution is an example of regional and ethnic dialects coinciding. Williamson, later in Part 2, brings up regional versus ethnic influences in black speech; she suggests that some of the black language features now seen as ethnic in northern cities were originally regional, common to both black and white southerners.

The relative nature of a "standard" language or dialect is investigated further by McDavid, in the next article.

**129**

Many Americans are unaware that they and their friends speak a variety of English which can be called a dialect. Many even deny it and say something like this: "No, we don't speak a dialect around here. They speak more harshly and strangely out East and down South, but we just don't have anything like that in *our* speech."

Most Southerners know that people from other parts of the country are either pleased or annoyed by their Southern pronunciations and expressions. Many Easterners are aware of the reactions of people from west of the Alleghenies to typical Eastern speech patterns. On the other hand, many Midwesterners, for some reason, seem oblivious to the fact that Americans from other areas find something strange about the vocabulary, pronunciation, and grammar characteristic of the Midwest.

People tend to describe the differences between their speech and that of others in certain conventional terms. *Harshness* and *nasalized drawl* are often used to describe the speech of any area other than that of the speaker. Another popular term, *guttural*, is also used with little precision. Strangely enough, many people will insist that they hear a *guttural* quality in the speech of another person *even though they cannot define the term.*

Linguists who specialize in the study of dialects describe American speech systematically and with precision. They avoid terms like *harsh* and *dull*, for such words are closer to condemnation than description, and terms like *soft* and *musical*, for they are too general to be useful. Like many common English terms, these words have been used so widely that it is difficult to say exactly what they *do* mean.

How, then, can linguists go about describing dialect differences systematically and precisely? Perhaps we should begin with what we already know. In an age in which people often move from one area of the country to another, it is rather common for us to have neighbors or classmates whose dialect may be somewhat "different." Furthermore, the summer (or winter) vacation has enabled many of us to enter different dialect areas. Television and radio have brought speakers from many social and geographical dialect areas into our homes. We may begin, then, by recognizing that there *are* dialect differences.

Besides the facts, however, we also begin with attitudes. Since language is a form of social behavior, we react to a person's speech patterns as we would react to any of his actions. If his dialect differs from our own, we may consider him quaint, naive, stupid, suave, cultivated, conceited, alien, or any number of other things. Most frequently, however, our attitude toward the outsider tends to be negative, since, after all, he is not one of *our* group. Recently a graduate school professor at a large Midwestern university asked his students to describe various unidentified persons whose voices were recorded on tape. The class described one voice as rustic and uncultivated. The voice was that of their professor!

It is clear, then, that most people recognize dialect differences of some sort and have certain feelings or attitudes toward them. A classic example of this recognition and reaction occurred during a survey of Illinois speech conducted in 1962. Many people from the middle of the state and most from the southern part pronounced *greasy* something like *greezy*. On the other hand, people in the northern counties of the state pronounced the word *greecey*. The northern Illinois informants felt that the southern pronunciation was crude and ugly; it made them think of a very messy, dirty, sticky, smelly frying pan. To the southern and midland speakers, however, the northern pronunciation connoted a messy, dirty, sticky, smelly skillet.

Which of the two pronunciations and reactions are right? The answer is easy: The southern Illinois pronunciation and reaction are appropriate in southern Illinois, and the northern Illinois pronunciation and reaction are proper in northern Illinois. Educated *and* uneducated speakers say *greezy* in southern Illinois. Educated *and* uneducated speakers say *greecey* in northern Illinois. Although we must not be surprised that people tend to believe their own way is the "right way," it should be clear that there are two acceptable pronunciations of this word in Illinois, reflecting different dialects. . . .

## DIFFERENCES IN PRONUNCIATION

[If] you practice writing the sounds you hear [using phonetic symbols,[1]] you can start to determine certain things about other speakers. Begin by writing short words, dictated by your teacher or your classmates. *Do not be influenced by the spelling of the word.* Listen only for its sound and write it using the phonetic symbols. People do not hear sounds in exactly the same ways, so it should not surprise you if the students in a given class produce several different acceptable transcriptions. The following words will provide good practice for you:

1 [Ed.'s note: Phonetic symbols are provided in the Appendix.]

| coat    | ringing |
|---------|---------|
| cats    | wilt    |
| boom    | late    |
| beans   | hike    |
| catches | then    |
| thick   | should  |
| sox     | money   |
| dogs    | rumor   |
| how     | joy     |
| boil    | judges  |

Remember that a good ear for sounds is not developed right away. You may wish to practice with other transcription exercises, or you may simply write phonetically the words used by teachers, classmates, television performers, or members of your family. If classmates or friends from a different part of the country are willing to serve as informants, have them pronounce the following words:

| WORD | NORTHERN | MIDLAND | SOUTHERN |
|------|----------|---------|----------|
| 1. cr*ee*k | ɪ and i | ɪ (north Midland) i (south Midland) | i |
| 2. p*e*nny | ɛ | ɛ | ɪ—(Southwest) |
| 3. M*a*ry | ɛ e (parts of eastern New England) | ɛ | e |
| 4. m*a*rried | æ (east of Appalachians) ɛ (elsewhere) | ɛ | ɛ |
| 5. s*i*ster | ɪ | ɪ (eastern) | ɪ (eastern) |
| 6. *o*range | *a* (east of Alleghenies) ɔ | *a* and ɔ | *a* and ɔ |
| 7. tomat*o* | o | ə | o or ə |
| 8. c*oo*p | u | u (NM), ʊ (SM) | ʊ |
| 9. r*oo*f | ʊ | u and/or ʊ | u |

. . .

Consonants sometimes will give clues to the dialect a person speaks. The following generalizations may be helpful:

| Word | Northern | Midland | Southern |
|------|----------|---------|----------|
| 1. h*u*mor | hɪumər | yumər | hɪumər or yumər |
| 2. wa*sh* | waš or wɔš | wɔrš or wɔɪš | wɔš or wɔɪš or waš |
| 3. wi*th* | wɪð and wɪθ (N.Y., Chicago, Detroit=wɪt working class) | wɪθ | wɪθ |
| 4. grea*sy* | grisɪ | grizɪ | grizɪ |
| 5. b*a*rn | bɑrn (Eastern North=bɑn) | bɑrn | bɑrn (East Coast=bɑn) |
| 6. *th*ese | ðiz (N.Y., Chicago, Detroit=diz working class) | ðiz | ðiz |

.   .   .

There are two recordings you can use for practice, or just for listening to differences. One, *Americans Speaking,* is published by the National Council of Teachers of English, with six long selections spoken by educated adults. The other is *Our Changing Language,* published by McGraw-Hill (Webster Division), containing twelve short selections spoken by junior high school and high school students. Other recordings are in prospect.

## DIFFERENCES IN VOCABULARY

Words are interesting to almost everyone. Through his vocabulary a person may reveal facts about his age, his sex, his education, his occupation, and his geographical and cultural origins. Our first reaction may be to imagine that all speakers of English use the same words. Nothing could be further from the truth; our language contains a vast number of synonyms to show different shades of meaning or reveal as much of our inner feelings as we want to. Some of these vocabulary choices are made deliberately. We use other words, however, without really knowing that our vocabulary is influenced by our audience.

### Age

Certain words tell how old we are. For example, many people refer to an electric refrigerator as an *ice box* despite the fact that in most parts of our country ice boxes have not been in common use for many years. Older natives of some Northern dialect areas still may call a frying pan a *spider,* a term which remained in the vocabulary of the older generation long after the removal of the four legs which gave the descriptive title. Frying pans no longer look like four-legged spiders, but the name remains fixed in the vocabulary of certain people. . . .

### Education

A person also reveals his educational background through his choice of words. It is no secret that learning the specialized vocabulary of psychology, electronics, or fishing is necessary before one becomes fully accepted as an "insider," and before he can fully participate in these areas. Much of what a student learns about a course in school is shown in his handling of the vocabulary of the subject. It is also true, however, that a person's choice of words is not nearly as revealing of education as his grammar and pronunciations are.

### Occupation

The specialized vocabulary of occupational groups also appears in everyday language. Truck drivers, secretaries, tirebuilders, sailors, farmers, and members of many other occupations use such words. Linguists who interview people for *The Linguistic Atlas of the United States and Canada* have found that the calls to certain animals, for example, illustrate what might be called farm vocabulary, particularly for the older generation of farmers (city dwellers obviously have no particular way of calling sheep or cows from pasture). Even within farming areas, furthermore, vocabulary will reveal specialization. Recent Illinois language studies showed that a male sheep was known as a *buck* only to farmers who had at some time raised sheep.

### Origins

It is common knowledge that certain words indicate where we are from. Northerners use *pail* for a kind of metal container which Midlanders refer to as a *bucket. Pits* are inside cherries and peaches of Northerners ; *seeds* are found by some Midlanders. It is amusing to some people, furthermore, that as a general rule horses are said to *whinny* or *whinner* in Northern dialect areas, whereas they *nicker* in some of the Midland parts of our country.

Customs are also revealed in our vocabulary. The *county seat* is relatively unknown in rural New England, where local government is handled at the town meeting.

The special names for various ethnic or national groups, whether joking or derogatory, are an indication of the settlement patterns of an area. If a person has the terms *Dago, Kraut,* or *Polack* in his active vocabulary, it is quite likely that he lives among or near Italians, Germans, or Polish people. Sometimes the nickname of a specific immigrant group becomes generalized to include most or all newcomers. Such a case was recently noted in Summit County, Ohio, where some natives refer to almost all nationality groups as *Hunkies,* regardless of whether or not they come from Hungary. That this practice has been with us for many years is shown in a comment by Theodore Roosevelt that anything foreign was referred to as *Dutch.* One nineteenth century politician even referred to Italian paintings as "Dutch daubs from Italy." [2] . . .

## Language and Prestige: "Standard English"

RAVEN I. McDAVID, Jr.

McDavid makes clear how arbitrary the choice of a "standard" language can be, as he briefly traces the fashions in English from its early status as "the language of barbarians" to its American diversification into many different regional standards —each of which is locally regarded as the natural way to speak. In the next article, however, Labov mentions the reservations many Americans have about their own speech; he calls this "linguistic insecurity" and relates it to socioeconomic groups.

The basic idea we Americans seem to act upon is that there is a right way to speak and a wrong way to speak. We are somewhat confused about the details of rightness and wrongness; we feel most comfortable with people who speak the way we do, but we may also attempt to sound like prestigious people in our own region, and we often suspect that our own speech doesn't measure up to the high standards of Truest Correctness. The origins of our notions about correctness are further investigated by Herndon, in Part 3, who provides a brief intellectual history of British and American attitudes toward language.

[2] H. L. Mencken, *The American Language,* abridged and revised by Raven I. McDavid, Jr. (New York: Knopf, 1963), p. 371.

Anyone who has seriously studied the history of the English language—or indeed of any other language—will realize that what happens to be a prestigious form of language at a given time is largely the result of a series of historical accidents. Though some have hinted that a language may have special virtues—Benjamin Lee Whorf, for instance, suggested that Hopi might be better than English for dealing with vibration phenomena—one can conclude that all languages have the same potentiality for expressing all the range of human experience, and that any language (given the right kind of creative genius to use it) can be the vehicle of what we sometimes call "great literature." The reverence we feel for Greek as a language is associated with the culture of the Hellenic, Alexandrian, and Byzantine civilizations, not with anything intrinsic in any period of the Greek language itself. Our linguistic and cultural isolation prevents us from realizing that Arabic was the vehicle of the greatest civilization in the Mediterranean world from the seventh till the twelfth century. We are but dimly aware that since 1800 the achievements of Western civilization have been made available to monolinguals who speak such tongues as Indonesian, Turkish, Czech, and Finnish; we are more familiar with the technological success of the Israelis whose national tongue was fitted for modern civilization after more than two thousand years of disuse except as a liturgical language and has proved itself adequate for everything from aeronautics to zoology. As we become more sophisticated, we realize that what is the prestigious variety of a given tongue may vary from one century to another. English was the language of barbarians when it was first carried to the British Isles; shortly afterward, however, the northern variety—Northumbrian—became the vehicle of a distinguished culture. Then, with Northumbria overrun by the Northmen, prestige shifted southward to Mercia; a little later, to Wessex in the southwest; and finally, after all varieties of English lost prestige under the Norman Conquest, to London where still a further prestige variety arose. And with the exception of Scots—and not a complete exception at that—every variety of standard English since that time has borne the imprint of what has become standard in London.

There are two qualifications that we need to make to clarify the influence of the London standard. First of all, London English itself has changed in many ways since its preeminence was established. All of the long vowels and diphthongs have changed; some have fallen together and others have arisen. The inflections have been greatly simplified, with some categories disappearing altogether and others becoming more uniform in their expression. New syntactic devices have developed; if English does not have— and it never has had—the variety of verb inflections for tense that Latin possessed, it has developed a much more complicated system of verb phrases than anything we find on the European continent. English has lost many words and gained many more. The half-million entries in a so-called "unabridged" dictionary are but the tip of the lexicographical iceberg, for it is estimated that fifty thousand chemical compounds are discovered and named every year. There is not—and may never be—a complete inventory of all the slang words that have been used in English since printing was developed. Moreover, it is a hopeless task to consider what went on in the thousand previous years of English, for few words of what we would now call slang found their way into the limited records set down by those few who had mastered the arcane skill of writing. Of the words that do survive in the language from the fifth century onward, almost every one has somehow changed its range of meaning—even such verbal auxiliaries as *can* and *may, shall* and *will,* or such prepositions as *of* and *with.*

The other qualification to our reflections on the influence of London English is that there is no single variety of English that we can call standard to the exclusion of other varieties. In a review of Mark M. Orkin's *Speaking Canadian English,* I have taken the author to task for setting up a contrast between "Standard English" and "General American." Leaving the latter term aside, I observe that to him "Standard English" seems to be restricted not merely to what is sometimes referred to as "Received Standard," Southern British, or "Public School English," but to the subspecies of it that A. S. C. Ross, Nancy Mitford, and their journalistic playmates chose to designate as *U,* the usage of the hereditary aristocracy. I had to remind Orkin— or at least the readers of the journal for which I was writing the review—that *U* was not coterminous in its application with even the body of speakers of Received Standard, and that many people in England have excellent cultural credentials, excellent education, and often titles of nobility, but do not speak that subvariety of the standard usage of Southern Britain, much less command the ineffable subtleties attributed by Ross and Miss Mitford to *U.*

If we go elsewhere in the world, we discover that there is even less reason to regard one variety of the language as the unique bearer of a culture. In Canada and the United States, in Australia and New Zealand and South Africa, and in dozens of areas within these grander subdivisions of the English-speaking world, there are people who grow up acquiring the best usage of the best representatives of local cultural traditions. Leaving aside the usage of other nations, the cultural facts are that there is inherently nothing to place the usage of Massachusetts (eastern or western) above that of Minnesota, that of New York above that of New Orleans, that of Texas above that of Tennessee, that of Virginia above that of California. The American presidency has spoken in the accents of the Virginia Piedmont, of central Ohio, of Vermont, of Iowa transplanted to the San Francisco Bay area, of the Hudson Valley, of Western Missouri, of Boston, of southeast Texas, and of Southern California—all within the last half century when broadcasting has made a candidate's accent instantly accessible to a national audience.

Yet the intellectual demonstration that any variety of language is intrinsically as good as any other, for all human purposes, is not always matched by visceral acceptance of this argument. Of the presidential worthies we have mentioned, every one had his way of speaking severely criticized by his countrymen, sometimes by members of the opposition party, sometimes by his nominal followers. Possibly the most cruel ridicule in recent years was that which Eastern and Middle-Western newspapers bestowed on the speech of Lyndon B. Johnson; "Old Cornpone" was one of the more printable epithets used to describe his speech, which was compared unfavorably to that of his more glamorous predecessor, John Kennedy. Yet Kennedy's own speech was not above criticism; in a discussion with students at the University of Kentucky, Albert H. Marckwardt discovered that they responded favorably to Johnson's speech as that of a familiar, sincere type of person with whom they could feel at ease; they distrusted the speech of the Kennedy clan as that of cold, arrogant, ruthless manipulators. It is simply the speech to which one has become accustomed that inspires the favorable reaction. The reactions of the Kentucky students were not dissimilar to those I once had toward the speech of other regions than my native South Carolina; indeed, within South Carolina itself, we of the Piedmont region were frequently amused and bewildered by the exotic speech of the Charleston area, even though we knew that the social order of Charleston—and hence the speech of representatives of that social order—was something to be admired by all those with any feeling for standards. For outsiders we had other feelings, rare as were our contacts. New Englanders we adjudged—as the Kentucky students did the Kennedys—as cold and calculating and arrogant; New Yorkers as unpleasantly aggressive; eastern Virginians as a bit pompous. For Middle Westerners we had little to say, perhaps because the routes of travel brought few of them into our neighborhood; but the feeling could hardly have been one of respect, since one of the folk comments in South Carolina is that the educated Middle Westerner talks like the uneducated Southerner—both of them having the strongly constricted postvocalic /-r/ that has been lacking in the educated speech of London and Boston and Richmond and Charleston and (until recently) New York.

As geographic mobility has increased, it has not always been a blessing, even to the educated migrant, since he has to wrestle with the prejudices his new neighbors have toward his way of speaking. And if he is white and a native speaker of English, he has none of the obvious cues of race or ethnicity to win the sympathetic ear of teachers or counselors who suspect that only willfulness prevents him from instantly adopting local speechways. That he may himself come from a cultural environment with traditions quite different from those of his new community is rarely admitted; Middle Westerners are often astounded that schoolchildren in the South are expected to use *sir* or *ma'am* in addressing teachers or older people; and Southern parents may become enraged on learning that their children have been reprimanded by Michigan teachers for using these normal tokens of respect. . . .

# The Reflection of Social Processes in Linguistic Structures

WILLIAM LABOV

Have you ever been in great danger or near death? In answering a question like that, you probably would not pay close attention to your pronunciation; you would be absorbed in what you were saying, not how you were saying it. On the other hand,

if asked to read aloud in front of other adults, you probably
would pay quite a bit of attention to your pronunciation.

William Labov elicited several speech styles from New York
speakers by (among other techniques) asking these New
Yorkers the question posed in the last paragraph and having
them read stories and word lists aloud. The resulting variation
in their speech is a major topic in this article. New Yorkers have
a sound system that allows an [r] to be dropped from certain
words and phrases. New Yorkers do pronounce [r] in words
like *bread* and *forest,* because these [r]'s are followed by vowels.
Likewise, in the phrase *for each of us* the [r] will be pronounced,
because the sound that follows it is a vowel—the first sound
in *each.* But in words like *beard* and phrases like *for Don
and me,* a consonant follows the [r]; an [r] in this position has
traditionally been dropped. However, around 1940 some New
Yorkers began using these [r]'s part of the time, apparently
at random: "it is a matter of pure chance which one
comes to his lips" (see Labov's footnote 4).

In the early 1960s William Labov showed that it was not
a matter of pure chance. He found clear patterns in the use of
this [r], patterns that were related to the socioeconomic background of the speaker and to casual versus formal styles of
speech. It turns out that all the socioeconomic groups in New
York drop these [r]'s; how frequently they drop the [r]'s, and
the way they respond to more and less formal situations, make
up the differences among these various groups.

In the next article Joos deals with style in vocabulary and
sentence structure. In Part 4, Fromkin and Rodman explain fully
the system of pronunciation rules that make up a speaker's
sound system.

The procedures of descriptive linguistics are based upon
the conception of language as a structured set of social norms.[1]
It has been useful in the past to consider these norms as invari-
ants, shared by all members of the speech community. However,
closer studies of the social context in which language is used
show that many elements of linguistic structure are involved in
systematic variation which reflects both temporal change and
extra-linguistic social processes. The following discussion presents some results of these studies which bring linguistics into
close contact with survey methodology and sociological theory.

---

[1] This paper is based upon a presentation given in a panel discussion
on sociolinguistics, at a meeting of the Eastern Sociological Society, in
Boston, April 12, 1964.

As a form of social behavior, language is naturally of interest to the sociologist. But language may have a special utility for the sociologist as a sensitive index of many other social processes. Variation in linguistic behavior does not in itself exert a powerful influence on social development, nor does it affect drastically the life chances of the individual; on the contrary, the shape of linguistic behavior changes rapidly as the speaker's social postion changes. This malleability of language underlies its great utility as an indicator of social change.

Phonological indexes—based upon the elements of the sound system of a language—are particularly useful in this respect. They give us a large body of quantitative data from relatively small samples of speech: from only a few minutes' conversation, on any topic, we may derive reliable index scores for several variables. To a large extent, the variation on which these indexes are based is independent of the conscious control of the subject. Furthermore, phonological systems show the highest degree of internal structure of all linguistic systems, so that a single social process may be accompanied by correlated shifts of many phonological indexes.

The examples to be cited below are drawn from a study of the social stratification of English in New York City, and particularly a linguistic survey of the Lower East Side.[2] This survey was based upon a primary survey of social attitudes of Lower East Side residents, carried out by Mobilization for Youth in 1961.[3] The original sample of the population of 100,000 consisted of 988 adult subjects. Our target sample was 195 of these respondents, representing about 33,000 native English speakers who had not moved within the previous two years. Through the assistance of Mobilization for Youth, and the New York School of Social Work, we had available a large body of information on the social characteristics of the informants, and we were able to concentrate entirely on their linguistic behavior in this secondary

---

[2] A complete report on this survey is given in "The Social Stratification of English in New York City," my Columbia University dissertation, 1964. The development of phonological indexes, and correlation with a complex set of social variables, represent continuations of techniques first developed in "The Social Motivation of a Sound Change," *Word*, 19 (1963), 273–309, which dealt with linguistic changes on the island of Martha's Vineyard, Massachusetts.

[3] Details on the sampling procedures and other methods utilized in this survey are provided in *A Proposal for the Prevention and Control of Delinquency by Expanding Opportunities* (New York, N.Y., Mobilization for Youth, Inc., 214 East Second St., 1961).

survey. Eighty-one per cent of the target sample was reached in the investigation of language on the Lower East Side.

New York City presents some exceptionally difficult problems for the study of linguistic systems: New Yorkers show a remarkable range of stylistic variation, as well as social variation, to such an extent that earlier investigators failed to find any pattern, and attributed many variables to pure chance.[4] To study social variation, it was first necessary to define and isolate a range of contextual styles within the linguistic interview. The context of the formal interview does not ordinarily elicit casual or spontaneous speech; the methods which were developed to overcome this limitation were crucial to the success of the investigation. The fact that we did succeed in defining and eliciting casual conversation is shown in the convergence of these results with other studies which utilized anonymous observations, and also in the consistency of the patterns of stylistic variation which were found.

As one example we may consider the phonological variable (r) in New York City.[5] In the traditional New York City pattern, /r/ is not heard in final position, nor before consonants. The words *guard* and *god* are homonyms: [gɒ:d] and [gɒ:d]. So also, *bared* and *bad* are homonyms: "I [bɛ:əd] my [a:m]; I had a [bɛ:əd] cut." In recent decades, a new prestige form has appeared in the speech of native New Yorkers, in which /r/ is pronounced. The phonological index used to measure this variable is simply the percentage of words with historical /r/ in final and preconsonantal position, in which /r/ is pronounced. Thus we find a lower middle class man, 22 years old, using 27% /r/ in careful conversation: an (r) index of 27. In less formal contexts, in casual speech, he uses no /r/ at all: (r)-00. In the more formal direction, he shows (r)-37 in reading style, (r)-60 in reading lists of

---

[4] "The pronunciation of a very large number of New Yorkers exhibits a pattern in these words that might most accurately be described as the complete absence of any pattern. Such speakers sometimes pronounce /r/ before a consonant or a pause and sometimes omit it, in a thoroughly haphazard fashion. . . . The speaker hears both types of pronunciation about him all the time, both seem almost equally natural to him, and it is a matter of pure chance which one comes to his lips." A. F. Hubbell, *The Pronunciation of English in New York City* (New York, Columbia University Press, 1950), 48.

[5] The convention of notation which is adopted here is as follows: (r) represents the *variable*, as opposed to the phonemic unit /r/ or the phonetic unit [r]. A particular value of the variable is shown as (r-1) or (r-0), while an average index score is shown as (r)-35. In this case, (r-1) usually coincides with the phonemic unit /r/, and the more familiar notation /r/ is used instead of (r-1).

words, and (r)-100 in reading pairs of words in which his full attention is given to /r/: *guard* vs. *god, dock* vs. *dark*, etc. An upper middle class subject may show the same pattern at a higher level of (r) values; a working class speaker at a much lower level.

We may consider another variable, one which is not peculiar to New York City: the pronunciation of *th* in *thing, think, through, bath*, etc. The prestige form throughout the United States is a fricative, scraping sound: [θ]. In many areas, many speakers occasionally use stops, *t*-like sounds in this position: "I [tɪŋk] so; [sʌmtɪŋ] else." Even more common is an affricate, a blend of stop and fricative: "I [tθɪŋk] so; [sʌmtθɪŋ] else." The phonological index for (th) assigns "0" to the fricative, "1" to the affricate, and "2" to the stop; thus an index of (th)-00 would indicate the use of only fricatives, and an index score of (th)-200 only stops. A working class man, for example, might show an index score of (th)-107 in casual speech, -69 in careful conversation, -48 in reading style. A middle class woman might show a score of (th)-20 in casual speech, and -00 in all more formal styles.

Although there is a great range in the absolute values of these variables as used by New Yorkers, there is great agreement in the *pattern* of stylistic variation. Almost eighty per cent of the respondents showed patterns of stylistic variation consistent with the status of consonantal /r/ as a prestige marker for (r), and stops and affricates for (th) as stigmatized forms.

This pattern of stylistic variation is primarily of concern to linguists and to students of the ethnography of speaking. However, it is closely associated with the pattern of social stratification in New York City. The pattern of stylistic variation, and the pattern of social variation, enter into the complex and regular structure which is seen in Figure 1.

Figure 1 is a class stratification diagram for (th), derived from the behavior of 81 adult respondents, raised in New York City.[6] The vertical axis is the scale of average (th) index scores. The horizontal axis represents four contextual styles. The most

[6] The main body of informants who were interviewed in detail with the linguistic questionnaire consisted of 122 subjects. Forty-one of these were residents of New York City who were born and raised outside of the city in the critical pre-adolescent years. These informants provided a valuable control in studying language changes and patterns peculiar to New York City. The high degree of regularity and agreement shown by the 81 New York City informants contrasted sharply with the irregular pattern of responses of the non–New Yorkers: in many cases, the trends shown by the New York informants were reversed by the others.

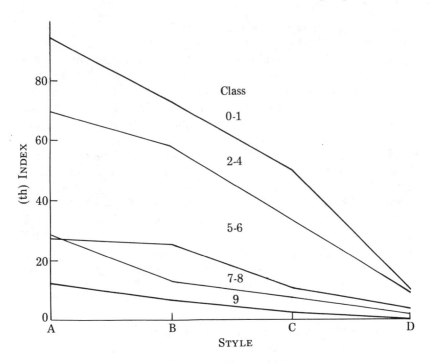

FIGURE 1. *Class stratification of a linguistic variable with stable social significance: (th) in* thing, through, *etc.*

informal style, casual speech, is shown at the left as A; B is careful conversation, the main bulk of the interview; C is reading style; D is the pronunciation of isolated words. The values on the diagram are connected by horizontal lines, showing the progression of average index scores for socio-economic class groups. These groups are defined as divisions of a ten-point socio-economic scale, constructed by Mobilization for Youth on the basis of their data in the primary survey. The socio-economic index is based on three equally weighted indicators of productive status: occupation (of the breadwinner), education (of the respondent), and income (of the family).[7]

Figure 1 is an example of what we may call *sharp stratification*. The five strata of the population are grouped into two larger

[7] The original survey utilized the education of the breadwinner, rather than that of the respondent. It was felt that the linguistic survey should utilize the respondent's education as an indicator, since this might be more closely tied to language behavior than to other forms of behavior. However, the over-all correlations of linguistic behavior and socio-economic class were not affected by this change: there were just as many deviations from regular correlation produced by the change as eliminated by it.

strata with widely different use of the variable. Figure 2 is a class stratification diagram which shows a somewhat different type of stratification. The vertical axis is the phonological index for (r), in which 100 represents a consistent *r*-pronouncing dialect, and 00 a consistent *r*-less dialect. The horizontal axis shows five stylistic contexts, ranging from casual speech, at A, careful speech at B, reading style at C, isolated words at D, and at $D^1$, the reading of word pairs in which /r/ is the sole focus of attention: *guard* vs. *god, dock* vs. *dark.* This structure is an example of what we may call *fine stratification:* a great many divisions of the socio-economic continuum in which stratification is preserved at each stylistic level. Other investigations of /r/ carried out in New York City support the following general hypothesis on the fine stratification of (r) : *any groups of New Yorkers that are ranked in a hierarchical scale by non-linguistic criteria will be ranked in the same order by their differential use of (r).*

The status of /r/ as a prestige marker is indicated by the

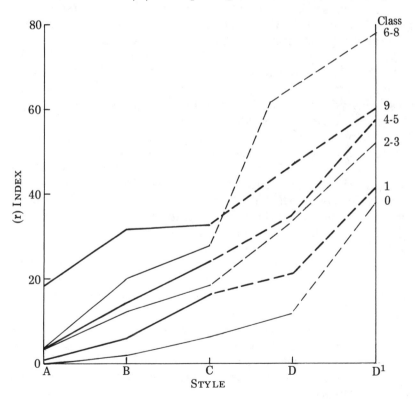

FIGURE 2. *Class stratification of a linguistic variable in process of change: (r) in* guard, car, beer, beard, board, *etc.*

general upward direction of all horizontal lines as we go from informal to formal contexts. At the level of casual, every-day speech, only the upper middle class group *9* shows a significant degree of *r*-pronunciation. But in more formal styles, the amount of *r*-pronunciation for other groups rises rapidly. The lower middle class, in particular, shows an extremely rapid increase, surpassing the upper middle class level in the two most formal styles. This cross-over pattern appears at first sight to be a deviation from the regular structure shown in Figure 1. It is a pattern which appears in other diagrams: a similar cross-over of the lower middle class appears for two other phonological indexes—in fact, for all those linguistic variables which are involved in a process of linguistic change under social pressure. On the other hand, the social and stylistic patterns for (th) have remained stable for at least 75 years, and show no sign of a cross-over pattern. Thus the hyper-correct behavior of the lower middle class is seen as a synchronic indicator of linguistic change in progress.

The linear nature of the ten-point scale of socio-economic status is confirmed by the fact that it yields regular stratification for many linguistic variables, grammatical as well as phonological. The linguistic variables have been correlated with the individual social indicators of productive status—occupation, education and income—and it appears that no single indicator is as closely correlated with linguistic behavior as the combined index. However, an index which combines occupation and education—neglecting income—gives more regular stratification for the (th) variable. For education, there is one sharp break in linguistic behavior for this variable: the completion of the first year of high school. For occupation, there are sharp differences between blue-collar workers, white-collar workers, and professionals. If we combine these two indicators, we obtain four classes which divide the population almost equally, and stratify (th) usage regularly. This classification seems to be superior to the socio-economic scale for analysis of variables such as (th) which reflect linguistic habits formed relatively early in life. However, the combined socio-economic index, utilizing income, does show more regular stratification for a variable such as (r). Since /r/ is a recently introduced prestige marker in New York City speech, it seems consistent—almost predictable—that it should be closely correlated with a socio-economic scale which includes current income, and thus represents most closely the current social status of the subject.

Figure 3 shows the distribution of (r) by age levels, a distribution in *apparent time* which indicates a sudden increase in

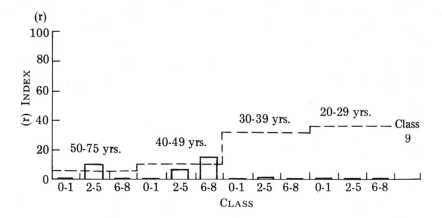

FIGURE 3. *Development of class stratification of (r) for casual speech in apparent time.*

real time of the social stratification of (r) in every-day speech. The upper middle class usage is indicated by the horizontal dotted line. The usage of other class groups—0-1, lower class; 2-5, working class; 6-8, lower middle class—is indicated by the series of vertical bars at each age level. For the two oldest age levels, there is little indication of social significance of /r/. But beginning with those under 40 years old, there is a radically different situation, with /r/ acting as a prestige marker of upper middle class usage only. This sudden change in the status of /r/ seems to have coincided with the events of World War II.

So far, we have been considering only one aspect of social stratification: the differentiation of objective behavior. In the recent studies of New York City, the complementary aspect of social stratification has also been examined: social evaluation. A subjective reaction test was developed to isolate unconscious social responses to the values of individual phonological variables. In these tests, the subject rates a number of short excerpts from the speech of other New Yorkers on a scale of occupational suitability, and cross-comparisons of these ratings enable us to isolate the unconscious subjective reactions of respondents to single phonological variables. Figure 4 shows the percentage of subjects who displayed reactions which were consistent with the status of /r/ as a prestige marker. We see that all subjects between 18 and 39 years old showed agreement in their positive evaluation of /r/, despite the fact (as shown in Figure 3) that the great majority of these subjects do not use any /r/ in their every-day speech. Thus sharp diversification of (r) in objective perfor-

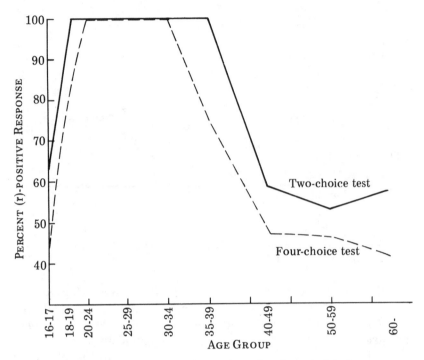

FIGURE 4. *Development of social evaluation of (r) in two subjective reaction tests.*

mance is accompanied by uniform subjective evaluation of the social significance of this feature. On the other hand, the subjects over 40 years old, who show no differential pattern in their use of (r), show a very mixed pattern in their social evaluation of /r/.

This result is typical of many other empirical findings which confirm the view of New York City as a single speech community, united by a uniform evaluation of linguistic features, yet diversified by increasing stratification in objective performance.

The special role of the lower middle class in linguistic change has been illustrated here in only one example, the cross-over pattern of Figure 2. When Figure 3 is replicated for increasingly formal styles, we see that in each age level, the lower middle class shows the greatest tendency towards the introduction of *r*-pronunciation, and in the most formal styles, goes far beyond the upper middle class level in this respect. A great deal of evidence shows that lower middle class speakers have the greatest tendency towards linguistic insecurity, and therefore tend to adopt, even in middle age, the prestige forms used by the youngest members of the highest ranking class. This linguistic insecurity is shown by the very wide range of stylistic variation used by lower middle class speakers; by their great fluctuation within a given stylistic context; by their conscious striving for correctness; and by their strongly negative attitudes towards their native speech pattern.

Another measure of linguistic insecurity was obtained by an independent approach, based on lexical behavior. The subjects were presented with eighteen words which have socially significant variants in pronunciation: *vase, aunt, escalator,* etc. Each word was pronounced in two alternate forms, such as [veɪz—vɑːz], [æ'nt—ɑ'nt], [ɛskəleɪtə—ɛskjuleɪtə]. Respondents were asked to select the form they thought was correct. They were then asked to indicate which form they usually used themselves. The total number of cases in which these two choices differed was taken as the index of linguistic insecurity. By this measure, the lower middle class showed much the greatest degree of linguistic insecurity.

Social stratification and its consequences are only one type of social process which is reflected in linguistic structures. The interaction of ethnic groups in New York City—Jews, Italians, Negroes and Puerto Ricans—is also reflected in these and other linguistic variables. For some variables, New York City Negroes participate in the same structure of social and stylistic variation as white New Yorkers. For other variables, there is an absolute differentiation of white and Negro which reflects the process of social segregation characteristic of the city. For example, there is a Southern phonological characteristic which merges the vowels /i/ and /e/ before nasals: *pin* and *pen, since* and *sense,* are homonyms: "I asked for a straight [pɪn] and he gave me a writing [pɪn]." In New York City, this phonological trait has been generalized throughout the Negro community, so that the younger Negro speakers, whether or not they show other Southern characteristics in their speech, regularly show this merger. Thus this linguistic characteristic acts as an absolute differentiator of the Negro group, reflecting the social processes which identify the racial group as a whole. Similar phonological characteristics can be found which mark the Puerto Rican group.[8]

Segregation of Negro and white may be seen in aspects of linguistic behavior quite distinct from the phonological system. Our investigation of New York City speech includes a number of semantic studies: one of the most fruitful of these concerns the

[8] Most New Yorkers differentiate the vowel of *can* as in "tin can" from that of *can* as in "I can." None of the Puerto Rican subjects interviewed showed a consistent use of this phonemic distinction.

semantic structures which revolve about the term *common sense.*
This term lies at the center of one of the most important areas
of intellectual activity for most Americans. It is a term frequently
used, with considerable affect; its meaning is often debated, and
questions about common sense evoke considerable intellectual
effort from most of our subjects. Negroes use the term *common
sense,* but also an equivalent term which is not a part of the native
vocabulary of any white speakers. This term is *mother-wit,* or
*mother-with* [mʌðɝ·wɪθ]. For a few white speakers, mother-wit
is identified as an archaic, learned term: but for Negroes, it is
a native term used frequently by older members of the household, referring to a complex of emotions and concepts that is quite
important to them. Yet Negroes have no idea that white people
do not use *mother-wit,* and whites have no inkling of the Negro
use of this term. Contrast this complete lack of communication
in an important area of intellectual activity with the smooth
and regular transmission of slang terms from Negro musicians
to the white population as a whole.

The process of social segregation springs from causes and
mechanisms which have been studied in detail. However, the opposing process of social integration is less obvious, and on the
plane of linguistic structure, it is not at all clear how it takes
place. Consider the semantic structure of *common sense.* When
we analyze the semantic components of this term, its position in
a hierarchical taxonomy, and its relation to coordinate terms in
a semantic paradigm, we see great differences in the semantic
structures used by various speakers.

This diversity can best be illustrated by contrasting two
types of responses to our questions on common sense, responses
which usually fall into two consistent sets. Respondent A may
think of *common sense* as just "sensible talk." If he understands
the cognitive content of an utterance, that to him is common
sense. Respondent B considers common sense to be the highest
form of rational activity, the application of knowledge to solve
the most difficult problems. Do most people have common sense?
A says yes, B says no. Who has a great deal of common sense? A
thinks that doctors, lawyers, professors have the most. B thinks
that uneducated people are more apt to have common sense, and
immediately calls to mind some highly educated people with no
common sense at all. If we say "two and two make four," is that
an example of common sense? A says yes, B says no. Can we say
that a person is intelligent, yet has no common sense? A says no,
because intelligence is the same as common sense. B says yes, common sense and intelligence are quite different. A believes that if

someone can be called *smart*, he would also have common sense; B sees no connection between smartness and common sense. Can one have *wisdom*, and yet no common sense? A says yes, B says no.

The extreme differences between types A and B, which are not independent of social stratification, lead us to question the possibility of semantic integration. Can such individuals, who have radically opposed semantic structures for *common sense*, be said to understand one another? Can the term *common sense* be used to communicate meaning between these speakers? Some writers (particularly the followers of General Semantics) feel that native speakers of English usually do *not* understand one another, that such opposing structures inevitably lead to misunderstanding. The results of our studies so far lead me to infer the opposite. People do understand one another: semantic integration seems to take place through a central set of relations of equivalence and attribution upon which all English speakers agree. With only a few exceptions, all subjects agree that *common sense* falls under the super-ordinate *judgment:* it is "good judgment." Equally high agreement is found in the collocation of *practical,* or *every-day,* with *common sense.* We have no simplex term to describe the quality of "not being learned from books," yet there is also a very high degree of agreement in this attribute of *common sense.*

If semantic integration takes place, it must be by a social process in which extreme variants are suppressed in group interaction to favor central or core values. The continuing studies of these semantic patterns are designed to throw light on the problem as to whether such a mechanism exists, and how it might operate.

This discussion has presented a number of aspects of language behavior in which linguistic structures are seen to reflect social processes. In the over-all view, there is a wide range of benefits which may be drawn from the interaction of sociological and linguistic investigations. These may be considered under three headings, in order of increasing generality:

1. Linguistic indexes provide a large body of quantitative data which reflect the influence of many independent variables. It does not seem impractical for tape-recorded data of this type to be collected and analyzed by social scientists who are not primarily linguists. Once the social significance of a given linguistic variant has been determined, by methods such as those outlined above, this variable may then serve as an index to measure other forms of social behavior: upward social aspirations, social

mobility and insecurity, changes in social stratification and segregation.

2. Many of the fundamental concepts of sociology are exemplified in the results of these studies of linguistic variation. The speech community is not defined by any marked agreement in the use of language elements, so much as by participation in a set of shared norms; these norms may be observed in overt types of evaluative behavior, and by the uniformity of abstract patterns of variation which are invariant in respect to particular levels of usage. Similarly, through observations of linguistic behavior it is possible to make detailed studies of the structure of class stratification in a given community. We find that there are some linguistic variables which are correlated with an abstract measure of class position, derived from a combination of several non-isomorphic indicators, where no single, less abstract measure will yield equally good correlations.

3. If we consider seriously the concept of language as a form of social behavior, it is evident that any theoretical advance in the analysis of the mechanism of linguistic evolution will contribute directly to the general theory of social evolution. In this respect, it is necessary for linguists to refine and extend their methods of structural analysis to the use of language in complex urban societies. For this purpose, linguistics may now draw upon the techniques of survey methodology; more importantly, many of the theoretical approaches of linguistics may be re-interpreted in the light of more general concepts of social behavior developed by other social sciences. The present report is intended as a contribution to this more general aim. It is hoped that the main achievements of linguistic science, which may formerly have appeared remote and irrelevant to many sociologists, may eventually be seen as consistent with the present direction of sociology, and valuable for the understanding of social structure and social change.

## The Styles of the Five Clocks

MARTIN JOOS

"You guys shut up!" and "Could I have everyone's attention, please?" mean very much the same thing. But a sergeant making an announcement to a room full of generals knows which

form of address to choose in order to avoid unpleasant consequences to his career. In this book, we use the term *style* to refer
to a form of language chosen to meet social expectations. In
the preceding article, Labov shows that New Yorkers have four
styles in their use of the sound [r]; the sound is used more
frequently in a formal style than in an informal one. In the present
article Joos discusses five possible styles in American English,
related to the topic, the setting, and the audience involved. You
may be interested in building your own theory of the number
and kind of styles used by people you know.

English usage guilt feelings have not yet been noticeably
eased by the work of linguistic scientists, parallel to the work
done by the psychiatrists. It is still our custom unhesitatingly
and unthinkingly to demand that the clocks of language all be
set to Central Standard Time. And each normal American is
taught thoroughly, if not to keep accurate time, at least to feel
ashamed whenever he notices that a clock of his is out of step
with the English Department's tower-clock. Naturally he avoids
looking aloft when he can. Then his linguistic guilt hides deep
in his subconscious mind and there secretly gnaws away at the
underpinnings of his public personality.

English, like national languages in general, has five clocks.
And the times that they tell are not simply earlier and later; they
differ sidewise too, and in several directions. Naturally. A community has a complex structure, with variously differing needs
and occasions. How could it scrape along with only one pattern
of English Usage?

STYLE: Here are the five clocks to which we shall principally
devote our attention. They may be called "higher" and "lower"
for convenience in referring to the tabulation; but that doesn't
mean anything like relative superiority.

> frozen
> formal
> consultative
> casual
> intimate

With a single exception, there is no law requiring a speaker
to confine himself to a single style for one occasion; in general,
he is free to shift to another style, perhaps even within the
sentence. But normally only two neighboring styles are used
alternately, and it is anti-social to shift two or more steps in a

single jump, for instance from casual to formal. When the five styles have been separately and comparatively described, the details of shifting will be obvious.

The two defining features of consultative style are: (1) The speaker supplies background information—he does not assume that he will be understood without it; (2) The addressee participates continuously. Because of these two features, consultative style is our norm for coming to terms with strangers—people who speak our language but whose personal stock of information may be different.

But treating the listener as a stranger is hard work in the long run; therefore we sooner or later try to form a social group with him. Our most powerful device for accomplishing this is the use of casual style. Casual style is for friends, acquaintances, insiders; addressed to a stranger, it serves to make him an insider simply by treating him as an insider. Negatively, there is absence of background information and no reliance on listeners' participation. This is not rudeness; it pays the addressee the compliment of supposing that he will understand without those aids. On the positive side, we have two devices which do the same job directly: (1) ellipsis, and (2) slang, the two defining features of casual style.

The purpose of ellipsis and the purpose of slang are the same; but they are opposite in their description and opposite in their history. Ellipsis is a minus feature and is very stable historically; slang is a plus feature and is absolutely unstable. Yet both signify the same: that the addressee, an insider, will understand what not everybody would be able to decipher.

Ellipsis (omission) makes most of the difference between casual grammar and consultative grammar. "I believe that I can find one" is proper (though not required) in consultative grammar, but casual English requires a shorter form, say "I believe I can find one" if not the still more elliptical "Believe I can find one." "Thank you" from "I thank you" has been promoted all the way to formal style, while "Thanks" from "Many thanks" or "Much thanks" (Shakespeare) has been promoted only to consultative. Aside from such little shifts in the tradition, ellipsis is stable: the elliptical expressions in use today can nearly all be found in Shakespeare, for instance "Thanks."

As an institution, slang is also ancient; but each individual slang expression is, on the contrary, necessarily unstable. The reason is obvious. Because the utility of any slang expression for classing the addressee as an insider (or excluding an unwanted listener as an outsider) depends on the fact—or at least the polite fiction—that only a minority of the population understands this bit of slang, each slang expression is necessarily ephemeral; for when that fiction has become transparent with age, its purpose is foiled, and then the useless slang is abandoned while new slang has to be created to take its place.

Besides these two pattern devices—ellipsis and slang—casual style is marked by an arbitrary list of formulas, all very stable, which are learned individually and used to identify the style for the hearer's convenience. "Come on!" has been one of these identifiers since before the time of Shakespeare (*The Tempest* I, ii, 308). Each style has its own list of such conventional formulas, which we may call "code-labels" because they serve both to carry part of the message and to identify the style. Consultative code-labels include the standard list of listener's insertions "yes [professorial for *yeah*], yeah, unhunh, that's right, oh, I see, yes I know" and a very few others, plus the "well" that is used to reverse the roles between listener and speaker.

Both colloquial styles—consultative and casual—routinely deal in a public sort of information, though differently: casual style takes it for granted and at most alludes to it, consultative style states it as fast as it is needed. Where there happens to be no public information for a while, a casual conversation (among men) lapses into silences and kidding, a consultative one is broken off or adjourned. These adjustments help to show what sort of role public information plays in the two colloquial styles: it is essential to them both.

Now in intimate style, this role is not merely weakened; rather, it is positively abolished. Intimate speech excludes public information. Definition: An intimate utterance pointedly avoids giving the addressee information from outside of the speaker's skin. Example: "ready" said in quite a variety of situations, some of them allowing other persons to be present; note that this could be equivalent to either a statement or a question.

The systematic features of intimate style are two, just as in the other styles: (1) extraction; (2) jargon. Both are stable, once the intimate group (normally a pair) has been formed. Extraction: the speaker extracts a minimum pattern from some conceivable casual sentence. Extraction is not ellipsis. An elliptical sentence still has wording, grammar, and intonation. Intimate extraction employs only part of this triplet. Our printed "Engh" represents an empty word, one that has no dictionary meaning but serves as a code-label for intimate style. (The parallel word in casual style, spelled "unh," has a different vocal quality.) There is, however, a message meaning; this is conveyed by the intonation, the melody, with which "Engh" is spoken. The speaker has extracted this intonation from a possible casual sentence, and that is all he uses of the grammatical triplet "wording, grammar, intonation." Once more, this is not rudeness; this pays the addressee the highest compliment possible.

Intimate style tolerates nothing of the system of any other style: no slang, no background information, and so on. Any item of an intimate code that the folklore calls "slang" is not slang but jargon—it is not ephemeral, but part of the permanent code of this group—it has to be, for intimacy does not tolerate the slang imputation that the addressee needs to be told that he is an insider. The imputations of all other styles are similarly corrosive. Accordingly, intimate codes, or jargons, are severely limited in their use of public vocabulary. Each intimate group must invent its own code. Somehow connected with all this is the cozy fact that language itself can never be a topic in intimate style. Any reaction to grammar, for instance, promptly disrupts intimacy. . . .

Describing formal style by departure from consultative style, the crucial difference is that participation drops out. This is forced whenever the group has grown too large. A competent manic is able to convert a tête-à-tête into a formal assembly; but normal persons maintain consultation up to a group-size of approximately six, which sets the limits on the size and composition of a "committee" in the English-speaking sense. Beyond that, parliamentary law is requisite, i.e., a division into active and chair-warming persons.

Non-participating is also forced whenever a speaker is entirely uncertain of the prospective response. Thus conversations between strangers begin in formal style; among urbane strangers in English-speaking cultures, the formal span is only the ceremony of introduction.

Formal style is designed to inform: its dominating character, something which is necessarily ancillary in consultation, incidental in casual discourse, absent in intimacy. The formal code-labels inform each hearer that he is in a formal frame, is not to make insertions but must wait until authorized to speak, and is being given time to plan reactions—as much as half a century. The leading code-label is "may," any message requiring either "might" or "can" in other styles is suppressed or paraphrased, giving "May I help you?" and "We may not see one another for some time," the consultative equivalent of which was cited previously. We may most economically label an introduction as formal by saying "May I present Mr. Smith?"—or petrify a child by saying "No, you may not." Originally, the well-placed "may" was as effective as a hat-pin.

Form becomes its dominant character. It endeavors to employ only logical links, kept entirely within the text, and displays those logical links with sedulous care. The pronunciation is explicit to the point of clattering; the grammar tolerates no ellipsis and cultivates elaborateness; the semantics is fussy. Formal text therefore demands advance planning.

The defining features of formal style are two: (1) detachment; (2) cohesion. One feature, of the highest importance, is retained from the basal styles: intonation. Since the audience hears the text just once, any deficiency in the intonation is dangerous, any major defect is disastrous. Lack of intonation, as in print, is simply a blank check; but false intonation will mulct the listener in triple damages.

# First-Language Influences on Ethnic Dialects: Spanish and Navajo

MURIEL R. SAVILLE

Saville explains some major differences between English and Spanish, and between English and Navajo; in each case, there are differences between the two languages in sound systems, sentence structures, and meaning. Her article has both a broad use and a narrower one: it tells us where we can expect to find variation in the ethnic dialects of English spoken by native speakers of Spanish and by native speakers of Navajo, and it also helps teachers predict trouble spots in their students' control of English. Dale, in the following article, discusses phonological and syntactic structures in another ethnic dialect, Black English. Penfield's article in Part 1 gives important background for both of these articles on ethnic dialects, since it suggests ages at which students can and cannot acquire completely native-speaker control of second languages and dialects.

Before we categorize these three groups as having ethnic dialects, we should add some reservations. First, none of the suggestions we are making are intended to apply to every Mexican-American, or Navajo American, or black American. We are talking about large numbers of speakers in these ethnic groups, but by no means all speakers. Second, the word *ethnic* can apply to anyone. We all recognize that a white American visiting another country is a member of a minority ethnic group. The same person in America is still a member of an ethnic group, whether or not that group is in the majority.

Most linguistically different children in the United States come from homes where a nonstandard dialect of English is spoken or where the primary language is Spanish, French, or one of the many American Indian languages. The particular problems that children with [Spanish and Navajo] language backgrounds have with English are considered below as are the reasons such problems can be predicted from linguistic analysis.

## SPANISH

Disadvantaged children with Spanish-language backgrounds present a major educational challenge to many schools, particularly in New York and the Southwest. The degree of language handicap exhibited by these children in an English-language classroom setting is sufficiently great to explain much of their academic underachievement and their high dropout rate. Contrasts between English and Spanish have been well described by linguists, and Spanish-speaking children have so far received most of the attention in elementary-school programs for teaching English as a second language. More reading and oral language materials for them will be published soon.

Not all Spanish-speaking children have the same language system any more than all English-speaking children do. Some of their families have come to the United States from Puerto Rico, Cuba, and various parts of Mexico. Others have lived for generations in parts of the United States where various dialects of Spanish have developed. When one considers that there are social dialects within the regional ones, the language problem seems very complex. There has been sufficient research to show that these dialectal differences in Spanish influence the children's use of English, but no comprehensive analysis is yet available.

In general the Spanish sound system does not contrast /š/ and /č/, and substitution or interchange of these English phonemes is the most obvious error Spanish-speaking children make in pronouncing English words. They may often say /čuw/ for *shoe* or /šer/ for *chair*. Spanish has one phoneme that covers the range of both English /b/ and /v/, and it often sounds as if the children say /beriy/ for *very* and /kəvərd/ for *cupboard*. Other common substitutions are /s/, /f/, or /t/ for /θ/; and /z/, /v/, or /d/ for /ð/. Consonant clusters cause many problems, particularly when they contain a sibilant, such as /s/.

Spanish uses only five vowel phonemes; children learning English must distinguish several more. The range of Spanish /i/ includes the vowel sounds of *mit* and *meat;* /e/ those of *met* and *mate;* /u/, those of *pull* and *pool;* /o/, those of *coat* and *caught;* and /a/ covers a range that includes the vowel sounds of *cut* and *cot.*

There are several basic differences in the grammatical structures of Spanish and English that cause interference for a pupil learning English as a second language.[1] The verb-noun pattern of *es un hombre* must be equated with the noun-verb-noun pattern of *this is a man.* Similarly, the interrogative-verb pattern of *¿qué es?* is patterned in English as interrogative-verb-noun, *what is that?* A difference in word order is seen in the following examples: *la mano derecha* (D-N-Adj) : *the right hand* (D-Adj-N) ; *le da el sombrero* (IO-V-DO) : *he gives him the hat* (S-V-IO-DO) ; *¿está abierta una ventana?* (V-Adj-N) : *is a window open?* (V-N-Adj). A relationship that has been indicated by word order in *la cabeza de un perro* must be indicated by inflection in *a dog's head;* the situation is reversed in the case of *dará,* which is expressed in English as *he will give.* Many Spanish-speaking children transfer the use of double negatives from Spanish to English. It is good Spanish to say *no hay nada en la mesa,* but the sentence literally translated is *there's not nothing on the table.*

The semantic structure of English also presents a number of problems for speakers of Spanish. There are many cognates in the two languages. The most difficult new words to learn are the "false friends," words that sound the same but have different meanings. An example is the Spanish verb *asistir,* which means in English *to attend* and not *to assist.*

---

[1] Fred Brengelman, "Contrasted Grammatical Structures in English and Spanish" (Unpublished paper, Fresno State College, 1964).

Teachers often comment that their Spanish-speaking pupils read without expression. To understand and correct the real problem they should first know that the Spanish intonational system has one less degree of stress than the English system, different rhythm and stress patterns, and different intonational contours. A Spanish-speaker will pronounce every syllable for about the same length of time, shorten English stressed syllables, put the stress on the wrong syllable, and not reduce vowels in unstressed syllables. He will use a rising pitch for a confirmation response and a low-mid-low pitch pattern for statements instead of the mid-high-low contour usual in English.

Improper intonation in reading English questions and exclamations may be partly a problem with symbols. If the pupil has learned to read in Spanish, he is used to the signals ¿ and ¡ at the beginning of questions and exclamations, respectively. Because the initial signals are missing in English he may get close to the end of these constructions before he realizes that they are questions or exclamations.

Most of the problems Spanish-speaking children have in learning to read and spell English words are due to the different correspondences between sounds and symbols. Vowels cause the greatest difficulty; pupils could conceivably write *cat* for *cot*, *mit* for *meat*, and *met* for *mate*. They might read *fine* as /fine/ instead of /fayn/ and *but* as /buwt/ instead of /bət/. These reading and spelling errors cannot be corrected unless the pupils can first consistently hear and use the vowel phonemes of English. The symbols can then be related to these sounds.

A similar problem may be noted in arithmetic if pupils have learned to write numerals in Mexico or one of several other countries. They will write 1 as *1* and 7 as *7*. Consequently, teachers and pupils may confuse 1's and 7's in problems and answers. . . .

## NAVAJO

A number of unrelated languages are spoken by the more than half a million Indians who live on reservations in the United States. Many groups have adopted some form of English as a primary language, and some continue to use the languages of their ancestors. On the Navajo reservation, forty-thousand pupils are now attending schools and the number increases each year. The teaching of English is recognized there as one of the most serious problems in education and one that must be solved as part of the assault on generally low wages, high unemployment rates, and poor living conditions.

The specific problems Navajo children have with English are considered here because the Navajos are the largest tribe in the United States. Their problems, as well as those of speakers of Spanish and French, depend on the points of contrast between their language and English, and thus cannot be generalized to include all Indian languages. These points should serve to indicate, however, the types of problems that may be encountered by speakers of languages completely unrelated to English.

There are many differences between English and Navajo both in the articulation of sounds that have similar positions in the phonemic systems of the two languages and in the articulation of sounds that occur in one language but have no correspondents in the other.

Navajo speakers do not distinguish between English /p/ and /b/ and usually substitute their own slightly different /b/ for both. This sound never occurs in syllable final position in Navajo, however, so they often substitute /ʔ/ (a glottal stop) for final /-p/ or /-b/ or reduce all final stops to the Navajo /-d/. This /d/, which sounds like the /t/ in /stap/, is also typically substituted for English /t/ or /d/ in initial position. The /ʔ/ is frequently substituted for stopped consonants and added before initial vowels, making Navajo speech sound choppy to speakers of English. In Navajo there are no correspondents to /f/, /v/, /θ/, /ð/, and /ŋ/.

The primary differences between the vowel systems are the use of vowel length and nasalization to distinguish meaning in Navajo and the greater variety of vowel sounds in English. The vowels /æ/ and /ə/ do not occur in Navajo and are the hardest for pupils to learn. Navajo-speakers must also learn to distinguish among English /o/, /u/, and /uw/.

English consonant clusters present a major problem for Navajo-speakers, who often substitute similar affricates for them. Much of the Navajos' difficulty with noun and verb inflections may be traced to their failure to hear or produce final consonant clusters.[2]

Tonal pitch in Navajo serves as the only distinctive feature to differentiate meaning in such words as /nílí/ *you are*, /nilí/

[2] Mary Jane Cook and Margaret Sharp, "Problems of Navajo Speakers in Learning English," in *Language Learning*, XVI, Nos. 1 and 2 (1966), 21–30.

*he is,* /át²í/ *he does,* /at²í/ *he is rich,* /azéé²/ *mouth,* and /azee²/ *medicine.* Whereas Navajo uses fixed tones with relation to vowels and syllabic nasals to distinguish meaning, English uses a variety of sentence pitch patterns, or intonational contours. Navajo-speakers must learn to disregard the pitch of individual phonemes. On the other hand, English makes use of stress to distinguish meaning in some words, whereas stress is never distinctive in Navajo.

The use of a rising sentence inflection to indicate interrogation or the use of other types of pitch to convey, for example, the connotation of surprise is either not possible in a tone language, is not used as a mechanism for this purpose, or is used in a different way. Particles in Navajo convey meanings expressed by intonation in English. For instance, /da²-iš/ and /-ša/ added to Navajo words signal questions, /-ga²/ gives emphasis, and /-²as/ indicates disbelief. Navajos may speak and read English without the appropriate modulations and inflections because they are unaccustomed to the use of intonation to express meaning in these situations.[3]

Other very general phonological problems that teachers of Navajo children should concentrate on are the voicing of stops, the production of most consonants in final position, and the production of glides.

Many features of English syntax are difficult for Navajo-speakers. Articles and adjectives are very troublesome because, with a few exceptions, they do not exist in Navajo. The idea of prettiness would be expressed by a verb and conjugated "I am pretty, you are pretty," and so forth. English adjectives present problems in both their word order and comparative patterns. Few Navajo nouns are inflected for plural; thus a common type of error in English is *four dog.* Possessive -*s* is also a problem, since the Navajo pattern for *the boy's book* would be *the boy his book.* English third-person pronouns are commonly confused. Navajo /bí/ translates as any of the following: *he, she, it, they, him, her, them, his, her, its, their.* This means that gender, number, and case distinctions must all be learned. Navajo makes other distinctions among third-person pronouns not found in English, however, such as distance from the subject. There are also numerous and complicated differences in the verb structure.

[3] Robert W. Young, "A Sketch of the Navaho Language," in *The Navaho Yearbook* (Window Rock, Ariz.: Navaho Agency, 1961).

Even if a Navajo child has mastered the phonological and syntactic components of the English language, he is faced with a semantic system that categorizes experience in a very different way. English often uses several unrelated words to describe something that is seen as different aspects of the same action in Navajo; or one word to describe an action seen as unrelated events. For example, if the object of each action is the same, the English verbs *give, take, put,* and several others are translated by one Navajo verb stem that means roughly "to handle." Different Navajo verb stems will be used for *to handle* depending on the shape of the object.

There has been no interference from written Navajo because the language has been recorded only by linguists and missionaries. Programs are now under way to teach reading and writing to Navajos in their native language. A standardized orthography has been developed. Questions concerning its possible interference with learning the English writing system have been raised, but some leading educators agree that basing the orthography on the Navajo language itself is a far more important consideration than any interference with English that may result.[4] . . .

Finally, there are still some individuals who believe that the purpose of language instruction is to eradicate nonstandard English. This attitude has contributed to the resistance of many children to the speech model prescribed in school. There are those who do not wish to adopt the middle-class pattern as their language system but prefer to retain that of their friends and family. They can communicate more effectively in their neighborhoods if they use their nonstandard dialect or native language. Teachers have the best chance for success in teaching English to these children if they try to *add to* rather than replace the dialect or language of the home.

The children should be made aware of other levels of language and of the difference their use can make in occupational opportunities, but their own patterns of speech should not be rejected as "sloppy" or inferior. The goal of language instruction for disadvantaged children should be to enable them to achieve sufficient flexibility to communicate easily on more than one level and in diverse situations.

[4] Sirarpi Ohannessian, *Conference on Navajo Orthography* (Washington, D.C.: Center for Applied Linguistics, 1969).

# Dialect Differences and Black English

PHILIP S. DALE

Look at the drawing of dialects as overlapping systems, in the introduction to Part 2. In the present article, Dale describes some of the nonoverlapping rules that identify one particular dialect: an ethnic dialect widely known as Black English. This term is very carefully defined by Dale, making clear that Black English is only one of many black dialects.

It is important to realize that we are discussing Black English at a time when we do not have complete information on either white dialects or other black dialects. Linguistics has simply not had the money or the manpower to survey all American dialects. So Dale's description should be taken as an attempt to spell out the rules that define Black English, but not a rigid claim that every one of these rules appears in Black English and Black English alone. The following article by Williamson brings up a number of language rules often taken as defining Black English that turn out to exist in southern white dialects as well.

There are some technical terms like *present progressive* and *deep structure* in this article. Some of these will be clear from context and examples. Others, like *deep structure,* are briefly dealt with in the overview of language in the general introduction, and are explained in detail in Part 3.

## ATTITUDES TOWARD DIALECT DIFFERENCES

A language is a coherent system of rules, and each dialect is also a coherent system of rules. And these systems have a great deal in common with each other. They are not exactly foreign languages, but they confront each other linguistically as equals, as alternative dialects of the same language.

Social class dialects are simply dialects like any other kind of dialect. Unfortunately, they have not always been viewed in this way. There is a strong tendency to see nonstandard [1] dialects as the result of isolated deviations from the standard language, resulting from failure to master the standard dialect. This failure in turn may be blamed on inadequate environment, genetic differences, or other factors.

---

[1] "Nonstandard" here refers to any dialect other than the one spoken by the dominant social class under fairly careful conditions. The term is entirely nonevaluative.

Social values and attitudes with respect to language are not only strong but also remarkably stable. Even revolutions fail to change them in most cases. In Amercan society, even the most radical and revolutionary figures do not use nonstandard syntax in speaking or in print. Of course it is traditional for politicians to sprinkle a little of the vernacular into their public speeches. But this is almost always in the form of vernacular vocabulary items, seldom in matters of pronunciation and even more rarely in syntax. The same phenomenon appears to be happening in the American black nationalist movement. There is a new trend to use some aspects of the nonstandard dialect [in formal situations], but [they are] almost always vocabulary items, not sentence construction.

To put this in different words, the entire linguistic community often shares attitudes toward dialects. In Quebec, both English and French are spoken. English-speaking Canadians hearing tapes of individuals speaking French Canadian and English, judge the speakers of English to be more intelligent, more dependable, kinder, more ambitious, better looking, and taller. Given the all too human tendency toward self- and group-glorification, this is not too surprising. The remarkable fact is that French Canadians respond in approximately the same way; that is, they respond more favorably to English speakers than to French Canadian speakers. The negative evaluation of French Canadian is shared by both communities in Quebec (Lambert, 1967). Similarly, although the vowel in *mad, bad,* and *glad* is pronounced in many different ways in New York City, there is general agreement that the higher the tongue (pronouncing the vowel closer to that of *beard*), the lower the status of the speaker. These two examples are both instances of a phenomenon that has long been familiar to sociologists: the adoption of majority norms by members of the minority, even when they are highly unfavorable to the minority. . . .

These attitudes can, and do change. French-speaking Canadians have become increasingly concerned with preserving their linguistic heritage, and so have many black Americans. But the changes are slow. Often an educated, culturally conscious elite can change its view, but it will have difficulty in affecting the majority of the group.

It is often the case that the people who most strongly condemn a form in the speech of others are among the people who are most likely to use it in their own casual speech. This is undoubtedly due to the fact that they are the ones who are struggling most actively to overcome this trait and are therefore most conscious of it. This situation often leads to what has been called **hypercorrect speech**—adopting the standard form even more strongly than the high prestige group. In studies of the pronunciation of *r* in such words as *heard, guard,* and *car,* lower middle-class speakers sharply increased their pronunciation of *r*. In reading sentences, their score was almost identical to that of upper middle class speakers; and in reading word lists, it actually exceeded that of upper middle class speakers. This tendency for such speakers to strongly condemn the nonstandard form is particularly important for the educational process, since American school teachers have traditionally been drawn from the lower middle class (although this is increasingly less true).

Of course there is no logical reason or necessity for such unfavorable attitudes. There are many situations in the world which demonstrate that a pluralistic situation can exist successfully. It often happens, for example, that the language used in school is not the native language of the children. Swahili is the school language in continental Tanzania (formerly Tanganyika), although a substantial proportion of the children in this region are not native speakers of Swahili. The Kerman area of Iran is an example of a pluralistic dialect situation. Kermani Persian is the native dialect of the children, while Standard Persian is the dialect of the schools. There is no stigma attached to speaking Kermani when the child is with his family or friends, but Standard Persian is used in school and with people from other areas of Iran.


## BLACK ENGLISH

In several areas of the United States, nonstandard dialects are associated with ethnic group membership. In the southwestern part of the country, and in parts of New York City, a nonstandard dialect arises as the result of contact between Spanish and English speakers. In many areas, a similar problem exists for American Indians. But the most widespread case is that of the dialect spoken by many black Americans. This is the only such dialect to be considered here, primarily because it is the one case for which there is some reliable, useful sociolinguistic knowledge. Virtually all of this is due to the work of [William] Labov in New York City and William Stewart in Washington,

D.C. This dialect is often called "Black English." I am hesitant to use this term because not all black Americans speak it, nor are the features of Black English entirely confined to black speakers. It is a convenient abbreviation and like all convenient abbreviations, somewhat false. However, it is shorter than "Nonstandard Negro English" or "Black Nonstandard English."

From a linguistic point of view, the differences between Black English (BE) and Standard English (STE) are not great. In general, the deep structures of sentences and the underlying representations of lexical items are the same in the two dialects. And so are most of the rules that operate on them: transformations on deep structures and phonological rules on underlying representations. Some rules are different, however; a rule may be present in one dialect but not the other, or the conditions for a rules application may differ. We will consider a few of the most obvious differences. . . .

In STE, the present progressive is marked in two ways; *He is going* contains the auxiliary *be* and the affix-*ing*. In BE, only the second element is necessary: *he goin' home*. In the so-called present perfect, *I have lived here* is the STE form, while either *I have live here* or *I lived here* is permissible in BE. Some possessives do not contain the *'s* marker; *This is John mother* in BE, in contrast to *This is John's mother* in STE. Notice that because of the order of the nouns, the BE form is unambiguous in referring to the mother of John. When the second noun (the object possessed) is deleted, the BE form does mark the possessive with *'s*: *This is John's* is the possessive, whereas *This is John* has a quite different meaning.

In the three constructions just discussed, STE marks a feature twice (*be* + *ing* for the present progressive, *have* + *en* for the present perfect, and *'s* + order for the possessive), whereas BE marks the feature just once. The converse also occurs. Double and triple negatives, as in *Didn't nobody see it*, are common in BE, just as in Russian. *Or either* is sometimes used in BE as just *either* is used in STE. Neither dialect should be viewed as a "simplified" version of the other.

Agreement between subject and verb in person and number is not obligatory in BE; *She have a bike* and *They was going*. Many common irregular verbs are not marked for the simple past tense. For example, the past tense forms of *come* and *see* are *come* and *see*, respectively. This is not to be interpreted as the lack of a past tense or as an indication that the speakers of BE do not have a concept of the past. The two tenses are negated differently : *I don't see it* is the present tense, whereas *I ain't see it* is the past tense form of the negation.

There are some cases where BE makes a grammatical distinction that STE does not make or that can be indicated in STE only by use of a complex construction. The most important of these is the use of the uninflected form of *be* to indicate habitual or general state. *He be workin'* means that he generally works, perhaps that he has a regular job. *He be with us* means that he is generally with us, perhaps that he lives here. In contrast *he workin'* can mean simply that he is working at this moment and *he with us*, that he is here now.

The verb *be* (in its inflected forms) is often not present in constructions which call for *be* in STE. These constructions include sentences with predicate nouns, *he a friend,* predicate adjectives, *he tired,* and the present progressive tense described above, *he workin' with us.* This absence of *be* has been interpreted by some linguists as a difference in deep structure between the two dialects. The simplest explanation for the absence of *be* in the surface structure is the assumption that *be* is not present in the deep structure. However, there is evidence that this interpretation is not correct. The verb *be* does appear in many contexts : as the last word in a sentence—*There he is* (not *There he*) and *I'm smarter* (*than he*) ; in tag questions and in negatives—*He ain't here, is he?*; in the past tense—*she was here;* and in other contexts. These facts indicate that *be* is present in the deep structure, but that it is deleted, by a transformation or transformations in certain specified contexts in the process of conversion, to the surface structure. The verb *be* is deleted in just those cases where contraction is possible in STE—*He's a friend, He's tired, He's with us,* but not *\*There he's* or *\*I'm smarter than he's.* The absence of *be* may be viewed as a result of contraction to *he's* by the same rule that exists in STE, followed by deletion of a final *s,* which is a very common phenomenon in BE.

*David, he say "Here I come"* illustrates the common use of a pronoun following the noun subject of a sentence in BE. This is called **pronominal apposition** and does occur infrequently in STE. It serves to focus attention on the "topic" of the sentence.

Labov has asked speakers of BE to repeat the sentence *Ask Albert if he knows how to play basketball.* The most common response is the production of *Ask Albert do he know how to play basketball.* In English direct questions, [the] declarative *He knows how to play basketball* has a corresponding direct question of the form *Does he know how to play basketball?*. But when this is an indirect question, that is, embedded in a sentence, the question is of the form *If he knows how to play basketball.* The question transformation and the transformation which supplies *do* if necessary do not apply in STE. But in BE, these transformations are applied consistently to both direct and indirect questions. Here we have a common kind of difference between dialects; not the present or absence of a transformation in a dialect but, simply, a change in the conditions under which it is applied. A similar difference exists for imperatives. The direct imperative *Don't do that* becomes *I told you not to do that* in STE but retains its form in BE, *I told you don't do that.*

In addition to these and other syntactic differences between STE and BE, there are many phonological differences. It is probably the phonological differences that [sometimes] make the dialects almost mutually unintelligible. Many of these differences concern consonants at the ends of words. The liquid *r* is dropped before consonants and at the ends of words. As a result, *sore* and *saw* are **homophones** (words pronounced alike), as are *court* and *caught*. Similarly, *l* may be omitted in the same contexts. Thus, *toll* and *toe* are homophones, as are *help* and *hep*.

Consonant clusters at the ends of words are often simplified,[2] especially if the cluster ends with *t, d, s,* or *z. Past* and *passed* are homophones with *pass; called* with *call; hits* with *hit,* and so on. In many of these cases it is not easy to determine if this is a phonological difference or a syntactic one. Is the final *d* of *called* deleted because of a phonological rule or because the simple past tense is not inflected in BE? Is the *s* of the third person singular form *hits* deleted because of a consonant cluster simplification rule or because number agreement is not obligatory between subject and verb? Both views account for some of the evidence and leave other forms unexplained.

In most cases, there is no distinction between [i] and [ɛ] before nasals and liquids; *pin* and *pen* are homophones, as are *cheer* and *chair*. Often the sounds [ay] and [aw] are changed to the simple vowel [a]. In this case, *find, found,* and *fond* are homophones.

The fricative φ in final position is changed to f; thus *with* and *bath* are pronounced wlf and baef, respectively.

It is still a matter of disagreement whether differences in

---

2 [Ed.'s note: This rule also appears in many white dialects; however, the frequency of its use may differ.]

pronunciation, that is, phonetic representations, are due to differences in underlying representation or to differences in the phonological rules that convert underlying representations into phonetic representations. This is a question that has important implications for the teaching of reading. . . . However, it does seem clear that the majority, even if not all, of the differences are in the rules, and that in these cases the underlying representations are the same in both dialects. An example of such a difference follows.

Many speakers of BE pronounce *risk* as [rɪs] and test as [tɛs]. From consideration of these forms alone there is no evidence that the final consonant is present in the underlying representations of these words. The most common plural forms for these words are [rɪsəz] and [tɛsəz]. Again, it does not appear that the final consonants are present. But suppose a suffix, -*y* or -*ing*, is added. Now the forms are pronounced [rɪskiy] and [tɛstɪn], in which the final consonants are present. The final consonants sometimes appear even in the root word, when it is followed by a word that begins with a vowel. The conclusion that the consonant is indeed present in the underlying representation appears difficult to reconcile with observed plural forms. However, if the phonological rules are formulated in the proper order, all the observed forms can be explained simply.

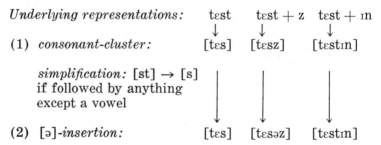

*Underlying representations:*     tɛst     tɛst + z     tɛst + ɪn
                                      ↓          ↓             ↓
(1) *consonant-cluster:*          [tɛs]     [tɛsz]       [tɛstɪn]

    *simplification:* [st] → [s]
    if followed by anything
    except a vowel

(2) [ə]-*insertion:*              [tɛs]     [tɛsəz]      [tɛstɪn]

the STE rule that inserts the vowel [ə] between two consonants produced at approximately the same location in the mouth; it produces the observed phonetic representations

There are also vocabulary differences between BE and STE. A surprisingly high proportion of slang expressions in STE originate in BE. Probably some words and expressions that occur in both dialects have different meanings, and this contributes to the difficulty of communication. "More research is needed" is a cliche, but nonetheless true for being a cliche.

# Selected Features of Speech:
# Black and White

JUANITA V. WILLIAMSON

Does "Black English" exist? In the preceding article Dale has suggested that it does, and he has described some characteristics of this dialect. Now Williamson points out that the speech of many white southerners contains the same structures that have been attributed to Black English.

This does not necessarily mean that there is no such thing as Black English, however. In the first place, Williamson's article is responding to previous research that focused on only a few features of speech; there may be other characteristics of Black English that do not appear in the English of southern whites. In the second place, any ethnic group that moves from one region to another, and that stays together as an ethnic group in the new locale, transforms a regional dialect into an ethnic dialect; Black English does exist as an ethnic dialect in many northern cities. Last, and perhaps most important, Labov's work has shown us that the language of a social group is not always defined by the complete presence or absence of some linguistic rule; these dialects can be defined instead by the frequency with which the rule operates. So the answer to "Does 'Black English' exist?" is not a simple yes or no; Dale, Williamson, and Labov all have important evidence to offer in arriving at an accurate picture of Black English.

There has been in recent years an increasing interest in the speech of American Negroes. Many of the journals, among them *Americans Speaking* and the journals of the National Council of Teachers of English and of the National Education Association, have published at least one article which deals with their speech. The articles usually discuss a limited number of phonological and/ or grammatical features which seem to set the speech of Negroes apart from that of other speakers of American English. One such article is Beryl Bailey's "Toward a New Perspective in Negro Dialectology" (*American Speech,* October 1965, pp. 171–177). In her article Professor Bailey analyzes selected structures found in the speech of Negroes: the absence of the copula (zero copula), the marked forms which are "past and future," the negation markers *ain't* and *don't,* and the treatment of *there* and "possessive *their.*" One or more of these structures is usually in-

cluded in most treatments of the grammar of the speech of
Negroes.

Professor Bailey's analysis is based upon the speech of Dude,
the narrator in Warren Miller's *The Cool World* (Boston, 1959).
The rationale for using a fictional character as her informant rests
upon the belief that "an author regularly packs his dialogue with
those features which he knows to be the most distinctive in the
dialect which his characters speak."

It is of interest to compare the four features of Dude's
speech, which Professor Bailey discusses, with those of Paul Valentine, a klansman and the author of an article entitled "Look
Out Liberals: Wallace Power Gonna Get You," which appeared
in the Fall, 1968, issue of *Katallagete Be Reconciled,* the Journal
of the Committee of Southern Churchmen (Nashville, Tennessee,
pp. 34–37). An editorial note accompanying the article states
that "Paul Valentine is the pseudonym of a Christian who has
operated for years in the Southern Klan. He employs by choice
the raw words of militant alienation." The article is written just
as the author might have spoken it.

In Dude's speech, Professor Bailey points out that the zero
copula, that is, the omission of the verb *be,* occurs before adjectives as in:

> I sure they aroun.
> You afraid of jail bait Big Man?

before nouns as in:

> She a big woman not skinny like my mother.
> He one of us all right.

before adverbs and prepositional phrases as in:

> I in a big hurry.
> Did you find out anything while you over in they territory?

after the filler subjects *there* and *it* as in:

> "It the truth." She say.
> They a lot of people on this street have Stomach Trouble.

In Valentine's speech the zero copula also occurs before adjectives and nouns, as may be seen in the following:

> Bobby, I think you right about that.
> You dumb and you crazy.
> I think that funny as hell.
> I say you hate and you violent. . .

We just about the most stubborn, onery bunch of. . .
They somethin else which we given a whole lot a thought.
He our mean and ugly bastard.[1]

*There* occurs several times before *is* in fairly emphatic, positive statements such as the following: "They is black niggers, yellow niggers, white niggers, and for all I know they is blue niggers somewhere."

The second feature Professor Bailey treats is the marked forms which are "past and future." She states that in Dude's speech it "appears that *was* is reserved for events that are completely in the past, while *been* extends from the past up to, and even including the present moment. *Be* is a simple future, with *gonna* the intentional future." The following are among the examples she gives to illustrate the use of these four forms:

> . . .you just end up scared like you was walkin down a empty street at night.
> . . .you was the sweetest baby so good.

> He bin inside too much.
> You been smokin without me?

> "You be back." Priest say lookin at me.
> "We be waiting for you." Little Flower say.
> Things gonna be a lot different aroun here now Duke in command.
> I sure you gonna contribit some of you earned money to your mother.

Valentine uses *was, been, be,* and *gonna* in a like manner, as the following examples show:

> Now Bobby was able to carry four or five states for Barry.
> Bobby he was real strong for Goldwater.

> You been to college.
> You been stealin our country blind.
> You been forgettin about our problems.

> I be back and catch you next time.
> We still be rollin.
> I think it be close.
> I think it be a generation or more. . .[2]
> We gonna do this because you not fit to run it.
> We gonna let you live knowin what you done to the country.

[1] No adverbs or prepositions occur after the zero copula in "Look Out Liberals."

[2] *Be* occurs in another sense also in Valentine's speech, as may be seen in the following: "Barry he be half Jewish."

I gonna agree with every thing you say. . .
You gonna whine and moan. . .
So George, he gonna have to cut hard. . .

The third feature of Dude's speech which Professor Bailey discusses is the use of *ain't* and *don't* as negation markers. She states that her analysis reveals that the "American Negro system has a curious deployment of the negative markers *don't* and *ain't. Ain't* is used consistently in non-verbal predications and before the tense markers," and this is also the form "preferred before the progressive *-in* form of the verb." She indicates that *don't* may be used in all other cases. The following are among the examples she gives:

"I aint afraid of nothin."
That piece aint been worth no fifteen dollas since you was a
    little boy Priest.
He aint comin back.
He aint gonna get no money out of it.
I dont know why he done it.
I dont care if they aint room for him.

Valentine uses *ain't* without any verbal form following it in the same manner that Dude uses it. It also occurs in his speech before the *-in/-ing* form of the verb. *Don't* is used in the same way Dude uses it:

It ain't hardly a secret.
It ain't quite so slick as ours.
Some of you ain't gonna be able to live with that.
We ain't kidding and we ain't quitting, we ain't turning
    back.
It don't work that way.
He don't tell folks what to do.

To support her fourth point, that in Dude's speech *there* and *their* occur as *they*, Professor Bailey lists the following examples:

They must be over a 100 books in they apartment.
They jus ain't no place in a gang for girls.
Everybody look down at they feet.
In the day time those places full of kids and they mothers.

In "Look Out Liberals," *there* occurs as *they* in the following:

How come they is so many of us?
They is black niggers. . .

Valentine's and Dude's speech patterns are noticeably similar. The question which arises, however, is that of whether the patterns Valentine uses in his article are representative of his speech and/or that of white speakers who live in the area where he lives, the South,[3] or whether what appears in his article is a mishmash he has created.

Since what has been dealt with up to this point is written material, it is of value to look at the dialogue found in fictional works written by authors who deal with the Southern scene and at the representations of Southern speech in articles and magazines. An examination of the dialogue found in William Faulkner's *Light in August,* "Spotted Horses," and *Sanctuary;*[4] Catherine Marshall's *Christy;*[5] Flannery O'Connor's "A Good Man Is Hard to Find," "The Life You Save May be Your Own," and "The Artificial Nigger";[6] John Steinbeck's *The Grapes of Wrath;*[7] Wilbur Daniel Steele's "How Beautiful With Shoes";[8] Percy Walker's *The Moviegoer;*[9] Robert Penn Warren's *All the King's Men* and "Blackberry Winter"[10] reveals that the four features discussed by Professor Bailey and found in Valentine's speech are used by some of the characters in these works.[11] Examples are given below.

Examples of the use of the zero copula:

"You mighty right it is." (*The Moviegoer,* p. 119)
"Name Lucynell Carter. . . ." ("The Life You Save May Be Your Own," p. 498)

---

[3] The South here includes all of the states usually thought of as Southern, and whose governors belong to the Southern governors conference. Some of these states (or parts of them) are actually a part of the South Midland speech area.

[4] *Light in August,* Modern Library edition (New York, 1950); "Spotted Horses," in *The Faulkner Reader* (New York, 1954), pp. 434–482; *Sanctuary,* Vintage Book edition (New York, 1958).

[5] Avon edition (New York, 1967).

[6] "A Good Man Is Hard to Find," in *An Introduction to Literature,* ed. Sylvan Barrett et al. (Boston, 1967), pp. 281–294; "The Life You Save May Be Your Own," in *Literature,* ed. Walter Blair et al. (Chicago, 1959), pp. 497–505; "The Artificial Nigger," in *Short Fiction,* ed. James R. Frakes and Isadore Traschen (Englewood Cliffs, 1959), pp. 101–118.

[7] Bantam edition (New York, 1939).

[8] In *Literature, Form and Function,* ed. P. Albert Duhamel and Richard Hughes (Englewood Cliffs, 1965), pp. 429–439.

[9] New York, 1960.

[10] *All the King's Men* (New York, 1947); "Blackberry Winter," in *Literature, Form and Function,* ed. P. Albert Duhamel and Richard Hughes (Englewood Cliffs, 1965), pp. 419–429.

[11] Only the speech of white characters is given. Not all of the structures, of course, are found in any one of the works.

"Name Tom Shiftlet," he murmured. ("The Life You Save May Be Your Own," p. 498)

"You the chairman?" I asked the other fellow. (*All the King's Men*, p. 60)

"Six of us Holts in school." (*Christy*, p. 84)

"Mission house round the bend now," the old man said blithely. (*Christy*, p. 127)

"Settin chair over yan," he volunteered. (*Christy*, p. 162)

Examples of the use of *was, been, gonna,* and *be* (*Gon* occurs in some works instead of *gonna*) :

"So they was Flem's horses." ("Spotted Horses," p. 467)

"They wasn't as advanced as we are." ("The Life You Save May Be Your Own," p. 500)

"It's nothing so sweet," Mr. Shiftlet continued, "as a boy's mother. My mother was a angel of God." ("The Life You Save May Be Your Own," p. 504)

"And I been a decent Baptist all my life, too." (*Sanctuary*, p. 258)

"We been here a long time without a girl." (*Grapes of Wrath*, p. 7)

"I been most everything." ("A Good Man Is Hard to Find," p. 291)

"I been rackin' my lungs out for you." ("How Beautiful With Shoes," p. 431)

"You been messing in politics a long time, Judge." (*All the King's Men*, p. 50)

"Time gonna come for some folks this year," another man said. ("Blackberry Winter," p. 425)

"You gonna git ice cream." (*The Grapes of Wrath*, p. 374)

"You gon behave yourself." (*The Moviegoer*, p. 134)

"We gon stay right here." (*The Moviegoer*, p. 134)

"Don't know himself where he be." (*Christy*, p. 98)

"That be a sealed bargain, fair and square . . ." (*Christy*, p. 85)

Examples of the use of *ain't* and *don't:*

"There ain't nobody there." ("How Beautiful With Shoes," p. 435)

"They ain't got nothing out of this trip." ("Spotted Horses," p. 438)

"That car ain't run in fifteen years," the old woman said. ("The Life You Save May Be Your Own," p. 498)

"Ain't nobody giving me money." (*The Moviegoer*, p. 96)

"You ain't been into my beer have you boy?" (*Sanctuary*, p. 245)

"Now ain't Mr. Duffy a card?" (*All the King's Men,* p. 17)
"You know, when this conscience business starts, ain't no
telling where it'll stop . . ." (*All the King's Men,* p. 52)
"It ain't any of my bizness, I'm the sheriff." (*All the King's
Men,* p. 59)
"It ain't no secret," he said. (*All the King's Men,* p. 60)
"How you know you ain't following the tracks in the wrong
direction?" ("The Artificial Nigger," p. 112)
"Don't see good no more." (*Christy,* p. 176)
"Lucy don't favor drinking," Willie said quietly. (*All the
King's Men,* p. 20)
"Even a fool gal don't have to come as far as . . ." (*Light
in August,* p. 22)

Examples of the use of *they* for *there:*

"They's a looney loose out of Dayville Asylum . . ." ("How
Beautiful With Shoes," p. 430)
"They was a big dance in Shawnee." (*The Grapes of Wrath,*
p. 5)
"They was a guy paroled . . ." (*The Grapes of Wrath,*
p. 22)
"They ain't no need to hurt her feelings." (*The Grapes of
Wrath,* p. 369)

Mary Washington Cable in "Jesse Stuart's Writings Pre-
serve a Passing Folk Idiom" (*Southern Folklore Quarterly,* Vol.
XXVII, September, 1964, pp. 157–198), gives a list of vocabulary items which show the "range and depth of Stuart's grasp
of his native folk speech." The following occurs in the list:

they: expletive, there. "I was afraid they would be trouble
there."

The quoted speech in two Memphis, Tennessee, newspapers,
*The Commercial Appeal* and the *Memphis Press-Scimitar;* in
*The Best of Hillbilly,* a collection of articles from Jim Comstock's
*West Virginia Hillbilly,* edited by Otto Whittaker (New York,
1969) ; and in three articles dealing with Southerners, "George
Branch Kentucky," (*Look Magazine,* Dec. 2, 1969, pp. 49–67),
"My Brother Lyndon," by Sam Houston Johnson (*Look Maga-
zine,* March 4, 1969, pp. 25–33), and "The People of Cades Cove
(Tennessee)," by William O. Douglas (*The National Geographic,*
July, 1962, pp. 60–95) include some of the structures discussed
in this paper. John Steinbeck in *Travels With Charley* (New
York, 1965) records the speech of persons he talks with on his
travels around the country. He visits several Southern states;

several of the structures occur in his representation of Southern speech.

Examples of the use of the zero copula:

"Rails too thick." ("Cades Cove," p. 67)
"Only five families left." ("Cades Cove," p. 93)
"This your house," the reporter asked. (*The Commercial Appeal*, Dec. 3, 1968)
"You partial, coach?" (*Memphis Press-Scimitar*, June 5, 1969)
"Not many folks in the Cove." ("Cades Cove," p. 67)

Examples of the use of *was, been,* and *gonna:*

"I tuk a look and shore 'nuf that was a big rattler." ("Cades Cove," p. 63)
"They wasn't clean." (*Travels With Charley*, p. 223)
"Where you been, Nellie?" (*Travels With Charley*, p. 224)
"They been coming since dawn . . ." (*Travels With Charley*, p. 225)
"Where you been keeping yourself?" (*The Commercial Appeal*, Feb. 19, 1969)
". . . wuz it the way the squirrels been out early and . . .?" (*Hillbilly*, p. 166)
"He ain't gonna run against you." ("My Brother Lyndon," p. 57)

Examples of the use of *ain't* and *don't:*

"Ain't these cheerleaders something?" (*Travels With Charley*, p. 203)
"I just ain't used to this." ("George Branch Kentucky," p. 37)
"I ain't got no strength no more." ("George Branch Kentucky," p. 32)
"But it ain't such a bad road." (*Hillbilly*, p. 183)
"I don't know what's wrong with this country." ("George Branch Kentucky," p. 28)
"It don't beat normal." ("George Branch Kentucky," p. 29)
"She don't like snakes." ("Cades Cove," p. 66)

Examples of the use of *they* for *there:*

"They's no greater life on earth . . ." ("George Branch Kentucky," p. 28)
"They's a class that's livin' and a class what's daid and don't know it." ("George Branch Kentucky," p. 33)
"They's times I hurt so bad I don't even know whur I'm at." ("George Branch Kentucky," p. 33)

In a column, written by a Southerner, in which the activities of Mississippi are reported, an imaginary conversation between T. X. Payer and Capitol Observer, which takes place on the first floor of the Capitol (Jackson, Mississippi) is recorded (*The Commercial Appeal,* November 30, 1969). The conversation includes sentences that have no copula, no auxiliary, and in which *been* is the only verb:

> Mr. C. O. went on, "You ever been in that place?" "You gettin' sarcastic," said C. O. "You some kind of lobbyist or something, who do you represent anyway?"

It is of interest to note what those trained to observe and record speech have written about these features. Fewer studies have been made of Southern speech than of the speech of other areas east of the Mississippi River. Those made deal primarily with the phonological features of the region. Bits of information about some of the grammatical features dealt with here can, however, be found in them. Some information can also be found in studies which deal with the speech of other areas.

One of the major reference grammars sheds some light on the sentence type which has no copula. George O. Curme in *Principles and Practices of English Grammar* (New York, 1947, pp. 23, 106) states that this sentence type is "quite common" in colloquial speech and gives the following examples:

> Our sister dead!
> Everything in good order.

E. Bagby Atwood in *A Survey of Verb Forms in the Eastern United States* (Ann Arbor, 1953, p. 26) shows that *have* is often missing in the speech of many persons in the phrase "I (have) been thinking." He states that "the /v/ is often lost through assimilation." Raven I. McDavid, Jr. and Virginia G. McDavid point out in "Grammatical Differences in the North Central States" (*American Speech,* February, 1960, pp. 5–19) that this omission is common in the North Central States also. They say that despite "the disapproval of handbooks and self constituted authorities certain forms occur everywhere in the speech of all social groups." One of these is "I been thinking." [12]

Professor James McMillan in "Vowel Nasality as a Sandhi Form of the Morphemes *-nt* and *-ing* in Southern American"

---

[12] Since *was* is used in all varieties of American English in discussing events which are "completely in the past," no comments on *was* are given in this section of the paper.

(*American Speech,* April, 1939, pp. 120–123) describes the various forms of *going* which occur in the speech of Southerners. Like other American English speakers they can say *gonna* [gonə] or [gʌnə]. In addition they have a form [gõ] in which the [o] is nasalized. "I'm going to do it" may be realized as "[a.m gõ] do it." They have a third form [o] which occurs only with the first person singular. Thus, "I'm going to do it" may also be realized as "[a·mo] do it." Carmelita Klipple in "The Speech of Spicewood, Texas" (*American Speech,* October, 1945, pp. 187–191) shows that this form is also found in Texas.

The negative form *ain't* is found in all sections of the United States. Its wide use is attested to by the many articles that appear defending or damning it. It is used to mean *am not, is not, are not, have not,* and *has not.* Professor Archibald A. Hill, of the University of Texas, in "The Tainted Ain't Once More" (*College English,* January, 1965, pp. 298–303) discusses the long history of the form, points out that he uses it, and describes the circumstances under which he does. Raven I. McDavid points out in "The Position of the Charleston Dialect" (*The Publication of the American Dialect Society,* April, 1955, pp. 35–49) that *ain't* is used in colloquial speech by the educated and socially prestigious in the South. McDavid and McDavid in the article referred to above also show that *ain't* and *hain't* occur side by side as negatives of both *have* and *be* in the North Central States.

*Don't* is a negative form used everywhere in all varieties of American English. Its use as a third person singular present tense form is generally frowned on by English teachers, but this usage is widespread. Kemp Malone states in "Current English Forum" (*English Journal,* February, 1950, pp. 104–105) that he has "heard *don't* for *doesn't* innumerable times from persons of good breeding and high cultivation. This form is well established in English colloquial speech, and has been for years." He states also that he has "heard it often in the mouths of highly educated people (Ph.D.'s in English among them). . . ." E. Bagby Atwood in *A Survey of Verb Forms of the Eastern United States* (p. 28) shows that "he don't" is used by both the educated and the uneducated. The evidence shows that the use of *ain't* and *don't* by Americans is no "curious deployment"; it is rather just one of the patterns found in American English.

John Sargeant Hall, in the *Phonetics of the Great Smoky Mountains American Speech* (Monograph, New York, 1942, p. 26), indicates that *there* is pronounced as *they* in that region. He says that *there* often appears as *they* [ðe] in such uses as,

"They come a snow that day." Carmelita Klipple shows also that *there* is pronounced as *they* in Texas: *"There* is heard as *they* so often that apparently *they* has come to be used for *there."* She gives the example: "Are they a pencil on the table?"

Are the structures presently in use in the South? The following examples taken from my files on Southern speech show that they are. All of them were recorded on tape or taken down in phonetic notation as the speakers were talking.[13] All of the speakers are white; all of the material has been gathered since 1967.

Examples of the use of the zero copula:

You just beautiful. (*professor of English, Southern university*)
Roger, you all excited. (*well-dressed shopper in a supermarket*)
He mad. (*professor of English, Southern university*)
They right over here. (*clerk in a department store*)
Here your keys. (*clerk in a cleaning establishment*)
You my buddy. (*man on a bus*)
He over there. (*high-school English teacher*)
We still on the Mid-South title. (*bank employee*)
Y'all from Nashville and . . . (*Member, Tennessee legislature*)
They never anybody there. (*diner in a motel*)

In the film *William Faulkner* (available through the University of Mississippi), in which Faulkner himself is featured, Faulkner says to a resident of Oxford, "Gilbert, you lame."

Examples of the use of *was, been, be,* and *gonna:*

It was a colored guy there. (*housewife*)
You was on that route. (*bus driver*)
See how things was. (*ticket-seller in Knoxville bus station*)
I been sleeping with a pistol by my side. (*secretary, State university*)
I been south. (*clerk in a department store*)
First time I been in four hours. (*man in bus station*)
I been had it. (*bus driver*)
Thisn be all right. (*customer in department store*)
She be fifteen in November. (*man talking to a clerk in a department store)*
I be glad to help you. (*clerk in a department store*)
Think how cool you are and you be cool. (*customer in a department store*)

13 All of the material was recorded by the writer.

That be all? (*clerk in a supermarket*)

Examples of the use of *gonna*, [aˑmo], [gō]

We gonna lose a lot of manpower. (*university professor*)
You gonna hear the people. (*federal employee*)
[aˑmo] try this one on. (*customer in a department store*)
[aˑmo] run over here, while you get . . . (*customer in a department store*)
I hope this not [gō] be true. (*member, men's service club*)
They [gō] have a big moon day celebration. (*bus driver*)

Faulkner says, in the film mentioned above, "We [gō] get the big one this time."

Examples of the use of *ain't* and *don't:*

They ain't doing no good. (*bus driver*)
I ain't [gō] bring you nothin. (*clerk in a shoe store*)
I ain't fixed it. (*teen-ager on a bus*)
Naw I ain't out; you out. (*young girl telling a story*)
I don't wanta see no splashdown. (*clerk in a store*)
You don't want none. (*clerk talking to another clerk*)
She don't like it short. (*clerk talking to a customer*)
It don't look good. (*man in a bus station*)

Examples of the use of *they* for *there* and *their:*

They's [ðez] been a controversy going on. (*high-school English teacher*)
They's [ðez] enough difference. (*book company representative*)
They [ðe] was a lot of people didn't know where they was at. (*retired airlines pilot*)
They [ðe] was another guy making . . . (*bus driver*)
. . . express they [ðe] feeling. (*book company representative*)
They have they [ðe] religious convictions. (*high-school English teacher*)
We hear they [ðe] idea. (*policeman*)
In they [ðe] life . . . (*university professor*)

The above examples show that Valentine's representation is clearly no mishmash. Whether he himself uses these structures cannot, of course, be ascertained; they are, however, found in the Southern region, most certainly in Tennessee, Alabama, North Carolina, Georgia, Virginia, Kentucky, Texas, Mississippi —and even Missouri, a border state. There are examples in my files from all of these.

That the four features are found in Dude's speech is no surprise, for most Negroes, wherever they might live outside the South, migrated to that place from the South. And it should be no surprise that they carried their Southern language patterns with them.

## Black Views of Language Use: Rules of Decorum, Conflict, and Men-of-Words

ROGER D. ABRAHAMS

In the preface to Joos's article on style, we mentioned a sergeant who is addressing a roomful of generals; he has a choice between "You guys shut up" and "Could I have your attention?" We know what his choice will be, assuming he wants to remain in the army. He chooses what to say in response to social expectations.

There are also ethnic-group expectations about the use of language; many of these operate at a less conscious level than do social expectations. We can become aware of these by noticing our surprise when one of them is not met; for instance, I never fail to be surprised when my friend from Bombay ends our telephone conversations by simply hanging up.

Abrahams talks about ethnic differences in the way blacks and whites use language, differences that can easily be misinterpreted unless they are understood as being parts of different cultures.

The United States, in spite of its democratic ideals, is essentially a pluralistic state; that is, rather than being a true "melting pot" ours is a nation in which communities with widely differing cultural perspectives only coexist. They are able to persist as separate cultural enclaves because one culture is dominant and the others, perforce, subordinate. This means not only that we have second-class citizenship from the political and social point of view, but that the basis of this discrimination is cultural. This is more insidious because it is often unconscious and results in inequities that go unrecognized. . . .

These cultural inequities are proclaimed and maintained by the creation of stereotypes. Stereotypes arise in almost any culture-contact situation. They are a response of an anxiety experienced by both groups involved, and they are developed on both sides. Stereotypes focus on those very areas in which the two groups most often make contact. But rather than directing themselves at the communication inherent in the contact situation, the stereotype emphasizes those places where communication is impossible because the group doing things doesn't do things correctly or it doesn't have the right attitude toward matters of extreme importance to the group imposing the stereotype. A stereotype will always exhibit the bias of the group that fashions it.

A classic case of communications failure arising out of the mutual imposition of stereotypes by two cultures coming into contact is discussed by Erving Goffman in his analysis of what he calls "interaction ritual":

> The Western traveler used to complain that the Chinese could never be trusted to say what they meant but always said what they felt their Western listener wanted to hear. The Chinese used to complain that the Westerner was brusque, boorish, and unmannered. In terms of Chinese standards, presumably, the conduct of a Westerner is so gauche that he creates an emergency [of maintaining face], forcing the Asian to forgo any kind of direct reply in order to rush in with a remark that might rescue the Westerner from the compromising position in which he has placed himself (p. 17*n*).

Here the Chinese and the Westerner have confronted each other with different modes of personal interaction, and because the two cultures carried different senses of decorum there resulted an impairment of communication and the beginning of stereotype configurations on both sides. Stereotypes so often begin in this way, focussing upon different communications-decorum systems. The New World Negro has often been called garrulous and unrestrained in his linguistic behavior by whites with whom he has come into constant contact because, in certain situations, he continued to use the elaborate mode of address system brought by him from Africa. Typical in this regard are the comments made by the English traveler, John Stewart, in the 19th century, in his book *A View of the Past and Present State of Jamaica:*

> Although the proverbial sayings of negroes have often much point and meaning, they, however, no sooner begin to expatiate

and enter more minutely into particulars, than they become tedious, verbose, and circumlocutory, beginning their speeches with a tiresome exordium, mingling with them much extraneous matter, and frequently traversing over and over the same ground, and cautioning the hearer to be attentive, as if fearful that some of the particulars and points on which their meaning and argument hinged should escape his attention. So that by the time they arrive at the peroration of their harangue, the listener is heartily fatigued with it, and perceives the whole which has been said, though it may have taken up half an hour, could have been comprised in half-a-dozen words (p. 264).

Clearly we have here an instance of failure of communication on the deepest level, for the Negro was using what he thought to be the mode of address most appropriate to the occasion, but he was condemned rather than appreciated for this act of decorum.

Another more recent instance of this type of intercultural failure of communication between whites and Negroes is the "problem" encountered by white teachers of Negro children of eye-avertance. In many Negro communities young children have learned that meeting an older person's gaze is a sign of hostility or defiance. Therefore, when called upon by the teacher in class, they look away from her when responding. If the question asked is not directed to the individual student, the teacher will tend not to notice the direction of the gaze. But if the question is directed at a specific student, the eye-avertance will commonly be interpreted by the teacher as evidence that something sneaky has been going on, or that the student is being arrogant or disrespectful. This is an especially great problem for speech therapists, for they must often have the child watch their lip movements. One inventive therapist recognized the source of the problem and has learned to have the child look into a mirror at her reflection, thus preserving decorum while serving efficiency.

Cultural differences of this sort, when encountered in the contact situation, contribute heavily to the development of a stereotype. . . .

A stereotype, as we most commonly understand the term, is the result of a negative typing procedure in which those attitudes and activities which are valued and which are threatened because of unconscious forces within the group are put into negative form and projected onto the other group (Williams, p. 40). In most cases, this must simply be regarded as the way in which disparate groups react to each other, and therefore it is a phenomenon which, in our shrinking world, is something to regret. But in cases where the two groups live side by side, as with blacks and whites, and they are served by the same government and economic systems, the procedure becomes dangerous as a barrier to communications.

Furthermore, the stereotyped group is stigmatized. By imputing negative traits to Negroes and then by telling stories in illustration, whites have learned to enjoy vicariously the Negro's supposed freedom from social constraint, and to reject the blacks for these same characteristics. Unless we are willing to learn to understand other cultures in our midst, thus breaking down this kind of stereotyped thinking, we will be incapable of fulfilling our professed high intentions.

This study is an attempt to break down the stereotype of the American Negro by exploring certain aspects of Negro culture that commonly, when encountered by whites, bring about a stereotype response. To do this it is necessary to look at what that stereotype is and how it undermines efforts at integration, however well-intentioned those efforts might be. Many of the effects are self-evident, or have been commented upon so often that to repeat the arguments would be impractical and self-defeating. Rather, I would like to focus on ways in which the ethnocentric attribution of stereotype traits have operated in perhaps the most important realm of the American experience— in education. . . .

## LANGUAGE

One of the statements most often repeated by white elementary teachers about "them"—their Negro charges—is that they have no verbal resources and, because of this, no language ability. This is commonly followed by one of two rationalizing statements: either "these poor children have never been taught to speak correctly" or "they couldn't have developed verbal skills since they come from families with so many children that there isn't any time for communication with their parents." . . . Both of these statements are ethnocentric in the extreme, even if they are well-meaning. . . .

In the United States, rather than viewing the various types of Negro speech as different dialectal corruptions of English, it is more meaningful to view them as one creole language, whole unto itself, which has been progressively gravitating toward the

regional English dialects with which it has come into contact
(W. Stewart, 1967, 1968). . . .

Furthermore . . . there is not only a different language at
work here but a different attitude toward speech and speech
acts. We are just beginning to recognize that we don't know
very much about information-passing among Negroes; but we
can predict with a reasonable degree of accuracy that the subjects
and methods of communication of knowledge and feeling will be
quite different from white middle-class norms. The implications
of such differences are of obvious importance to teachers of
Negroes, especially since they have been operating on the assumption that no cultural differences existed in this area.

One of the basic variations in the passing on of information is in regard to who communicates with whom, and in what
recurrent situations; this brings us back to the second ethnocentric judgment commonly made by teachers—that Negro
children are not verbal because they don't have a chance to
communicate with parents. This attitude makes the assumption
that the only communication channel useful for educational development is that which arises between adults and children. This
is a natural outgrowth of the image that teachers have of themselves (ratified by the community, of course) that they are sur-
rogate parents. But with children who are not subject to the
middle-class family system, this places them immediately at a
disadvantage, both in relation to the teacher who has these expectations, and in regard to the educational system in general.

The fact is that most of the lower-class black children who
come into the classroom have a well-developed sense of language
and its power to pass on information and to control interpersonal
relationships; but the children derive this language skill not from
social interaction with adults (with whom they have been taught
to be silent) so much as with other children. This situation is
dictated by the custom of care, in which younger children are
placed in the care of older ones; it is also assisted by the practice
of street play which has older children teaching the younger
both verbal and motor play routines. In this milieu, children
learn the power of words in the development of their sense of
self. They learn the importance of banter, the power of the
taunt, the pleasure of playing with words. They develop vocabulary and other skills in active contest situations, for the purpose
of winning a verbal game and gaining esteem from their group.
If they have little informational exchange with adults, they have
a great deal of language-learning play with fellow children, a

factor usually ignored in the classroom. Indeed, Negro children find, when they go into school, that the language skills they have learned are in a tongue that is despised as substandard and performed in a manner that is regarded as hostile, obscene, or arrogant. They learn very quickly that the easiest way of getting by in the classroom is to be quiet—and so they are accused of being nonverbal. This derogation of language and language skills, furthermore, does little for the development of self-confidence.

If this weren't enough, even the best-intentioned language arts teachers commonly carry a further prejudice into the educational encounter with black pupils. It is firmly felt by them that reading is a skill that is the key to learning, that words are *things* that one must learn to recognize on the printed page or blackboard because such recognition will open up the repositories of knowledge, books. The often unconscious assumption made by these teachers is that all children will share the attitude that books are valuable things. But not only do most lower-class Negro children not share this feeling (since like most lower-class people most never encounter much reading material around the house or on the streets) but they don't commonly recognize words as things. Words to them are rather devices to be used in performances. Consequently, the argument that one must learn to read and then write in order to find one's way into the wonderful world of books is totally lost on children from such a background. They have not been concerned with the kinds of information contained in books, the kind that middle-class adults pass on to children, and that teachers expect to feed students.

But this does not mean that the lower-class black child brings no cultural resources into the classroom—they are just *different* resources. He brings a verbal skill, which, if recognized by the teacher, can be of considerable value in the development of an understanding of language. But to capitalize upon this fund, the child must be allowed to speak, even if this violates the usual sense of decorum the teacher carries into class with her. The teacher must further learn to understand the communication system with which she is dealing, both as it relates to adult-child situations and to those between peers. Once this system is recognized it appears obvious (as it did to Herbert Kohl when he taught Harlem children) that one can teach writing by showing the children how much more permanent and pleasurable are their verbal performances when written down. Once the value of words as records of speech events has been shown, the reading of other people's performances in book form will come naturally. By attacking the problem this way, the teacher will have served education in two ways. First, the child has been allowed to develop his own resources without having them exhibited as substandard; therefore he has been permitted to retain and develop his self-respect. Second, he has been taught to speak in an appropriate classroom manner (giving him a sense of the appropriateness of different kinds of language), then write, and then read, and he has thus been led to a point where he has been offered a cultural choice. He has learned to recognize alternatives and to make discretions, which I understand are the aims of our educational process. All of this has been achieved through a recognition of cultural variability on the part of the teacher. The only way this can be achieved, however, is through an understanding of the cultural heritage of the black children (and by this heritage, I *don't* mean spirituals or jazz, but those expressions of culture that the children know from their own immediate experience). The only way this cultural relativity can be learned is by breaking through the barriers to understanding erected by stereotyped thinking. . . .

## MEN-OF-WORDS

There are many ways in which Negro expressive culture reflects [a conflict] orientation. Reports of elaborate "cutting" or "jam" sessions in which musicians compete in musical terms are legion in writings on the roots of jazz, and similar contests can be observed between dancers, singing groups, even preachers. Words are especially valued as power devices, and men-of-words performers find ready audiences on street corners, in bars and pool halls, at parties, virtually wherever two or more people have congregated.

This kind of word show has often been witnessed by white observers, but seldom appreciated or understood because the recognition of beauty based on wit is something that whites do not fully share. A recent dramatic demonstration of just such an understanding gap arising from cultural disparity is to be found in the biography of Cassius Clay, *Black Is Best*, by the white sportswriter, Jack Olsen. In the first chapter, Olsen reports at great and fascinating length, a sample day's activities of the Muhammed Ali organization. Muhammed is surrounded by a chorus of amen-sayers and constantly holds forth for their benefit. He is a man-of-words of dimension and brilliance, but the nature of his rapport with his audience is missed by Olsen because of the culture gap. We read of Muhammed sermonizing in a preacher's voice, telling jokes, boasting, improvising a poem, narrating commentary for a film, singing, reminiscing, calling home, and generally keeping everyone entertained. Through all of this, Olsen patronizingly describes how Clay repeats himself, how he does not really extemporize poems but "repeats" ones made up for another occasion with the addition of only a few lines, how he turns every subject of conversation back on himself, and how completely and defensively self-centered the boxer is. But in spite of Olsen's moralizing, a picture of a powerful man-of-words in an oral culture shines through, a person capable of capturing and holding his audience's interest and admiration for days on end.

Another Negro man-of-words, Dick Gregory, has written his own story, and in this we get more of an inside view of such performers. He tells in various parts of the book how he developed his technique of humor through aggressive verbal contests. For instance, in his childhood he often found himself involved in contests of wit but seldom winning.

> I got picked on a lot around the neighborhood; skinniest kid on the block, the poorest, the one without a Daddy. I guess that's when I first began to learn about humor, the power of a joke.
>
> "Hey, Gregory."
>
> "Yeah."
>
> "Get your ass over here, I want to look at that shirt you're wearing."
>
> "Well, uh, Herman, I got to . . ."
>
> "What you think of that shirt he's wearin', York?"
>
> "That's no shirt, Herman, that's a tent for a picnic."
>
> "That your Daddy's shirt, Gregory?"
>
> "Well, uh . . ."
>
> "He ain't got no Daddy, Herman, that's a three-man shirt."
>
> "Three-man shirt?"
>
> "Him 'n' Garland 'n' Presley (his brothers) supposed to be wearing that shirt together."
>
> At first . . . I'd just get mad and run home and cry when the kids started. And then, I don't know just when, I started to figure it out. They were going to laugh anyway, but if I made the jokes they'd laugh *with* me instead of *at* me. I'd get the kids off my back, on my side. So I'd come off that porch talking about myself.
>
> "Hey, Gregory, get your ass over here. Want you to tell me and Herman how many kids sleep in your bed."
>
> "Googobs of kids in my bed, man, when I get up to pee middle of the night gotta leave a bookmark so I don't lose my place."

Before they could get going, I'd knock it out first, fast, knock out those jokes so they wouldn't have time to set and climb all over me. . . . And they started to come over and listen to me, they'd see me coming and crowd around me on the corner." [1]

With both Gregory and Muhammed Ali we see nearly all of the primary attributes of the man-of-words, the importance of inserting the performer in the midst of his performance, emphasized through the constant use of the first-person pronouns, the strong interaction between performer and audience, the identification of the performer with the item being performed, and most important, the development of performance technique in a contest atmosphere (Abrahams, 1964; 1968). This kind of self-deprecation, for instance, can become something of a boast in its use of hyperbole, and therefore the voicing of one humorous complaint can lead to a rejoinder and a casual remark becomes a battle of wits.

## CONTESTS AND PLAYING THE DOZENS

I'm so broke, I couldn't buy a crippled crab a crutch if I had a forest of small trees.

. . .

Yeah, well I'm so broke, I couldn't buy a mosquito a wrestling jacket, and *that's* a small fit.

My soles are so thin that if I stepped on a dime I could tell whether it's heads or tails.

I'm so hungry my backbone is almost shaking hands with my stomach.

I'm so hungry I could see a bow-legged biscuit walk a crooked mile.

I'm so broke, if they were selling Philadelphia for a penny, I'd have to run, afraid they would sell it to the wrong person. [2]

---

[1] From the book *Nigger: An Autobiography* by Dick Gregory with Robert Lipsyte. Copyright © 1964 by Dick Gregory Enterprises, Inc. Reprinted by permission of E. P. Dutton & Co., Inc.

[2] The texts of the boasts and dozens come from my own Philadelphia collection (printed in part in *Deep Down in the Jungle*, pp. 241–242) and from a group of students in Huston-Tillotson College, Austin, Texas, January 1967. These students were from East Texas, Houston, and Chicago. All informants were under age 30.

However, most contests of this sort do not generally turn back on the performer in this self-deprecating fashion. The boast is the norm, and if deprecation is involved it is commonly directed at another. We can see this in a number of traditional verbal forms, perhaps most clearly in "playing the dozens." There are two ways of playing: the "clean dozens" and the "dirty dozens." The clean dozens commonly involve a series of clever insults:

> Now dig. Your house is so small, the roaches have to walk sideways through the hallways.
>
> Your mother is so small she can do chin-ups on the curb.
>
> Your mother is so fat, she has to have a shoehorn to get in the bathtub.
>
> Man, you're so dark, you need a license to drink white milk.
>
> If electricity was black, your mother would be a walking powerhouse.
>
> You look like death standing on a street corner eating life-savers.

In the clean dozens some of the insults are directed at the other's mother, but most are directly personal. On the other hand, in the dirty dozens, the mother of the other person is almost always the subject of the slur, and she is commonly subject to aspersions of illicit sexual activity, usually with the speaker. Thus, the dirty dozens involve insults that also serve as boasts. . . .

The dozens provides the boy, who has commonly been raised in a matrifocal household, with a technique for "cutting the apron strings" by attacking another's mother knowing that his own mother will be attacked in turn (Abrahams, 1964, pp. 49–59). It also allows him practice in bringing aggressive language into artful form. This kind of verbal aggression is part of a larger system of "hidden language" which utilizes techniques of argument by indirection—called "signifying" in many black groups—which is tremendously important in the daily lives of lower-class Negros.

> *But most important for our present concerns, playing the dozens provides, in expressive form, a statement of behavior conceived on a model of aggressive interpersonal activity but in a framework of useful and entertaining competition. The dozens can be viewed as the model of other verbal activities, for it presents a pattern of on-going, open-ended, competitive behavior which need not have a winner or a loser to justify the performance, since the competition is entertainment in itself. But be-*

*cause no winner and loser are declared,[3] there is a sense of the incomplete and the perpetual about this type of activity, when compared with white, middle-class expectations for such performances. We expect a routine or story to have a beginning, middle, and end, an expectation obviously not completely shared by Negro audiences. Furthermore, this pattern of on-going competition is observable in nearly all such activities, the most obvious being the jam-session, for seldom do we have the declaration there of winner and loser. Rather, competition provides the atmosphere by which performers can best perform.*

## BEAUTIFUL PERFORMERS

The competitive frame of reference gives the performer a position in black society which is extremely difficult for whites to understand. Because such performers are able to assert their power confidently and to embody it in such aggressive motives, they find an audience which is willing to give its undivided attention for very long periods of time. Furthermore, because the performer asserts hostility in a world of license and gets away with it, he provides a model of behavior for all others who find themselves similarly coerced and similarly conflict-minded. Consequently, the black audience thinks of *performers* as "beautiful" as opposed to white use of the esthetic term in reference not to the artist but to a work of art. In other words, Negroes use the term in relation to good performers rather than to effective performances. To call someone beautiful is not to talk about physical characteristics so much as style, which means primarily the ability to compete successfully in a hostile environment.

This use of "beautiful," an esthetic value word, is expanded then into an ethical position. Those who can function well in handling the recurrent problem of interpersonal or intergroup hostility are conceived of as being successful in artistic terms. This use of "beautiful" is simply one example of the utilization of esthetic terminology for ethical purposes.[4] "Jazzy," "Swinging," "Cool," "Soul," all derive from emotional affect words from the good musical performance experience. All of them have been appropriated as descriptive of personality, and all turn on a per-

[3] It is not meant here that no one is considered the winner of such contests, for certain men-of-words are regarded as inevitable cappers. Their best caps are celebrated in their group in legendary stories. But each engagement is not ended with a declaration of winner or loser.

[4] This is paralleled by the use of the word "ugly" meaning "bad" especially in interpersonal situations.

son's ability to handle recurrent problems through their exhibition of the proper style of toughness and resilience.

This is why those expressive performers who have been able to overcome the obstacles are "culture heroes" in a sense that no performer could ever be in the white world.[5] They have confidence in battle; they wear their warrior's image comfortably, something which not many blacks are able to do (Keil, p. 20). And if such performers combine ability with words with effective acts— as with Cassius Clay, Dick Gregory, Adam Clayton Powell, Willie Mays (at least early in his career), and "Sugar" Ray Robinson— then they assure themselves a place in the black pantheon. To be a hero, one must be willing to do battle for one's prestige, bullystyle, to take on all comers at any time, to engage in an apparently never-ending series of conflicts.


## TOASTS

This quality of enduring and eternal conflict is observable not only in the way in which the performers present themselves but also in the deeds of the heroes they celebrate. The never-ending battle is encountered and enjoyed by the central characters of those poetic improvisations called "toast" or "toastës" by street-corner talkers.

These epic fictions are performed in rhymed couplets, are commonly multi-episodic, and chronicle the deeds of various types of heroes.[6] Toasts are widely found among American Negroes, especially in the cities and in prisons. Many of them seem merely to present a central character in a series of situations in which he can show his abilities with words or actions. Seldom do his activities have the kind of dramatic climax we find in European literature; rather, he is presented as a "bully of the town" whose adversaries are numberless. This point is emphasized by the fact that in various tellings of these heroic toasts, incidents and confrontations are added and subtracted at will, and not just in the

---

[5] Conversely, villains' names such as "Uncle Tom" and "Steppin Fetchit" come from performers who don't act in the approved manner.

[6] I have described the presentation and compositional elements of toasts and printed a number of representative texts from South Philadelphia in *Deep Down in the Jungle*, pp. 99–173. See also Hughes and Bontemps (1959); Hughes (1966); Galoob (1963); Owens (1966). The techniques described by Olsen in his book on Cassius Clay make it obvious that Ali's poetizing is derived from toasting (pp. 7–10).

middle of the actions but also at the end. It is common, for instance, to tack on a visit to hell by the hero and a confrontation with the Devil and his family, such as we find in the toast about the only survivor from the wreck of the *Titanic*. This is made possible because of the improvised compositions of these poems in true epic style (Lord).

## Shine and Stackolee

I don't know, but I think I will
Make my home in Jacksonville.
I don't know, but so they say,
The tenth of May was a hell of a day.
The captain and his mates were mumbling a few words
As the great *Titanic* knocked hell out of that first iceberg.
Up popped Shine from the decks below,
And said, "Captain, the water is at my boilerroom door."
He said, "Get, Shine, and do your act!
I've got forty-two pumps to keep the water back."
But before Shine could mumble another word
The great *Titanic* knocked hell out of that second iceberg.
Over went Shine and he began to swim,
Three thousand millionaires looking dead at him.
The Captain jumped up from the deck and called,
"Shine, oh Shine, please save poor me,
I'll make you richer than any Shine will ever want to be."
Shine said, "Your money is good as far as I can see,
But this ain't no shit for me.

. . .

Shine swam for three days and three nights
When up popped the whale from the bottom of the sea,
And said, "You black motherfucker, you're trying to outswim me."
Shine said, "You swim good and you swim fast,
But you'll have to be a swimming motherfucker to catch my black ass."
When news got to Washington the great *Titanic* had sunk
Shine was on the corner of hun'ed and twenty-fifth street already half drunk.

. . .

Shine, in his abilities to engage in repartee in the midst of this trying situation, and in his apparently superhuman physical capacities, is a good representation of one type of Negro hero. But we are not given any feeling that his achievements in any of these arenas are permanent; rather we are left with the feeling that he must go on to further challenges, further victories.

# REFERENCES

ABRAHAMS, ROGER D. 1964. *Deep Down in the Jungle . . . Negro Narrative Folklore from the Streets of Philadelphia.* Hatboro, Pa., Folklore Associates.

———. 1968. "Public Drama and Common Values in Two Caribbean Islands." *Trans-Action,* July/August, 62–71.

GALOOB, DEBRA. 1963. "Back in '32 When Times Was Hard." *Riata* (student literary magazine of the University of Texas), Spring, 24–33.

GOFFMAN, ERVING. 1967. *Interaction Ritual.* New York, Doubleday & Co.

GREGORY, DICK, with ROBERT LIPSYTE. 1965. *Nigger.* New York, Pocket Books (reprint edition).

HUGHES, LANGSTON. 1966. *The Book of Negro Humor.* New York, Dodd, Mead and Co.

HUGHES, LANGSTON, and ARNA BONTEMPS. 1959. *The Book of Negro Folklore.* New York, Dodd, Mead and Co.

KEIL, CHARLES. 1966. *Urban Blues.* Chicago, University of Chicago Press.

LORD, ALBERT M. 1960. *The Singer of Tales.* Cambridge, Mass., Harvard University Press.

OLSEN, JACK. 1967. *Black Is Best: The Riddle of Cassius Clay.* New York, Dell Publishing Co. (reprint edition).

OWENS, TARY. 1966. "Poetry from the Texas Prisons." *Riata* (student literary magazine of the University of Texas), Spring, 22–23.

STEWART, JOHN. 1823. *A View of the Past and Present State of Jamaica.* Edinburgh, Oliver and Boyd.

STEWART, WILLIAM. 1968. "Continuity and Change in American Negro Dialects," *Florida FL Reporter,* Vol. 6, No. 1 (Spring 1968), pp. 3–4, 14–16, 18.

———. 1967. "Sociolinguistic Factors in the History of American Negro Dialects," *Florida FL Reporter,* Vol. 5, No. 2 (Spring 1967), pp. 11, 22, 24, 26, 30.

WILLIAMS, ROBIN M., JR., with JOHN P. DEAN and EDWARD A. SUCHMAN. 1964. *Strangers Next Door: Ethnic Relations in American Communities.* Englewood Cliffs, N.J., Prentice-Hall, Inc.

# Cognition and Language Variation

## Language and General Intelligence

ERIC H. LENNEBERG

Is language the result of general intelligence? (I am speaking
of "language" as the ability to create and understand sentences,
not of the ability to say something profound with those sentences.)
Lenneberg offers evidence that suggests it is not. Further study
of this question might begin with Lenneberg's important book
*The Biological Foundations of Language* (New York: Wiley, 1967).

. . . I would like to propose . . . that the ability to acquire
language is a biological development that is relatively independent of that elusive property called intelligence. I see evidence
for this view in the fact that children acquire language at a time
when their power of reasoning is still poorly developed and that
the ability to learn to understand and speak has a low correlation
with measured IQ in man. Let me elaborate on this latter point.

In a recent study Lenneberg, Nichols, and Rosenberger
(1964) studied the language development of 84 feeble-minded
children raised by their own parents in a normal home environment. The basic results are represented diagrammatically in
Fig. 1. IQ figures, as measured by standard instruments, de-
teriorate with chronological age in the mentally retarded, even

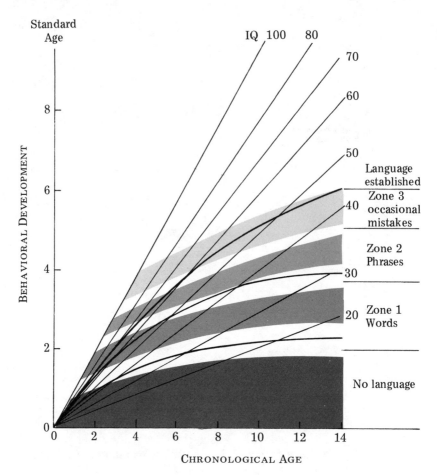

FIGURE 1. *Relationship between speech development and IQ. The curved lines show empirically determined "decay rates" of IQ in the mentally retarded. The shadings indicate language development. An individual whose IQ at a given age falls into the dark area at the bottom has no language. If he falls into the lighter areas, he is in one of three stages of language development and will develop further until his early teens, his progress depending upon both his IQ and his age. If he falls into the white area above, he is in full command of language. After age 12 to 13 speech development "freezes." (Data based on a follow-up study of 61 mongoloids and 23 children with other types of retarding disease.)*

though there is objective growth in mental age up to the early teens, after which time mental development is arrested.

Language begins in the same manner in retardates as in the normal population. We found that it is impossible to train a child with, say, mongolism to parrot a complicated sentence if he has not yet learned the underlying principles of *syntax*. However, the general principle underlying *naming* is grasped at once and immediately generalized. Naming behavior may be observed even in low-grade idiots; only individuals so retarded as to be deficient in stance, gait, and bowel control fail to attain this lowest stage of language acquisition. . . . Children whose IQ is 50 at age 12 and about 30 at age 20 are completely in possession of language though their articulation may be poor and an occasional grammatical mistake may occur.

Thus, grossly defective intelligence need not implicate language; nor does the *absence of* language necessarily lower cognitive skills. For instance, congenitally deaf children have in many parts of the world virtually no language or speech before they receive instruction in school. When these preschoolers are given nonverbal tests of concept formation they score as high as their age peers who hear (Furth, 1961; Rosenstein, 1960; Oléron, 1957). From these examples it appears that language and intelligence are to some extent at least independent traits.

## REFERENCES

FURTH, H. The influence of language on the development of concept formation in deaf children. *J. Abnorm. Soc. Psychol.*, 1961, 63: 386–389.

LENNEBERG, E. H., I. A. NICHOLS, and E. F. ROSENBERGER. Primitive stages of language development in mongolism. *Proc. Assoc. Res. Nerv. Ment. Disease*, 42 (1964):119–137.

OLÉRON, P. *Recherches sur le developpement mental des sourdes-muets*. Paris: Centre National de la Recherche Scientifique, 1957.

ROSENSTEIN, J. Cognitive abilities of deaf children. *J. Speech Hearing Res.*, 1960, 3:108–119.

# The Advantages of Being Bilingual

WALLACE E. LAMBERT

Problems experienced by bilingual children in American schools have sometimes led to speculation that being bilingual is confusing or otherwise cognitively handicapping; one such speculation is the "balance theory, that is, the theory that most people are unable to learn two languages simultaneously as well as monolinguals learn one by itself . . ." [1] That the "balance theory" is inadequate has been shown by this selection and other work by Wallace Lambert and his colleagues in Montreal. For instance, Peal and Lambert (1962) found significant differences in *favor* of bilinguals on nineteen out of twenty-four measures of intelligence and achievement.[2] (It should be noted that when the bilinguals and monolinguals were matched for nonverbal IQ and socioeconomic status, there were no differences in verbal IQ.)

America has always been multicultural, but we Americans have not always been aware of this. Awareness and acceptance of "cultural pluralism" is now growing; Lambert thinks that this new attitude may favor the development of bilinguals who are encouraged to feel competent and comfortable in both of their languages and cultures, instead of being forced into making a choice of allegiance to one or the other speech community.

Link's brief report, later in this section, should suggest to us one source of the view that bilingualism is a disadvantage. Tests written in English have been administered to all children, regardless of the children's amount of control over English. Test administrators have then accepted whatever scores were produced, just as though the test scores accurately represented these children's understanding and intelligence. The problem here lies not in the children, but in the tests and in our own blind acceptance of their scores.

My argument is that bilinguals, especially those with bicultural experiences, enjoy certain fundamental advantages which, if capitalized on, can easily offset the annoying social tugs and pulls they are normally prone to. Let me mention one of these advantages that I feel is a tremendous asset. Recently, Otto Klineberg and I conducted a rather comprehensive international study of the development of stereotyped thinking in children. . . . We found that rigid and stereotyped thinking about in-groups and out-groups, or about own groups in contrast to foreigners, starts during the pre-school period when children are trying to form a conception of themselves and their place in the world. Parents and other socializers attempt to help the child at this stage by highlighting differences and contrasts among groups, thereby making their own group as distinctive as possible. This tendency, incidentally, was noted among parents from various parts of the

[1] John Macnamara, *Bilingualism and Primary Education: A Study of Irish Experience* (Chicago: Aldine Publishing Co., 1966), p. 19.

[2] Elizabeth Peal and Wallace E. Lambert, "The Relation of Bilingualism to Intelligence." *Psychological Monographs: General and Applied*, 76, No. 27 (1962), 1–23.

world. Rather than helping, however, they may actually be setting the stage for ethnocentrism with permanent consequences.
The more contrasts are stressed, the more deep-seated the stereotyping process and its impact on ethnocentric thought appear to
be. Of relevance here is the notion that the child brought up bi-
lingually and biculturally will be less likely to have good versus
bad contrasts impressed on him when he starts wondering about
himself, his own group, and others. Instead he will probably be
taught something more truthful, although more complex: that
differences among national or cultural groups of peoples are
actually not clear-cut and that basic similarities among peoples
are more prominent than differences. The bilingual child in other
words may well start life with the enormous advantage of having a more open, receptive mind about himself and other people.
Furthermore, as he matures, the bilingual has many opportunities to learn, from observing changes in other people's reactions
to him, how two-faced and ethnocentric *others* can be. That is,
he is likely to become especially sensitive to and leery of ethnocentrism.


## BILINGUALS AND SOCIAL CONFLICTS

This is not to say that bilinguals have an easy time of it. In
fact, the final investigation I want to present demonstrates the
social conflicts bilinguals typically face, but, and this is the major
point, it also demonstrates one particular type of adjustment that
is particularly encouraging.

In 1943, Irving Child investigated a matter that disturbed
many second-generation Italians living in New England: what
were they, Italian or American? Through early experiences they
had learned that their relations with certain other youngsters in
their community were strained whenever they displayed signs of
their Italian background, that is, whenever they behaved as their
parents wanted them to. In contrast, if they rejected their Italian
background, they realized they could be deprived of many satis-
factions stemming from belonging to an Italian family and an
Italian community. Child uncovered three contrasting modes of
adjusting to these pressures. One subgroup rebelled against their
Italian background, making themselves as American as possible.
Another subgroup rebelled the other way, rejecting things American as much as possible while proudly associating themselves
with things Italian. The third form of adjustment was an apathetic withdrawal and a refusal to think of themselves in ethnic

terms at all. This group tried, unsuccessfully, to escape the conflict by avoiding situations where the matter of cultural background might come up. Stated in other terms, some tried to
belong to one of their own groups or the other, and some, because
of strong pulls from both sides, were unable to belong to either.

Child's study illustrates nicely the difficulties faced by people
with dual allegiances, but there is no evidence presented of second-generation Italians who actually feel themselves as belonging
to both groups. When in 1962, Robert Gardner and I studied another ethnic minority group in New England, the French-Ameri-
cans, we observed the same types of reactions as Child had noted
among Italian-Americans. But in our study there was an important difference.

We used a series of attitude scales to assess the allegiances
of French-American adolescents to both their French and American heritages. Their relative degree of skill in French and in
English were used as an index of their mode of adjustment to
the bicultural conflict they faced. In their homes, schools, and
community, they all had ample opportunities to learn both languages well, but subgroups turned up who had quite different
patterns of linguistic skill, and each pattern was consonant with
each subgroup's allegiances. Those who expressed a definite preference for the American over the French culture and who negated
the value of knowing French were more proficient in English
than French. They also expressed anxiety about how well they
actually knew English. This subgroup, characterized by a general
rejection of their French background, resembles in many respects
the rebel reaction noted by Child. A second subgroup expressed a
strong desire to be identified as French, and they showed a greater
skill in French than English, especially in comprehension of
spoken French. A third group apparently faced a conflict of cultural allegiances since they were ambivalent about their identity,
favoring certain features of the French and other features of the
American culture. Presumably because they had not resolved the
conflict, they were retarded in their command of both languages
when compared to the other groups. This relatively unsuccessful
mode of adjustment is very similar to the apathetic reaction noted
in one subgroup of Italian-Americans.

A fourth subgroup is of special interest. French-American
youngsters who have an open-minded, nonethnocentric view of
people in general, coupled with a strong aptitude for language
learning are the ones who profited fully from their language
learning opportunities and became skilled in both languages.

These young people had apparently circumvented the conflicts and developed means of becoming members of both cultural groups. They had, in other terms, achieved a comfortable bicultural identity.

It is not clear why this type of adjustment did not appear in Child's study. There could, for example, be important differences in the social pressures encountered by second-generation Italians and French in New England. My guess, however, is that the difference in findings reflects a new social movement that has started in America in the interval between 1943 and 1962, a movement which the American linguist Charles Hockett humorously refers to as a "reduction of the heat under the American melting pot." I believe that bicultural bilinguals will be particularly helpful in perpetuating this movement. They and their children are also the ones most likely to work out a new, non-ethnocentric mode of social intercourse which could be of universal significance.

# The Research Non-Basis for "Restricted Codes"

NANCY AINSWORTH JOHNSON

The idea that children from low socioeconomic classes suffer from a kind of linguistic-cognitive deprivation is currently widespread in the American academic community; for instance, a movie about preschool children (four and five years old) states that they "gain an impressive verbal—and therefore mental—control over their environment" when they "master the word *not*"; [1] this film also suggests that the children conceived of objects "floating in random limbo" before they were taught to use speech patterns approved by the film's makers. This "verbal deprivation" theory probably lies behind the behavior of the teacher pictured

[1] "Demonstration in Language Skills," produced, ironically enough, by the B'nai B'rith Anti-Defamation League, no date. As Klima and Bellugi show in Part 1, children know the meaning of *not* well before they are four years old.

in "A Visit to a California Classroom," by Gumperz and Hernández-Chavez, presented later in this section.

The "verbal deprivation" theory is rooted in the work of Basil Bernstein, a British sociologist. Bernstein's writings from 1958 through 1973 show an acceptance of the theory that language controls thought, and a simplistic application of this theory to the language behavior of working-class and middle-class speakers in London. For instance, his 1973 claims that working-class speakers show a "particularistic" language code rest largely on taped discussions in which working-class speakers used a greater number of personal pronouns than did middle-class speakers. Bernstein claims that pronouns are "context-specific" —uninterpretable outside of context—and therefore "particularistic" as opposed to the "universalistic" code used by middle-class speakers. The lower-class speakers have a "restricted code," Bernstein concludes. My article attempts to raise a number of questions about Bernstein's terms, assumptions, and methods.

From 1958 to the present, the work of British sociologist Basil Bernstein has influenced American views of the relationships among language, social class, and the ability to think. Bernstein's major suggestion is that children from low socioeconomic classes exhibit a "culturally induced backwardness transmitted by the linguistic process" (Bernstein, 1970, p. 37); he names this "backwardness" a "restricted code" and contrasts it with an "elaborated code" supposedly possessed by middle-class speakers.

This theory has influenced American sociology, anthropology, education, and psychology. For example, the following passages appear in a major psychology text on child development, frequently used in preparing college students to teach in the public schools:

> . . . [T]he most relevant research dealing directly with social-class differences in language training is that of the English educational sociologist Basil Bernstein, of the University of London. His findings were based on British subjects but they would seem to be valid for American lower- and middle-class families as well. Bernstein's systematic observations highlight the sharp contrasts between what he has labeled the *restricted* language of the lower class and the *elaborated* codes or messages of the middle class. . . . [In the lower-class language,] only *low levels of conceptualization and differentiation are involved,* and attention is directed toward "the *concrete* here and now". . . . In this kind of speech *there is little evidence of reasoning.* . . . [In] elaborated language, typical of the middle class . . . [a] wider, more complex range

of thought is communicated. [Mussen, Conger, and Kagan, 1969, pp. 311–313; emphasis added.]

Labov (1970) has provided powerful arguments against Bernstein's suggestion that elaborate middle-class linguistic styles reflect cognition that is superior to that of lower-class speakers. Although Labov briefly describes Bernstein's research, no one has discussed in detail the nature and quality of that research.[1] I believe that such detail will support Labov's call for a reassessment of Bernstein's theories and of the major educational programs they have inspired (e.g., Bereiter and Engelmann, 1966; see also Jensen, 1968 and 1969).

Bernstein's views have been published in several forms: only three articles report his research on language in detail (1958, 1962a, and 1962b). His other articles summarize previous research, offer his latest statements of his views and their relevance, and attempt to answer critics. Here we will look closely at the evidence gathered in the three articles that report research projects, and we will look at two of the summarizing articles (1970 and 1972) for Bernstein's own words as to recent developments in his thinking.

Three questions are important here: first, exactly what claims did Bernstein make about the cognitive abilities of lower-class speakers? Second, what evidence does he offer as support for his claims? Third, what actual differences in the use of language by social groups may have inspired Bernstein to formulate his theories?

## WHAT BERNSTEIN SAID

There are several reasons for taking a close look at Bernstein's claims between 1958 and 1970 about the cognitive abilities of working-class speakers. To begin with, Bernstein himself has attempted to disown the "verbal deficit" and "compensatory education" proposals that have been cited in his work (1970, pp. 52–56; 1972, pp. 136–149), and there is widespread belief that his work has indeed been misinterpreted by the "verbal deprivation"

---

[1] Lawton's (1968) review of this research accepts without question most of the assumptions and methods this paper will criticize, though it does offer some criticism of Bernstein's terminology and other relatively minor aspects of his work. See, for example pp. 93–95 in Lawton; here Lawton accepts Bernstein's assumption that pauses in speech reflect the quality of cognitive activity taking place.

theorists in America—belief that Bernstein never implied that lower-class children cannot think as well as middle-class children can. I think that, in fairness to those who have interpreted Bernstein's work, the record should show that from 1958 through 1970 he did suggest—and rather strongly—that speakers in lower socioeconomic groups lack important cognitive abilities due to their "restricted codes." Far more important than just setting the record straight is the need to question the continuing influence of these suggestions. Some of these suggestions now have been dropped by Bernstein; they do not appear directly in his 1972 article. But he did not repudiate them there—they were simply left unmentioned. Since the 1958–1970 articles are still very much in circulation, it seems important to review and then evaluate their claims about cognitive abilities.

A final reason for looking at the exact nature of these claims is that Bernstein's writing style is often unusually difficult to follow. It was probably this density of prose that led one researcher to suggest taking a look at *Lawton's* analysis of Bernstein's writings "for [an] accurate statement of what *Bernstein* actually said" (Carroll, 1973, p. 174). Even Lawton—an admirer and student of Bernstein's—is not always sure of the meaning of Bernstein's statements (see Lawton, 1968, pp. 84 and 90, for example). Perhaps the best way to reach some agreement as to what Bernstein said is to look directly at his writings. Of course, the quotes that follow are only brief excerpts from a large body of writing; it might be objected that they have been taken out of context. My reply would be that a careful study of Bernstein's articles until 1970 will show that their context actually strengthens the impression (given by these excerpts) that Bernstein sees working-class speakers as lacking the ability to think as well as do middle-class speakers. Here are his own words about cognition and "restricted codes" (emphasis added) :

In 1958:

> Working-class speakers do not merely place different significances upon different classes of objects, but *their perception is of a qualitatively different order* (p. 160).
>
> Working-class speakers show a preference for *descriptive* rather than an analytical cognitive process (p. 160).
>
> The working-class child is sensitive to the content of objects . . . . where there is sensitivity to content *only the simplest logical implications . . . will be cognized* . . . . at best crude causal connections are made (pp. 168–169).

In 1962a:

> [T]he content of the speech is likely to be *concrete, descriptive, and narrative rather than analytical and abstract* (p. 33).
>
> ["Elaborated codes" and "restricted codes"] entail *qualitatively* different verbal planning orientations which control . . . *levels of cognitive behavior* (p. 44).

In 1962b:

> A shift from narrative or description [a restricted code] to reflection [an elaborated code] . . . [is a shift] from the *simple ordering* of experiences to *abstracting* from experience (p. 235).
>
> [A] higher proportion of the preposition "of" . . . [may confirm an earlier suggestion] that an elaborated code would be associated with greater selection of prepositions symbolising *logical relationships* than with those indicating [nearness in space or time] (p. 235).
>
> The non-specificity implied by "they" is a function of the *lack of differentiation* and the subsequent *concretising* of experience which characterises a restricted code as a whole. . . . What appears to be lacking is [an] intervening series of successive levels of *abstraction* (p. 234).

In 1970 Bernstein does attempt to renounce some of the progeny of his earlier articles:

> Because his code is restricted does not mean that a child is non-verbal, nor is he in the technical sense linguistically deprived. . . . There is nothing, but nothing, in dialect as such, which prevents a child from internalizing and learning to use universalistic meanings [elaborated code] (pp. 56–57).

But in that same article he reaffirms his earlier views of working-class cognitive abilities:

> This restricted code orients its speakers to a *less complex conceptual hierarchy*. . . . Working-class children's *difficulty with abstract concepts* . . . may result from the limitations of a restricted code. . . . Such a code will emphasize . . . *the concrete rather than the abstract* (p. 29).

In 1972:

> The middle-class *tight logical ordering of semantic space* . . . may result from the middle-class mother relating to general principles and their reasoned consequences [p. 144].

Bernstein's major emphasis in this last article is on two terms which did, in previous articles, suggest that working-class speakers are cognitively inferior to middle-class speakers. Though in 1972 he has broadened the meaning of these terms—*universalistic*

and *particularistic*—he has not fully abandoned his earlier definition for them; and this definition suggested that working-class
speakers are less able to differentiate themselves from others of
their class than are middle-class speakers.

> In contrast to the working-class speaker, the middle-class speaker
> proceeds to individualize his meanings, he is differentiated from
> others like a figure from its ground. . . . The "I" stands over the
> "we" [pp. 140–141].

It seems to me undeniable that, from 1958 through at least
1970, Bernstein has indeed suggested that working-class speakers
do not think as well as do middle-class speakers; and I cannot
interpret his 1972 work as a significant change in this basic
message.

## EVIDENCE OF "RESTRICTED CODES"

The next question is, what evidence does Bernstein have for
his claims? Here are Bernstein's three major sources of evidence
for restricted codes: vocabulary, pauses, and pronouns.

### The Ability to Analyze—Evidence: Vocabulary

In 1958 Bernstein gave a group of working-class teenage
boys two tests, the Mill Hill Vocabulary Scale Form 1 Senior
(1945) and a test of nonverbal abilities, the Raven Progressive
Matrices (1938). He suggests that the vocabulary test measures
"purely linguistic problems of a conceptual or categorizing order," while the nonverbal test measures "the ability to solve certain non-linguistic problems" (pp. 167–169). The boys' scores
on the vocabulary test were "depressed" in relation to their scores
on the nonverbal test; Bernstein sees the discrepancy between
their two scores as suggesting that members of the working-class
prefer "a descriptive rather than an analytical cognitive process"
(p. 160), and that they "do not merely place different signifi-
cances upon different classes of objects, but . . . their perception
is of a qualitatively different order" (p. 160); their "cognitive
differentiation" is comparatively undeveloped.

I would not wish to deny that there is any relationship whatever between "cognitive differentiation" and vocabulary size.
What "cognitive differentiation" may consist of, however, is far
from clear; about all we can be sure of is that any relationship
between it and vocabulary would be complex indeed. Is it valid

for Bernstein to assume that scores on his vocabulary test do measure perception, cognitive differentiation, and preference for an analytical cognitive process?

What does a vocabulary test actually test? To what extent does it simply measure the amount of exposure to these words the test-taker has had? If I give you a vocabulary test with the term *Daltonism* on it and you fail to choose the correct definition, does that imply that your cognitive differentiation has not developed to the point of including the meaning of *Daltonism?* What if I now give you a different test, including the meaning of *Daltonism* under an alternative term, *color-blindness,* and you now choose the correct definition—did your cognitive differentiation expand to include the meaning of the term?

It seems highly likely that the 1945 Mill Hill vocabulary test, which Bernstein gave to working-class teenagers in 1958, was designed by members of the British middle class. The middle class is in control of British education now, according to Bernstein; surely they were in control of it in 1945. How well would a member of this 1945 middle class do on a vocabulary test designed by working-class teenagers in 1958? Being American, I am not familiar with British working-class vocabulary terms; but I am familiar with some terms from American non-middle-class vocabularies. I can imagine how well a middle-class American might do if tested on terms like *pocho* and *signifying,* from those non-middle-class vocabularies.

The final point to be made about this evidence drawn from vocabulary is that Bernstein himself has repudiated it. In the 1970 article he says, "Notice that these codes are not defined in terms of vocabulary or lexical selection" (p. 31). This is a very curious statement, since in the same article he speaks of "restricted codes" as lacking differentiation of vocabulary (p. 33). A search through his previous articles turns up this comment in 1958: ". . . the important determining factor here is the nature of the words . . . , not necessarily the size of vocabulary . . ." (p. 161). But the vocabulary test he administered presumably measured exactly that—size of vocabulary. This contradiction within Bernstein's work can be clarified only by further explanation from him.

As we will see below, in his 1962b article Bernstein did believe that the kind of words used (pronouns) are important; and in 1972 he still bases much of his current definition of "restricted codes" on the use of pronouns in his 1962 data. This 1962 data also contained pauses, important in supporting "restricted codes."

### *The Ability to Abstract: Pauses and Pronouns*

The idea that lower-class speakers can deal better with "the concrete" than with "the abstract" ties together a great deal of Bernstein's work; it was a major claim of his 1958–1970 writings, and it survives—though in modified form—in his 1972 work.

The terms *abstract* and *concrete* are used without definition or example in most of this work. This is, of course, a major problem; it leads to serious errors, e.g., those of Lawton (1968).

"Abstract speech" might have at least two meanings; it could be either (1) speech in which someone goes through the intellectual process of abstracting, or (2) speech in which abstract words like "beauty" as opposed to concrete terms like "apple" are used. The first meaning has no necessary relationship to the second; abstraction (an intellectual process) can be expressed in either concrete or abstract words. In fact, some of our best writers prefer to express their ideas in concrete terms (see Orwell, 1946). Yet Lawton—in an attempt to measure abstract thinking—collects written work from students of both social classes and judges it partially on the basis of whether or not the student who is told to write on "home" mentions his own, concrete home "not at all" or "all the time" (1968, pp. 111–112). Lawton makes other attempts to separate "the concrete" from "the abstract" in these samples; but Leacock (1972) would suggest that the philosophical and psychological synthesis of "the concrete" and "the abstract" is so great as to make such efforts to quantify abstract thinking largely futile.

Let us set aside the second meaning of "abstract speech" as clearly not a matter of cognitive ability, and look at Bernstein's work on the mental process of abstracting as related to language.

Even if we assume that a distinction can be made between "concrete" and "abstract" thinking, we find that Bernstein's evidence on this point contains some fatal weaknesses.

In 1962 Bernstein tape-recorded group discussions among working-class speakers and group discussions among middle-class speakers. He then counted the pauses in the speech of each class group; the middle-class group paused more often than the lower-class group.

PAUSES. Another researcher had suggested that people pause in their speech more often when "summarizing (abstracting and generalizing . . .) . . . than during description" (Bernstein,

1962a, p. 42).[2] Bernstein turned this suggestion around: if abstracting leads to pausing, then pausing must indicate that abstracting is going on. This logic is invalid; A may cause B, but that does not mean that B always represents A. People may indeed pause while abstracting. But they may also pause for many other reasons; the pauses Bernstein counted may have occurred for any of these other reasons.

Of these various reasons, one is particularly important: when people have never met before, discussion among them probably takes place in a more formal style, at a slower pace than does discussion among people who are more familiar with one another. In checking the methods Bernstein used to gather his information on pauses, we find this statement:

> It was thought that the working-class groups would find the test situation threatening and that this would interfere with their speech and consequently all working-class groups had two practice discussions (one a week) before the test discussion. This was not the case with the middle-class groups. . . . (1962a, p. 37).

Bernstein's data on pauses came from taping of groups' discussions; the groups of working-class speakers had all met and held a similar discussion twice before, while the groups of middle-class speakers had not. Either the invalid theory that pauses indicate analysis, or the grossly unsophisticated research mistake of giving some speakers different treatment than other speakers, would have been enough to make all this evidence on pauses utterly inadequate as support for "restricted codes."

PRONOUNS. In 1970, some new terms relating to the concrete versus the abstract began to appear in Bernstein's work: *context-specific* and *context-free*. He also mentions the "communality" of working-class speech use. Later, in 1972, *context-free* and *context-specific* are important to Bernstein's use of *particularistic* and *universalistic*.

Where do these terms come from, and what do they mean? Apparently the basis for these terms and claims is a count of pronouns in Bernstein's taped discussions, supplemented by a count of pronouns in Hawkins's (1969) tentative findings about children of the two social classes. Hawkins suggested that working-class children use pronouns more often than middle-class children. Bernstein found in his own 1962a data (analyzed in Bernstein,

---

[2] This research (Goldman-Eisler, 1958) seems to me to have inadequate bases for this suggestion; but the suggestion itself is plausible. What Bernstein makes of it is not.

1962b) that middle-class speakers used the pronoun "I" more often than did the lower-socioeconomic-class speakers (pp. 234–235).

From this use of pronouns Bernstein draws his new terms. In 1970 he cites a paragraph constructed by Hawkins—not actually uttered by any working-class speaker—as showing the "context-specific" orientation of the working-class; only in pronouns does this paragraph differ from the corresponding paragraph constructed to represent middle-class speech (1970, p. 26; 1972, p. 141). Of course, without the context of a sentence, a pronoun is ambiguous; "they were playing" could refer to three people or twenty. So Bernstein suggests that working-class speech is "particularistic" or "context-specific," tied to the context of the utterance; we must know the context in order to disambiguate the pronoun. His own data on greater use of "I" by the middle-class speakers, in his taped 1962 discussions, also come into play as support for the "context-specific," as opposed to "context-free," orientation of the working class. For, says Bernstein in 1970, "an elaborated code will arise wherever the culture or subculture emphasizes the 'I' over the 'we' " (p. 33). This claim again appears in 1972; in the middle-class "elaborated code," "the 'I' stands over the 'we' " (p. 141). The middle-class use of "I" in Bernstein's taped discussion supposedly represents freedom from the concrete details of the particular context in which speech is uttered. Can we accept this use of pronouns as evidence for the existence of "elaborated" and "restricted" codes? Is this simplistic interpretation of this pronoun usage correct?

Anyone can suggest interpretations of pronoun usage. For instance, I might suggest that greater use of the pronoun *I* on the part of the middle-class British speakers shows their inability to control selfishness and egocentricity. Or we might look at the history of English; at one time, English had a singular form of pronouns, a dual form of pronouns to refer to two people, and a plural form of pronouns. We have lost the dual form. Does this mean that English speakers no longer have the ability to conceive of duality? Have our mental faculties declined in this way? The divorce rate among English speakers can be shown to have risen since the loss of this pronoun; is this a result of our inability to clearly conceive of duality?

We could speculate about the cognitive process symbolized by the use of *you* for both singular and plural second-person references. Does the lack of separate forms for singular *you* and plural *you* in northern dialects of American English mean that northern speakers cannot clearly differentiate between one person being addressed and many being addressed? Are southern speakers better equipped to make this distinction cognitively because their language makes that distinction, using *you* for the singular and *you-all* for the plural?

Bernstein's attempts to interpret pronoun use as directly paralleling cognition show lack of familiarity with the literature critical of the Whorf hypothesis, the theory that language determines thought. Since Lenneberg's (1953) powerful criticism of such claims, most of the 1940s–1950s supporters of the Whorf hypothesis have reconsidered their positions (see Haugen, 1973, for an annotated bibliographic guide to this process of renunciation). Lenneberg suggests that Whorfian speculations about linguistic control over our thought processes are just that—speculations. We must ask for more evidence than speculation as affirmation of Bernstein's "restricted code" suggestions.

Bernstein has intertwined Whorfian speculations such as "the 'I' stands over the 'we' " with another suggestion—that use of pronouns fails to spell out the background information that may make speech easier to understand. Though we must reject his Whorfian speculations as groundless, the second suggestion deserves more examination.

There definitely is a need to spell out background information in some situations. Joos has called the kind of speech that meets this need "consultative style." If, indeed, working-class speakers do not use this style in appropriate situations, that lack may cause them problems in school.

The trouble with Bernstein's claims on this point is that he lacks evidence for those claims; a simple count of pronoun usage is not evidence of lack of this style. In order to show such a lack, he must show this pronoun usage to be inappropriate to the situation. The situation must be one in which "consultative style" is called for, and each pronoun must be considered in the context of the discussion—if its antecedent has already been made clear, its use is not inappropriate. "Consultative style," as well as formal styles in general, will be discussed further in the final section of this paper.

### Other Mental Abilities—Evidence: Sentence Structure

Finally, we should mention two of Bernstein's themes throughout these articles: nonverbal communication and simple syntactic structures. The first of these themes holds that lower-class speakers have to rely on nonverbal communication (body language) because their expression through the verbal channel is restricted (Bernstein, 1958, pp. 164 and 168; 1962a, p. 33; 1970, p. 32). The evidence for this claim is simply nonexistent. Bernstein has not studied nonverbal communication at all. Researchers who have studied it (e.g., Birdwhistell, 1970) believe that all humans use this channel of communication extensively. This claim by Bernstein—which has been widely repeated—rests on no evidence at all.

The second theme Bernstein repeats throughout his first four articles is that of "the simplification and rigidity of the syntax of a restricted code" (1970, p. 32). In his 1962b analysis of the taped conversations gathered in 1962a data, Bernstein finds greater complexity in middle-class speech; there were more embedded sentences (e.g., relative clauses) in the speech of the middle-class speakers than in that of the working-class speakers.

The informality of Bernstein's working class groups, due to previous meetings, would probably account for their less formal, simpler syntax in these third meetings. However, let us assume that middle-class speakers do commonly use more complex sentences than do working-class speakers.[3] Does simple sentence structure imply inferior cognition?

No. In fact, as Labov (1970; pp. 165–169) has pointed out, complex sentences may contain empty rhetoric, thrown out as a smokescreen to make the content seem more impressive or to disguise the fact that the content is confused, contradictory, or even nonexistent. Surely all of us have suffered through lectures, books, and articles that illustrate this point.

Speaking of complex syntactic structure in articles, it should be noted that the syntactic structure used by Bernstein himself changed *toward* simplicity during the time from 1958 to 1972. The 1972 article is written in a simpler style than were the 1958, 1962a, 1962b, and 1970 articles. In fairness to him I should point out that in the 1972 article he has dropped all mention of simple syntax as an attribute of these "codes." At the same time, he does not say in 1972 that his views have changed on this point.

This 1972 article contains a number of changes; all direct claims about inferior cognitive abilities are dropped, as are claims about use of nonverbal communication. In fact, in 1972 Bernstein offers many comments about compensatory education that are

---

[3] Other researchers have reported this finding, e.g., Lawton 1963 and 1964.

perfectly sound. But in 1972 he hardly begins to acknowledge the extent and nature of his own previous claims: "my own writings have sometimes been used (and *more often abused*) in support of compensatory education" (p. 136; emphasis added); "The concept *restricted code* has been equated with linguistic deprivation, or even with the nonverbal child" (p. 140).

In these statements Bernstein apparently disavows any strong connection with the concepts "linguistic deprivation" and the "nonverbal" child, in spite of the massive foundation for those claims laid in his work. Abandoning one's previous claims is always difficult, and I admire his decision to drop, in 1972, some of his themes from earlier work. But failure to acknowledge the themes of cognitive-linguistic deprivation and nonverbal communication in his earlier work, and failure to specifically repudiate those themes, leaves these earlier articles free to exert more influence in the directions that even Bernstein now deplores.

I believe that Bernstein developed his theory on the basis of some facts about social-class differences in the use of language; I believe, however, that he incorrectly grouped these differences with some other features of language not related to social class. Our effort to understand social-class differences that do appear in language use will be hampered until we can put simplistic Whorfian speculations completely behind us.

## SOCIAL-CLASS DIFFERENCES IN LANGUAGE USE

### *Being Articulate*

There may be social-class differences in speakers' ability to be articulate—to explain their feelings and thoughts. Bernstein probably intends to treat being articulate when he speaks of "elaborating discrete intent," communicating individual responses. But this ability is not basically related to social class. The *topic* being discussed and the speaker's *practice* in discussing are probably the two important factors in articulate speech; is this topic one the speaker has information on? Has the speaker talked about it before?

If there is a connection between social class and the ability to articulate individual responses (and Bernstein offers no proof whatsoever that there is), it may result from two facts: (1) that education provides practice in articulating responses; and (2) that part of the *definition* of lower socioeconomic classes is *lack* of education, in comparison with the middle class. It should not surprise us, then, to find that working-class speakers are less articulate then middle-class speakers. I wonder, however, if there is in fact a lack of the ability to articulate on the part of working-class speakers. (I repeat: we have no evidence either way on this question.) Perhaps the topic being discussed will turn out to be the major significant variable in being articulate; and our problem, in that case, will be designing research that will cover topics in which speakers of differing social classes have expertise.

Finally, there are undoubtedly further distinctions to be made in defining the ability to be articulate. For instance, talking at length may succeed in communicating ideas; but this route to "being articulate" can certainly be unfavorably compared with more efficient ways of expressing oneself. On this point, as on the general topic of being articulate, we simply do not yet have reliable data—in fact, we have very little data of any kind.

### Styles and "Speech Variants"

This final topic of my paper is perhaps the most difficult to write about; there is no well-established description of the sort of language variation to be discussed here, though there are many excellent individual contributions to description of these variables. It is probably this lack of established terminology that has led to the extensive debate over Bernstein's work, which offers the terms *restricted code* and *elaborated code* for describing the variation sociolinguists are currently puzzling over.

Martin Joos's term *style*, referring to changes in language that are made in response to social expectations, is the best-known label for the general type of language variation that Bernstein probably had in mind as he wrote about "restricted" and "elaborated codes." [4] Kochman (1969) and Labov (1970) interpret Bernstein as referring to a formal style in his discussion of "elaborated codes"; certainly a formal style is involved in Bernstein's claims, for formal styles show both relatively complex sentence structure and the Latinate vocabulary that often is called for by vocabulary tests such as the one Bernstein used in his early research.

---

[4] I am indebted to Rudolph Troike and Roger Abrahams's introduction to the Joos article, "The Styles of the Five Clocks," in their *Language and Cultural Diversity in American Education* (Englewood Cliffs, N.J.: Prentice-Hall, 1972) for pointing out this connection.

It may be that speakers become adept in using formal styles during the years they spend in our educational system. Since, as we just discussed in relation to being articulate, more years of education are a major part of the defining characteristics of the middle class, it would not be surprising if middle-class speakers have more control over a formal style than do lower-class speakers. But if years in school do teach formal styles, we would expect to find a *relative* difference in control over these styles, not an absolute difference between classes—for children of both classes do attend school, though for differing lengths of time. And recent research has shown that lower-class children do indeed show control over formal styles—control that grows increasingly greater during higher grades in school. Troike (1972) points out receptive control and DeStefano (1974) finds productive control over formal styles on the part of children in low socioeconomic classes. DeStefano finds that this control increases with years in school.

This relative difference sounds very much like the "difference in contexts and conditions" that evoke use of "elaborated codes" in Bernstein's view. When we specify Joos's "consultative style" as the equivalent, among formal styles, of Bernstein's "elaborated code," Joos's and Bernstein's definitions agree even more. In "consultative style," "the speaker supplies background information—he does not assume that he will be understood without it" (Joos, 1972, p. 146) ; in Bernstein's latest version of "elaborated codes," "the meanings are freed from context and so understandable by all" (Bernstein, 1972, p. 142). Viewing Bernstein's "codes" as styles is corroborated, also, by Bernstein's repeated statement that the codes are "verbal planning orientations" that determine which of the many optional syntactic constructions a speaker will choose to express his message ; just this kind of planning seems to me to occur in producing styles.

But Bernstein also says that his "codes" are not the same as "speech variants. . . . A speech variant is a pattern of linguistic choices which is specific to a particular context" (1970, p. 56). Since these "speech variants" are then defined in a way that suggests they are styles, Bernstein himself seems to reject the possibility that his work refers to styles.

At this point, I could present further statements from Bernstein's work about what he did mean ; but his statements in regard to "speech variants" and other possibly relevant language elements are vague and self-contradictory. Further quotes and speculations about his meanings would, I think, tell us no more about language even if they succeeded in telling us more about Bernstein's views about language.

It seems to me that the notions of "elaborated" and "restricted codes" were almost certainly inspired by contrasts in control over formal styles, along with variation in being articulate about school subjects. Bernstein presents little, if any, evidence about social class differences in use of styles. The only relevant data he has was contaminated by differences in his treatment of the two class groups; though middle-class speakers used more complex syntax in their taped discussion, they had had no "practice" sessions. However, let us assume for the sake of argument that middle-class speakers do have more control over formal styles than do working-class speakers.

Styles are not directly representative of cognition; the same thing can be said in two styles. A presidential press secretary recently said to a reporter, "We have not made a judgment as to the appropriate response to your question." A press conference was in progress; television cameras were focused on him; at least 35 people were in the room listening to him. Half an hour earlier, on the telephone with an old friend in the press corps, the press secretary might have said, "We haven't figured out what to tell you," with the same meaning. Styles relate to audience, topic, setting, and other variables studied by sociolinguists (see Gumperz and Hymes, 1964), not to the ability to think.

It seems quite plausible that social-class differences in language use could be related to some of the problems lower-class children confront in a basically middle-class school. The questions are (1) what differences are there, and (2) what is the significance of each of these differences? The second question—about *significance* of language differences—is the crucial one. This paper has attempted to show that the differences examined by Bernstein do not have the significance he ascribes to them. Perhaps we should abandon the terms *restricted* and *elaborated codes*— with their long history of association with cognitive deficits—and turn our attention to other terms and other theoretical models for explanations of the complex and important relationships between language and social class.

## REFERENCES

BEREITER, CARL and SIEGFRIED ENGELMANN. 1966. *Teaching Disadvantaged Children in the Preschool.* Englewood Cliffs, N.J.: Prentice-Hall.

BERNSTEIN, BASIL. 1958. "Some Sociological Determinants of Perception," *British Journal of Sociology,* 9, 159–174.

BERNSTEIN, BASIL. 1959. "A Public Language: Some Sociological Implications of a Linguistic Form." *British Journal of Sociology,* 10, 311–326.

BERNSTEIN, BASIL. 1960. "Language and Social Class." *British Journal of Sociology,* 11, 271–276.

BERNSTEIN, BASIL. 1961. "Social Class and Linguistic Development: A Theory of Social Learning," in *Education, Economy, and Society,* eds. A. H. Halsey, J. Floud, and A. Anderson. New York: Free Press.

BERNSTEIN, BASIL. 1962a. "Linguistic Codes, Hesitation Phenomena, and Intelligence," *Language and Speech,* 5, 31–46.

BERNSTEIN, BASIL. 1962b. "Social Class, Linguistic Codes, and Grammatical Elements," *Language and Speech,* 5, 221–240.

BERNSTEIN, BASIL. 1970. "A Sociolinguistic Approach to Socialization: With Some Reference to Educability," in *Language and Poverty,* ed. Frederick Williams. Chicago: Markham Publishing Company.

BERNSTEIN, BASIL. 1972. "A Critique of the Concept of Compensatory Education," in *Functions of Language in the Classroom,* eds. Courtney Cazden, Dell Hymes, and Vera John. New York: Teacher's College Press.

BIRDWHISTELL, RAY L. 1970. *Kinesics and Context.* New York: Ballantine Books.

CARROLL, JOHN. 1973. "Language and Cognition: Current Perspectives from Linguistics and Psychology," in *Language Differences: Do They Interfere?,* eds. James L. Laffey and Roger W. Shuy. Newark, Del.: International Reading Association.

DESTEFANO, JOHANNA S. 1974. "Productive Language Differences in Fifth-Grade Black Students' Syntactic Forms," in *Language and the Language Arts,* eds. Johanna S. DeStefano and Sharon E. Fox. Boston: Little, Brown and Company.

GOLDMAN-EISLER, FRIEDA. 1958. "Speech Production and the Predictability of Words in Context," *Quarterly Journal of Experimental Psychology,* 10, 96–106.

GUMPERZ, JOHN J. and DELL HYMES, eds. 1964. *The Ethnography of Communication.* Special issue of *American Anthropologist,* 66, No. 6, Part 2.

HAUGEN, EINAR. 1973 (in manuscript). "Linguistic Relativity," in "Bilingualism, Language Contact, and Immigrant Languages in the United States: 1956–1970," to appear in *Current Trends in Linguistics,* Vol. 10, ed. Thomas Sebeok. The Hague: Mouton.

HAWKINS, P. R. 1969. "Social Class, the Nominal Group and Reference," *Language and Speech,* 12: 125–135.

JOOS, MARTIN. 1972. "The Styles of the Five Clocks," in *Language and Cultural Diversity in American Education,* eds. Roger D. Abrahams and Rudolph C. Troike (Englewood Cliffs, N.J.: Prentice-Hall, 1972), pp. 145–149.

KOCHMAN, THOMAS. "Culture and Communication: Implications for Black English in the Classroom," in *Linguistic-Cultural Differences and American Education*, Alfred C. Aarons, Barbara Y. Gordon, and William A. Stewart, eds. Special issue of *The Florida F-L Reporter*, 7, No. 1.

LAWTON, DENIS. 1963. "Social Class Differences in Language Development," *Language and Speech*, 6: 120.

LAWTON, DENIS. 1968. *Social Class, Language, and Education*. London: Routledge and Kegan Paul.

LEACOCK, ELEANOR BURKE. 1972. "Abstract Versus Concrete Speech: A False Dichotomy," in *Functions of Language in the Classroom*, eds. Courtney Cazden, Dell Hymes, and Vera John. New York: Teachers College Press.

LENNEBERG, ERIC. 1953. "Cognition in Ethnolinguistics," *Language*, 29, 463–471.

MUSSEN, P. H., JOHN J. CONGER, and JEROME KAGAN. *Child Development and Personality*, 3rd ed. New York: Harper & Row.

ORWELL, GEORGE. 1950. "Politics and the English Language," in *Shooting an Elephant, and Other Essays*. New York: Harcourt Brace Jovanovich.

TROIKE, RUDOLPH. 1972. "Receptive Bidialectalism: Implications for Second-Dialect Teaching," in *Language and Cultural Diversity in American Education*, eds. Roger D. Abrahams and Rudolph C. Troike. Englewood Cliffs, N.J.: Prentice-Hall.

# Applications for the Study of Language Variation

## A Visit to a California Classroom

JOHN J. GUMPERZ AND
EDUARDO HERNÁNDEZ-CHAVEZ

"Verbal deprivation" as a theory may be boring or abstract.
As a source of stereotyping, however, it goes into effect every
day in the California classroom discussed here. For evaluation
of the "verbal deprivation" theory, see the Johnson article
immediately preceding this one.
In Part 4, three articles deal with reading in relation to
children who speak nonstandard dialects.

. . . [S]ocial findings based on incomplete data or on populations different from those for which they were intended, may
themselves contribute to cultural misunderstanding. . . . Rosenthal has shown that teachers' expectations have a significant
effect on learning (1969), and psychological experiments by
Williams (1969) and Henrie (1969) point to the role that dialect
plays in generating these expectations. When expectations
created by dialect stereotypes are further reinforced by mis-
applied or inaccurate social science findings, education suffers.

Imagine a child in a classroom situation who in a moment of special excitement shifts to black speech. The teacher may have learned that black speech is systematic and normal for communication in Afro-American homes. Nevertheless, intent as she is upon helping the child to become fully bilingual, she may comment on the child's speech by saying, "We don't speak this way in the classroom," or she may ask the child to rephrase the sentence in standard English. No matter how the teacher expresses herself, the fact that she focuses on the form means that the teacher is not responding to the real meaning of the child's message. The child is most likely to interpret her remark as a rebuff and may feel frustrated in his attempt at establishing a more personal relationship with the teacher. In other words, by imposing her own monostylistic communicative norms, the teacher may thwart her students' ability to express themselves fully. An incident from a taperecorded language session in Black Language Arts will illustrate the point.

Student:   (reading from an autobiographical essay) This lady didn't have no sense.

Teacher:   What would be a standard English alternate for this sentence?

Student:   She didn't have any sense. But not this lady: *she didn't have no sense.*

Classroom observation of first-grade reading sessions in a racially integrated California school district illustrates some of the problems involved. Classes in the district include about 60 percent White and 40 percent Chicano, Black, and Oriental children. College student observers find that most reading classes have a tracking system such that children are assigned to fast or slow reading groups and these groups are taught by different methods and otherwise receive different treatment.

Even in first-grade reading periods, where presumably all children are beginners, the slow reading groups tend to consist of 90 percent Blacks and Chicanos. Does this situation reflect real learning difficulties, or is it simply a function of our inability to diagnose reading aptitude in culturally different children? Furthermore, given the need for some kind of ability grouping, how effective and how well adapted to cultural needs are the classroom devices that are actually used to bridge the reading gap?

One reading class was divided into a slow reading group of three children, and a second group of seven fast readers. The teacher worked with one group at a time, keeping the others busy with individual assignments. With the slow readers she concentrated on the alphabet, on the spelling of individual words, and on supposedly basic grammatical concepts such as the distinctions between questions and statements. She addressed the children in what White listeners would identify as pedagogical style. Her enunciation was deliberate and slow. Each word was clearly articulated with even stress and pitch, as if to avoid any verbal sign of emotion, approval or disapproval. Children were expected to speak only when called upon, and the teacher would insist that each question be answered before responding to further ideas. Unsolicited remarks were ignored even if they referred to the problem at hand. Pronunciation errors were corrected whenever they occurred, even if the reading task had to be interrupted. The children seemed distracted and inattentive. They were guessing at answers, "psyching out" the teacher in the manner described by Holt (1965) rather than following her reasoning process. The following sequence symbolizes the artificiality of the situation:

> Teacher: Do you know what a question is? James, ask William a question.
>
> James: William, do you have a coat on?
>
> William: No, I do not have a coat on.

James asks his question and William answers in a style which approaches in artificiality that of the teacher, characterized by citation form pronunciation of [ey] rather than [ə] of the indefinite article, lack of contraction of "do not," stress on the "have," staccato enunciation as if to symbolize what they perceive to be the artificiality and incomprehensibility of the teacher's behavior.

With the advanced group, on the other hand, reading became much more of a group activity and the atmosphere was more relaxed. Words were treated in context, as part of a story. Children were allowed to volunteer answers. There was no correction of pronunciation, although some deviant forms were also heard. The children actually enjoyed competing with each other in reading, and the teacher responded by dropping her pedagogical monotone in favor of more animated natural speech. The activities around the reading table were not lost on the slow readers, who were sitting at their desks with instructions to practice reading on their own. They kept looking at the group, neglecting their own books, obviously wishing they could participate. After a while one boy picked up a spelling game from a nearby table and began to work at it with the other boy, and they began to argue in a style normal for black children. When their voices were raised, the teacher turned and asked them to go back to reading.

In private conversation, the teacher (who is very conscientious and seemingly concerned with all her children's progress) justified her ability grouping on the grounds that children in the slow group lacked books in their homes and "did not speak proper English." She stated they needed practice in grammar and abstract thinking and pronunciation and suggested that, given this type of training, they would eventually be able to catch up with the advanced group. We wonder how well she will succeed. Although clearly she has the best motives and would probably be appalled if one were to suggest that her ability grouping and her emphasis on the technical aspects of reading and spelling with culturally different children is culturally biased, her efforts are not so understood by the children themselves. Our data indicate that the pedagogical style used with slow readers carries different associations for low middle class and low-income groups. While whites identify it as normal teaching behavior, low-income blacks may associate it with the questioning style of welfare investigators and automatically react by not cooperating. In any case, attuned as they are to see meaning in stylistic choice, the black children in the slow reading group cannot fail to notice that they are being treated quite differently and with less understanding than the advanced readers.

What are the implications of this type of situation for our understanding of the role of dialect differences on classroom learning? There is no question that the grammatical features of black dialects discovered by urban dialectologists in recent years are of considerable importance for the historical study of the origin of these dialects and for linguistic theory in general, but this does not necessarily mean that they constitute an impediment to learning. Information on black dialect is often made known to educators in the form of simple lists of deviant features with the suggestion that these features might interfere with reading. There is little if any experimental evidence, for example, that the pronunciations characteristic of urban Black English actually interfere with the reading process. Yet the teacher in our classroom spent considerable time attempting to teach her slow readers the distinction between *pin* and *pen*. Lack of a vowel distinction in these two words is widespread among

Blacks but also quite common among Whites in Northern California. In any case, there is no reason why homophony in this case should present more difficulty than homophony in such words as 'sea' and 'see' and 'know' and 'no' or that created by the midwestern dialect speaker's inability to distinguish 'Mary,' 'marry,' and 'merry.'

## REFERENCES

HENRIE, SAMUEL N., JR. 1969. "A Study of Verb Phrases Used by Five Year Old Non-Standard Negro English Speaking Children." Unpublished Ph.D. dissertation, University of California, Berkeley.

HOLT, JOHN CALDWELL. 1964. *How Children Fail.* New York: Pitman.

ROSENTHAL, ROBERT. 1968. *Pygmalion in the Classroom.* New York: Holt, Rinehart and Winston.

WILLIAMS, FREDERICK. 1969. "Psychological Correlates of Speech Characteristics: On Sounding 'Disadvantaged.'" Unpublished ms., Institute for Research on Poverty, University of Wisconsin, Madison, Wisconsin, March 1969.

## 22,000 "Retarded Children" Face Second Chance

TERRY LINK

Why do we put so much trust in numbers? Test results mean nothing if the test itself is faulty. Link reports on the fate of children who have been classified according to their scores on a test, regardless of whether or not they understood the test. Damage to the self-image of these children—not to mention the educational setbacks they suffered—must have been severe.

This is not an isolated instance. Many states have been guilty of this sort of classification. In one state, parents had to go all the way to the state supreme court in order to force school officials to stop testing native speakers of Spanish with IQ tests written in English.

It seems to me that we must begin evaluating testing (such as that Link describes) and research (such as Bernstein's

research on "restricted codes") rather than continuing to
accept at face value the graphs and numbers that label schoolchildren. Such evaluation may not be easy, but the price we
pay for shirking that task is actually paid not by us, but by
children like those described by Link in this article.

Soledad, California—Nine children in this rural town 160
miles south of San Francisco were recently "graduated" from a
public school class for the mentally retarded.

They were in it on the strength of their first intelligence
tests, in which they had attained dismal scores ranging from
thirty to seventy-two. Incapable of absorbing more, they had
been kept busy cutting out paper figures.

But when they were retested recently they had made dramatic gains, an average of fifteen points each. They averaged
seventy-five in the verbal section of the IQ test and eighty-four
in the performance section.

Unfortunately, their lawyers charge, the difference in scores
wasn't a miracle of pedagogy but a horrible instance of injustice.
The children—all youngsters from largely Spanish-speaking
families—had been classified as mentally retarded on the strength
of English-language IQ tests.

Worse, it was no isolated slip-up, say lawyers for the California Rural Legal Assistance foundation.

They have begun legal action which promises to bring retesting in Spanish for the 22,000 California Chicano kids who
were classified as retarded after they flunked English IQ tests.

The class in which the Soledad children were placed had
one teacher and thirteen pupils, twelve of them Mexican-American. According to eleven-year-old Maria, one of the plaintiffs,
most of the pupils' time was spent doing "baby stuff"—coloring
and cutting pictures out of magazines.

School districts receive about $550 extra in state aid for
each pupil enrolled in such classes.

The children were retested when the California Rural Legal
Assistance foundation sent Victor Ramirez, a certified school
psychologist from San Diego, to retest them in Spanish.

The day he arrived in Soledad, he found only nine of the
fourteen children available for retesting. Of the nine, seven now
scored above the seventy points which the state of California
uses to classify retarded children. One scored on the dividing
line and the ninth scored three points below.

The most dramatic—or pathetic—case was eight-year-old Diane, who had scored thirty in her first IQ test. (This score should indicate that Diane was so retarded that she couldn't even take care of herself physically—which she obviously could.) In Spanish, Diane's score jumped from thirty to seventy-nine.

The children, whose names were withheld, range in age from eight to thirteen. They are mostly the children of farm-workers and live in a labor camp maintained by the city of Soledad. They also share a Mexican heritage and an imperfect grasp of middle-class English.

The parents of one had already protested to school authorities the placement of their child in a class for retarded children, without success.

A suit was filed against the state board of education in behalf of the nine retested children and five other Soledad children who were threatened with placement in the retarded class. It asked that they be placed in normal classes and be given special tutoring to make up for what they had missed.

It also asked the retesting in Spanish of all California's 22,000 Chicano children placed in classes for the retarded.

The fourteen children got both the transfer and tutoring they asked.

The state board of education has also agreed to retest in Spanish those children who scored between 50 and 70 ("educables"), but not those who scored between 30 and 50 ("trainables"), arguing that the 30–50s are "probably bona fide mentally retarded," in the words of one school official.

# Doublespeak: Dialectology in the Service of Big Brother

JAMES SLEDD

The angry tone of Professor Sledd's writing may reflect anger he sees in people who feel that forced bidialectalism programs label their dialects as inferior. I believe such anger to be legitimate and important; whatever language program a school may adopt, that program must not suggest—directly or indirectly—that some dialects are inferior to others.

I do question, however, some of Professor Sledd's sub-arguments. For instance, he accepts the suggestion that a second dialect cannot be taught until we have a complete description of the second dialect, and then points out that we have no such description and it may be quite a while before we do have one— if ever. But the original suggestion may be unsound. The dialects in question overlap to a great extent. Do we have to have a description of the huge core of shared linguistic features in order to teach a second dialect? Would not a description of most of the differences provide quite a bit to teach?

But the question of whether we are able to teach a "standard dialect" is not at all the same as the question of whether we *should* teach these "standard" language features and require that they be used everywhere but in the home. Professor Sledd presents a powerful argument for the position that no speaker with "nonstandard" dialect features should be forced to give them up. Though Professor Sledd uses those black speakers who have "nonstandard" dialects as his example, his argument really applies to all of us—for none of us speaks a dialect that would be accepted as "standard" in all the regions and all the social groups that make up this country.

## A SHORT HISTORY OF DOUBLESPEAK

It was only a few years ago that Prof. Dr. Roger W. Shuy, then of Michigan State University, discovered American dialects.[1] In a little book which James R. Squire, Executive Secretary of the National Council of Teachers of English, described as "a valuable resource" for teachers increasingly concerned with "the study of the English language in our schools" (Shuy, "Fore-word"), Dr. Shuy informed the profession that in Illinois "a male sheep was known as a *buck* only to farmers who had at some time raised sheep" (p. 15) and that "the Minneapolis term *rubber-binder* (for rubber band)" was spreading into Wisconsin (pp. 36–37). He also declared that Southerners pronounce *marry* as if it were spelled *merry;* that they pronounce *fog* and *hog* like *fawg* and *hawg;* that they have a final /r/ in *humor;* that they make *which* identical with *witch* and rhyme *Miss* with *his;* etc. (pp. 12–13).

[1] Roger W. Shuy, *Discovering American Dialects.* (Champaign, Illinois: National Council of Teachers of English, 1967.)

But one does not expect high scholarship from a popularizing textbook, and though Dr. Shuy's discoveries made no great noise in the world of dialectology, the fault was not his alone. As he himself pointed out, American dialect studies were becoming "both more complex and more interesting," and new questions were being asked.

> Twenty or thirty years ago dialect geographers were mainly concerned with relating current pronunciations, vocabulary, and grammar to settlement history and geography. In the sixties, the problems of urban living have attracted attention, including social dialects and styles which need to be learned and used to meet different situations. We need more precise information about the dialects which set one social group apart from another. (Shuy, p. 63)

One might say metaphorically that the dialectologists, like millions of their compatriots, had left the farm for the big city. There they had discovered the blacks—and were making the best of it. In September, 1967, Dr. Roger W. Shuy was no longer a teacher in East Lansing, Michigan, but a Director of Urban Language Study in Washington, D.C.

The trouble with the blacks, as it seemed to the nabobs of the National Council, was that they didn't talk right and weren't doing very well in school. But they were also raising considerable hell with the police; and since the traditional self-righteous pontification against the South showed little promise of quelling riots in Chicago, Detroit, or New York, the greater Powers of the North had assumed a beneficent air and (as one stratagem) had employed a band of linguists and quasi-linguists who would pretend to help black folks talk like white folks on all occasions which the Northern Powers thought it worth their while to regulate. This was the origin of bidialectalism, biloquialism, or— in "good plain Anglo-Saxon"—doublespeak. No missionary enterprise of recent times has been more profitable—for the evangelists.

Readers in search of a longer and more reverential history may find it in many sources, including at least six volumes in the Urban Language Series, under the general editorship of Dr. Roger W. Shuy, now Director of the Sociolinguistics Program of the Center for Applied Linguistics. They are particularly directed to the volume entitled *Teaching Standard English in the Inner City*, which Dr. Shuy has edited with his colleague Ralph W. Fasold (Washington, D.C.: Center for Applied Linguistics, 1970). Further light is shed by other collections of essays, notably the special anthology issue of *The Florida FL Reporter* which appeared in 1969 under the title *Linguistic-Cultural Differences and American Education;* the report of the twentieth annual Round Table Meeting at Georgetown, *Linguistics and the Teaching of Standard English to Speakers of Other Languages or Dialects;* and Frederick Williams' anthology *Language and Poverty: Perspectives on a Theme.* Professor Williams includes a recent essay by the British sociologist Basil Bernstein, who in his own way is also somewhat critical of doublespeak; and readers interested in Bernstein's earlier work will find it reviewed by Denis Lawton in *Social Class, Language and Education.* By all odds the best of the bidialectalists is the genuinely distinguished linguist William Labov of Columbia University, whose little book *The Study of Nonstandard English* includes a selected bibliography. Recently, the apostles of doublespeak have been vexed by more numerous and more vocal objectors, and perhaps there is just a hint of admitted failure in the shifting of attention by some biloquialists from doublespeak to the teaching of reading. Linguists, educationists, and others have addressed themselves to reading problems in memorial volumes like *Reading for the Disadvantaged,* edited by Thomas D. Horn, and *Language & Reading,* compiled by Doris V. Gunderson.[2]

## THE MONEYED BANKRUPT

It is sad to report that the results of such vast activity have been disproportionately small. The biloquialists themselves

[2] To list the cited works more formally: Alfred C. Aarons, Barbara Y. Gordon, and William A. Stewart, eds., *Linguistic-Cultural Differences and American Education.* Special anthology issue of *The Florida FL Reporter,* Vol. 7, No. 1 (Spring/Summer, 1969).

James E. Alatis, ed., *Linguistics and the Teaching of Standard English to Speakers of Other Languages or Dialects.* Report of the Twentieth Annual Round Table Meeting on Linguistics and Language Studies. (Washington, D.C.: Georgetown University Press, 1970.)

Frederick Williams, ed., *Language and Poverty: Perspectives on a Theme.* (Chicago: Markham Publishing Company, 1970.)

Denis Lawton, *Social Class, Language and Education.* (New York: Schocken Books, 1968.)

William Labov, *The Study of Nonstandard English.* (Champaign, Illinois: National Council of Teachers of English, 1970.)

Thomas D. Horn, ed., *Reading for the Disadvantaged: Problems of Linguistically Different Learners.* (New York: Harcourt Brace Jovanovich, Inc., 1970.)

do not claim to have produced substantial numbers of psychologically undamaged doublespeakers, whose mastery of whitey's talk has won them jobs which otherwise would have been denied them. In fact, the complete bidialectal, with undiminished control of his vernacular and a good mastery of the standard language, is apparently as mythical as the unicorn: no authenticated specimens have been reported.[3] Even the means to approximate the ideal of doublespeaking are admittedly lacking, for "the need for teaching materials preceded any strongly felt need for theoretical bases or empirical research upon which such materials could be based" (Fasold and Shuy, *op. cit.*, p. 126). Consequently, there are relatively few teaching materials available (*ibid.*, p. 128), and those that do exist differ in theory, method, content, and arrangement (Walt Wolfram, in Fasold and Shuy, p. 105). In the words of Director Dr. Shuy,

> A majority of the materials currently available for teaching standard English to nonstandard speakers rest on the uneasy assumption that TESOL techniques [for teaching English as a second language] are valid for learning a second dialect. They do this without any solid proof. We do not have a viable evaluation tool at this time nor are we likely to get one until the linguists complete their analysis of the language system of nonstandard speakers. Most current materials deal with pronunciations although it has long been accepted that grammatical differences count more heavily toward social judgments than phonological or lexical differences.[4]

Taken literally, that confession would mean that the biloquialists will never be able to tell their patrons whether or not their costly teaching materials are any good, because a complete analysis of any language, standard or nonstandard, is another unattainable ideal. The best of existing descriptions of what is called Black English are only fragments, sketches of bits and pieces which have caught the eye of Northern linguists un-

---

Doris V. Gunderson, compiler, *Language & Reading: An Interdisciplinary Approach.* (Washington, D.C.: Center for Applied Linguistics, 1970.)

[3] Labov has repeatedly said as much, most recently in "The Study of Language in its Social Context," *Studium Generale*, 23 (1970), p. 52. "We have not encountered any nonstandard speakers who gained good control of a standard language, and still retained control of the nonstandard vernacular." The goodness of the acquired control of the standard language will not easily be assumed by students of hypercorrection, readers of H. C. Wyld on "Modified Standard," or teachers of Freshman English in state universities.

[4] Roger W. Shuy, "Bonnie and Clyde Tactics in English Teaching." In Aarons, Gordon, and Stewart, *Linguistic-Cultural Differences and American Education*, p. 83.

familiar with Southern speech.[5] Advocates of doublespeak must therefore admit that they have still not produced the "absolutely necessary prerequisite to English teaching in such situations, . . . the linguistic analysis and description of the nonstandard dialect." [6]

## CAUSES OF FAILURE

At this juncture the irreverent might be tempted to ask a question. If happy, accomplished, and fully employed doublespeakers are not swarming in Northern cities, if tried and tested materials for teaching more of them remain scarce, and if complete descriptions of the relevant dialects are not going to exist while we do, then one might ask just what the biloquialists have been doing with the money and manpower which the Establishment has provided them or whether (more suspiciously) the Establishment really want them to do anything or just to give the impression of a great society on the march toward new frontiers.

One naughty answer would be that the biloquialists have been so busy convening, conferring, organizing, advertising, and asking for more that their intellectual activities have suffered. There is even some expert testimony to this effect:

> A recent national conference on educating the disadvantaged devoted less than five percent of its attention during the two days of meetings to the content of such education. Practically all of the papers and discussion centered on funding such programs, administrating them and evaluating them. (Shuy, in Fasold and Shuy, p. 127)

But so elementary a naughtiness is only a partial answer, and in part unfair. It is unfair specifically to William Labov and

---

[5] Readers may satisfy themselves of the truth of this proposition by examining the table of contents in Walter A. Wolfram's *Sociolinguistic Description of Detroit Negro Speech* (Washington, D.C.: Center for Applied Linguistics, 1969) or by reading Wolfram and Fasold, "Some Linguistic Features of Negro Dialect," in Fasold and Shuy, *Teaching Standard English*, pp. 41ff. A much more extensive work is the *Study of the Non-Standard English of Negro and Puerto Rican Speakers in New York City* by Labov, Paul Cohen, Clarence Robins, and John Lewis (2 vols.; Columbia University, 1968); but Chapter III of their first volume, "Structural Differences between Non-Standard Negro English and Standard English," is very far from a "complete" grammar of either dialect.

[6] William A. Stewart, "Urban Negro Speech: Sociolinguistic Factors Affecting English Teaching." In Aarons, Gordon, and Stewart, *Linguistic-Cultural Differences*, p. 53.

his associates, who have taught us a great deal, not just about current American English, but about the theory and practice of descriptive and historical grammar; and it does not sufficiently emphasize the extenuating circumstance that well-meaning sloganeers may be trapped by their own slogans as they try to do in a few years a job that would take a generation.

Since the Powers prefer the appearance of social change to the reality, it was not hard to hook governments and foundations on the alleged potentialities of doublespeak as if those potentialities had been realized already or would be on a bright tomorrow; but when the advertisements had brought the customers, the delivery of the actual goods turned out impossible. Nobody knows what the biloquialists admit they would have to know about dialects of English to make doublespeak succeed; and besides this general ignorance (which some of them have manfully attacked), the biloquialists are working under some special disadvantages. It is always hard for people who have not taught much to talk about teaching (though ingenious youths like Dr. Peter S. Rosenbaum can sometimes manage it),[7] and it is hard for linguists who have not heard much Southern speech to talk about speech which is basically Southern: they are constantly discovering distinctive characteristics of "the Negro vernacular," like "dummy *it* for *there*," which the most benighted caucasian Christian spinster in Milledgeville, Georgia, could assure them are commonplace among poor whites.[8]

---

[7] Dr. Rosenbaum's oration on the twentieth Round Table report deserves special attention, but lack of space forbids an attractive excursus. A couple of quotations will suggest the orientation of this already eminent "linguistic engineer." (1) "*Learning* means acquiring new or improved control over one's environment. *Teaching* means structuring or manipulating an environment so that a learner through experience in this environment can with facility acquire the desired control" (p. 112). Just how this statement applies to a class in *Beowulf* may be left to Dr. Rosenbaum to explain. (2) "In experimental computerized versions of such an environment being developed by IBM Research, the tutor is a computer itself, communicating with a student by means of a terminal station equipped with a typewriter, tape recorder, and image projector" (p. 116). It would be unkind to blame the tutor computer for Dr. Rosenbaum's prose, since it is well known that he received conventional humanistic instruction at MIT; but even acknowledged masters of inanity might envy the following sentence: "As is understood by all, some students are weaker than others" (p. 114). An antiquated antiquarian (perhaps unduly vexed by the "structuring or manipulating" of the now well-oiled Gulf beaches) must ask forgiveness for doubting that a man who can write like that is likely "to devise a new classroom regime capable of satisfying all major language learning environment criteria" (p. 117).

[8] William Labov, *The Study of Nonstandard English*, p. 27; Flannery O'Connor, "A Good Man Is Hard To Find," in *Three by Flannery O'Connor* (New York: New American Library, n.d.), pp. 133, 139, 142, 143.

There are other difficulties, too, which hamper not only the biloquialists but all practitioners of large-scale linguistic engineering (the jargon is contagious). Linguistics in the '60s and early '70s has been unsettled by new theories, whose advocates are openly skeptical of oversold "applications"; and even in favorable circumstances "interdisciplinary" efforts like biloquialism are always slow to take effect, often hampered by disagreements among the congregation of prima donnas, and sometimes disappointingly unproductive.

Quite as loud as the general lamentation over the failure of "interventionist" programs for the disadvantaged are the debates among the interveners. Thus, to the devotees of applied linguistics, both the Englishman Bernstein and the American partners Engelmann and Bereiter are sinners against the light,[9] but neither Bernstein nor Engelmann has rushed headlong to confession. On the contrary, both are recalcitrant.

For all his talk about restricted and elaborated codes (talk which has won him a retinue of American disciples), Bernstein still sees no reason to interfere with nonstandard dialects:

> That the culture or subculture through its forms of social integration generates a restricted code, does not mean that the resultant speech and meaning system is linguistically or culturally deprived, that its children have nothing to offer the school, that their imaginings are not significant. It does not mean that we have to teach these children formal grammar, nor does it mean that we have to interfere with their dialect. There is nothing, but nothing, in dialect as such, which prevents a child from internalizing and learning to use universalistic meanings.[10]

Obviously, Bernstein has little in common with the biloquialists except the tendency to talk smugly about *we* and *they* and what *we* have to do to *them*. Engelmann, equally godlike, ranks "The Linguistic and Psycholinguistic Approaches" under "Abuses in Program Construction" and dismisses both:

> It is not possible to imply statements about teaching from the premises upon which the linguist and the psycholinguist operate. Attempts to use linguistic analysis as the basis for teaching reading have produced the full range of programs, from paragraph reading to single-sound variations. The linguist's entire theoretical preamble, in other words, is nothing more than an appeal used to

---

[9] See Labov's "Logic of Nonstandard English," reprinted by Williams in *Language and Poverty* from the twentieth Round Table report.

[10] Basil Bernstein, "A Sociolinguistic Approach to Socialization: With Some Reference to Educability," in *Language and Poverty*, p. 57.

sanction an approach that derives from personal preferences, not from linguistic principles.[11]

Unless the Powers are willing to subsidize all interveners equally, such disagreement indicates that at least some seekers of funds should get no more funding for the evaluating of their administrating; and the unfunded (to close this selective catalogue of disagreements) are likely to include some linguists, for linguist can differ with linguist as vigorously as with psychologist or sociologist. Marvin D. Loflin, for example, transmogrifies all Southern whites to pluriglots when he finds "Nonstandard Negro English" so unlike the standard speech of whites "that a fuller description . . . will show a grammatical system which must be treated as a foreign language." [12] Similarly, William A. Stewart finds enough "unique . . . structural characteristics" in "American Negro dialects" to justify the bold historical speculation that the Negro dialects "probably derived from a creolized form of English, once spoken on American plantations by Negro slaves and seemingly related to creolized forms of English which are still spoken by Negroes in Jamaica and other parts of the Caribbean." [13]

Perhaps it may be so. At any rate, when Stewart's theory is questioned he is quick to denounce what he calls "the blatant intrusion of sociopolitical issues into the scientific study of Negro speech"; [14] and his sociopolitical rhetoric, if not his linguistic evidence, has been so convincing that his conclusions are sometimes confidently repeated by persons whose linguistic sophistication is considerably less than his.[15]

Yet Loflin and Stewart have not had everything their own way among linguists. Raven McDavid is presumably one of Stewart's blatant intruders of sociopolitical issues into virginal science:

> Even where a particular feature is popularly assigned to one racial group, like the uninflected third-singular present (*he do, she have, it make*)—a shibboleth for Negro nonstandard speech in urban

[11] Siegfried Engelmann, "How to Construct Effective Language Programs for the Poverty Child," in *Language and Poverty*, p. 118.

[12] "A Teaching Problem in Nonstandard Negro English," *English Journal*, 56.1312-1314, quoted by Wolfram, *A Sociolinguistic Description of Detroit Negro Speech*, p. 13.

[13] "Toward a History of American Negro Dialect," in Williams, *Language and Poverty*, p. 351.

[14] "Sociopolitical Issues in the Linguistic Treatment of Negro Dialect," in Alatis, *Linguistics and the Teaching of Standard English*, p. 215.

[15] For example, Muriel R. Saville, "Language and the Disadvantaged," in Horn, *Reading for the Disadvantaged*, p. 124.

areas—it often turns out to be old in the British dialects, and to be widely distributed in the eastern United States among speakers of all races. It is only the accidents of cultural, economic, and educational history that have made such older linguistic features more common in the South than in the Midland and the North, and more common among Negro speakers than among whites.[16]

William Labov is equally firm in rejecting Loflin's theory of nonstandard Negro English as a foreign language:

> In dealing with the structure of NNE, we do not find a foreign language with syntax and semantics radically different from SE [Standard English]: instead, we find a dialect of English, with certain extensions and modifications of rules to be found in other dialects. . . . Striking differences in surface structure were frequently the result of late phonological and transformational rules.[17]

No amount of funding can conceal the fact that somebody, in arguments like these, has got to be wrong.

## THE SHIFT TO READING

If the shift from doublespeak to interdisciplinary assaults on reading does hint at some sense of failure among the disunited sloganeers of overambitious biloquialism, their choice of a second front will not redeem their reputation as skillful strategists. The familiar tactic of concealing the failure to keep one promise by making another is unlikely to succeed if the second promise is less plausible than the first; and promises to give everyone "the right to read" are notoriously hard to make good on, even for the linguist in his favorite role of universal expert.

The perusal of books on reading like those edited by Horn and Gunderson leaves one considerably sadder, therefore, but little wiser, than when he began. The inquisitive amateur soon accepts the experts' repeated assertion that little is known—and gets tired of their plea for more research and full employment:

> After decades of debate and expenditures of millions of research dollars, the teaching of reading remains on questionable psychological and linguistic grounds. When one looks at the research on reading over the past half century, the sheer volume of the literature and the welter of topics and findings (and lack of findings)

---

[16] Raven I. McDavid, Jr., "Language Characteristics of Specific Groups: Native Whites," in *Reading for the Disadvantaged*, p. 136.

[17] Labov, *et al.*, *A Study of the Non-Standard English of Negro and Puerto Rican Speakers in New York City*, II. 339, 343.

is incredible. Yet, we are sore put to name even a few trustworthy generalizations or research based guides to educational practice. Eleven widely different methods, represented by a variety of materials, were tested in some five hundred classrooms of first grade children during 1964–1965. Summary reports . . . revealed that by and large methods and materials were not the crucial elements in teaching first grade children to read.

At the present time we need research into every aspect of the education of the disadvantaged.[18]

If the amateur educationist is already an amateur linguist, he probably already knows Labov's opinion that "the major problem responsible for reading failure" in the ghettos "is a cultural conflict," not dialect interference.[19] He is thus surprised only by the source of Dr. Roger W. Shuy's quite unsurprising statement "that learning to read has little or nothing to do with a child's ability to handle Standard English phonology." [20] A Southern amateur who has consorted with Australians, for example, or vacationed among Lake Country farmers, hardly needs linguistic enlightenment to know that the oddest speech is perfectly compatible with the reading of internationally acceptable English. And the mere happy innocent who cares nothing for either linguistics or pedagogy, if he has reflected at all on what he does when he reads, will know that reading is not just a "language art." The essential processes, even in reading parrot-like without understanding, are inference and judgment in what Kenneth S. Goodman has called "a psycholinguistic guessing game"; [21] and most of the linguistic entrepreneurs can claim no special competence in such matters.

## SOMNIGRAPHY AND EUPHEMISM

To anyone with a normal dislike for solemn inanity, the contribution of linguistics to the teaching of reading is thus a less promising subject than the sleep-writing and professional euphemism which mark the work of the biloquialists and the

[18] Richard L. Venezky, *et al.*, Harry Levin, and William D. Sheldon, in Gunderson, *Language & Reading*, pp. 37, 123, 266, 271.

[19] William Labov and Clarence Robins, "A Note on the Relation of Reading Failure to Peer-Group Status in Urban Ghettos," in *Language & Reading*, p. 214.

[20] "Some Language and Cultural Differences in a Theory of Reading," *Language & Reading*, p. 80.

[21] "Reading: A Psycholinguistic Guessing Game," *Language & Reading*, pp. 107–119.

inhabitants of schools of education. The name *biloquialism* is itself as fine an instance of verbal magic as one could want. Because nobody likes to admit that his speech makes other people laugh at him or despise him, *dialect* has become a dirty word. Hence its compounds and derivatives, like the older *bidialectalism*, must go too—the hope being, one imagines, that if the name goes the thing will vanish with it. For such wizardry, *doublespeak* is the perfect label.

Educationists make as much fuss over the euphemism *the disadvantaged* as the linguists do over *biloquialism*. They have not contented themselves with the one weasel-word, but have matched it with a number of others: *the culturally different, the linguistically different, the culturally deprived, the intellectually deprived, the culturally antagonized* (Horn, *Reading for the Disadvantaged*, pp. v, 11). It is a touch of genius that after choosing a word to obscure his meaning, a writer can then debate what he means by it. Thomas D. Horn concludes that anybody can be disadvantaged, even when he thinks he is in the catbird seat:

> Any individual may be disadvantaged socially, economically, psychologically, and/or linguistically, depending upon the particular social milieu in which he is attempting to function at a given time. Indeed, he may be completely oblivious to his disadvantaged condition and perceive others in the group as being disadvantaged rather than himself.[22]

Horn's readers will not deny their intellectual deprivation.

Somnigraphy, the art of writing as if one were asleep, is as zealously cultivated by biloquialists and educationists as euphemism. Sleep-writing must be distinguished from New High Bureaucratian (NHB), which is grammatical and has a meaning but obscures it by jargon. At its best, somnigraphy is neither grammatical nor meaningful; but no sentence can qualify as somnigraphic unless either its meaning or its grammar is somehow deviant. The following statement approaches the degree of vacuity necessary to somnigraphy; but since its distinctive feature is pompous scientism, it is probably to be treated as NHB:

> Commands or requests for action are essentially instructions from a person A to a person B to carry out some action X at a time T.

---

[22] *Reading for the Disadvantaged*, p. 2. Observe the opening for the educationist to decide who gets the works in school because he's disadvantaged without knowing it.

$$A \rightarrow B:X!/T$$

Somnigraphy in the pure state is more easily recognizable:

Illogical comparison: "The selection of informants in this study is more rigid than the original study."

Tautology rampant: "Before a nonconsonantal environment the presence of the cluster-final stop, for all practical purposes, is categorically present in SE."

Failure of agreement: "The difference between the Negro classes appear to be largely quantitative for monomorphemic clusters."

The dying fall: "That we see linguists, psychologists, sociologists, educators, and others exercising varying definitions of language and language behavior, is important to know."

Chaos and Old Night: "Much of the attention given to the sociocultural aspects of poverty can be seen in the kinds of causes and cures for poverty which are often linked as parts of an overall *poverty cycle* (Figure 1)." [But neither the attention to poverty, nor the cures for it, can be found in the cycle itself.]

The *like/as* syndrome: "English, as most languages, has a variety of dialects."

Self-contradiction: "The nativist position carries with it the concept of a distinction between a child's linguistic knowledge and all of the varied facets and factors of his actual speaking and listening behaviors, one factor of which is the aforementioned knowledge." [That is, the child's knowledge both is and is not a part of his behavior.]

Scrambled metaphor: "In brief the strategy is to prepare the child for candidacy into the economic mainstream." [Sooner or later, we will read about the aridity of the mainstream culture—probably sooner.]

Fractured idiom: "Goodman (1965) and Bailey (1965), along with Stewart (esp. 1969), have all discussed the possibility of interference from the dialect on acquiring the ability to read." [And let no man interfere on their discussion.]

The unconscious absurd: ". . . both the linguists and sociologists . . . were relatively free from . . . cross-fertilization. . . ."

Lexical indiscretion: "As long as one operates in terms of languages and cultures conceived as isolates, internally discreet, . . ."

Flatus: "Middle-class children emitted a larger number of
. . . self-corrections than the lower-class children did."

The cancerous modifier: "Mrs. Golden's program, as with
most of the teaching English as a second language to Negro
nonstandard English speakers programs, relies on pattern
practice. . . ." [Sounds like somebody needs it.]

Confusion of map with territory: "The rule for the absence
of *d* occurs more frequently when *d* is followed by a consonant than when followed by a vowel."

The genteel thing: "To improve one's social acceptability
to a middle class society, working class people should focus
primarily on vocabulary development."

The intense inane: "Reading is a process of recognizing that
printed words represent spoken words and is a part of the
total language spectrum."

The shipwrecked question: "How do the separate and disparate experiences of individuals lead to a common acceptance of general meaning but which also permit differences
of interpretation?" [God only knows.]

Circumblundering a meaning: "The educational world has
generally thought of language as lexicon and it is not surprising that they would equate cultural adjustment to the
words of the city. . . ."

The undefining definition: "By underlying structure here
I mean that ability which even beginning readers have which
enables them to avoid misreading via any other manner
than by the phonological, and grammatical rules of their
native language."

The arresting title: "Economic, Geographic, and Ethnic
Breakdown of Disadvantaged Children."

Opposites reconciled: "One obstacle, lack of skill in the use
of standard American English, has increasingly been recognized as a major contributing factor to the success of a
child beginning his formal education."

## WHY THE POWERS PAY

That exhibit, which could be enlarged at will, is neither
cruel nor insolent nor joking. The insolence is that the perpetra-
tors of such writing should set themselves up as linguists and
teachers of standard English. The cruelty is that people who
think and write so badly should be turned loose upon children.
The level of simple competence in the use of words is simply

low among biloquialists, and to the old-fashioned English professor who still believes that a man's sentences (not his dialect) are a good index to his intelligence, that fact demands an explanation.

The obvious answer is that governments and foundations have put up so much money for doublespeak that they have not been able to find good people to spend it; but that answer simply shifts the question to another level. Why do our rulers act like that? Why should they employ verbicides in the impossible and immoral pursuit of biloquialism? Well-meaning incompetence may characterize many biloquialists; but incompetence has no direction, follows no party line unless some other force is guiding—and the drift of biloquialism is too plain to be accidental. There must be, somewhere, an inhumanity that shapes its ends.

The explanation does not require that inhumanity should be reified in a body of conspirators or that the making of educational policy, at any level, should be viewed as the conscious, intelligent adaptation of public means to private ends. In their dealings with black people, most middle-class white linguists in the United States may be expected to act like most other middle-class whites. Their probable motivations include a real desire to do good, some hidden dislike, some fear, and the love of money and status. Foundation men, bureaucrats, and politicians may be expected to share those foibles; and precisely because the whole conglomerate is shaped and moved by the same forces, it cannot move beyond its limits.

The appeal of doublespeak is that it promises beneficent change without threat to existing power or privilege. If doublespeak were to succeed, the restive communities of the poor and ignorant would be tamed; for potential revolutionaries would be transformed into the subservient, scrambling, anxious underlings who constitute the lower middle class in a technological society. Their children, if there should be a next generation, would rise to be its linguists, its English teachers, and its petty bureaucrats; and doublespeak would be justified by Progress. If doublespeak should fail, as it must, large numbers of young blacks can still be assured that it was they who failed, and not their white superiors; and the blacks' presumed failure in not doing what they could not and should not do can be used against them as a psychological and political weapon.[23] In either event,

[23] See Wayne O'Neil, "The Politics of Bidialecticalism," from which I have borrowed the ingenious idea that educational failure might still be political success for the backers of doublespeak.

the white Powers have nothing to lose by their exercise in cosmetology. Both their conscience and their supremacy will be clear.

## THE FORM OF THE ARGUMENT

The essential argument for such an explanation should be stated formally enough to keep the issues plain. As a hypothetical syllogism, the argument would look like this:

Unless the biloquialists and their sponsors were misled by their presumed self-interest, they would not pursue the impossible and immoral end of doublespeak so vigorously—or defend themselves for doing it.

But they do pursue, etc.

Therefore they are misled. . . .

Less pedantically, nobody insists on trying to do what he can't and shouldn't do unless there's something in it for him somewhere.

It is the consequent of the major premise that needs attention.

## THE IMPOSSIBILITY OF DOUBLESPEAK

The impossibility of establishing doublespeak in the real world has already been argued: the necessary descriptions of standard and nonstandard dialects are nonexistent, and materials and methods of teaching are dubious at best. It may be added here that competent teachers of doublespeak are a contradiction in terms. For tough young blacks, the worst possible teacher is a middle-class white female; and a middle-class black female may not be much better, since she is nearly as likely as her white counterpart to look down on her lower-class students. Such condescending culture-vendors have no chance whatever of neutralizing the influence of the world outside the classroom, a world where ghetto youngsters have few occasions to use such standard English as they may have learned and where, if they did use it, they might find the effort unrewarding. Their peers would blame them for trying to talk like white people, and they would hardly be compensated for such isolation by any real increase in "upward mobility." The black college graduate who makes less money than a white dropout is a sad familiar figure.

Teachers of standard English may be sure, then, of resistance from teen-age students in the ghettos, and unless they are more tactful than the biloquialists, they may be sure of resistance from black adults as well. On the issue of doublespeak the black community is undoubtedly divided. Blacks who have made it into the middle and upper classes, and many black parents, want to see young people make it too. They consider the ability to use "good English" a part of making it (though in reality good English is far less important to success on the job than a great many other qualifications). At the other extreme are the tough teen-agers, the adults who secretly or openly share their values, and some of the more militant community leaders; while in between there are probably a good many blacks of various ages for whom the white world's insistence on its standard English sets off an internal conflict between pride and self-hate.

But the black community is not at all divided in its opposition to doctrines of white supremacy, whether politely veiled or publicly announced. No black of any age is likely to be much pleased by condescension and the calm assumption of superiority:

> First, there has been the general attitude, common even among some linguists, that nonstandard speech is less worthy of interest and study than varieties of speech with high prestige. . . . As this relates to the speech of Negroes, it has been reinforced by a commendable desire to emphasize the potential of the Negro to be identical to white Americans. . . .[24]

> Even if it were possible to "stamp out" nonstandard English, changing the students' language behavior completely might be detrimental to their social well-being. They may need the nonstandard for social situations in which it is appropriate.[25]

> More than the foreign-language student, more than the native speaker of standard English, the second-dialect student needs to know his teacher considers him truly "worth revising." [26]

The neighbor-loving speech which ended with the last quotation was soon followed, understandably, by an angry outburst from a black auditor:

> I am outraged and insulted by this meeting. . . . I would like to know why white people can determine for black people what is standard and what is nonstandard.

[24] William A. Stewart, "Urban Negro Speech," in Aarons, Gordon, and Stewart, *Linguistic-Cultural Differences*, p. 51.
[25] Irwin Feigenbaum, "The Use of Nonstandard English in Teaching Standard," in Fasold and Shuy, *Teaching Standard English*, p. 89.
[26] Virginia F. Allen, "A Second Dialect Is Not a Foreign Language," in Alatis, *Linguistics and the Teaching of Standard English*, p. 194.

But two of the linguists present did not get the message—the plain message that it must no longer be whites only who "conduct the important affairs of the community." The first of them rebuked the young lady rudely, once in the meeting and once in a "subsequent written comment"; he rapped about "rapping" on sociolinguists and using phony ploys "in political confrontations." The second, in a display of caucasian tact, congratulated her on expressing herself "in perfectly standard grammar."

If those who set themselves up as teachers of teachers behave like that, they may succeed in uniting the divided black community—uniting it against the advocates of doublespeak. Whatever the black community does want, it does not want to be led by the nose.

## THE IMMORALITY OF DOUBLESPEAK

The biloquialist, of course, makes a great fuss about giving the child of the poor and ignorant, whether black or white, the choice of using or not using standard English. "He should be allowed to make that decision as he shapes his decisions in life." [27] But the biloquialist obviously sees himself as the determiner of the decisions which other people may decide, and the choice he deigns to give is really not much choice after all. In the name of social realism, he begins by imposing a false scheme of values, of which "upward mobility" is the highest; and he then sets out to make the child "upwardly mobile" by requiring hours of stultifying drill on arbitrary matters of usage, so that in situations where standard English is deemed appropriate the child may choose between "Ain't nobody gon' love you" and "Nobody is going to love you." *Appropriate* will be defined by the white world, which will also fix the punishment if the liberated doublespeaker prefers his own definition. Ain't nobody gon' love him if he does that.

The immorality of biloquialism is amply illustrated by such hypocrisy. Assuring the child that his speech is as good as anybody else's, publicly forswearing all attempts to eradicate it, and vigorously defending the individual's free choice, the biloquialist would actually force the speech and values of the middle-class white world on children of every class and color.

---

[27] John C. Maxwell in "Riposte," *English Journal*, 59 (November, 1970), p. 1159.

By *upward mobility* he means getting and spending more money, wasting more of the world's irreplaceable resources in unnecessary display, and turning one's back on family and friends who are unable or unwilling to join in that high enterprise. Every day, by his loud-voiced actions, the biloquialist would tell the child to build his life on that rotten foundation.

But *tell* is too mild a word: *force* is more accurate. *Force* is more accurate because the schoolchild would not have a choice between wasting his precious days (with the biloquialists) in the study of socially graded synonyms and (with intelligent teachers) learning something serious about himself and the world he lives in; and besides, when schooldays were over, the young doublespeaker could not really choose between his vernacular and his imperfectly mastered standard English. In every serious transaction of an upwardly mobile life, the use of standard English would be enforced by the giving or withholding of the social and economic goodies which define upward mobility. The upwardly mobile doublespeaker would be expected to eradicate his vernacular except in some darkly secret areas of his private life, of which eventually he would learn to be ashamed; and his likely reward for such self-mutilation would be just enough mobility to get him stranded between the worlds of white and black. There he could happily reflect on the humanitarianism of the Great White Expert who saves the oppressed from militancy and sends them in pursuit of money and status, which literature, philosophy, religion, and the millennial experience of mankind have exposed as unfit ends for human life. "That doesn't seem very humane from where I sit." [28]

## ON NOT LOVING BIG BROTHER

But the present argument against biloqualism is not a militant argument (though biloquialists have called it one in the attempt to discredit it with a label they think is frightening), and it is not primarily a humanitarian argument (though biloquialists have called it inhumane). Our new teachers of reading cannot read well enough to tell Mill from a militant. The argument here is the argument of an unashamed conservative individualist. With his own eyes the arguer has seen British working people,

[28] *Loc. cit.* But I bet you guessed.

and chicanos, and black Americans humiliated by contempt for their language and twisted by their own unhappy efforts to talk like their exploiters. An expert is no more needed to prove that such humiliation is damaging or such efforts an expense of spirit than a meteorologist is needed to warn of the dangers of urinating against the wind; but the weight of the argument rests mainly on the fact that if any man can be so shamed and bullied for so intimate a part of his own being as his language, then every man is fully subject to the unhampered tyrants of the materialist majority. To resist the biloquialist is to resist Big Brother, and to resist him for oneself as well as others. Big Brother is not always white.

In all the variety of his disguises, Big Brother is very near at hand today. In one form he is Basil Bernstein, whose notions about restricted and elaborated codes (as they are interpreted or misinterpreted by Bernstein's American disciples) might vulgarly be taken as supporting an injunction to get the pickaninnies away from their black mammies; in another form he is the arrogant dogmatist Siegfried Engelmann, the amoral educational technologist with a big stick.

The biloquialist follows neither Engelmann nor Bernstein, but his own high-sounding talk should not be taken at face value, either. Doublespeak is not necessary to communication between users of different dialects, since speakers of nonstandard English generally have passive control of standard, if only through their exposure to television; the biloquialist himself assures us that no dialect is intrinsically better than any other; and his announced devotion to freedom of choice has already been exposed as phony, like his promise of social mobility through unnatural speech. When the biloquialist's guard is down, he too can talk the language of dialect-eradication, which he officially abhors:

> . . . attempting to eliminate this kind of auxiliary deletion from the speech of inner-city Negro children would be a low-priority task.[29]

Behind the mandarin's jargon and self-praise lies the quiet assumption that it is his right and duty to run other people's lives.

The mandarin will go a long way to make other people see that his good is theirs, so that his values may prevail among the faceless multitude. As educator, his aims are not always educational, but may be as simple as keeping young people off the labor

---

[29] Fasold and Wolfram, "Some Linguistic Features of Negro Dialect," in Fasold and Shuy, *Teaching Standard English*, p. 80.

market by keeping them in school, though he tacitly admits that he has planned nothing to teach them there:

> The problems of finding suitable programs will be complicated if, as educators anticipate, education is made compulsory for students until they reach the age of eighteen. Educators will be forced to adapt programs for the group of young people from sixteen to eighteen who under the present system have dropped out of school.[30]

Yet the mandarin's ends, he thinks, justify almost any means.

> Intelligence and verbal skills within the culture of the street is prized just as highly as it is within the school:—but the use of such skills is more often to manipulate and control other people than to convey information to them. Of course it is the school's task to emphasize the value of language in cognitive purposes. But in order to motivate adolescent and preadolescent children to learn standard English, it would be wise to emphasize its value for handling social situations, avoiding conflict (or provoking conflict when desired), for influencing and controlling other people.[31]

> Between 5 and 10 percent of the 62,000 children in this city in the American midlands are taking "behavior modification" drugs prescribed by local doctors to improve classroom deportment and increase learning potential. The children being given the drugs have been identified by their teachers as "hyperactive" and unmanageable to the point of disrupting regular classroom activity.[32]

> Bettye M. Caldwell . . . has proposed "educationally oriented day care for culturally deprived children between six months and three years of age." The children are returned home each evening to "maintain primary emotional relationships with their own families," but during the day they are removed to "hopefully prevent the deceleration in rate of development which seems to occur in many deprived children around the age of two to three years." [33]

---

[30] Robert J. Havighurst, "Social Backgrounds: Their Impact on Schoolchildren," in Horn, *Reading for the Disadvantaged*, p. 12.

[31] William Labov, "The Non-Standard Vernacular of the Negro Community: Some Practical Suggestions," ED 016 947, p. 10.

[32] Robert M. Maynard, "Children Controlled by Drugs," despatch from Omaha to *The Washington Post*. In *The Austin American*, June 29, 1970, p. 1. Yet they jail the kids for smoking pot.

[33] Labov, "The Logic of Nonstandard English," in Alatis, *Linguistics and the Teaching of Standard English*, pp. 28–29. Labov, who here as usual is much above his fellow biloquialists, is criticizing Bettye M. Caldwell's article "What Is the Optimal Learning Environment for the Young Child?" in the *American Journal of Orthopsychiatry*, 37 (1967), pp. 8–21. *Ortho* is a bit optimistic when the proposal is to disrupt the families of mothers whom Bettye M. Caldwell has judged inadequate.

The Defense Department has been quietly effective in educating
some of the casualties of our present public schools. It is hereby
suggested that they now go into the business of repairing hundreds of thousands of these human casualties with affirmation
rather than apology. Schools for adolescent dropouts or educational
rejects could be set up by the Defense Department adjacent to
camps—but not necessarily as an integral part of the military. If
this is necessary, it should not block the attainment of the goal
of rescuing as many of these young people as possible.[34]

In June the Camden (N.J.) Board of Education hired *Radio Corporation of America* to reorganize its entire school system. According to *Education Summary* (July 17, 1970), the management
contract for the first year of the USOE pilot project requires that
RCA "be responsible for identifying Camden's educational needs;
specifying priorities organizing demonstration projects; training
school personnel for functions they can't perform adequately now;
organizing the system on a cost-effectiveness basis; and arranging
for objective valuation of results." [35]

There is not much doubt that the use of such means will
corrupt whatever end is said to justify them. It is not, for example, a super-abundance of new teachers which now keeps them
from finding jobs, but the government's decision to pay for war
in Viet Nam and not for education. To solve this financial problem, school boards are encouraged to choose education on the
cheap. When they make their bargains with the big corporations,
the corporations get direct control both of education and of whatever money the school boards do spend. The corporations can thus
keep up their profits; teachers are made subservient automatons;
and the country is delivered from the danger that either teachers
or students might occasionally think. Disrupted families, drugged
students, schools run by business or the military—these are the
typical products of Big Brother's machinations.

The role of the biloquialist in our educational skin-flick is

[34] Kenneth B. Clark, quoted by George H. Henry in reviewing Alvin
C. Eurich's *High School 1980* in the *English Journal*, 59 (1970), p. 1165.
Henry's review is a splendid denunciation of manipulators inside and out-
side the NCTE.

[35] Edmund J. Farrell, "Industry and the Schools," NCTE *Council-
Grams*, 31 (Special Issue for November, 1970), pp. 1–3. Farrell takes a
strong stand against the takeover by industry—with the natural consequence
that Robert F. Hogan, Executive Secretary of the Council, warns readers to
"keep in mind that the point of view is Mr. Farrell's, not a reflection of
Council policy or position." When George Henry called it likely "that English will find itself taken over by the USO—Foundation—Big Business—
Pentagon Axis," he also said that the appeasing executives of the Council
complain only mildly of such barbarian invasions, "because by virtue of being high in the Council one is eligible for a place in the Axis" (Henry, *op.
cit.*, pp. 1168–69). But unlike RCA, Henry is not an objective evaluator.

not outstanding: he is not a madam, just a working girl. His commitment, however, to the corrupt values of a corrupt society makes him quite at house with the other manipulators, and his particular manipulations have their special dangers because a standard language can be made a dangerous weapon in class warfare.

Standard English in the United States is a principal means of preserving the existing power structure, for it builds the system of class distinctions into the most inward reaches of each child's humanity: the language whose mastery makes the child human makes him also a member of a social class. Even rebellion demands a kind of allegiance to the class system, because effective rebellion, as the world goes now, requires the use of the standard language, and the rebel is not likely to master the standard language without absorbing some of the prejudice that it embodies. In the United States, the child "knows his place" before he knows he knows it, and the rebellious adult is either coöpted into the ruling class or has to fight to get a hearing. Biloquialism makes capital of this situation.

Big Brother and his flunkies are in control now; there is no doubt of that. But they have not won the last battle as long as resistance is possible, and resistance is possible until Big Brother makes us love him—if he can. If resistance saves nothing else, it saves the manhood of the unbrainwashed resister. The conservative individualist opposes biloquialism just because he does believe in individuality, to which liberty is prerequisite. "Tell the English," a bad poem says, "that man is a spirit." He is; and he does not live by beer alone; and the *radix malorum* is the businessman's morality of "getting ahead," which the biloquialist espouses when he argues that "right now, tomorrow, the youngster needs tools to 'make it' in the larger world." [36]

Both physically and spiritually, *that* "larger world" is unfit for human habitation.

## WHAT TO DO

The biloquialist's favorite counterpunch, when he is backed into a corner, is the question "If not biloquialism, what?" and he pretends, if his critic does not spin out a detailed scheme for curing all the ills of education, that in the absence of such a

36 Right again: John C. Maxwell, *English Journal*, 59 (1970), p. 1159.

scheme doublespeak remains the best available policy for English teachers. The pretense is foolish, like doublespeak itself. Whatever English teachers ought to do, they ought not to follow the biloquialist, and the mere establishment of that fact is a positive contribution. To know what's not good is part of knowing what is.

The cornered biloquialist will often make his question more specific. It's all very well, he will concede, to expose linguistic prejudice as an instrument of repression and to work for social justice, though he himself may not be notably active in either cause; but in the meantime, he asks, what will become of students who don't learn standard English?

The beginning of a sufficient reply is that the advocate of doublespeak must answer the question too, since there are probably more biloquialists than doublespeakers whom they have trained. In the foreseeable future there will always be distinctions in speech between leaders and followers, between workers at different jobs, residents of different areas. And in a healthy society there would be no great harm in that. Millions of people in this country today do not speak standard English, and millions of them, if they are white, have very good incomes. But in job-hunting in America, pigmentation is more important than pronunciation.

There is not, moreover, and there never has been, a serious proposal that standard English should not be taught at all, if for no other reason than because its teaching is inevitable. Most teachers of English speak it (or try to speak it); most books are written in it (somnigraphy being sadly typical); and since every child, if it is possible, should learn to read, schoolchildren will see and hear standard English in the schools as they also see and hear it on TV. Inevitably their own linguistic competence will be affected.

The effect will be best if teachers consciously recognize the frustrations and contradictions which life in a sick world imposes on them. Because our ruling class is unfit to rule, our standard language lacks authority; and because our society has been corrupted by the profit-seeking of technology run wild, an honest teacher cannot exercise his normal function of transmitting to the young the knowledge and values of their elders. In fact, the time may come, and soon come, when an honest teacher can't keep his honesty and keep teaching. At that point, he must make his choice—and take the consequences. So long, however, as he stays in the classroom, he must do his imperfect best while recognizing its imperfection, and must find in that effort itself his escape from alienation.

Specifically, and without pretense:

1. We English teachers must have—and teach—some higher ambition than to "get ahead." We have the whole body of the world's best thought to draw on. The daringly old-fashioned amongst us might even recommend the Ten Commandments.

2. We should do all we can to decentralize power, to demand for ourselves and for other common men some voice in shaping our own lives. Reason enough to say so is the truism that men are not men unless they are free; but if the practical must have practical reasons, we all can see that in education as in everything else, conditions vary so much from state to state, from city to city, from city to country, from neighborhood to neighborhood, that no one policy for the whole nation can possibly work. Decisions about our teaching must *not* be passed down, as they now are, from a tired little mediocre in-group, who in the best of circumstances are so involved in the operation of the professional machinery that they can't see beyond its operation. A useful rule of thumb might be to never trust a "leader in the profession."

3. As politically active citizens, we must do whatever we can to end the social isolation of "substandard speakers," so that differences in speech, if they do not disappear of themselves, will lose their stigmatizing quality.[37]

4. As English teachers we should teach our students (and if necessary, our colleagues) how society uses languages as its most insidious means of control, how we are led to judge others— and ourselves—by criteria which have no real bearing on actual worth. We must stigmatize people who use dialects as stigmatiz-

---

[37] For such suggestions I have been told both that I believe that English teachers can change the world by political action, perhaps by revolution, and at the same time (because I oppose biloquialism) that I advocate "do-nothingness." Though I hope I have more awareness of human tragedy than to believe that the NCTE, or RCA, or even an Educational Laboratory can abolish pain, I would certainly not teach English if I did not believe that to some small extent English teachers indeed can change the world. If I did not believe that English teachers can act politically for good, by parity of reasoning I would not bother to attack the evil politics of doublespeak. On the subject of revolution, I wrote in the essay which has been criticized as perhaps inciting to revolt that "the only revolution we are likely to see is the continued subversion, by the dominant white businessman, of the political and religious principles on which the nation was founded" (*English Journal* 58, p. 1312). I leave it to the objecting and objectionable biloquialist to reconcile the conflicting charges of do-nothingism and political activism, but I do resent the suggestion that I consider English teachers brave enough to start a revolution. I have never entertained such a false and subversive idea in my life.

ing; and if that means that we as correctness-mongers get blasted too, then we deserve it.[38]

5. We should teach ourselves and our white students something about the lives and language of black people. For communication between dialects, receptive control is what matters. In the United States, most black children are already likely to understand most kinds of English that they hear from whites. Presumably white people have the intelligence to learn to understand the blacks. The Center for Applied Linguistics may even be capable of learning that white ignorance is a bigger obstacle to social justice than black English is.

6. In teaching our students to read and write, our aim should be to educate them, to open and enrich their minds, not to make them into usefully interchangeable parts in the materialists' insane machine. We should know and respect our children's language as we demand that they know and respect our own. And we should make no harsh, head-on attempt to *change* their language, to make them speak and write like us. If they value our world and what it offers, then they will take the initiative in change, and we can cautiously help them. But we must stop acting as the watch-dogs of middle-class correctness and start barking at somnigraphy.

7. As teachers and as citizens, we must defend the freedom of inquiry and the freedom of expression. Neither is absolute, and it is often hard to strike a balance between the demands of the society that pays us and the intellectual duties of our calling. It is clear, however, that subservience to government and indifference to social need will alike corrupt inquirer and inquiry and thus endanger the freedoms that no one else will cherish if we don't. When we allow our choice of studies to be governed by government subsidy, we have committed ourselves to the ends of the subsidizers. When pure curiosity guides us, we tacitly assert that the satisfaction of curiosity is more important than any other purpose that our research might serve. Along both roads we are likely to meet the amoral intellectual, whether for hire or

---

[38] This suggestion has nothing to do with the self-seeking proposal by foolish linguists that the English language should be made the center of the English curriculum. I would indeed teach prospective teachers of English in the schools a good deal more about their language than they are usually taught now; but only a biloquialist would believe—or pretend to believe— that to suggest a college curriculum in English for prospective English teachers is to suggest the same curriculum for every schoolchild. A "language-centered curriculum" for the schools would be a disaster.

self-employed. The prime contention of this indirect review is that the biloquialist, by his acquiescence in the abuse of standard English as a weapon, forfeits some part of the respect which otherwise would be inspired by achievements which are sometimes brilliant, like Labov's. For despite the politican's scholar who says that scholarship is politicized when scholars question his privy politics, scholars *are* teachers, and scholar-teachers citizens.

## Language Variation and Teaching

The articles in Part 2 provide evidence against four widely held beliefs about language variation.

First: the belief that there is one "pure" English language, and that all variation from that way of speaking is incorrect or even pathological, has made language variation a source of concern to many parents, teachers, and school administrators. No one conspired to promote this belief; it has been part of our culture for hundreds of years, as Herndon's article in Part 3 suggests.

A second belief about language variation, more sophisticated than the first one, recognizes that every language is made up of dialects. But this view assumes that there is one "standard" dialect that is everywhere the same. Occasionally this view goes further, assuming that this "standard" dialect contrasts only with "nonstandard dialect"—as if only these two ways of speaking existed.

A third misunderstanding about language variation can arise from some of the material written recently about "Black English." This writing has sometimes been interpreted as offering to its readers only two choices: one, the belief that there is no such thing as a separate black dialect of English, or two, the belief that such a dialect not only exists but is largely separate from other dialects of English.

Finally, the "verbal deprivation" theory inspired by Basil Bernstein's [1] writings on "restricted codes" has become a source

---

[1] Bernstein has repudiated the "verbal deprivation" theory, but his writings from 1958 to 1970 do provide the basis for many of its claims about language and cognition, as my article in this section points out.

of misunderstanding about language variation. Its acceptance by educators such as Bereiter and Engelmann (1966) has led to widespread belief that children with non-middle-class language systems are cognitively handicapped.

In reply to these four beliefs, we can draw from the articles in Part 2 four suggestions with interesting and important implications for the content of a language program and for understanding between teachers and their students. Articles elsewhere in this book reinforce some of the evidence Part 2 provides for these suggestions.

**SUGGESTION I:** There is no such thing as one unvarying English language; language variation is not only normal but inevitable.

*Central Article:* William Labov, "The Reflections of Social Processes in Linguistic Structures": Labov finds four major kinds of language variation—loss of /r/ before consonants is a *regional* language feature of New York City, and the frequency of this loss is a *social* language feature there; there are terms such as "mother-wit" whose presence or absence is an *ethnic* language feature in the city; and *stylistic* variation takes place within these regional, social, and ethnic dialects.

*Supporting Evidence in Other Articles:*

Shuy, Williamson: regional dialects—Shuy finds northern, midland, and southern regional dialects in American English; Williamson points out differences between northern and southern white dialects, as part of her argument on another point.

Saville, Dale, Abrahams: ethnic dialects [2]—Saville predicts the influence Spanish and French as first languages will have on the English dialect of children in these ethnic groups; Dale describes phonological and syntactic features in a major black dialect of English; Abrahams finds some sociolinguistic features common to many black speakers.

Joos: stylistic variation—finds language features (such as vocabulary terms and pronunciations) that can be grouped into five styles: frozen, formal, consultative, casual, and intimate.

[2] This variation is often dealt with as part of "social dialects," but I am making a distinction between "social dialects" and "ethnic dialects"; see the Introduction to Part 2.

Fries, Rigg: temporal variation—language continually changes as time passes; this *temporal* variation is caused by distance in time rather than by distance in geographic space or social space.

## Implications for Teaching

AGE OF STUDENTS. A great deal of interesting work on language variation can be done in middle-school, junior-high-school, and high-school classrooms; most of the following suggestions are for those ages. Opinions vary about the suitability of this study for children in elementary schools. Troike, in Part 1, mentions young children who show awareness of language variation. He suggests that bidialectalism (if it is desired) should be taught in elementary school because the brain undergoes changes making language-learning more difficult as the child grows older (cf. Penfield, Part 1). However, young children who have no difficulty in absorbing language via natural exposure may have difficulty studying it in the abstract; and young children may show a tendency to ridicule any language difference pointed out to them, defeating the major purpose of bidialectalism. Problems with teaching bidialectalism will be discussed further in relation to Suggestion II.

STUDYING REGIONAL, SOCIAL, AND ETHNIC DIALECTS. Dialects vary in three kinds of language characteristics: phonology, syntax (including semantics), and sociolinguistic traits. The quickest way to discover the language characteristics of your own dialect is to move out of your usual geographic area, social area, or ethnic group and listen to differences between your speech and the speech around you in the new environment. For Americans, perhaps the best teacher of this sort is a trip to England.

In order to study regional dialects, students who grew up in the community can listen to those who have moved into the community for language differences, and those who have moved in can describe the differences they noticed when they arrived. Again, these activities must be presented carefully in order to avoid ridicule of anyone's dialect. It may be safest to concentrate on dialects entirely different from those of the students; records and tapes with British speakers singing or reading poetry and plays are easy to find. For instance, a great deal of rock music has been recorded by British musicians. The National Council of Teachers of English has a tape recording of regional dialects in the United States, called "Americans Speaking"; this is an inexpensive and valuable resource. Some of John Kennedy's speeches can be found on recordings. Or students might create their own tapes by sending to a school elsewhere in the country tapes of themselves reading a passage such as the one used in "Americans Speaking," together with blank tapes and copies of the passage to be recorded and returned. Socioeconomic information about the speakers could also be traded, but this can be a sensitive topic and must be handled delicately.

Older students can study dialects in literature. *Huckleberry Finn* is a classic example: Huck's speech shows features of a social dialect—Huck's education is limited, and his father's occupation and income are very low on the social scale (to put it mildly). Jim's speech shows features of an ethnic dialect—a Negro dialect used in the South during the time being portrayed in *Huckleberry Finn*. And all the characters in the book show features of a regional dialect (southern American English) used then.

But the study of dialect in literature can run into two problems. Students may feel condescending toward the dialects they read, and they may accept a stereotyped description of either the dialect or its user. Both of these problems may be dealt with by beginning with literature that includes ridicule or stereotyping of the students' own language behavior. British authors sometimes show condescension toward American dialects, condescension that not infrequently borders on ridicule; I remember one story in which a British husband and wife shared a joke—they used common American pronunciations such as "grosheries" for "groceries" and "noo" for "new." Another story mentioned that some character's accent had "betrayed" the fact that he was American; and yet another showed a highly educated, well-to-do American as growling, "Say, mister!" at intervals throughout his conversation with an aristocratic Briton.

Students who read derisive accounts of American dialects should be encouraged to resist these characterizations. They should be encouraged to feel language pride based on the knowledge that American English is not inferior to British English—it is merely different. Perhaps these same students can then learn to treat other American dialects as having no inherent superiority or inferiority to their own. And reading stereotyped descriptions of their own language may bring home the point that stereotypes often are highly inaccurate.

After gaining some perspective on dialects in literature, high-school students might be interested in studying the way Dashiell Hammett uses social dialects to characterize cops and crooks in novels such as *The Maltese Falcon* (of Humphrey Bogart fame) and *The Thin Man*. Raymond Chandler makes similar use of dialect differences in *The Long Goodbye*.[3] Other literature using dialects is not difficult to find.

We have been discussing dialects in general, and how they may be studied. But one kind of dialect—an ethnic dialect—requires some special discussion. It is true that the dialects of different ethnic groups vary in syntax and phonology, just as regional and social dialects do. However, ethnic dialects differ from one another in a third dimension—sociolinguistic rules—to a greater extent than do regional and social dialects.

Before discussing this third kind of variation, we should establish a definition of "ethnic group"; this term refers to groups of people who share basic cultural traits, not to groups of people who belong to the same racial group. In the United States there are many ethnic groups; this country is multicultural. Of course, there is a great deal of overlap among the cultural views and rules of these ethnic groups, just as there is a great deal of overlap in the linguistic rules of differing American dialects; but there are also many dissimilarities among American cultural groups. These dissimilarities are often overlooked. The same people who would never fail to look for and respect cultural differences when visiting another country will fail even to look for cultural differences between themselves and members of other ethnic groups within America.

Of course, none of us wants to dehumanize another person by setting him completely apart from us or by seeing him as primarily part of an ethnic group rather than as an individual. But to ignore—or even deny—ethnic group differences has some unfortunate effects. In the first place, it may be as dehumanizing to insist that another group is identical to your own as it is to insist that that group is entirely different from your own. In both cases the implication is that the only proper and desirable way of living is that of your own group; anything different would be unacceptable.

Secondly, ignorance of differences can lead to misinterpretations of cultural signals. Abrahams points out the misreading of some black children's eye-averting as a sign of respect toward teachers; a white teacher may interpret this behavior as evi-

[3] Midwestern students who believe their speech to be the national "newscaster standard" will be surprised to find that "anyways," standard to them, is attributed to some very unpleasant characters in this detective literature.

dence of shame or guilt. Another example: a nine-year-old white boy was playing with a black friend of the same age. The black child said, "Your momma is fat!" "She is not!" replied the white child. "Okay, then she's thi-is skinny!" was the reply, said while holding up palms that almost touch. At this point the angry white child threw his arms around his friend and fell forward on top of him, starting a fight that ended in tears. Abrahams would suggest that one child was playing "the dozens," a game of ritual insults that is not supposed to provoke physical fighting; but the other child had no such language game in his culture, and responded according to his understanding that insults must be avenged.

Literature can give a high-school class some information on sociolinguistic differences between cultural groups. For instance, Maya Angelou's autobiography, *I Know Why the Caged Bird Sings,* suggests to me that the rules for responding to questions may differ between some white and black subcultures:

> We have a saying among Black Americans which describes Momma's caution. "If you ask a Negro where he's been, he'll tell you where he's going." . . . If an unaware person is told a part of the truth (it is imperative that the answer embody truth), he is satisfied that his query has been answered. If an aware person . . . is given an answer which is truthful but bears only slightly if at all on the question, he knows that the information he seeks is of a private nature and will not be handed to him willingly. Thus direct denial, lying and the revelation of personal affairs are avoided.[4]

Of course, sociolinguistic roles can be studied directly by interviewing people of varying subcultures, just as syntax and phonology are studied. The class might make up a brief questionnaire asking whether informants had noticed ethnic differences in greeting, questioning, or bargaining, and asking for examples. Data gathered with this questionnaire would help the class narrow its focus to only one of these language events. Eventually the class could formulate the differences it has found as a beginning ethnography of speaking in contrasting subcultures. For instance, two graduate students distributed to black informants questionnaires asking about greeting behavior among whites. The responses suggested that whites' greeting styles seem cold to these black speakers; whites often "fail to acknowledge you as a

---

[4] Maya Angelou, *I Know Why the Caged Bird Sings* (New York: Bantam Books, 1971), pp. 164–165. © 1970. Reprinted by permission of Random House, Inc.

person" in situations where other blacks would offer a warm greeting.[5] There is a common sociolinguistic rule among whites that prohibits direct greeting of people who have not yet been introduced to the speaker by a third person: it may be that the black informants of this study have a differing cultural rule for offering greetings and beginning conversations. One teacher [6] in a mostly black Los Angeles junior high school told of constant conflict between students and white staff over the amount of noise students could make during class. The faculty in general believed that no learning could take place unless the noise level was quite low, and teachers spent much of their time and energy trying to lower the noise level. Abrahams might suggest that this noise level was high because of the high value many blacks place on verbal abilities. If teachers could work with this value rather than against it, they might be able to lead students toward valuing several kinds of verbal abilities—including persuasive writing as well as persuasive speaking, for example.

STUDYING STYLES. As Joos suggests, styles and style-shifting in response to social expectations seem to be a normal part of every community. In fact, style-shifting is important in defining a *speech community;* according to Labov, a *speech community* is a group of people who show by their style shifts that they share some beliefs about the appropriate language style for certain situations, even though their actual speech behavior may differ in many ways.

Students of many ages can listen to their parents, to television and radio, and to each other in order to find out what sort of speech community they live in, in terms of styles. For students of junior-high and older ages, gathering data the way Labov did may be an excellent group project. Cassette tape recorders are widely available. After individually gathering some examples of style variation, the class can choose one or two style markers (like preconsonantal /r/ in the New York study). Then they construct (1) a brief questionnaire that asks for age, sex, ethnic group, education and occupation, and places lived; and (2) a brief paragraph that contains the style marker(s) chosen. Groups of students can participate in interviewing teachers from other classes, neighbors, and so on. In each interview, the person is

---

[5] Dayna Reynolds found this evaluation on the part of black students at Lansing Community College, Lansing, Michigan (unpublished ms., Michigan State University, 1975).

[6] James Herndon, *The Way It Spozed to Be* (New York: Simon & Schuster, 1968).

first asked whether he has ever been in great danger or near death, then asked (orally) the questions on the questionnaire, and then asked to read the paragraph. This process should uncover casual, careful, and formal oral styles, respectively. Comparing these styles with the social information gathered with questionnaires will yield a picture of the local speech community; local newspapers might be interested in publishing this sketch of language habits.

One final note about this project: people being interviewed should be approached tactfully about some possibly sensitive aspects of participating. Though Labov had statistics on income of his informants, students may decide not to request that sort of personal information from their subjects. Having informants read a list of word pairs should also be carefully considered before it is included in the project, since an informant may feel at that point that the structure of the interview has been an attempt to catch him using nonprestigious speech habits. In fact, the entire process of having your language studied can be felt as a dehumanizing procedure, and gathering data does not justify putting informants through that sort of experience. Problems like this can be discussed extensively by students (perhaps debated or written about). One possible solution is a carefully worded initial request for the informant's participation, explaining the purpose of the survey truthfully but without going into enough detail to radically affect informants' behavior.

A less rigorous method of studying styles might be more suitable for an introduction to the topic. Older students can look for style changes on local news reports, and then play the roles they've seen—the city councilman being interviewed, the reporter who did the interviewing. City officials are prone to use formal markers in both vocabulary and phonology. In vocabulary, look for "involved in," "in terms of," "developing," "aspects of," "activity," "facility," and "situation": "In terms of our situation with regard to the other school systems in the state, we are involved in developing a program that will provide three new facilities for physical education activity." In phonology, listen for heavy stress on prepositions and on forms of the verb "to be": "The city council *is* interested *in* developing a program *to* meet the needs *of* our citizens." Another possibility is use of cassette recorders in man-in-the-street interviews, with students playing the role of reporters for a class newspaper; passersby are asked for their opinions on weighty subjects. But this sort of project would call for careful handling—the difference between this (imaginary) class newspaper and any real school newspaper should be stressed.

The number and type of styles a person can use is called one's *linguistic repertoire*. Since most children can already switch styles to some extent by the time they are 8 or 9 (see Troike's article in Part 1), students of a wide age range can investigate the styles in their own communities and repertoires. Of course, the approach will have to vary with the students' age and with the makeup of the community. One possible way of introducing a conscious awareness of styles to young students is role-playing. At age seven, my daughter and her friends all demonstrated ability to use "teacher" styles as opposed to "student" styles, including different gestures, intonation, and loudness. "Teachers" gave commands instead of making requests, and "students" did the opposite; "teachers" used such markers of a formal style as "you will not" instead of "you won't." But it may be that young students will show ability to play these roles, making many style switches, without being able to view these changes in the abstract —without, that is, being able to name what they are doing, or otherwise consider style-switching apart from the situations in which they are making the switches. Older students, of course, will be able to do this. They might enjoy taking the roles of governor, mayor, city councilor, or police chief as they are interviewed by student "reporters."

**SUGGESTION II:** There is no one, unvarying "standard" dialect of American English.[7]

*Central article:* Raven McDavid, "Language and Prestige: 'Standard English.'" McDavid points out the variation that has taken place in "standard" language as time has passed, and he brings up the regional variation in "Standard English" in America.

*Supporting Evidence in Other Articles:*

Shuy: "Standard" dialects vary from one geographic region to another.

Joos: There is usually variation in styles within one person's dialect, because no one style of speech is appropriate to all of the many social situations people take part in during daily life.

[7] It should be made very clear that the articles I cite here as evidence for my "Suggestion II" were not necessarily written with the intent of making exactly the point I am making here.

Rigg (Part 3) : Four versions of the same biblical text, written at four stages in the history of English, illustrate the constant, inevitable change that language undergoes as time passes (this could be called *temporal variation*).

## Implications for Teaching

"STANDARD ENGLISH." This term is often used without any definition, giving rise to the impression that there is general agreement as to its meaning; and it is often used as though "Standard English" were a completely separate language from other, "nonstandard" dialects.

To take up the last point first, we can refer to Figure 1 and Figure 2 in the Introduction to Part 2; dialects are *not* entirely separate systems—they are overlapping language systems, having in common a huge core of language features (such as words, pronunciations, sentence structures). Speakers of two dialects of English generally can understand one another quite well, given some exposure time and an attitude favorable toward other speakers' social groups. What really is at issue in many discussions about "standard" and "nonstandard" language is a relatively brief list of "nonstandard" language features.

General agreement on the contents of this list is lacking. In phonology, the list differs from region to region. In syntax, there is some national consensus as to "nonstandard" features; "ain't," negative concord (the "double negative"), and some verb forms (*He don't*) are examples. But even this limited consensus is subject to change; for instance, each of the three "nonstandard" features just mentioned has been perfectly standard in the past—in fact, "He don't" and "ain't" were the high-prestige forms in England until the early 1900s. Society changes, and with it language sanctions change also. Even when some language feature is stigmatized as "nonstandard," it may be used without being noticed if the speaker who uses it has an admired social identity; the social identity seems to affect the listeners' expectations, and the listeners then hear what they expect to hear rather than what was actually said.[8]

A final point about "Standard English": as Joos makes clear, language that is appropriate for one situation can be inappropriate for another. If we use "standard" to mean "accepted as appropriate," what is standard among one group of people will not

---

[8] I am indebted to David DeCamp for this suggestion (personal communication, University of Texas, 1973).

always be standard among another group. Language appropriate for one topic will not be appropriate for another. This sort of variation can also be called stylistic variation; "Standard English," then, will vary even within one geographic region and at one time in history.

Even if agreement has been reached as to the "standard" language features that are valued in one area and the formal situations in which they are to be used, two problems still face the teacher: distinguishing form from content, and confronting the special problems associated with "bidialectalism" programs that attempt to teach a second dialect.

DISTINGUISHING FORM FROM CONTENT. As Labov has pointed out, a middle-class vocabulary does not necessarily signal thought or reasoning superior to that indicated by a less prestigious set of words:

> All too often, standard English is represented by a style that is simultaneously overparticular and vague. The accumulating flow of words buries rather than strikes the target. It is this verbosity which is most easily taught and learned, so that words take the place of thoughts, and nothing can be found behind them. [1970, p. 171.]

Teachers at all levels should encourage students to think about what is behind the surface of a sentence; for instance, how should we evaluate the statement of an air force officer being interviewed about bombing—"It's not *bombing*, it's *air support*"? Teachers themselves need to look for originality and strength in writing and speaking before looking for the vocabulary and mechanics of "Standard English." Compare these two sentences:

(1) I am one individual who has had an opportunity to thoroughly enjoy the wonder of an airplane landing.

(2) I used to live near an airport, and every time I saw a plane make a three-point landing, I got a million goosebumps on my left neck.

The first sentence communicates little of the writer's experience; the second—written by a nine-year-old child—leaves the reader with a visual and tactile image strong enough to be remembered hours later.

As teachers in a time of revision of school curricula, textbook material, and even social attitudes, we often look for something safe to teach students—something widely agreed upon. The mechanics of writing "Standard English" seem to offer that safety: sentences must begin with a capital letter, punctuation must be used correctly, and, most of all, words must not be misspelled. Certainly these mechanics have a place in our schools; "King Henry walked and talked eloquently ten minutes after his head was cut off" needs the punctuation that makes it "King Henry walked and talked eloquently; ten minutes after, his head was cut off." But do these mechanics deserve the proportion of time they often receive? How important are they? The "King Henry" example just mentioned is highly artificial; how often is punctuation really important to communication?

After they have watched and thought about the way language is used in their community, students can begin to form their own, class-designed set of standards for various types of writing and speaking. It is important to stay honest in helping students design these standards. Students of all ages (including those of us who teach) have been affected by old-style handbooks that give only two choices of language use—acceptable and unacceptable. Really old handbooks name these "correct" and "incorrect" English (or "good grammar" and "bad grammar"), and newer-old handbooks call them "Standard English" and "nonstandard dialect," linking the two with school and home, respectively. Students can arrive at a much more useful set of standards than this two-part set by looking at newspapers, listening to television, observing the way adults use language in differing situations, and finally choosing styles appropriate to several types of occasions. Judy's article in Part 1 is relevant to this search.

Two examples of artificially inflexible language standards are spelling requirements and conventions imported from Latin. Spelling tests are given throughout our school system, from the first grade on up. Certainly no one would suggest that an entire page of misspelled words should be ignored. But how serious are a few misspellings? My college students—many of them destined to become executives and lawyers—misspell words on every test and every paper assigned to them. How much misspelling is dangerous to your health?

Another type of convention, frequently introduced during the last years of high school, includes several arbitrary taboos that go back to the influence of Latin upon early English grammarians; this influence on our written language can be best understood after reading Herndon's article in Part 3. These grammarians tried to make English similar to Latin. For instance, in English the infinitive (unmarked form) of a verb is usually given as two words, e.g., "to eat." But in Latin and its descendants, the infinitive is one word; in French, "manger" is the infinitive corresponding to the English "to eat." Naturally, a one-word infinitive like "manger" is never torn apart in order to allow the insertion of an adverb within it. Therefore, according to the Split Infinitive Taboo, the English infinitive should never be "split" by an adverb between "to" and the verb form: "totally to abolish" is correct, "to totally abolish" is incorrect. Often writers can avoid the issue by using 'to abolish totally," but sometimes the only word order that sounds like English is the one with an adverb between "to" and the verb. In any case, why must our schools perpetuate a completely groundless "rule"? These arbitrary conventions should be reassessed.

BIDIALECTALISM. One kind of educational program currently being proposed attempts to teach "Standard English" (as defined in the geographic area involved) to speakers whose dialect contains nonstandard features. Gaining functional control over two dialects is called "bidialectalism"; Sledd's article attacks programs that attempt to enforce a goal of bidialectalism for students whose dialects include nonstandard features.

Should students be taught how to change their speech when it does not conform to the "standard" pattern of the community? Arguments on this point are usually of two kinds, ethical and pragmatic. The pragmatic argument for bidialectalism says that a student should be able to switch into a formal or semiformal style in finding and keeping a good job. The pragmatic argument against bidialectalism suggests that teaching a second dialect is very difficult (perhaps impossible—see Penfield, Part 1) and that nonstandard language features are not the major source of discrimination anyway—the major source of discrimination is prejudice against the social or ethnic group of the job applicant.

The ethical or moral argument for bidialectalism is that schools have a responsibility to equip a student for success in society; they have wronged the student if they fail to teach the basic tools for doing this. The ethical argument against bidialectalism is that it may damage the student's self-concept by implying that his language is inferior; like ragged, faded old clothes, it is appropriate for home use but not for school or office. This argument rests on the fact that a person's language is used to represent his or her self to the world, and criticism of language is usually felt as criticism of the self.

The question of whether children are being forced to replace one dialect with another while in school, as opposed to receiving instruction in the second dialect but having the option of continuing to use their native dialect, is important in evaluating "bidialectalism" programs. It seems to me that Sledd, in Part 2, clearly is directing his argument against the policy of *forcing* use of a "standard" dialect. Troike, in Part 1, suggests that children should have a choice in this matter.

Penfield's article on limitations of language acquisition and Troike's article on receptive bidialectalism, in Part 1, make two more important points about this question: first, there are limitations on our ability to switch dialects; and second, you do not have to be able to produce a dialect in order to understand it. In order to find the limits of reasonable requests for learning second dialects, teachers should ask all dialect groups in the classroom to learn features of a second dialect. Students will discover their receptive abilities to understand a second dialect, and the problems of trying to produce it. However, it cannot be overemphasized that care must be taken to avoid situations that could end in ridicule of anyone's dialect.

Lambert's article here in Part 2 suggests that a speaker does best in two languages when he can identify with both of the groups speaking these languages; probably that condition is true of speakers learning new dialect features as well. One implication of this point may be that asking a speaker to completely stop using his native dialect except at home and a few other occasions —e.g., on the playground—is felt as a request that the speaker renounce his identification with his entire background, including family, friends, and ethnic identification. If this is the case, some of our bidialectalism programs may be asking far too much of their students. Perhaps teaching by exposure, as suggested in the summary article to Part 1, would avoid this pitfall.

**SUGGESTION III:** "Black English," as defined by Dale in this section, is neither an entirely separate language nor a dialect identical to that of white speakers.

*Central Article:* Philip Dale, "Dialect Differences and Black English"; Dale lists the phonological and syntactic features of this major black dialect, features that differ from many white dialects.

*Supporting Evidence in Other Articles:*
Abrahams: sociolinguistic differences—in the use of language and in speakers' attitudes toward language—exist

between the black speakers and white speakers described by Abrahams.

Williamson: whites in the South often use several syntactic features that in the North are used only by blacks.

Baratz; Goodman and Buck (Part 4) : Baratz gives evidence of differences among various black and white dialects; Goodman and Buck present research evidence that the differences between most black and white dialects are not great enough to hinder reading comprehension.

## Implications for Teaching

DOES "BLACK ENGLISH" EXIST? Dale describes a dialect often called "Black English," a dialect having phonological and syntactic differences from most northern white dialects. Abrahams then describes sociolinguistic differences between many black and white speakers. Williamson, however, brings up the fact that some of the syntactic rules of "Black English" are also used by many white speakers in the South.

Does Williamson's article prove, then, that "Black English" does not exist? There are several reasons for suggesting that it does not, although it does provide some very important data on the overlap between white and black dialects in the South and on the question of whether or not reading materials for black children should be written in a black dialect.

In the first place, regardless of similarities between black and white dialects in the South, the salient fact for educators in the North is that differences do exist there. In the North, then, we can say that the dialect described by Dale does exist. There Black English is a major black dialect, used where large groups of black speakers live together in an ethnic community. Black speakers who grow up outside such communities, of course, may have a dialect that shows little or no influence from Black English. But those people who do stay in the community will continue to learn the dialect spoken around them, in the same language-learning process that takes place all over the world (see Slobin and Gough, Part 1).

Secondly, even in the South there may be some differences between dialects of black and white speakers, differences not covered by Williamson's article. For instance, Williamson did not deal with phonological differences at all. Furthermore, some of the language features now shared by black and white speakers in the South may originally have been characteristics of black speech—not rooted in any white dialect.

Another important point is that made by Labov in relation to social dialects in New York City: differences between dialects can be a matter of frequency of use of a language feature, not the absolute presence or absence of the feature. Even if whites and blacks in the South do share language rules, one group may use a certain rule far more often than does the other group. And finally, a group of speakers may be thought to have the option of viewing their form of speech as a separate language. Some languages in other parts of the world are divided by political or national affiliations; though two slightly different languages would technically be regarded as dialects of the same language, their speakers choose to regard them as separate because the speakers feel themselves to belong to differing political or social identities.

In any case, Black English—like all other dialects of English—is a fully systematic, legitimate language system in its own right. The fact that it overlaps with other English dialects is irrelevant to that basic truth.

Williamson's article does, however, raise some questions for educators. For instance, some educators have suggested that the child who speaks Black English should learn to read a text written in that dialect. If, as Williamson suggests, it turns out that some southern whites share many important language features with speakers of Black English, then these speakers might also be considered candidates for special texts. If, however, an examination of school achievement records discloses that these southern whites show no significant problems in learning to read—in contrast to the reading problems often attributed to black children—perhaps the search for a cause of these problems should be directed somewhere other than toward language differences. Abrahams suggests, here in Part 2, that sociolinguistic differences may contribute to problems like these and that teachers can not only overcome these differences but actually use the differences to their advantage in teaching.

Speakers of Black English are very often considered as possibly needing to learn "standard" English. Problems with this approach have just been discussed, under Suggestion 2.

DESCRIBING BLACK ENGLISH. It is important to look at the details of claims made about Black English and other dialects having some "nonstandard" features. Frequently the differing characteristics of the two dialects are somewhat exaggerated.

For instance, two columns of sentences are often contrasted, one supposedly representing "Standard English" and one the "nonstandard" dialect being discussed: the "Standard English" column will have a sentence containing uncontracted auxiliary verbs such as "will not" where the "nonstandard" sentence has "won't"; and the "Standard English" sentence will have "going to" where the "nonstandard" sentence has "gonna." The fact is, of course, that virtually all speakers of American English use "won't" and "gonna."

It is usually helpful to separate the traits attributed to any dialect into at least three categories: phonological differences, syntactic differences, and differences that might belong to either of the first two categories—such as omission of the "s" in "He's leaving," which might occur because of a syntactic difference or because of a phonological rule that deletes [s] at the end of a word. Dale discusses this particular instance of dialect difference between Black English and most white dialects, showing that it is probably a phonological difference. Since phonological differences are not as likely to affect meaning as are syntactic differences, they are usually considered relatively unimportant. Dale suggests that phonological differences can add up to produce mutual unintelligibility between Black English and many white dialects. However, a listener's receptive language abilities are usually able to overcome even large numbers of phonological differences, given time and a favorable attitude toward the speaker. On the other hand—as Penfield's work in Part 1 suggests—it may be extremely difficult for a speaker to change the language he produces, after age 12 or 13. Perhaps, then, the most successful approach a teacher can take to dialect differences will be one that develops the receptive abilities of all the students involved.

**SUGGESTION IV:** Language and cognition are not related in the simple, direct way recent "verbal deprivation" theorists have suggested; neither bilingualism nor use of a nonprestige dialect appears to handicap a child cognitively.

*Central Article:* Johnson, "The Research Non-Basis for 'Restricted Codes'": Bernstein's "restricted code" hypothesis, the inspiration of much of "verbal deprivation" theory, was based on invalid assumptions and unacceptable research methods.

*Supporting Evidence in Other Articles:*

Lenneberg: There is no direct connection between language and general intelligence as measured with IQ tests.

Lambert: Students who are fully bilingual, with a positive attitude toward both of the speech communities they participate in, achieve at least as well in school as do monolingual students.

The relationship between language and cognition is not yet well understood. However, claims have been made about this relationship, and these claims have affected educational programs throughout the United States; the question is, do we have evidence to support these claims?

It appears that some very far-reaching claims have been made on the basis of some very short-reaching evidence. That, at least, is the conclusion of my own article about Basil Bernstein's "restricted code" hypothesis, which has inspired many of the "verbal deprivation" theories widely accepted during the 1960s. Of course, Bernstein and some of his followers have, during the last few years, modified their claims about cognition to some extent; but Bernstein has not repudiated his earlier, influential suggestions, and these suggestions have caused teachers to expect linguistic "backwardness" in children speaking a dialect with nonstandard features. Gumperz and Hernández-Chavez illustrate vividly the result of such expectations. Teachers should expect professional literature to continue accepting the "verbal deprivation" theory for several years more, since it takes time for counterarguments to diffuse throughout the educational system. They should resist characterizations of children as being "verbally deprived," remembering the evidence from Part 1 that all children acquire language in the same way and that linguistic structure is present at all times in children's language. Teachers can conclude from the articles in Part 2 that variation in language is normal and inevitable, not a sign of perceptual difficulty. And Lenneberg, here in Part 2, points out that language is largely independent of intelligence. In regard to both perception and intelligence, then, it would be a mistake to accept current suggestions that language differences represent cognitive differences.

Describing and testing cognitive processes—if it is finally achieved—will surely be a complex process, not a simple matter of testing vocabulary, or counting speech pauses, or counting pronouns, as Bernstein did. Other examples of simplistic "tests" of cognitive abilities are easy to find in professional literature.

Teachers can and should approach this literature with a great deal of suspicion. In the past we have been far too prone to accept the results of any test without considering its exact nature. Perhaps the most dramatic evidence of our society's thoughtless trust in tests is given by Link's report on thousands of school-children who have been placed in classes for the retarded because their scores on an IQ test were low—an IQ test given in English, although the children were native speakers of Spanish.

## REFERENCES

ANGELOU, MAYA. *I Know Why the Caged Bird Sings.* New York: Bantam Books, 1971.

BEREITER, CARL, and SIEGFRIED ENGELMANN. *Teaching Disadvantaged Children in the Preschool.* Englewood Cliffs: N.J.: Prentice-Hall, 1966.

LABOV, WILLIAM. "The Logic of Nonstandard English," in *Language and Poverty,* ed. Frederick Williams. Chicago: Markham Publishing Co., 1970.

# 3
# MODERN GRAMMARS

## Introduction

### "GRAMMAR" AND "GRAMMATICAL"

*Grammar* in *modern grammars* means "description of a language." *Grammar* also means, in this book, the system of language rules that a speaker uses to create and understand sentences; when linguists use the terms *ungrammatical* and *grammatical,* they are talking about violations of or conformity with these internalized rules. In Part 3, Fromkin and Rodman give examples of ungrammatical and grammatical utterances. Sentences that are ungrammatical, in the linguist's sense, are uncommon in our speech and are usually noticed. Apparently Tank McNamara (in the cartoon on the next page) has occasionally announced to his news audience that he intends to present "norts spews"; this was an ungrammatical phrase, using the wrong phonetic form for the words "sports news." Every English-speaker who heard Tank laughed or otherwise noted his mistake, because each of them knew the language rules of English. These are the rules linguists try to write, for both the sound system and the syntax of a language.

If you have read Part 1, you have already seen attempts

274

# TANK M<sup>C</sup>NAMARA

by Jeff Millar & Bill Hinds

© Universal Press Syndicate

to write language rules; McNeill and Bloom wrote rules for creating basic sentence structures (phrase structure rules), and Klima and Bellugi wrote rules for forming questions and negatives. And if you have read Part 2, you have seen differences between dialects described as differences in language rules. Dale, for instance, goes into detail about the phonological rules of Black English; Fromkin and Rodman, here in Part 3, give more description of phonological rules in English.

## CHANGE IN LANGUAGE

Before going into the details of modern descriptions of language rules, we should look briefly at the important fact of change in these rules. As Fries points out, change in language must be recognized as natural and inevitable. It is a kind of language variation (like regional and social dialects), and it too can be described with modern grammars. Rigg gives us four versions of the same Bible text: Old English, Middle English, Early Modern English, and Modern English. These illustrate the facts of linguistic change in English. Sounds have changed, spellings have changed; so has sentence structure and so has vocabulary.

Herndon then traces our attitudes toward language and our attempts to describe it, from the Greeks to the structural linguists.

## PRESCRIPTIVE AND DESCRIPTIVE GRAMMARS

### Prescriptive Grammars

*Prescriptive* grammars—beginning with the Greeks—have prescribed the form languages "ought" to take. When I say "language," I am thinking of linguistic rules, not of *rhetorical style* or *literary style* (as mentioned in the Introduction to Part 2). Rhetorical style certainly ought to be clear and effective, and literary style ought to be appropriate and aesthetically pleasing.

Prescriptive rules are called *usage rules*. They assert that certain language forms are wrong, such as *ain't* in speech and the "split infinitive" in writing. These assertions are simply social taboos, without any solid rationalization; the "split infinitive" and the insistence that prepositions should not appear at the end of sentences both come from the efforts of early English grammarians to make English more like Latin, which they regarded as a prestigious language. In Latin, infinitives are one word and therefore cannot be split. The functions that prepositions have in English are in Latin fulfilled by inflections affixed to word stems; since these inflections cannot appear alone, prepositions should not appear alone at the end of an English phrase or sentence. According to this prescriptive rule, "the house I went to" is incorrect and should be revised into "the house to which I went." An American magazine editor's attempt to use this rule in changing some of Winston Churchill's preposition use once prompted Churchill to remark, "This is the sort of English up with which I will not put."

### Descriptive Grammars

Today there are two major kinds of descriptive grammars, *structural* and *generative* grammars. Generative grammars are the more widely used, and the best known of these is transformational-generative grammar, often called simply *transformational grammar*.

As Herndon explains, structural grammars were dominant in the United States during the 1940s and 1950s. They stressed a scientific approach to language rather than an emotional, prescriptive one. In their attempt to take a scientific view of language, they gave special attention to aspects of language that could be observed; the sound systems of languages are more easily observed than are their systems of meaning, so in structural linguistics phonology—the study of sound systems—received more attention than did semantics. Laird, in Part 3, illustrates this approach; he attempts to define a sentence almost entirely in terms of sounds.

Structural grammarians are often accused of completely neglecting the role of meaning in language; this accusation is not accurate. In Part 3, Fries points out (in "Lexical and Structural Meaning") that structural linguists were interested in a particular kind of meaning—structural meaning.

By contrast, the transformational-generative approach presented by Fromkin and Rodman and by Liles considers all the underlying meaning of a sentence appropriate for description by linguists. The structural approach prefers to avoid dealing with certain kinds of meaning, but the transformational approach focuses directly on meaning of many kinds.

Another major contrast between the two approaches is that between what might be called a *process grammar* and an *analytical grammar;* structural grammars attempt to analyze sentences already formed, but generative grammars attempt to describe language as a process which forms sentences. A generative grammar might be thought of (somewhat irreverently) as a machine that cranks out sentences.

A third contrast between structural and generative grammars is that between attention only to language as it is uttered and attention to possible underlying elements of language as well. Structuralists tended to confine their explanations to the observable surface of language; generative grammarians discuss both a surface level of language and underlying relationships among phonemes and morphemes.

Both structural and generative grammars can be generally divided into attention to phonology and attention to syntax.

PHONOLOGY. Laird defines and discusses the important concept of *phonemes,* as it was understood and used by structuralists. Fromkin and Rodman modify the definition of *phoneme;* in generative phonology, *phonemes* are the underlying units of a sound system, and surface *phonetic* realizations are the sounds used in speech. In generative phonology, the prefix *in-* has two underlying phonemes: the first is a vowel, the second is a nasal,

/n/. But when the morpheme *in-* is added to a word like "plausible," the underlying /n/ phoneme becomes a surface phonetic [m].

SYNTAX. Laird, a structuralist, defines *morpheme* in basically the same way as it would be defined by Fromkin and Rodman and Liles, who are generative grammarians. *Morpheme* refers to a unit of meaning, such as the "-er" in "sweeter" and "greener."

But the two types of grammarians differ as to the appropriate way of describing sentence structure. Fromkin and Rodman define a sentence in terms of its constituents: a sentence is made up of a noun phrase (NP) and a verb phrase (VP). Laird's definition, however, rests on the sound structure of a sentence. There are other structural definitions of a sentence, and one branch of structural syntax did focus on sentence constituents; in fact, transformational-generative grammar grew out of that part of structural linguistics. But the contrast between Fromkin and Rodman's approach and Laird's approach illustrates the major differences, as we have listed them, between structural and generative descriptive grammars.

## APPLICATIONS

The application of transformational-generative analysis to teaching writing is discussed by Malmstrom and Weaver. Research in general has found little if any connection between knowledge of grammar (in the sense of a linguist's description of language) and ability to write well.[1] Recently, however, transformational grammar has been used to teach students to write sentences that are more complex than those they were previously writing. Malmstrom and Weaver discuss sentence complexity in relation to clarity and appropriateness. The summary article at the end of Part 3 continues this discussion.

Stalker points out that the generative approach to syntax can help beginning students understand poetry that includes ambiguous surface structures (those having more than one deep structure). It is the general approach of generative syntax

---

[1] See J. Stephen Sherwin, "Increasing Skill in Writing" (Chapter 3), in *Four Problems in Teaching English* (Scranton, Pa.: International Textbook Company [representing the National Council of Teachers of English], 1972), pp. 109–168. Sherwin reviews a great deal of literature on this topic before coming to the conclusion just stated.

Stalker refers to, however; his concern is to promote understanding of and pleasure in poetry, not to require students to complete tree diagrams for the poetry they read.

The summary article for Part 3 first discusses generative grammar and writing, and then suggests some ways of explaining dialect differences, using generative grammar as a descriptive tool. The distinctions made in modern grammars actually make the job of explaining language differences easier, rather than complicating the task of describing these differences. A teacher can understand dialect differences and evaluate them much more effectively when the general term *language* is understood as including several specific parts of language—phonemes, phonological rules, morphemes, phrase-structure and transformational rules. A dialect difference can be classified as fitting the definition of one of these subcategories of language, and the teacher can then decide what—if anything—can and should be done in the treatment of that difference in the classroom.

# The Emergence of
# Descriptive Grammars

## The Facts of Linguistic Change:
## Old, Middle, Early Modern, and
## Modern English Versions of One Text

A. G. RIGG, Editor

Changes that have already happened seem to be much easier to accept than changes that are now going on. Most of us look at the Old English text reprinted here and marvel at the perversity of a language system with so many word endings; *-e, -um, -an, -re,* and *-u* were all added to words to show relationships which we now show with other syntax signals, or not at all. For instance, now the subject of a verb is placed before the verb, the object after it; so word order shows whether *Fred hit Harry* or *Harry hit Fred.* In Old English, regardless of word order, the subject was marked with one inflectional ending and the object was marked with another. Another example of the complexity we have lost: in Old English there were eight types of strong (irregular) verbs, each with its own pattern of inflections. Now the overwhelming majority of our verbs are regular.

If we feel no need to mourn the loss of this intricate system, why do we react emotionally to the language change we see around us today? I always feel a little sad when I hear *infer* and *imply* used interchangeably, though as a linguist I know that this coming together of two meanings is natural. (Sometimes words completely switch meanings; the Old English word for *jaw* has now become *cheek,* and the word for *cheek* has now become *jaw.*) Apparently future differences concern us, though past differences do not.

In the next brief article, Fries tries to deal with our concern over current linguistic change; change, he points out, is part of what language is.

## OLD ENGLISH HEPTATEUCH

1 Ēac swylce sēo nǣddre wæs gēapre ðonne ealle ðā ōðre nȳtenu ðe God geworhte ofer eorðan. And sēo nǣddre cwæð tō ðām wīfe: "Hwī forbēad God ēow ðæt gē ne ǣton of ǣlcon trēowe binnan Paradīsum?" 2 Þæt wif andwyrde: "Of ðǣra trēowa wæstme ðe synd on Paradīsum wē etað, 3 and of ðæs trēowes wæstme þe is on middan neorxnawange God bebēad ūs ðæt wē ne ǣton, ne wē ðæt trēow ne hrepedon ðī lǣs ðe wē swelton." 4 Ðā cwæð sēo nǣdre eft tō ðām wīfe: "Ne bēo gē nāteshwōn dēade, ðēah ðe gē of ðām trēowe eton. 5 Ac God wāt sōðlīce ðæt ēowre ēagan bēoð geopenode on swā hwylcum dæge swā gē etað of ðām trēowe, and gē bēoð ðonne englum gelīce, witende ǣgðer gē gōd gē yfel." 6 Ðā geseah ðæt wīf ðæt ðæt trēow wæs gōd tō etenne, be ðām ðe hyre ðūhte, and wlitig on ēagum and lustbǣre on gesyhðe, and genam ðā of ðæs trēowes wæstme and geæt and sealde hyre were; hē æt ðā. 7 And heora bēgra ēagan wurdon geopenode; hī oncnēowon ðā ðæt hī nacode wǣron, and sywodon him ficlēaf and worhton him wǣdbrēc. 8 Eft ðā ðā God cōm, and hī gehȳrdon his stemne ðǣr hē ēode on neorxnawange ofer midne dæg, ðā

---

1 gēap(re): *more astute;* nȳten(u): *animals;* eorð(an): *earth;* forbēad (forbēodan): *forbade;* ǣton (etan): *pt. pl. subj., eat;* binnan: *within*

2 andwyrde: *answered;* wæstm(e): *fruit*

3 neorxnawang(e): *paradise;* bebēad (bebēodan): *ordered;* hrepedon: *pt. pl. subj., touch;* ðī lǣs ðe: *lest;* swelton: *pt. pl. subj., die*

4 nāteshwōn: *by no means;* dēade: *dead;* ðēah ðe: *although*

5 ēagan: *eyes;* engl(um): *angels;* witende: *knowing*

6 be ðām ðe: *as;* ðūhte: *seemed;* wlitig: *beautiful;* lustbǣre: *pleasant;* gesyhð(e): *sight;* genam: *took;* geæt: *ate;* sealde [sold]: *gave;* wer(e): *man*

7 bēgra: *gen., both;* oncnēowon: *knew;* ficlēaf: *figleaves;* wǣdbrēc [weeds, breeches]: *breeches*

8 gehȳrdon: *heard;* stemn(e): *voice;* ðǣr: *where;* behȳdde: *hid*

behȳdde Adam hine, and his wīf ēac swā dyde fram Godes gesihðe on middan ðām trēowe neorxnanwonges. 9 God clypode ðā Adam and cwæð: "Adam, hwær eart ðū?" 10 Hē cwæð: "Ðīne stemne ic gehīre, lēof, on neorxnawange, and ic ondrǣde mē, for ðām ðe ic eom nacod, and ic behȳde mē." 11 God cwæð: "Hwā sǣde ðē ðæt ðū nacod wǣre, gyf ðū ne ǣte of ðām trēowe ðe ic ðē bebēad ðæt ðū ne ǣte?" 12 Adam cwæð: "Ðæt wīf ðe ðū mē forgēafe tō gefēran, sealde mē of ðām trēowe and ic ætt." 13 God cwæð tō ðām wīfe: "Hwī dydestu ðæt?" Hēo cwæð: "Sēo nǣdre bepǣhte mē and ic ætt." 14 God cwæð tō ðǣre nǣddran: "For ðan ðe ðū ðis dydest, ðū bist āwyrged betwēox callum nȳtenum and wild-ēorum; ðū gǣst on ðīnum brēoste and etst ðā eorðan callum dagum ðīnes līfes. 15 Ic sette fēondrǣdene betwux ðē and ðām wīfe and ðīnum ofspringe and hire ofspringe; hēo tobrȳtt ðīn hēafod and ðū syrwst ongēan hire hō." 16 Tō ðām wīfe cwæð God ēac swylce: "Ic gemǣnifylde ðīne yrmða and ðīne geēacnunga; on sārnysse ðū ācenst cild and ðū bist under weres anwealde and hē gewylt ðē." 17 Tō Adame hē cwæð: "For ðan ðe ðū gehȳrdes ðīnes wīfes stemne, and ðū ǣte of ðām trēowe ðe ic ðē bebēad ðæt ðū ne ǣte, is sēo eorðe āwyrged on ðīnum weorce: on geswyncum ðū etst of ðǣre eorðan eallum dagum ðīnes līfes. 18 Ðornas and bremelas hēo āsprȳt ðē and ðū ytst ðǣre eorðan wyrta. 19 On swāte ðīnes andwlitan ðū brȳcst ðīnes hlāfes, oð ðæt ðū gewende tō eorðan of ðǣre ðe ðū genumen wǣre, for ðan ðe ðū eart dust and tō duste gewyrst.

## WYCLIFFITE (PURVEY)

1 But and the serpent was feller than alle lyuynge beestis of erthe, whiche the Lord God hadde maad. Which serpent seide to

10    gehīre: *hear;* lēof: *dear (one);* ondrǣde mē: *am afraid*
12    forgēafe: *pt. 2 sq., gave;* gefēra(n): *companion*
13    bepǣhte: *deceived*
14    āwyrged: *cursed;* wildēor(um): *wild animals;* gǣst (gān): *will go*
15    fēondrǣden(e): *enmity;* tōbrȳtt; *will break apart;* hēafod: *head;* syrwst (sierwan): *pr. 2 sg., will plot;* hō: *heel*
16    gemǣnifylde: *will multiply;* yrmð(a): *miseries;* geēacnung(a): *pregnancies;* sārnyss(e): *sorrow;* ācenst: *pr. 2 sq., will bear;* anweald(e): *power;* gewylt (gewealdan): *pr. 3 sq., will rule over*
17    weorc(e): *labor;* geswync(um): *toils*
18    bremel(as): *brambles;* āsprȳt [sprout]: *will produce;* ytst = etst; wyrt(a) [worts]: *plants*
19    swāt(e): *sweat;* andwlita(n): *face;* brȳcst (brūcan): *pr. 2 sq., have the use of;* hlāf(es) [loaf]: *bread;* oð ðæt: *until;* gewende: *turn;* gewyrst (geweorðan): *pr. 2 sq., will become*
1    feller: *more clever*

the womman, "Why comaundide God to ȝou, that ȝe schulden not ete of ech tre of paradis?" 2 To whom the womman answerde, "We eten of the fruyt of trees that ben in paradis; 3 sothely God comaundide to vs, that we schulden not ete of the fruyt of the tre, which is in the myddis of paradijs, and that we schulden not touche it, lest perauenture we dien." 4 Forsothe the serpent seide to the womman, "Ze schulen not die bi deeth; 5 for whi God woot that in what euere dai ȝe schulen ete therof, ȝoure iȝn schulen be opened, and ȝe schulen be as Goddis, knowynge good and yuel." 6 Therfor the womman seiȝ that the tre was good, and swete to ete, and fair to the iȝen, and delitable in biholdyng; and sche took of the fruyt therof, and eet, and ȝaf to hir hosebonde, and he eet. 7 And the iȝen of bothe weren openid; and whanne thei knewen that thei weren nakid, thei sewiden the leeues of a fige tre, and maden brechis to hem silf. 8 And whanne thei herden the vois of the Lord God goynge in paradijs at the wynd after myddai, Adam and his wijf hidden hem fro the face of the Lord God in the middis of the tre of paradijs. 9 And the Lord God clepide Adam, and seide to hym, "Where art thou?" 10 And Adam seide, "Y herde thi vois in paradijs, and Y drede, for Y was nakid, and Y hidde me." 11 To whom the Lord seide, "Who forsothe schewide to thee that thou were nakid?—no but for thou hast ete of the tre of which Y comaundide to thee that thou schuldist not ete." 12 And Adam seide, "The womman which thou ȝauest felowe to me, ȝaf me of the tre, and Y eet." 13 And the Lord seide to the womman, "Whi didist thou this thing?" Which answerde, "The serpent disseyued me, and Y eet." 14 And the Lord God seide to the serpent, "For thou didist this, thou schalt be cursid among alle lyuynge thingis and vnresonable beestis of erthe; thou schalt go on thi brest, and thou schalt ete erthe in alle daies of thi liif; 15 Y schal sette enemytees bitwixe thee and the womman, and bitwixe thi seed and hir seed; sche schal breke thin heed, and thou schalt sette aspies to hir heele." 16 Also God seide to the womman, "Y schal multiplie thi wretchidnessis and thi conseyuyngis; in sorewe thou schalt bere thi children; and thou schalt be vndur power of the hosebonde, and he schal be lord of thee." 17 Sothely God seyde to Adam, "For thou herdist the voys of thi wijf, and hast ete of the tree, of which Y comaundide to thee that thou schuldist not ete, the erthe schal

3   sothely: *truly;* perauenture: *by chance*
5   woot: *knows*
11   no but for: *not unless because*
15   aspies: *spies*
17   traueylis: *toils*

be cursid in thi werk; in traueylis thou schalt ete therof in alle daies of thi lijf; 18 it schal brynge forth thornes and breris to thee, and thou schalt ete eerbis of the erthe; 19 in swoot of thi cheer thou schalt ete thi breed, til thou turne aȝen in to the erthe of which thou art takun; for thou art dust, and thou schalt turne aȝen in to dust."

## KING JAMES

1 Now the serpent was more subtill then any beast of the field, which the Lord had made, and he said vnto the woman, Yea, hath God said, Ye shall not eat of euery tree of the garden? 2 And the woman said vnto the serpent, Wee may eate of the fruite of the trees of the garden: 3 But of the fruit of the tree, which is in the midst of the garden, God hath said, Ye shal not eate of it, neither shall ye touch it, lest ye die. 4 And the Serpent said vnto the woman, Ye shall not surely die. 5 For God doeth know, that in the day ye eate thereof, then your eyes shalbee opened: and yee shall bee as Gods, knowing good and euill. 6 And when the woman saw, that the tree was good for food, and that it was pleasant to the eyes, and a tree to be desired to make one wise, she tooke of the fruit thereof, and did eate, and gaue also vnto her husband with her, and hee did eate. 7 And the eyes of them both were opened, & they knew that they were naked, and they sewed figge leaues together, and made themselues aprons. 8 And they heard the voyce of the Lord God, walking in the garden in the coole of the day: and Adam and his wife hid themselues from the presence of the Lord God, amongst the trees of the garden. 9 And the Lord God called vnto Adam, and said vnto him, Where art thou? 10 And he said, I heard thy voice in the garden: and I was afraid, because I was naked, and I hid myselfe. 11 And he said, Who told thee, that thou wast naked? Hast thou eaten of the tree, whereof I commanded thee, that thou shouldest not eate? 12 And the man said, The woman whom thou gauest to be with mee, shee gaue me of the tree, and I did eate. 13 And the Lord God said vnto the woman, What is this that thou hast done? And the woman said, The Serpent beguiled me, and I did eate. 14 And the Lord God said vnto the Serpent, Because thou hast done this, thou art cursed aboue all cattel, and aboue euery beast of the field: vpon thy belly shalt thou goe, and dust

18   breris: *briars;* eerbis: *herbs*
19   swoot: *sweat;* cheer: *face*

shalt thou eate, all the dayes of thy life. 15 And I will put enmitie betweene thee and the woman, and betweene thy seed and her seed: it shall bruise thy head, and thou shalt bruise his heele. 16 Vnto the woman he said, I will greatly multiply thy sorowe and thy conception. In sorow thou shalt bring forth children: and thy desire shall be to thy husband, and hee shall rule ouer thee. 17 And vnto Adam he said, Because thou hast hearkened vnto the voyce of thy wife, and hast eaten of the tree, of which I commaunded thee, saying, Thou shalt not eate of it: cursed is the ground for thy sake: in sorow shalt thou eate of it all the dayes of thy life. 18 Thornes also and thistles shall it bring forth to thee: and thou shalt eate the herbe of the field. 19 In the sweate of thy face shalt thou eate bread, till thou returne vnto the ground: for out of it wast thou taken, for dust thou art, and vnto dust shalt thou returne.

## MODERN AMERICAN

1 Now the serpent was the most clever of all the wild beasts that the Lord God had made. "And so God has said that you are not to eat from any tree of the garden?" he said to the woman. 2 "From the fruit of the trees of the garden we may eat," the woman said to the serpent; 3 "it is only concerning the fruit of the tree which is in the middle of the garden that God has said, 'You may not eat any of it, nor touch it, lest you die.' " 4 But the serpent said to the woman, "You would not die at all; 5 for God knows that the very day you eat of it, your eyes will be opened, and you will be like gods who know good from evil." 6 So when the woman realized that the tree was good for food and attractive to the eye, and further, that the tree was desirable for its gift of wisdom, she took some of its fruit, and ate it; she also gave some to her husband with her, and he ate. 7 Then the eyes of both of them were opened, and they realized that they were naked; so they sewed fig-leaves together, and made themselves girdles. 8 But when they heard the sound of the Lord God taking a walk in the garden for the breezes of the day, the man and his wife hid themselves from the Lord God among the trees of the garden. 9 The Lord God called to the man. "Where are you?" he said to him. 10 "I heard the sound of thee in the garden," he replied, "and I was afraid, because I was naked; so I hid myself." 11 "Who told you that you were naked?" he said. "Have you eaten from the tree from which I commanded you not to eat?" 12 The man

said, "The woman whom thou didst set at my side, it was she who gave me fruit from the tree; so I ate it." 13 Then the Lord God said to the woman, "What ever have you done?" The woman said, "It was the serpent that misled me, and so I ate it." 14 So the Lord God said to the serpent,

> Because you have done this,
> The most cursed of all animals shall you be,
> And of all wild beasts.
> On your belly you shall crawl, and eat dust,
> As long as you live.
> 15 I will put enmity between you and the woman,
> And between your posterity and hers;
> They shall attack you in the head,
> And you shall attack them in the heel."

16 To the women he said,

> "I will make your pain at child-birth very great;
> In pain shall you bear children;
> And yet you shall be devoted to your husband,
> While he shall rule over you."

17 And to the man he said, "Because you followed your wife's suggestions, and ate from the tree from which I commanded you not to eat,

> Cursed shall be the ground through you,
> In suffering shall you gain your living from it as long
> as you live;
> 18 Thorns and thistles shall it produce for you,
> So that you will have to eat wild plants.
> 19 By the sweat of your brow shall you earn your living,
> Until you return to the ground,
> Since it was from it that you were taken;
> For dust you are,
> And to dust you must return."

Modern American version from J. M. Powis Smith and Edgar J. Goodspeed, *The Complete American Bible: An American Translation*. Copyright 1923, 1927, 1948 by The University of Chicago. Used by permission of The University of Chicago Press, publisher.

# Language and Change

CHARLES C. FRIES

A look at the preceding selection from Old and Middle English texts shows us that English has always been in a state of change, and—like all other languages—it will always be in such a state. Fries addresses the concern speakers of a language normally feel when they see their most familiar tool undergoing change; this change is not distortion from perfection, we must realize, but an inevitable part of language. The process of acquiring language leads to variation, as we saw in Part 1; language inevitably varies over distance (geographic or social), as we saw in Part 2. Now we add distance over time to the list of sources of language variation; but we call this temporal variation *linguistic change.*

All these variations—caused by distance over space, or over time, or between social groups—take place in the same language categories: phonology and syntax, with syntax including both words (and word parts) and their arrangement into sentences. Most of Part 3 presents some tools for describing language, its variation, and its use—terms and ideas that allow us to talk about parts of language instead of having to talk about the entire complex of structure and content taken in by the unqualified term *language.*

Before looking at the details of language structure, we see in Herndon's article a brief history of our own attitudes and approaches to language and to its description.

Constant change—in word meanings, in pronunciation, and in grammatical structure—is the normal condition of every language (as far as we know) spoken by a living people. The developing of a rigorous technique for the study of this change constituted the first step in "modern linguistic science" and has given us linguistic history. A hundred years of careful scientific study have been devoted to establishing the history of the English language from the time of the earliest recorded texts to the present time—a period of about a thousand years. This detailed history of English has upset many of our naïve and prescientific notions concerning language changes.

These changes, for example, are not corruptions that can or should be prevented—by academies, dictionaries, or grammars. They do not arise from the "mistakes" of the uneducated. In fact, the speech of the uneducated changes much more slowly than does the speech of the educated group. Nearly all the grammatical forms that are called "mistakes" in the speech of the uneducated are simply surviving forms from older periods of the English language. The double negative, for example, as in "They didn't take no oil with them," was in Old English the normal stressed negative. Chaucer often used the multiple negative. The Modern English equivalent of one sentence in his description of the Knight is "He never yet no unfit speech didn't say to no kind of man." The form *clumb* in "He clumb up a tree" is older than the Standard Modern English *climbed. Climb* is one of 129 so-called "strong" verbs that have, in Modern English, all changed to the pattern of the "weak" (regular) verbs. In similar fashion "She went down town *for to* buy a hat" and "It's three *mile* down the next road" survive from older periods of English in the speech of the uneducated.

At no time during the thousand years of the history of English are the recorded texts lacking in evidence of changes actually in progress. There are always points upon which usage is divided. But as far as the evidence goes, neither the practices of the uneducated nor the conscious choices of the educated have had any effect whatever upon these changes. From the point of view of history looking back, they fit into large patterns developing over long periods of time. . . .

[N]o words except highly technical words have precisely the same area of meaning in two languages. We must learn to live with the language as it is, not try to dodge or ignore the multitude of difficulties arising from its constant change.

## Two Thousand Years of Language Study

JEANNE H. HERNDON

If the Greeks had eight word classes ("parts of speech"), the Romans were certainly not going to settle for seven. So they created a category: interjections, like (in English) "Oh!" and "Aha!" Of course, "interjections" are quite different from other classes of words. But tradition must be served. And to this day, "English grammar" is often thought of as equal to a list of the seven (or eight) "parts of speech," with examples.

Herndon gives a brief history of our traditional, prescriptive views of language and then describes the rise of a more scientific, descriptive study of language structure. It is interesting to see prescriptive attitudes about "correctness" in language appearing as far back as the Greeks; language change was as threatening to them as it is to many of us. To realize that many changes in English have somehow triumphed over our urge to freeze language as we ourselves speak it, see the four versions of one Bible text that begin this section.

When one human being communicates with another by means of spoken language, it can safely be assumed that several distinct events have occurred. These are:

1. An ideational stimulus to the mind of the speaker
2. The formulation of a language statement by the speaker
3. The physical act of speaking
4. Sound waves in the atmosphere
5. The physical process of hearing
6. The mental sorting of the language statement by the hearer
7. Understanding the idea by the hearer

There are those who argue that the first two of these are so closely interrelated that they constitute a single event. The same argument is often given for considering the final two items to be a single event. It is not necessary to settle this dispute for our purposes. For the moment, let us arbitrarily settle upon the seven items or events above as a touchstone for the discussion of how language scholars have approached the problems of analyzing and describing the language around them.

## TRADITIONAL GRAMMAR THEORY

### The Greeks

The earliest known efforts of Western man to analyze the phenomena of language dealt only with steps one and two above.

Plato began by searching for the source of man's knowledge. There were, he thought, universal truths, universal ideas, that lay behind the language of the Greeks. He did not consider that other languages were in any way worthy of study or consideration; they were barbaric. The Greeks spoke several dialects but these, in Plato's view, were simply decayed or degenerate versions of a once-perfect system of communication. . . .

Aristotle, [by contrast,] believed that . . . language was arrived at by convention and agreement of the speakers of a given language. . . .

Somewhat later, in the great learning center of Alexandria, a scholar named Dionysius Thrax pulled all the fragmented ideas about Greek grammar into a single short work called *The Art of Grammar*. Written in the first century B.C., the grammar was only about 400 lines long and yet for twenty centuries it has influenced the work of countless grammarians in the formulation of grammars for virtually all the languages of Europe.

*The Art of Grammar* divided the Greek language into eight parts of speech—noun, verb, participle, article, pronoun, preposition, adverb, and conjunction—defined these in a variety of ways, and outlined the uses of each in sentences. Consideration was also given to letters and to syllables since, to Thrax and his contemporaries, language study meant the study of *written* language and the conventions of correctness established by great writers.

The Greeks established for the world of language study the first terminology for discussing their subject; they established the practice of analyzing written representations of human speech which was to become one of the hallmarks of traditional grammatical investigation and evaluation; and, finally, they established as a basic assumption the idea that there was a universally correct and acceptable logic of language for man to follow in expressing his ideas.

## The Romans

The Romans imitated the Greeks in linguistic matters as they did in many other areas of culture and learning. Some Romans, notably Julius Caesar and Quintilian, the rhetorician, raised questions of how far language scholars could go in setting up rules for the logic of language which differed from the way that the language was used by most of its speakers. This gap between scholarly rule and common usage widened into the distinct difference between the Latin of classical literature and the Vulgar (here meaning common) Latin spoken by the masses of Roman people. Still, the most influential works written on the grammar of Latin were to follow the pattern established by Thrax in writing of Greek.

The early standard Latin grammar was that written by Marcus Varro in the first century. A later work written by Priscian in the sixth century consisted of eighteen books on parts of speech and two on syntax. This was to be the basis for standard Latin grammars throughout medieval times when Latin was the international language of the learned.

It is important to note that the rigidly categorized parts of speech were notionally defined in some cases—as with the noun and verb—and described according to their function in others— as with the preposition and conjunction.[1] Latin grammarians found it necessary to adjust the eight parts of speech decreed for Greek. Latin had no articles, but since the Greeks had dictated that any self-respecting language had eight parts of speech, Latin grammarians replaced the category for articles with one for interjections. An extensive list of inflections had to be listed and classified for each part of speech. Conjugations and declensions were mandatory since the inflectional ending contained a part of the meaning of most words. For example, endings added to nouns indicated whether the noun was subject of the verb, direct or indirect object, the means of accomplishing the action, the result of an action, and so on. Verbs had literally dozens of inflectional endings. Each one signified some combination of person, number, tense, and mood. Every inflectional ending had to be categorized and defined; rules had to be established for the use of each and exceptions noted. The order in which words appeared in a sentence was of comparatively little importance since any nominal or verbal elements were clearly labeled with their function in the sentence by whatever inflectional endings they carried.

The Romans bowed to Greek precedent in setting up the grammatical rules for their language, and the practice spread with the Empire and, later, with the Church over all of Europe.

## The Medieval Period

Because Latin was the language of Church scholarship and of serious literature all through the Middle Ages, the vernaculars

---

[1] [Ed. note: A *notional* definition concerns meaning, as in the common definition of a noun as "the name of a person, place, or thing," while a *functional* definition concerns the role of the word class in sentences, as in the definition of conjunctions as words "that connect other words, phrases, and clauses."]

—the languages of the masses of uneducated people—that were to become the Romance languages, grew and developed without rules other than those established by usage and custom. Still, these languages were of Latin origin and when, with the rise of nationalism, each country felt the need of its own scholarly grammar, it was a comparatively easy task to fit these languages into the mold fashioned for classical Greek and modified slightly for classical Latin.

Among scholars, great emphasis was placed on orderly argumentation and logic, so it is not surprising that grammatical rules were held valid only when they adhered to logical system. Those who established rules for these languages made them adhere to strictly formulated logical principles dictated by Latin scholarship rather than attempting to fathom the logic or system that had developed as a part of each language.

## England

In England, too, classical grammatical concepts were brought to bear by those who sought to establish standards of usage for a language that had become a symbol of national identity and pride.

England was to have no language academy as did several other countries, but in the eighteenth century a number of influential men of letters and school masters began to have a regularizing effect on some of England's writers and, to a far greater degree, on her schools. It was an age marked by great reverence for the classical—in literature, art, architecture, even matters of fashion—and so it was natural that the grammarians sought the status of a classically correct grammar for their language.

The dictionary of Samuel Johnson and the school grammars of John Wallis, Robert Lowth, and Lindley Murray were not only aimed at establishing "correct" usage but at pointing out "errors." Their criteria for such decisions were often based upon a familiarity with the requirements of Latin grammar, which was secure in its centuries of scholarly prestige, rather than upon serious consideration of the somewhat different grammatical system used by native speakers of the English language.

The task of forcing English into the Latin grammar mold was doubly difficult because English is not derived from Latin but from old Germanic dialects. Undaunted by differences, these eighteenth-century grammarians equated English auxiliary verbs with Latin verb inflections and endowed English with a complete future tense and an almost totally alien subjunctive mood among other things. They forced the modal system derived from the Germanic into a variety of Latin categories. *Shall* and *will* became a part of the future tense; *may* became a part of the subjunctive mood. The Lowth and Murray grammars were the most widely used in England for several generations. Their pronouncements on matters of English grammar set standards of usage that left an indelible mark on the language itself.

These grammarians are often called *prescriptive grammarians* because their objectives were largely those of establishing rules to be taught to young students and by which literary efforts might be judged, at least in part.

## COMPARATIVE AND HISTORICAL LINGUISTS

In spite of the fact that most grammarians relied upon classical grammarians for method and classical languages for criteria of correctness, some new ideas were stirring in the field of language study in the eighteenth century. These new ideas were not to affect the work of school grammarians for several generations. But among these ideas are to be found the roots of a whole new approach to the problem of analyzing and describing language.

Many language scholars had noted similarities between various European languages; some languages had quite clearly developed from one variety or another of provincial Latin. It remained for an Englishman who was not primarily a language scholar to see relationships among the most widely dispersed of those languages which were later to be recognized as the Indo-European family of languages.

Sir William Jones had served in the colonial government of India and while there had studied Sanskrit. In 1786 he wrote of observing similarities between a remarkable number of vocabulary items in Sanskrit and their equivalents in European and Middle Eastern languages. He suggested that all these languages might have "sprung from some common source, which, perhaps, no longer exists."

Investigation of similarities and differences among languages is called *comparative linguistics*. As language scholars began to establish patterns of relationships among languages, their work came to be called *historical linguistics*. (These scholars were interested primarily in relationships among languages; they were concerned with matters of grammar only insofar as these might indicate relationships among languages and not as a matter of establishing rules of correctness.) Their research was simply a matter of gathering data, sorting and analyzing it. Their view of change was totally objective. They were only interested in what kinds of changes had occurred, not whether these changes were "right" or "wrong," "good" or "bad."

After two centuries of enormous amounts of language study, linguists have arrived at some very sweeping theories about the nature of the relationships among the many Indo-European languages. Stated in the simplest possible terms, the important points are these: (1) All these languages, developed from a single language which no longer exists. (2) Differences developed when groups of people who spoke this language moved apart and were separated for long periods of time. That is, one group moved into India and their language developed and changed to become Sanskrit; another group moved into southeastern Europe and their language grew into the ancestor of Greek; another group broke off and moved into northern Europe and their language changed in some respects to become the parent language of German, English, Danish and so on. (3) The fact that all these languages share a common heritage accounts for the fact that some similarities still exist in all of them.

Among the first linguists to make important comparative studies was a Danish scholar named Rasmus Rask, who compared Icelandic and Scandinavian languages and dialects. Another, Jacob Grimm, carried Rask's studies still further and proposed a theory to account for the differences he found among languages. Out of these and many other similar studies, grew the theory that languages not only change gradually, over long periods of time, but that they change systematically and that the changes are best traced through comparison of the sound systems of languages. . . .

In addition to broad grammatical concerns, grammarians such as Henry Sweet and Otto Jespersen placed great emphasis on the analysis of sounds used by speakers of English to communicate their thoughts. They saw that commonly used English spelling was an unacceptable means of representing the speech sounds made by speakers of English. Henry Sweet led the way for English grammarians seeking to establish a system of representing speech sounds with the greatest possible fidelity to their spoken form. The key requirement for such a system is that each symbol represent one and only one sound. Sweet's phonetic alphabet, like those proposed by other language scholars, placed greatest emphasis on the physical means of sound production. Consideration was given to such factors as whether a sound involved resonance or not, the parts of the vocal equipment—lips, tongue, teeth, and so on—shaping the sound, the degree to which the flow of air was constricted and the factors of lip-rounding or tenseness involved.

Grammarians dealing with English from the time of Sweet onward have been influenced to some degree by his work.

Traditional grammarians—and these included Sweet himself—still worked within the classical framework established for defining parts of speech and syntactic devices used by a speech community to communicate ideational or notional meaning. In addition, they began to add investigation of the sound systems of languages to their field of study. They worked from both the standpoint of the notional meaning and from the standpoint of the sound system of the language. The main framework of their analysis still rested on its traditional foundations but they recognized that speakers of English expressed their ideas in ways that were unique to English in some respects. They saw that matters of syntax and word order were more important to the grammar of English and the proportion of their work devoted to syntactic analysis increased accordingly.

They still attempted to sort the English language into parts of speech and syntactic functions by defining logical—or psychological—meanings expressed by speakers of English. Definitions of parts of speech still listed referents and syntactic function or meaning as well as accidence (the forms taken by a given part of speech). For example, nouns were the names of persons, places, states, qualities and other "things"; they served as subjects, objects, complements, and so on; and they showed singular and plural number and had a common and a genitive case.

Many English words and classes of words do not fit as neatly into this kind of classification as nouns. Some, such as prepositions, do not vary in form; some, such as *man, fancy, ship,* and *paint,* skip nimbly from one part of speech category to another; and some, such as gerunds, have the notional characteristics of more than one part of speech.

Consideration of syntactic or contextual characteristics presented these grammarians with even greater problems. Syntactic structures and functions do not lend themselves readily to simple, easily memorized notional definitions because English word order allows such an enormous range of distributional possibilities. Simply listing the possibilities is a formidable task; attempting to explain them in terms of what each means is an undertaking of staggering proportions. Those works that even approached a complete description of the grammar of English were the seven-volume work of Otto Jespersen and the five-volume work of Hendrik Poutsma.

While these lengthy works contain analysis of enormous quantities of examples and variations in the use of English, they are still open to criticism on the grounds that rigorously controlled methods of definition occasionally lapse into intuitive or "common sense" definition. This becomes especially troublesome when exceptions to a "rule" are at least as numerous and commonplace among speakers of the language as instances of compliance with the rule. For example, the future tense was said to be expressed by the use of the forms *shall* and *will* but English speakers are just as likely to indicate futurity by means of adverbs as in "The play opens tomorrow." Another thing that the exhaustive volume of traditional analysis did not obscure was the fact that the fundamental definitions were still, in many instances, circular. For example, a sentence was defined as a group of words expressing a complete thought and containing a subject and a predicate; subject and predicate were defined as being necessary parts of sentences. These definition problems still present difficulties for traditional grammarians.

# Structural and Generative Approaches to Language Study

## Phonemes, Morphemes, and Meaning

CHARLTON LAIRD

Laird presents a structuralist's quarrel with using meaning in a description of language. His definition of a sentence illustrates his views beautifully; it focuses on the intonation pattern of a sentence—something physical and measurable, instead of an elusive meaning. It is not quite true, however, that structuralists wanted to completely avoid dealing with meaning. In the next selection Fries, a prominent structuralist, makes a distinction between *lexical* meaning and *structural* meaning; he is interested in using only structural meaning in his description of language.

The two very important terms Laird introduces here are *phoneme* and *morpheme.* The term *phoneme* has been modified in transformational grammar, but the basic ideas these terms stand for have both become part of all current descriptions of language; they are important in the study of language acquisition, language variation, and reading presented in the rest of this book.

. . . Structural linguistics owes its origin to a desire to be scientific and its popularity in part to its use in teaching obscure languages during the recent war. Structuralists are aware that meaning and function are important in language, but they are aware, also, that these concepts lack scientific accuracy. Since every word has varying meaning for various people, how can the student rest a scientific description on meaning? Similarly, function is uncertain; for example, what are the kinds of modification, and if they are not distinguishable, how can they be defined? If these are not measurable, what is measurable? Structure, many linguists believe, is measurable. When one says, "A noun is the name of a person, place, or thing," he is talking demonstrable nonsense; but when he says, "A noun is one of a class made up partially of linguistic units which can be preceded by *the* or by *the* plus words of the general nature of *good, red,* and *magnetic,*" one is saying what is at least true. Very well, the structuralists determined, let us say anything we can about language that is demonstrably true, and say nothing we cannot prove. In the end we may get farthest in this way.

Accordingly, the structuralists studied language as objectively as possible. What, they asked, is significant and determinable in language? Meaning is significant, but in the present state of our knowledge it is not exactly determinable. Sound is significant and so determinable that it can be transformed into a variable band of light which can be broken into parts. It is so measurable and analyzable that machines have been built which can talk, but unfortunately a spectroscopic reproduction of human speech seems nearly as complicated as the speech itself, and thus far has not told us what we should like to know about grammar.

Here the structuralists were helped by the concept of the phoneme. They built upon the work of the phoneticians, of course, who had identified such bits of sound as [d]. Actually, [d] is not a unit. Speakers make a number of sounds which approximate [d]; in fact, if you will now say *dad,* although you probably cannot hear the difference, you will pronounce the first *d* in one way and the second in another. If you watch the motion of your tongue when you say the word, you will notice that your tongue works differently for the two sounds. But for speakers of English the sounds are considered the same, and consequently the structuralist can give himself a unit that is valid for English by defining all these sounds as a single phoneme, written between slanted lines, /d/. The two *d*'s are phonetically two sounds, but they are one phoneme because users of the language treat them as one. That is, roughly, a phoneme is a usable unit of sound. In other languages the same spread of sound might not be a phoneme. In Paiute, for example, speakers make no distinction between [d] and [t], which for that language become one phoneme. In another language sounds which are only one for us become two phonemes —one sound which we would spell *d* made with the tongue forward almost to the teeth and another made with it somewhat back. A word pronounced with one *d* will have a meaning different from one pronounced with another *d*, just as with us *dad* differs from *tat*, although a Paiute would not make the distinction.

Thus a phoneme is the spread of sound which becomes a working unit in a given language. But these phonemes can be used in sequence to form larger working units—*work* and *sing*, for example—which are called *morphemes,* units of form. *Work* and *sing* are words as well as morphemes, but *morpheme* is a more exact term than *word. Work* is one word and one morpheme, but *worker,* although it is one word, is two morphemes, /work-/ and /-er/. We can make a distinction between what are called *free* and *bound forms. Work* is a free form; it can be used by itself (*I work*), but /-er/ is a bound form, since, although it has a recognized use in the language, it must always be bound to another morpheme. It makes the difference in shape and use between *work* and *worker,* but /-er/ alone does not mean "one who does something." We cannot say, *A handyman is an er.* The structuralists also recognize *phrases,* made up of units like *in the well* and *workman,* which, although it is conventionally spelled as one word, is two forms, /work/ and /man/. But a phrase, also, is a form.

Forms belong to *form classes,* which may be defined as all of the shapes having the same privilege of occurrence; that is, are interchangeable in a construction. Since *man* and *boy* are interchangeable in *The man works, The boy works,* the two belong to the same form class. The whole is a construction, and the structuralists recognize, as the older grammarians did, that it is a predication which can be cut into a subject and predicate or a noun and a verb, depending upon the way the structuralist sets up his description of the language.

But the sort of sound difference which can be noticed in /d/ and /t/ is not the only distinction which can be observed in English discourse. Consider, for instance, the copybook sentence *King Charles walked and talked eloquently ten minutes after his head was cut off.* Repunctuated, the sentence makes somewhat better sense: _King Charles walked and talked eloquently; ten minutes after, his head was cut off._ The differences are only suggested by the changed punctuation. The structuralist would say that part of the difference arises from the pauses within the sentence, which he calls _junctures,_ of which he recognizes four in English: one like that after _king,_ a second like that after _after,_ a third like that after _eloquently,_ and a fourth like that afer _off._ They may be called respectively cross juncture, /+/, bar juncture, /|/, double bar juncture, /‖/, and double cross juncture, /#/. The last two may also be marked /↑/ and /↓/.

There are other differences. The _after_ in the second sentence is said more forcefully than that in the first sentence; that is, it has more stress. The structuralist recognizes three, or more frequently four, levels of stress: zero, //, which is usually not marked; tertiary, /ˈ/; secondary, /ˋ/; and primary, /ˊ/. But the tone of _after,_ the pitch of the voice, is different in the two sentences. In the first the tone holds rather low and level; in the second it starts higher and then drops. The structuralist usually recognizes four tones, which may be marked 1 2 3 or 4. For example, a common tone morpheme for _I will come tomorrow_ might be /21 31/, provided the whole sentence were _my sister cannot_

$$\underset{2\quad\ 1}{\qquad\qquad\qquad}\underset{3\ \ 1}{\qquad\qquad}$$

_come until Sunday, but I will come tomorrow._

Thus the structuralist finds that he needs relatively few concepts with which to describe any language, whether Swahili or the Chicago dialect of American English. A language is made up of working units of sound, phonemes; these are built into morphemes, some of which can be classified into form classes, having certain privileges of occurrence in constructions; the constructions can be further analyzed with degrees of tone, stress, and juncture. Described thus in one sentence, structural linguistics does not seem complicated, and it has the great advantage of being more precise than the older grammatical statement. For instance, a sentence becomes any group of words which structures with no other. A structuralist may be able to define subjects and verbs briefly and exactly. But pursued seriously and in detail, structural linguistics can become complicated, so complicated that only persistent students can hope to stagger through it, and so subtle that as yet the doctors do not agree. For example, in a recent and excellent textbook the author does not presume to define a simple sentence until after 335 pages of closely reasoned matter. He then provides a working definition to introduce his discussion, as follows:

> A sentence . . . is a sequence of segmental material occur-
> ing under a single pitch superfix. The superfix may or may not
> contain more than one pitch morpheme, but if there is more than
> one pitch morpheme, the pitch morphemes must be linked. A sen-
> tence must also have a stress superfix, which also may consist
> of several stress morphemes . . . [and] one or several segmental
> morphemes.[1]

This is a plausible definition of a sentence, although it must sound
like gibberish to anybody who has not worked through the preceding 335 pages or their equivalent. Furthermore, structuralists
commonly recognize sentences which have no subjects, but only
"subjectivals." They may define *oh* and *understand* as phrases,
*so* and *not* as clauses. They divide what are commonly called
prepositional phrases into various things, including complements
and discontinuous predicators. They may say that *Let's go, John,*
is a complex sentence, but that *John, let's go* is not, and that in
*The room was cool, the windows being open,* the participal element, *the windows being open,* is the independent portion of the
sentence, and *the room was cool* is dependent upon it. Statements
of this sort would, of course, horrify many a conventional grammarian.

# Lexical and Structural Meaning

CHARLES C. FRIES

> Fries explains one major structuralist view of the role
> meaning should have in a description of language. The
> distinction he explains has been widely used, under the terms
> *function words* or *structure words* for structural signals,
> and *form words* or *content words* for lexical meanings.

Structural linguistic procedures have led to a new view of
the nature of human language and thus to a new view of what
constitutes its basic functioning units. The structural approach

---

[1] Archibald A. Hill, *Introduction to Linguistic Structures* (New York:
Harcourt, Brace and Company, Inc., 1958), p. 336.

does not ignore meaning of any kind. It assumes that the chief social function of language is the communication of meanings in order to make possible the sharing of experience and the cooperation necessary to the existence of every social group. But the language itself is not the meanings—not the messages that are sent or received. The language is the code by which the meanings are signalled—the signals through which the communication of the message is achieved. The messages themselves can be communicated through any of the language codes.

In a language code there are at least two layers of signals, each functioning to communicate its own layer of meanings.

(a) *The layer of lexical meanings.* Given the same intonation patterns, the two sentences, *"The top of this pen was bent over"* and *"The top of this pan was bent over,"* differ solely in lexical meaning. *Pen* and *pan* are different "words" representing different things. The fact that *pen* and *pan* are different "words" is signalled by the distinctive difference in their vowel sounds.

(b) *The layer of structural meanings.* The two sentences following also differ in meaning. *"The top of this pen was bent over"* and *"Was the top of this pen bent over."* This is not, however, a difference in lexical meaning. The "words" are the same, but the contrast of the position of *was* in relation to *the top of this pen* signals a difference of structural meaning, i.e. of grammatical meaning.

All languages seem to have at least these two layers of meanings—lexical meanings signalled by "words," and structural meanings signalled by contrastive arrangements and forms of these "words." In other words, from this point of view, the *grammar* of a language consists of the constructive patterns of arrangements and forms that signal its layer of structural meanings.

But the functioning units of the contrastive patterns that signal the structural meanings that make our "sentences" are not "words" as mere lexical items, they are "words" which in the context of live language are formally marked as belonging to one of a small number of form-classes ("parts of speech"). The markers, not the meanings, signal the form-class. Even meaningless or "nonsense" words take on form-class meanings as a response to the markers. *Woggle* becomes a "thing" word with such markers as *"a woggle. . . . . . ," "two woggles."* With other markers *woggle* becomes an "action" word, "Two woggles *woggled* another woggle."

From this structural point of view, grammar deals only with those contrastive arrangements of form-classes that function as signals of structural meanings. In all languages the "words" of the utterances must occur in some order—a sequence in a time dimension. But in only a limited number of languages does a contrast of "position," in such a sequence, signal specific grammatical meanings. In Old English the meaning of "performer of action" in *þone beran slōh sē mann* is signalled by the forms *sē mann* (nominative) in contrast with the forms *þone beran* (accusative). The position of these words in the sequence has no grammatical signalling value. In the Modern English sentence, *The man killed the bear,* the contrastive "position" alone signals whether *the man* or *the bear* is the "performer" of the *killing.* The contrast of "position" was not a grammatical signal in Old English or in Latin. It is an important structural signal in Modern English.

For English, four major form-classes and a very small number of function words make up the units of the contrastive patterns that signal the whole range of structural or grammatical meanings. These structural signals operate independently of the lexical meanings of the "words." . . .

## Chomsky and the Creativity of Language

JOHN LYONS

Dots and dashes tapped out in Morse code may mean nothing to you; if I tap out a message, you may have no idea what meaning I am trying to communicate. But if you know the rules that relate these sounds to meaning, you will understand my message. And you will be able to create messages to me that I will understand.

This is not an advertisement for Morse code; it illustrates the process we all go through every time we say something or listen to someone else say something. Each of us knows the rules that relate sound to meaning, and we are each using those rules every time we create a sentence or understand one. These are the rules that Lyons is interested in, and these are the rules that are discussed in the selections on transformational grammar in this section.

To give a general example of these basic rules, let us look at four words arranged in a bloc: $\frac{Fred\ Harry}{sink\ saw}$ These words do not obey any sentence-structure rules we know; so, assuming that these words are part of a message, we have to imagine what structure they might have. It could be *Fred saw Harry sink* or *Harry saw Fred sink*. But which?

Both arrangements obey the rules of English sentence-building. The rules don't change; in each case, we understand that a noun before a verb is a subject, and a noun after the verb is an object. A speaker could use these rules to create either message—or an infinite variety of other messages.

Try keeping track of the number of sentences you create and understand in one day (including spoken and written ones). You may not get very far before conceding that these rules are a powerful tool.

[A] general property of human language . . . is its *creativity* (or "open-endedness"). By this is meant the capacity that all native speakers of a language have to produce and understand an indefinitely large number of sentences that they have never heard before and that may indeed never have been uttered before by anyone. The native speaker's "creative" command of his language, it should be noted, is in normal circumstances unconscious and unreflecting. He is generally unaware of applying any grammatical rules or systematic principles of formation when he constructs either new sentences or sentences he has previously encountered. And yet the sentences that he utters will generally be accepted by other native speakers of the language as correct and will be understood by them. (We must make allowances, as we shall see later, for a certain amount of error—hence the qualification implied by "generally" in the previous sentence—but this does not affect the principle that is under discussion here.) As far as we know, this creative command of language is unique to human beings: it is *species-specific*. Systems of communication employed by species other than man are not "open-ended" in the same way. Most of them are "closed," in the sense that they admit of the transmission of only a finite and relatively small set of distinct "messages," the "meanings" of which are fixed (rather as the messages that one may send by means of the international telegraphic code are determined in advance), and it is not possible for the animal to vary these and construct new "sentences." It is true that certain forms of animal communication (for example, the signaling "code" that is used by bees to indicate the direction and distance of a source of honey) incorporate the possibility of making new "sentences" by systematically varying the "signal." But in all instances there is a simple correlation between the two variables—the "signal" and its "meaning." For example, as K. von Frisch discovered in his celebrated work on the subject, it is by the intensity of their body movements that bees signal the distance of the source of honey from the hive; and this parameter of "intensity" is subject to infinite (and continuous) variation. This kind of continuous variation is also found in human language: for instance, one can vary the "intensity" with which the word *very* is pronounced in a sentence like *He was very rich*. But it is not this feature that is being referred to when one talks of the creativity of human language. It is the ability to construct new combinations of discrete units, rather than simply to vary continuously one of the parameters of the signaling system in accordance with a correspondingly continuous variation in the "meaning" of the "messages." . . . [Noam] Chomsky considers that the creativity of language is one of its most characteristic features and one that poses a particularly challenging problem for the development of a psychological theory of language use and language acquisition.

. . . It may be helpful if I summarize [a number of the more important general principles of linguistics]. Modern linguistics claims to be more scientific and more general than traditional grammar. It assumes that the "natural" medium for the expression of language is sound (as produced by the speech organs) and that written languages are derived from speech. The grammar of any language will comprise at least the following three interrelated parts: syntax, semantics, and phonology; and it should, among other things, account for the ability native speakers have to produce and understand an indefinitely large number of "new" sentences.

# Generative Syntax: Grammaticality, Phrase-Structure Rules

VICTORIA FROMKIN and ROBERT RODMAN

One branch of structural linguistics focused on *sentence constituents,* such as noun phrases, verb phrases, and their subparts. This study of sentence constituents eventually led to the linguistic theory known as *transformational-generative grammar.* Transformational-generative grammar describes language as a process of creating (generating) sentences and their subparts. In this selection Fromkin and Rodman first discuss the words *grammar* and *grammaticality* as they are used by linguists, and then present *phrase-structure rules*—a major part of any transformational grammar—which generate basic sentence types. In the following selection, Liles presents *transformational rules* which transform these basic sentence types into negative sentences or into questions. Then another selection by Fromkin and Rodman describes the *phonological rules* of a generative grammar, rules that account for the pronunciation of the syntactic structures that were generated by phrase-structure and transformational rules.

The term *deep structure* refers to a sentence that has been generated by phrase-structure rules but has not yet undergone the actions of transformational rules. The use of this term has become very widespread, and in the process its meaning has sometimes broadened; some writers use this term loosely, as identical to "underlying meaning." But in most technical literature about language, *deep structures* are thought of in relation to phrase-structure rules of the type described here by Fromkin and Rodman.

## GRAMMATICALITY

The meaning of a sentence is a synthesis of the meanings of the morphemes of which it is composed. But the morphemes cannot occur haphazardly in the sentence. *The dentist hurt my teeth* does not have the same meaning as *My teeth hurt the dentist,* and the string of morphemes *my the hurt dentist teeth* has no meaning at all even though it is made up of meaningful elements. There are rules in one's grammar that determine what morphemes are combined into larger grammatical units to get intended meanings, and how these morphemes are to be combined. These are the *syntactic rules* of the language. They permit

us to say what we mean, which, at least according to the March
Hare, is what we should do.

> "Then you should say what you mean," the March Hare
> went on.
> "I do," Alice hastily replied: "at least—at least I mean what
> I say—that's the same thing, you know."
> "Not the same thing a bit!" said the Hatter. "You might
> just as well say that 'I see what I eat' is the same thing as 'I
> eat what I see'!"
> "You might just as well say," added the March Hare, "that
> 'I like what I get' is the same thing as 'I get what I like'!"
> "You might just as well say," added the Dormouse . . .
> "that 'I breathe when I sleep' is the same thing as 'I sleep when
> I breathe'!"
> "It *is* the same thing with you," said the Hatter.

If there were no rules of syntax it wouldn't have mattered
whether Alice said "I say what I mean" or "I mean what I say."
Part of the meaning of a sentence, then, is determined by the
order of the morphemes. The syntactic rules of the grammar
specify, among other things, such order.

This is true in all languages. In Thai, for example, *mœœw
hĕn mǎa* means "The cat saw the dog," but *mǎa hĕn mœœw* means
"The dog saw the cat" and *hĕn mǎa mœœw* is not a sentence in
Thai and has no meaning. *Où est la télévision?* ("Where is the
television?") is a sentence in French. *\*Est la où télévision?* ("is
the where television?") is not a sentence in French. ɛha yɛ hū
("This place is spooky") is a sentence in Twi. *\*Yɛ ɛha hū* ("is
place-here spooky") is not a sentence in Twi.

Strings of morphemes which conform to the syntactic rules
of the language are called the **grammatical sentences** of the language, and strings which do not "obey" these rules are called
**ungrammatical.**

You don't have to study "grammar" or linguistics to know
which sentences are grammatical. Even a very young child knows
intuitively that *The boy kissed the girl* is a "good" sentence in
English but that something is wrong with the string *\*Girl the
kissed boy the.*

According to *your* knowledge of English syntax, which of
the following sentences would you mark with an asterisk (as
ungrammatical)?

a. Sylvia wanted George to go.
b. Sylvia wanted George go.
c. Sylvia heard George to go.
d. Sylvia hoped George go.

    e. Sylvia heard George go.
    f. Clarence looked up the number.
    g. Clarence looked the number up.
    h. Morris walked up the hill.
    i. Morris walked the hill up.

If the syntactic rules of your grammar are the same as those of our grammar (and we expect that they are), you "starred" as ungrammatical sentences b, c, d, and i. If we agree on the "grammaticality" of any of these sentences we must be making these decisions according to some rules which we know. Notice that the syntactic rules which account for our "intuitions" in these cases are not *just* "ordering" rules. They "tell" us, for example, that with the verb *wanted* we must use a *to,* but with *heard* we do not use a *to.* And they permit us to move the *up* in sentence f but not in sentence h.

    These examples show that the syntactic rules permit us to make judgments about the "grammaticality" of sentences. In other words, the sentences of a language are well-formed, grammatical strings, not just any strings of morphemes. And it is the *syntax* of the grammar which accounts for this fact.

    The syntactic rules also account for other linguistic judgments that speakers are able to make. Consider the following sentence:

    j. The Mafia wants protection from attack by the police.

You can't be sure whether the Mafia wants the police to protect them against the attack of some unnamed parties or whether the Mafia wants someone to protect them from the attack of the police. The double meaning (or ambiguity) of the sentence is not due to the occurrence of any homonyms or words with two meanings, as it is in the following sentence:

    k. Katerina gave Petruccio a sock.

In sentence k, Katerina may have given Petruccio an article of clothing or a punch. *Sock* has two meanings. But in sentence j the ambiguity can't be explained in this way; it must be due to the *syntactic structure* of the sentence. Your knowledge of the syntactic rules permits you to reconstruct sentence j as meaning either

    l. The Mafia wants the police to protect them from attack.
                          *or*
    m. The Mafia wants protection from being attacked by the police.

Sometimes the multiple meanings are not immediately apparent. But you can usually figure out which sentences are ambiguous because of your knowledge of the syntactic rules. . . .

## PHRASE-STRUCTURE RULES

We said above that everyone knows what a sentence in his language is. But what is it? Most schoolchildren learn that "every sentence has a subject and a predicate." That's a pretty good definition, and every speaker is aware of this even if he hasn't learned it consciously. All the ten strings of morphemes listed here as group 1 have subjects and predicates, and they are all sentences of English:

| | SUBJECT | PREDICATE |
|---|---|---|
| **1** a. | It | frightens me. |
| b. | Sally | frightens me. |
| c. | The man | frightens me. |
| d. | The fat man | frightens me. |
| e. | The fat man who is whistling | frightens me. |
| f. | He | fell. |
| g. | John | went fishing. |
| h. | Several friends of mine | threw a party. |
| i. | This book | is fascinating. |
| j. | Flying planes | can be dangerous. |

The subject may assume various forms, some more complex than others, but all of them are **referring expressions**; that is, they point out some entity. *John* points out the individual named John; *this book* points out a particular book; *it* points out something that the hearer is assumed to know (perhaps by previous discourse). Linguists call such expressions **noun phrases** (NP), since they contain at least one noun or pronoun.

The predicate is a **relating expression** in that it relates the subject to some action or some property. In sentences 1a to 1e, the various noun phrases (NPs) are related to the action "frighten." In sentence 1i, "this book" is related to the property of "being fascinating." Since the predicate always contains at least a verb (and may contain other elements, such as the direct object *me*) it is called a **verb phrase** (VP).

If every sentence of a language must include a noun phrase as subject and a verb phrase as predicate, the grammar must include a rule which can be stated as:

**1** Every Sentence (S) consists of a Noun Phrase (NP) and a Verb Phrase (VP).

This rule can be abbreviated, or stated formally as:

1′ S → NP   VP.

This reads: A Sentence "is a" (or "rewrites as") as Noun Phrase followed by a Verb Phrase. We know Rule 1 is a rule of English because it "explains" why the strings under sentence group 2 are not sentences: [1]

2  a. *frightens me
   b. *the man
   c. *the man that is whistling
   d. *jumped into the pool without his clothes on

The order of the NP and the VP must also be as given in the rule to account for the ungrammaticality of the sentences in group 3:

3  a. *frightens me it
   b. *frightens me the fat man
   c. *went fishing John
   d. *can be dangerous flying planes

Verb phrases may consist of subparts just as sentences do, as we can see from the sentences in groups 4 and 5.

4  a. The wind howled.
   b. The wind blew.

5  a. The wind frightened Mary.
   b. The wind frightened the girls.
   c. The wind frightened the little kitten.
   d. The wind frightened several old ladies who were drinking tea in the living room of the haunted house.

Notice that in the sentences of group 4 the verb phrase consists of a verb alone, but in those of group 5 the verb is followed by a noun phrase. Since these are all grammatical sentences in the language, the rule stating what a verb phrase is must account for this. This rule can be stated:

2 A Verb Phrase may consist of a Verb (V) alone, or of a Verb followed by a Noun Phrase.
2′ VP → V   (NP).

The parentheses in Rule 2′ denote that the NP is optional, that is, may or may not occur in a verb phrase. Rule 2′ really abbreviates two rules:

---

[1] Certain "subjectless" sentences . . . [may] actually [have] an "understood" subject.

2' a. VP → V.
   b. VP → V  NP.

As we add rules we are clearly defining what it is a speaker knows about sentences. If we just defined a sentence as consisting of an NP VP, that would not tell us what these two categories are. Furthermore we see by Rule 2' that all the expressions that can be subjects also have the potential of being objects of verbs (and vice-versa).[2] This is an important general property of language, for it allows speakers to reuse in a different context what they know already. When a child is learning his language he need only learn what a noun phrase is, and learn that an NP can occur either as a subject or an object. Furthermore, by using the same symbol, NP, in two rules we show that the same kinds of phrases occur in different parts of the structure.

Knowing the syntactic rules of English, you know that verbs may be in the *present tense* or the *past tense.*[3] We can express this knowledge by Rule 3:

**3** A verb consists of a verb *stem* and an abstract morpheme designating tense: present (Pres) or past (Past).

$$3' \ V \rightarrow V_{stem} \begin{Bmatrix} Pres \\ Past \end{Bmatrix}.$$

The braces, { }, indicate that either Pres or Past must follow the verb stem. Notice that once again we have used an abbreviating device which collapses two rules which could have been stated:

3' a. $V \rightarrow V_{stem}$ Pres.
   b. $V \rightarrow V_{stem}$ Past.

By writing one rule with braces we are able to state this more generally.

The rules "defining" a verb phrase or a sentence do not yet give enough information; we haven't said what a noun phrase is. Speakers of all languages know what constitutes a noun phrase

---

[2] There are, of course, restrictions which depend on the semantic and syntactic properties of the words used. This is why we said "have the potential." *Several old ladies frightened the wind* is an anomalous sentence, but *several old ladies* can occur as the subject NP in *Several old ladies frightened the little kitten.*

[3] The *future tense* in English is expressed by the use of the "auxiliary verbs" *shall, will,* and *going to,* not by changing the tense of the verb. Remember that we are not including all the rules of English syntax but merely illustrating what kinds of syntactic rules exist and what they do in the grammar.

even if they never heard the term *noun phrase*. They know the different linguistic forms that can be referring expressions, and they know that only that type of linguistic form can be a subject and occur in an environment like "_____ was lost" or be an object and occur in an environment like "Who found _____?"

> 6 a. The kitten was lost.          Who found the kitten?
>   b. The blond haired girl         Who found the blond-haired
>      was lost.                      girl?
>   c. It was lost.                   Who found it?
>   d. Sally was lost.                Who found Sally?

As the (c) sentences show, an NP may be a pronoun, since a pronoun (Pro) is a referring expression that can be a subject or an object. And the (d) sentences show that an NP can be a proper noun (the name of a *particular* person or place or object), for all proper nouns refer to someone or something and can serve as subjects or objects, as Alice pointed out:

> "What's the use of their having names," the Gnat said, "if they won't answer to them?"
> "No use to *them*," said Alice, "but it's useful to the people that name them, I suppose. If not, why do things have names at all?"

A noun phrase can also be a noun (N) preceded by such morphemes as *a, the, some, several, every, each, many, my,* and so on. Of these, we will only consider the articles (Art) *a* and *the*. An NP can of course be much more complex than what has been described so far, since it includes phrases such as *several old ladies who were drinking tea in the living room of the haunted house*.

NPs occur in all languages, although some of the details may differ. Thai, for example, has no articles (*phǒm hěn dèg* is literally "I see boy"), and in Danish the article follows the noun as a suffix (*bog*, "book"; *bogen*, "the book"). The particular rule which "rewrites" NP, that is, which states what it is, will differ somewhat from language to language, but all grammars will include an "NP rule."

An oversimplified version of the English NP rule may be stated:

> 4 A Noun Phrase may be a pronoun (Pro) or a proper noun ($N_{prop}$) or a noun (N) preceded by an article (Art) or a noun preceded by one or more adjectives (Adj) all of which are preceded by an article.

The more complicated these rules get, the more difficult it is to understand them when they are written out in this way. Formally we can abbreviate this rule as:

$$4' \ NP \rightarrow \begin{Bmatrix} Pro \\ N_{prop} \\ Art \ (Adj)*N \end{Bmatrix}.$$

Once more the braces designate the optional choice between a pronoun, a proper noun, and an expression containing a noun. When braces are used, one of the items enclosed must be chosen. That is, an NP must be something. Thus the braces differ from parentheses, which designate that the item enclosed may be selected or may be omitted. We added another device, the asterisk after the adjective, (Adj)*. This notation means "zero or more adjectives." It clearly states that a noun phrase of this type can include no adjectives (*the man*) ; one adjective (*the old man*) ; two adjectives (*the dirty old man*) ; three adjectives (*the bearded dirty old man*) ; ? adjectives (*the skinny, red-haired, lecherous, bearded, . . . dirty old man*).

Further evidence that Rule 4 is a syntactic rule of English comes from the fact that English speakers know all the expressions in group 7a are noun phrases, and that none of the expressions in group 7b are:

|  |  |  |
|---|---|---|
| 7 a. | he | the dwarf |
|  | you | a good boy |
|  | Sally | an elegant old table |
|  | Chicago | the cross-eyed bear |
|  | Waterloo | a noun phrase |
| b. | man the | run |
|  | the man old | a blue whale is abaft the binnacle |
|  | an it | of a mouse |
|  | the Sally | an oaken |

You know much more about noun phrases than is shown by this rule. You know, for example, that most nouns can be singular or plural (*boy/boys, man/men*),[4] and that a prepositional phrase can follow the noun (*the cousin of my aunt, the hole in the bottom of the sea*). Clearly a complete grammar of English would have to include all this syntactic information about noun phrases, verb phrases, prepositional phrases, and so on.

All the rules given so far have counterparts in other languages, although there may be certain differences. In Korean,

---

[4] Some nouns do not ordinarily specify "number," such as *rice* and *molasses*.

*The wind the girl frightened* is a sentence and the VP rule would look like:

> **2K** A Verb Phrase consists of a Verb alone, or a verb *preceded* by a Noun Phrase.
> **2'K** VP → (NP)   V.

The NP in French differs in detail from its English counterpart in that French adjectives normally follow the noun. Thus Rule 4'F would be part of the NP rule of French to account for the order in the following phrases:

> 8 a. le gateau délicieux     "the delicious cake"
>    b. une femme intelligente     "an intelligent woman"
> **4'F** NP → Art N (Adj).

Though languages may differ in such details, they all have referring phrases (NP) and relating phrases (VP), and their sentences must contain at least one of each. They all have nouns, pronouns, and verbs, and they all require the morphemes of a sentence to occur in certain orders specified by the rules of syntax.

Rules 1 through 4 are valid for English (though not complete), and every speaker "knows" these rules whether he is aware that he knows them or not. He wasn't ever taught them by his mother, his teachers, or anyone else. Nor did he learn them from a book (illiterate speakers of English know them also). The rules are a part of the syntactic system of the language, and they are "learned" by children when language is acquired.

These rules are called **phrase-structure rules.** They show us what a sentence is, what a noun phrase is, what a verb phrase is, and so on. They also show that sentences are more than strings of morphemes which follow one after the other. The morphemes are grouped into substructures called **constituents.** The constituents are in a hierarchical arrangement showing what each constituent is composed of. For example, the constituent *sentence* is composed of a noun phrase and a verb phrase; the constituent *verb phrase* may be made up of a single verb, or a verb followed by a noun phrase; a *verb* consists of a verb stem followed by a morpheme of tense. The phrase-structure rules also reveal *grammatical relations.* They tell us that the first noun phrase is the *subject* of the sentence, but a noun phrase that occurs after the verb is the *direct object* of the sentence. Knowledge of the grammatical relations of a sentence is crucial to comprehension of meaning: *cats eat bats* is quite different from *bats eat cats!*

A sentence can be represented in a diagram called a **phrase-structure tree** or a **phrase marker** that reveals the constituent structure and the grammatical relations. Such diagrams of sentences 9a, 9b, and 9c are shown in Figures 1, 2, and 3, respectively.

9 a. The wind howled.
   b. The wind frightened me.
   c. A cold wind brings cold rainy weather.

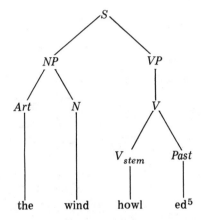

FIGURE 1. *Phrase marker of sentence 9a.*

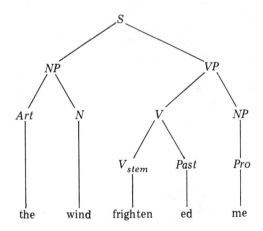

FIGURE 2. *Phrase marker of sentence 9b.*

[5] The phonetic representation of the grammatical morphemes like Past would be determined by the phonological rules of the language.

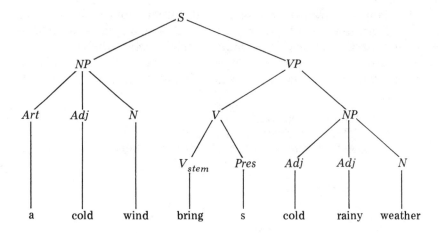

FIGURE 3. *Phrase marker of sentence 9c.*

Notice that such a phrase-structure tree (or phrase marker: PM) visually represents what you know about these sentences. Starting from the topmost structure of Figure 1, the tree shows that an S is composed of two parts, an NP and a VP, that the NP consists of an Art and an N, that the VP consists of a $V_{stem}$ and the tense Past. If you trace the "branches" of the tree from the bottom up, the diagram shows that *the* is an Art, that *wind* is an N, that *howl* is a $V_{stem}$, that *-ed* is the Past morpheme, that *the wind* is an NP, and *howled* is a V, and that *the wind howled* is an S. In addition, if you look at all three trees (Figures 1–3), you can see that *the wind, a cold wind, me,* and *cold rainy weather* are all NPs (since the label NP is at the points or *nodes* in the trees from which they all come). Of course you know this is true, but the diagrams reveal this knowledge.

These rules and the phrase-structure trees which can be constructed from them show what speakers know about the structures of the sentences of their language.

## Generative Syntax: Transformational Rules—Negation, Questions

BRUCE L. LILES

The syntax of a transformational-generative grammar usually contains two major kinds of language rules, phrase-structure rules (P-S rules) and transformational rules (T-rules), also called transformations. It may also contain lexical rules, sometimes called lexical-insertion rules.

In generating a sentence, the first rules to operate are the phrase-structure rules; the preceding selection by Fromkin and Rodman described the operation of these. After these phrase-structure rules have created a sentence-structure "tree," *lexical rules* may add lexical items (morphemes—e.g. word stems and endings) to the trees; however, some transformational grammars include addition of lexical items as the final part of the operation of phrase-structure rules. In either case, the sentence-structure "tree" created by P-S rules, complete with morphemes (however supplied) is called the *deep structure* of a sentence.

After a deep structure has been created, it is operated upon by transformational rules such as those given in this selection. As soon as the first transformational rule has been applied to the deep structure, it ceases to be a deep structure. After all the relevant T-rules have been applied, the sentence is said to be a *surface structure.* It is helpful to think of surface structures as surface syntactic structures, since they are not yet in final form; surface (syntactic) structures have to be operated upon by phonological rules before they reach a form a speaker might utter. Sample phonological rules are given in the following selection.

The phrase-structure rules Liles has used to create deep structures differ slightly from those used by Fromkin and Rodman; Liles's phrase-structure rules are listed in the Appendix.

## THE NEGATIVE TRANSFORMATION

The phrase-structure rules can produce the structures underlying such sentences as *Those boys might have been swimming in the lake* and *The manager wrote a letter.* They cannot produce such structures as the following:

1. The manager didn't write a letter.
2. Did the manager write a letter?
3. Who wrote a letter?
4. What did the manager write?
5. A letter was written by the manager.
6. Because the manager wrote a letter . . .
7. The letter that was written by the manager . . .
8. The letter written by the manager . . .

9. For the manager to write a letter . . .
10. The manager's having written a letter . . .

All of these structures seem to be related in some way to *The manager wrote a letter.* The same relationships are found in all of them: the manager is the one who performed the act of writing, and a letter is the result of this action. In spite of differences in form, there is a similarity in meaning in all the structures. Transformational rules are used to produce these changes in form.

Earlier we listed several sentence modifiers: *yes, no,* etc. To these we add *not,* which distinguishes a sentence such as *John could sing well* from the negative sentence *John could not sing well.* By selecting the SM [sentence modifier] *not,* we can derive a structure as shown [below]. This gives *not John past can sing well,* which is not grammatical. It would be grammatical if we changed the word order to *John past can not sing well (John could not sing well).* We now need to introduce two new terms: *deep structure* and *surface structure.* A structure generated only by phrase-structure and lexical rules, such as *not John past can sing well,* is a deep structure. A deep structure that has been transformed into a grammatical English sentence, such as *John could not sing well,* is called a surface structure. All grammatical English sentences are surface structures; underlying each one is a deep structure. . . . Both deep and surface structures are more abstract than we are presenting them here, since phono-

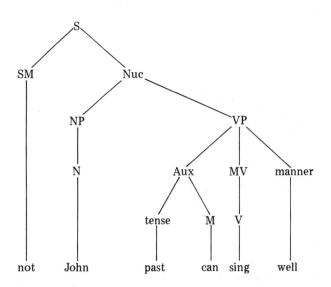

logical rules have not yet been applied. However, at this stage it is easier to follow the transformational rules if we use a form such as *not John could sing well* than the abstraction that is the actual deep structure.

All native speakers of English are capable of producing an infinite number of surface structures, or grammatical English sentences. Our purpose is not to teach you how to make negative sentences; any normal five-year-old can do that perfectly. Our main purpose in studying these structures is to learn to make accurate observations about how English operates. By *negative* we are referring to sentence negation, not word negation. *That is not probable* has the SM *not*. *That is improbable* does not have this SM and is, therefore, not part of this immediate study, although the processes we are employing in this chapter could easily be extended to account for such negative forms as *improbable*.

By selecting the optional SM *not*, we can generate a number of deep structures like those on the left below:

| | |
|---|---|
| 1. not Jerry could hear me | Jerry could not hear me. |
| 2. not Bill has received it | Bill has not received it. |
| 3. not they are going with us | They are not going with us. |
| 4. not they have been doing it | They have not been doing it. |

We need to formulate a rule to transform the deep structures on the left to the surface structures on the right. At first glance you might say something like "Move not to the position after the auxiliary." In the first sentence, *not Jerry could hear me*, this would work, but the third sentence would become *They are ing not go with us* (. . . the *ing* which accompanies the auxiliary *be* is part of the auxiliary). We must refine our observations. In the surface structure, the negative particle *not* follows part of the auxiliary, but not all of it. In fact, it follows only the first auxiliary after tense. In *not Jerry could hear me, could* is a case of *past + can. Can* is the first occurring auxiliary; therefore, *not* follows it in the surface structure. We use the abbreviation $Aux^1$ for the first auxiliary that comes after tense. In the following sentences $Aux^1$ has been marked:

1. they past *can* be ing go
2. we present *have* en eat
3. those dress Pl present *must* have en be red

So long as the auxilary contains something besides tense (a modal, *have,* or *be*), the first element following tense is Aux[1]. Our transformational rule for the correct placement of *not* should read something like this: "Move *not* to the position following the first auxiliary after tense." Since we will have a number of transformational rules, it will be advantageous to write them in a conventional abbreviated form. The rule can be stated as follows:

$$\text{not} + X + \text{tense} + \text{Aux}^1 + Y \Rightarrow X + \text{tense} + \text{Aux}^1 + \text{not} + Y$$

The information on the left of the arrow describes the structure to which the rule is applicable: one with the SM *not* and an Aux[1]. If either of these conditions is not met, the rule does not apply. The information on the right of the arrow describes the structure after the change has been made. The double arrow means that this is a transformational rule rather than a phrase-structure rule. Whereas phrase-structure rules merely expand elements, such as *Nuc*[1] into *NP* and *VP,* transformational rules rearrange, delete, add, or substitute elements, thereby altering the underlying structure of the sentence. The symbol $X$ stands for anything coming between *not* and *tense,* such as another sentence modifier or a noun phrase. Since the rule operates the same way regardless of what follows *not,* we can simplify our rule by using the symbol $X$ for any structure coming between *not* and *tense.* Similarly, $Y$ stands for anything following Aux[1]. This may be other auxiliaries, a verb, and anything that follows a verb. Since the same process applies regardless of what follows Aux[1], we can improve the rule by using the symbol $Y$ for this.

For the deep structure *not they present can hear you,* we can illustrate the rule in the following way:

| not | $X$ | tense | Aux[1] | $Y$ | |
|-----|------|---------|--------|------------|---|
| not | they | present | can | hear you | $\Rightarrow$ |

| $X$ | tense | Aux[1] | not | $Y$ |
|------|---------|--------|-----|----------|
| they | present | can | not | hear you |

This gives *They can not hear you,* after the phonological rules have been applied. This process can be illustrated with trees. Here is the deep structure:

---

[1] [Ed. note: Remember that Liles is referring to phrase-structure rules that are slightly different from those introduced by Fromkin and Rodman in the previous selection. His first P-S rule was $S \rightarrow (SM)\ Nuc.$ Then his second P-S rule expanded *Nuc: Nuc → NP VP.*]

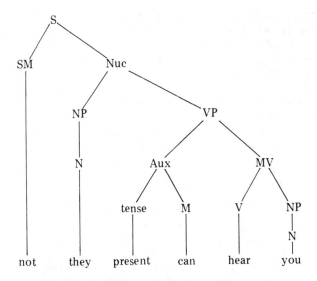

The negative transformation rearranges the tree to provide the following surface structure:

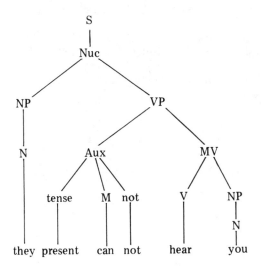

After the application of phonological rules, we have the sentence *They can not hear you.*

Before going further, you should practice with the following structures. Remember that you are trying to understand the process and the mechanics of the rule.

1. not those apples were smelling rotten
2. not Estelle would have done that
3. not you are reading fast enough
4. not Lucille will have finished by then
5. not we had heard the news

Some sentences have only tense in the auxiliary and, there-fore, no Aux[1]. For these sentences the rule we have given will not apply. We need to write new rules for these sentences; then we will see how we can modify the rule that we have already formulated. Examine the following deep structures on the left and their corresponding surface structures on the right:

1. not they are our friends     They are not our friends.
2. not Jane was friendly       Jane was not friendly.
3. not the bird was there      The bird was not there.

Like the sentences with Aux[1], these demand a rearrangement of the structure. This time *not* is placed after *be* instead of after an auxiliary. Notice that in these sentences *be* is not an auxiliary, since there is no verb following it and since there is no *ing* on the next word. The *be* in these sentences is part of the MV. We write this rule as follows:

$$\text{not} + X + \text{tense} + \text{be} + Y \Rightarrow X + \text{tense} + \text{be} + \text{not} + Y$$

This rule operates on the following deep structure:

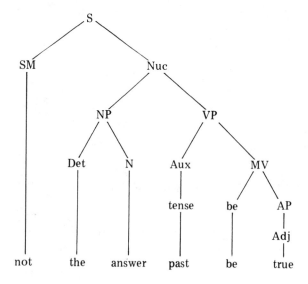

The rule transforms the deep structure into the following surface structure:

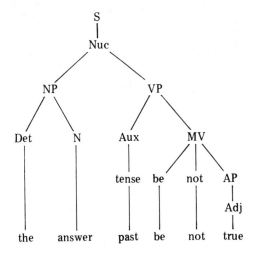

*The answer was not true.*

We have now covered those sentences with some element in the auxiliary in addition to tense; of the sentences with no such auxiliary, we have covered those that contain *be* as part of the MV. That leaves only those sentences with only tense in the auxiliary and with verbs other than *be* in the MV. The following structures illustrate the transformation involving these verbs:

1. not we play often       We do not play often.
2. not they taste the salt   They do not taste the salt.
3. not Terry eats early     Terry does not eat early.
4. not the janitor did it    The janitor did not do it.
5. not the man sees me     The man does not see me.

In the surface structure *not* comes before the verb and after tense, which is attached to *do*. If we omit *do* from the surface structure, we obtain the following:

1. We present not play often.
2. They present not taste the salt.
3. Terry present not eat early.
4. The janitor past not do it.
5. The man present not see me.

These are not grammatical sentences, since *not* cannot be altered to show a contrast between past and present. To provide a grammatical sentence, we add the word *do*. Although this word has no lexical meaning, it can carry the tense morpheme: *do* and *does* in contrast to *did*. These sentences require two rules:

$$\text{not} + X + \text{tense} + V + Y \Rightarrow X + \text{tense} + \text{not} + V + Y$$
$$X + \text{tense} + A + Y \Rightarrow X + \text{tense} + \text{do} + A + Y$$

The negative rule moves *not* between tense and the verb. In the second rule, *A* stands for any morpheme other than an auxiliary or a verb. Any time *tense* appears before any such morpheme, we add the word *do* to carry the tense. To convert the deep structure *not we present jump here* into a surface structure, we apply the negative and *do* transformations as shown in the following trees.

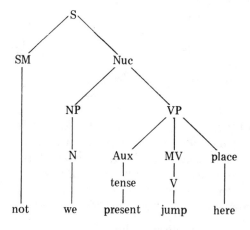

The negative transformation applies to this deep structure to produce the following *intermediate structure:*

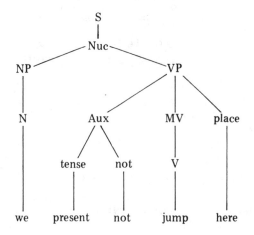

Now the *do* transformation applies to produce a surface structure:

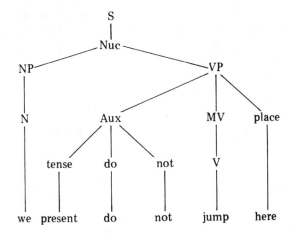

After the application of phonological rules this becomes *We do not jump here.*

We have now given three rules for the negative transformation in English, as follows:

$$\text{not} + X + \text{tense} + \text{Aux}^1 + Y \Rightarrow X + \text{tense} + \text{Aux}^1 + \text{not} + Y$$
$$\text{not} + X + \text{tense} + \text{be} \quad + Y \Rightarrow X + \text{tense} + \text{be} \quad + \text{not} + Y$$
$$\text{not} + X + \text{tense} + V \quad + Y \Rightarrow X + \text{tense} + \text{not} \quad + V \quad + Y$$

There is a great deal of repetition among these rules. We have a means of combining the three:

$$\text{not} + X + \text{tense} \begin{bmatrix} \text{Aux}^1 \\ \text{be} \\ V \end{bmatrix} Y \Rightarrow X + \text{tense} \begin{bmatrix} \text{Aux}^1 + \text{not} \\ \text{be} + \text{not} \\ \text{not} + V \end{bmatrix} Y$$

The square brackets indicate that corresponding items must be selected on both sides of the arrow. If *Aux¹* is selected on the left, then *Aux¹* + *not* must be selected on the right; if *be* is selected on the left, then *be* + *not* must be selected on the right; if V is selected on the left, then *not* + V must be selected on the right.

## QUESTION TRANSFORMATIONS

Transformation is the process that converts deep structures into surface structures. The negative transformation involves a rearrangement of structure, as when we move *not* to the position after the first occurring auxiliary or after *be*. In the case of sentences containing only tense in the auxiliary and a verb other than *be*, the word *not* is shifted to the position after tense, and then another transformation adds *do*. This second transformation involves addition, rather than rearrangement of structure. In addition to these two processes, a transformation may delete material from the deep structure:

> He can't sing well, but I can sing well.
> He can't sing well, but I can. (*sing well* is deleted)

Or it may substitute something for a morpheme in the deep structure:

> When Jane saw me, Jane screamed.
> When Jane saw me, *she* screamed.

Some transformations involve a combination of these four processes: rearrangement, substitution, deletion, and addition. Phrase-structure rules do not perform any of these processes; rather, they expand elements (NP, Aux, etc.) into their constituents.

English has two main kinds of questions: those that are answered *yes* or *no (Are you ready? Did he leave? Should I stop?)* and those that are answered by other words *(Where are you going? Whose book are you reading? What is her name?)*. It will become obvious as we go along that these two kinds of questions are formed differently. We call the first type *yes/no questions,* the second type *WH questions*, since many of them begin with words with the first letters *wh*. In addition, there are questions such as *Sue is going, isn't she?* and *Sue isn't going, is she?* Then there is the echo question: *You heard him come in?* We will not be treating these kinds of questions, although they can easily be handled by the same processes we use for yes/no and WH questions.

It would be possible to derive yes/no questions from related declaratives such as the following:

1. Tom is sick.                  Is Tom sick?
2. They have already left.       Have they already left?
3. He heard us.                  Did he hear us?

With this approach we would have the same morphemes in both structures (except for *do* in *Did he hear us?*), but the transformation would change the meaning of the sentence. *Is Tom sick?*

does not mean the same thing as *Tom is sick*. A principle of our grammar is that transformations affect the form of a structure but not the meaning. By means of the negative transformation we derived *He will not go* from *not he will go*, both of which have the same meaning. *He will not go* is not derived from *He will go*, but is merely similar to it.

Likewise, *Tom is sick* cannot be the deep structure for *Is Tom sick?* although the two are similar. Just as the idea of negation must be present in the deep structure of a negative sentence, so the idea of interrogation must be present in the deep structure of a question. This idea is expressed by the SM *Q*, which indicates that the structure is a question. More specifically, it may be interpreted as meaning "I request that you answer *yes* or *no* to the question. . . ."

The sentences on the left below are deep structures that have the sentence modifier Q; those on the right are surface structures:

1. Q she could sing well      Could she sing well?
2. Q the book has become wet      Has the book become wet?
3. Q the bell is ringing now      Is the bell ringing now?

The process of forming questions, like that of making negatives, is not new to you. When you were very young, you incorporated into the grammar that you were learning certain rules for forming questions and negatives. These rules are still part of your grammar, but you are probably not conscious of the intricacies of this grammar, and your observations about it may be inaccurate. You might say that you are moving the verb in front of the subject noun phrase to form a question. This process, of course, would give *Could sing she well?* for the first question above, and you would begin refining your observation, as you did in describing the negative transformation. Tense and the first auxiliary (tense + Aux[1]) have been placed in front of the noun phrase in the surface structure; Q has been deleted. This transformation, like the negative, involves a rearrangement of elements. This part of the yes/no rule can be written as follows:

$$Q + NP + \text{tense} + \text{Aux}^1 + X \Rightarrow \text{tense} + \text{Aux}^1 + NP + X$$

This rule will apply to a deep structure like this:

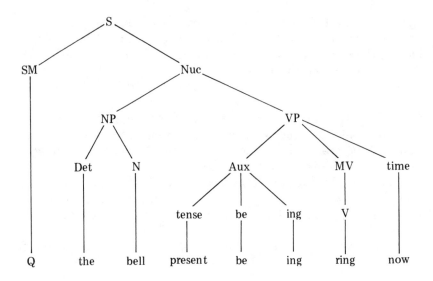

It produces the following surface structure:

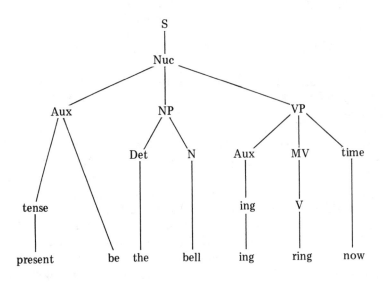

*Is the bell ringing now?*
    Now we will examine sentences with no Aux[1]:

|   |   |
|---|---|
| 1. Q the men are lucky | Are the men lucky? |
| 2. Q he was our supervisor | Was he our supervisor? |
| 3. Q Betty is at home | Is Betty at home? |

When tense is the only element of the auxiliary and the main verb is *be*, the subject noun phrase changes position with tense and *be*, and Q is deleted:

$$Q + NP + tense + be + X \Rightarrow tense + be + NP + X$$

So far we have seen a parallel between this transformation and the negative. Sentences with an auxiliary other than tense behave similarly to sentences with no such auxiliary but with *be* as the main verb. Sentences with only tense as the auxiliary and with verbs other than *be* behave differently under the negative transformation. Let us see whether this parallel is extended to the yes/no transformation:

1. Q John read my letter     Did John read my letter?
2. Q the teachers eat here     Do the teachers eat here?
3. Q she knows my name     Does she know my name?

If we omit the meaningless word *do* from the surface structures, we are left with structures such as *past John read my letter.* When there is no auxiliary other than tense and the main verb is not *be*, tense and the noun phrase change places, so that *Q she present know my name* becomes *present she know my name.* Since *present* cannot be attached to *she*, we apply the *do* insertion rule: *present do she know my name.* These steps can be shown as follows:

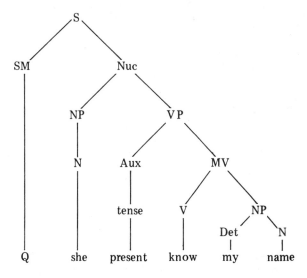

By the yes/no transformation this becomes:

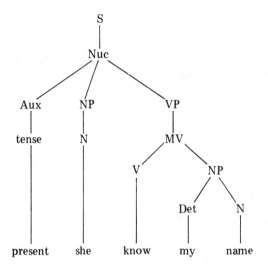

Then *do* insertion applies:

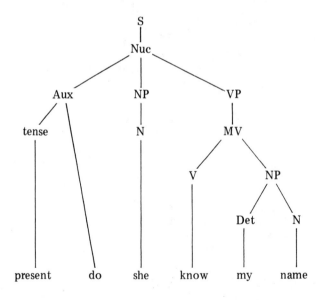

The complete rule for the yes/no transformation can be stated as follows:

$$Q + X + \text{tense} \begin{bmatrix} \text{Aux}^1 \text{ (not)} \\ \text{be (not)} \\ \text{(not) } V \end{bmatrix} Y \Rightarrow \text{tense} \begin{bmatrix} \text{Aux}^1 \text{ (not) } X \\ \text{be (not) } X \\ \text{(not) } X + V \end{bmatrix} Y$$

*Not* has been included in parentheses to allow for such sentences as *Isn't she going with us?*

According to our rules, we can have a deep structure like *Q not she is going with us.* We apply the transformations in the order (1) negative, (2) yes/no, (3) *do.* By negative we get the intermediate structure *Q she isn't going with us.* A structure like this that has had one or more transformations applied to it but which still is not a surface structure is called an *intermediate structure.* Then the yes/no transformation applies to produce the structure *Isn't she going with us?* Since tense can be attached to *be,* the *do* transformation is inapplicable.

Now let us examine the other kind of question, the WH question, as in *What is he saying?* This surface structure is derived from *Q he is saying something,* or preferably *Q he is saying* NP-WH. After the application of the yes/no transformation, we have the intermediate structure *Is he saying* NP-WH? The WH transformation substitutes the interrogative *what* for the noun phrase and shifts it to the beginning of the sentence: *What is he saying?* These processes are illustrated by the following trees. Here is the deep structure:

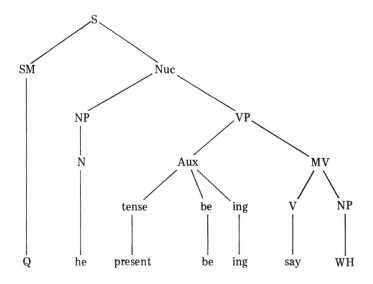

The yes/no transformation applies:

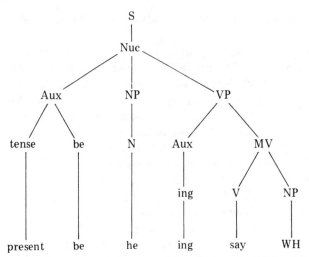

The WH transformation then shifts the NP with *WH* attached to it to the beginning of the sentence and substitutes *what:*

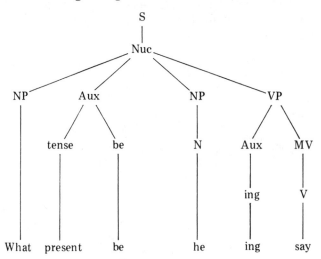

Notice the process in the following sentences. The ones on the left are intermediate structures that have undergone the yes/no transformation; those on the right have had the WH transformation applied to them:

1. are you reading NP-WH    What are you reading?
2. has she torn NP-WH    What has she torn?
3. were you giving it to NP-WH    Who(m) were you giving it to?

A noun phrase that has *WH* attached to it is replaced by *what* or *who* and moved to the beginning of the sentence.

If the noun phrase with WH-attachment is the object of a preposition, either the whole prepositional phrase or just the noun phrase may be moved. The choice is entirely stylistic, *What are you writing with?* being less formal than *With what are you writing?* We can express this transformation this way:

$$X + \text{(Prep) NP-WH} + Y \Rightarrow \text{(Prep)} \begin{Bmatrix} \text{who} \\ \text{what} \end{Bmatrix} X + Y$$

In the structure *are you reading NP-WH now,* X is everything before the noun phrase (*are you reading*) and Y is everything after it (*now*). Either X or Y may be nothing, as in *Are you reading NP-WH,* Y is nothing.

As we have stated the rule, there is no way of knowing whether *Q you saw NP-WH* will become *What did you see?* or *Whom did you see?* This choice between *who* and *what* depends on whether the NP has the feature [+ human] or not. The deep structure will attach to the NP not just WH, but also [+ human] or [— human]. The lexicon will give *who as* [+ human] and *what as* [— human].

But noun phrases are not the only structures that may have WH attachment. We may find it on an adverbial of place, as in *Where are you going?* which derives from *are you going Adv-p-WH.* Various adverbials may have WH attachment; the interrogatives that replace them are listed below, along with a possible answer:

| ADVERBIAL | REPLACEMENT | ANSWER |
|---|---|---|
| place (Adv-p) | where | there; in the yard |
| time (Adv-t) | when | then; tomorrow |
| manner (Adv-m) | how | carefully; with care |
| reason (Adv-r) | why | because of her; for me |

In addition to noun phrases and adverbials, determiners may have WH attachment. *Whose* replaces a possessive (*my, his, John's,* etc.) ; *which* (and sometimes *what*) replaces possessives or demonstratives. The WH transformational rule may be summarized as follows:

$$X \begin{bmatrix} \text{Adv-p-WH} \\ \text{Adv-t-WH} \\ \text{Adv-m-WH} \\ \text{Adv-r-WH} \\ \\ \text{Det-WH} + \text{N} \\ \\ \text{(Prep) NP-WH} \end{bmatrix} Y \Rightarrow \begin{bmatrix} \text{where} \\ \text{when} \\ \text{how} \\ \text{why} \\ \begin{Bmatrix} \text{whose} \\ \text{which} \\ \text{what} \end{Bmatrix} + \text{N} \\ \text{(Prep)} \begin{Bmatrix} \text{who} \\ \text{what} \end{Bmatrix} \end{bmatrix} X + Y$$

# Generative Phonology: Phonemes, Phonological Rules

VICTORIA FROMKIN and ROBERT RODMAN

Generative phonology describes two kinds of knowledge: knowledge of phonemes and knowledge of how to combine those phonemes into sequences. Phonemes are seen as underlying the phonetic form (sounds) of words and sentences. In much the same way that deep structures are operated upon by transformational rules, the underlying phonemic forms of words and sentences are operated upon by phonological rules, to result in the final phonetic representation of an utterance—the finished form that might be uttered by a speaker.

We can now summarize the creation of a sentence, as described in transformational-generative grammar. First, the phrase-structure rules generate a sentence structure, to which morphemes are added; the result is a *deep structure.* Then transformational rules operate on the deep structure; when all the relevant transformational rules have been applied, we have a *surface (syntactic) structure.* The sentence is then put in the form of phonemes, and these underlying phonemes are operated upon by phonological rules to produce the *surface phonetic form* of the sentence—that final form which could be uttered by a speaker. Remember, however, that we are not describing the mental process a speaker goes through; we are presenting a linguist's organization of the knowledge speakers have.

## PHONEMES: THE PHONOLOGICAL UNITS OF LANGUAGE

For a native speaker, phonological knowledge goes beyond the ability to produce all the phonetically different sounds of his language. It includes this, of course. A speaker of English can produce the sound [θ] and knows that this sound occurs in English, in words like *thin* [θɪn] or *ether* [iθər] or *bath* [bæθ].[1] An English speaker may or may not be able to produce a "click" or a velar fricative, but even if he can, he knows that such sounds are not part of the phonetic inventory of English. Many speakers are unable to produce such "foreign" sounds. A Frenchman simi-

[1] The use of brackets, [ ], as opposed to slashes, / /, is further explained on pages 335–336.

larly knows that the [θ] is not part of the phonetic inventory of French and often finds it difficult to pronounce a word like *thin* [θɪn], pronouncing it as [sɪn].

An English speaker also knows that [ð], the voiced counterpart of [θ], is a sound of English, occurring in words like *either* [iðər], *then* [ðɛn], and *bathe* [beð].

Knowing the sounds (the phonetic units) of a language is only a small part of one's phonological knowledge. The same set of phonetic segments can occur in two languages with different phonological systems. For example, . . . in English both aspirated and unaspirated voiceless stops occur. The aspirated stops [pʰ], [tʰ], and [kʰ] occur in the words *pill, till,* and *kill,* and the unaspirated stops [p], [t], and [k] occur in *spill, still,* and *skill.* If one pronounced *spill* with an aspirated stop, [spʰɪl], it would still be understood as *spill,* although someone hearing that pronunciation might wonder why the speaker was "spitting out" the word. [p] and [pʰ] (and the other pairs of voiceless stops) are different *phonetic* segments in English, but in spite of this, speakers consider them to be "the same." This is because the difference between the pairs of sounds is not **distinctive;** the substitution of one for the other does not change meaning. Even more than that, speakers of English "know" (unconsciously) when to produce an aspirated stop and when to produce an unaspirated stop; they know that aspirated voiceless stops occur at the beginning of a word, and unaspirated voiceless stops always occur after [s]. This is a fact about English phonology. There are two p-*sounds* which occur in English, but speakers consider the *two phonetic units* to be *one phonological unit,* which linguists call a **phoneme.**

Since the presence or absence of aspiration in English is *predictable,* aspiration is *nonphonemic;* it is a *redundant* feature of a voiceless stop which is always added in certain contexts.

When two sounds in a language are linguistically or phonologically distinctive—when the difference between them contrasts meanings—these two sounds are *separate phonemes* in the language. A phoneme is an abstract unit. We do not utter phonemes; we produce **phones,**—that is, phonetic segments.

We shall distinguish between these different kinds of segments by enclosing phonemes between two slashes, /p/, and phonetic segments (or phones) between square brackets, [pʰ] and [p]. [Previously we have] enclosed "broad transcriptions" in slashes. A phonemic transcription is like a broad transcription in the sense that all linguistically irrelevant (or predictable) features are ignored. A phoneme is, however, a unit of the phonological system of a language, and in this sense the "slash" notation represents more than a lack of phonetic detail. /p/, then, is a phoneme in English which is realized phonetically as either [p] or [pʰ]. When more than one phone is the phonetic realization of a single phoneme, these sounds have traditionally been called the **allophones** of the phoneme; [p] and [pʰ] are the allophones of the phoneme /p/.

These same phonetic segments occur in Thai, but they function differently in Thai and in English. In the chapter on phonetics we pointed out that whether a voiceless stop is aspirated or unaspirated in Thai is not predictable by a general rule. Both aspirated and unaspirated voiceless stops occur in the same position in different words:

[paa] "forest"     [pʰaa] "to split"

The presence of aspiration in Thai changes the meaning of the word, and it is therefore nonredundant; aspiration is a *distinctive* or *phonemic* feature in this language.

In English a general rule can be stated: "Voiceless stops are aspirated when they occur at the beginning of a word." This cannot be a rule in the phonology of Thai, as the examples above illustrate, since if we applied it to the word [paa] "forest" we would derive a different word, [pʰaa] "to split."

Thus, the same *sounds* may exist in two languages but they may function differently. Both English and Thai include the phones [p] and [pʰ]; but in English they represent one phoneme /p/, and in Thai they represent two phonemes /p/ and /pʰ/. Aspiration as a *phonetic* feature of sounds occurs in both languages. Since aspiration is predictable in English, it is nonphonemic; since it is not predictable in Thai, it is a distinctive phonemic feature of phonological units.

Knowledge of a language includes knowing which sounds are phonemic and which are not. That may sound very complicated and abstract. Yet every speaker "intuitively" knows that different sounds may represent a single abstract phoneme. When linguists describe the phonology of a language they attempt to make such intuitive knowledge explicit.

An examination of the phonological system of English reveals other such predictable nonphonemic properties of sounds.

Every speaker of English knows that an l-sound occurs in English. There must be a phoneme /l/, since *lake* means something different from *rake, make, bake, take, cake,* and so on. Most speakers of English also believe that the same /l/ occurs in *leaf* and *feel*, and *phonemically* this is true. *Phonetically*, however, the /l/ in *leaf* and the /l/ in *feel* differ. When you pronounce *leaf*, the back of the tongue is not raised; in the pronunciation of *feel* the back of the tongue is raised toward the hard palate or velum. If you say these words aloud and concentrate on the tongue position you may feel the difference. If you can't feel the difference, and if you find it difficult to hear the difference, it is not surprising. This reflects the truth of the statement that there is only one /l/ phoneme in English. Despite the phonetic differences, the two phones seem the same. An /l/ produced with the back of the tongue raised is called a "velarized *l*" (or "hard *l*"). In Russian there is a phonemic difference between these two sounds, but in English, just as with aspiration, velarization is *predictable* or *redundant* or *nonphonemic* or *nondistinctive* (all these terms are equivalent). In English, /l/ is velarized ([ɫ]) *only* when it occurs before a back vowel, as in *look, Luke, lock, load*, or when it occurs at the end of a word, as in *feel, fool, pal, pull, pill*. Thus, velarization is predictable by rule, and the two phonetic l-sounds [l] and [ɫ] represent allophones of the single phoneme /l/.

## SEQUENCES OF PHONEMES

> If you were to receive the following telegram, you would have no difficulty in correcting the "obvious" mistakes:
>
> BEST WISHES FOR VERY HAPPP BIRTFDAY
>
> because sequences such as BIRTFDAY do not occur in the language.
>
> —COLIN CHERRY, *On Human Communication*

We demonstrated above that one's knowledge of the phonological system includes more than knowing the phonetic inventory of sounds in the language. It even goes beyond knowing the phonemes of the language.

A speaker also knows that the phonemes of his language cannot be strung together in any random order to form words. The phonological system determines which phonemes can begin a word, end a word, and follow each other.

That speakers have knowledge of such sequential rules is not too difficult to demonstrate. Suppose you were given four cards, each of which had a different phoneme of English printed on it:

| /k/ | /b/ | /l/ | /ɪ/ |
|-----|-----|-----|-----|

If you were asked to arrange these cards to form all the "possible" words which these four phonemes could form, you might order them as:

| /b/ | /l/ | /ɪ/ | /k/ |
| /k/ | /l/ | /ɪ/ | /b/ |
| /b/ | /ɪ/ | /l/ | /k/ |

These are the only arrangements of these phonemes permissible in English. */lbkɪ/, */ɪlbk/, */bkɪl/, */ɪlkb/, etc., are not possible words in the language. Although /blɪk/ and /klɪb/ are not *existing* words (you will not find them in a dictionary), if you heard someone say:

"I just bought a beautiful new *blick*."

you might ask: "What's a 'blick'?" But if you heard someone say:

"I just bought a beautiful new *bkli*."

you would probably just say "What?"

Your knowledge of English "tells" you that certain strings of phonemes are permissible and others are not. After a consonant like /b/, /g/, /k/, or /p/ another similar consonant is not permitted by the rules of the grammar. If a word begins with an /l/ or an /r/, every speaker "knows" that the next segment must be a vowel. That is why */lbɪk/ does not sound like an English word. It violates the restrictions on the sequencing of phonemes.

Other such constraints also exist in English. If the initial sound of *church* begins a word, the next sound must be a vowel. [čat] or [čon] or [čækəri] are possible words in English, but *[člit] and *[čpæt] are not.

All languages have similar constraints on the sequences of phonemes which are permitted. Children learn these rules when they learn the language, just as they learn what the phonemes are and how they are related to phonetic segments. In Asante Twi, a word may end only in a vowel or a nasal consonant. /pik/ is not a possible Twi word, because it breaks the sequential rules of the language, and /ŋŋa/ is not a possible word in English for similar reasons, although it is an actual word in Twi.

Speakers of all languages have the same kinds of knowledge. They know what sounds are part of the language, what the phonemes are, and what phonemic and phonetic sequences may occur. The specific sounds or sound sequences may differ, but the phonological systems include similar *kinds* of rules.

## THE RULES OF PHONOLOGY

*No rule is so general, which admits not some exception.*
—ROBERT BURTON

*But that to come*
*Shall all be done by the rule.*
—SHAKESPEARE, *Antony and Cleopatra*

Everyone who knows a language knows the basic vocabulary of that language. This means he knows that an object like "pot" is represented by a given sequence of phonemes, /pat/. In other words, he knows both the sounds and the meanings of these linguistic units. This knowledge must be part of the way he "stores" these words in his mental dictionary, since when he wants to refer to the concept "pot" he doesn't produce the sounds [tʰap]. But he needn't represent the sounds of this word by including all the phonetic features of these sounds as we saw in the discussion on phonemes, as long as the relationship between the phonemic representation he has stored and the phonetic pronunciation is "rule-governed." The rules which relate the minimally specified phonemic representation to the phonetic representation form part of a speaker's knowledge of his language. They are part of his grammar. One such rule in the grammar of English was given above:

1 Voiceless stops are aspirated at the beginning of a word.

This rule makes certain predictions about English pronunciation. It specifies the class of sounds affected by the rule ("voiceless stops") and it specifies the context or phonemic environment of the relevant sounds ("at the beginning of a word"). Obviously both kinds of information must be given by a phonological rule, or we could apply it to the wrong class of sounds (for example, voiced stops) or in some environment where it is inapplicable (for example, after an /s/). Given this rule we can represent the words *pick, tick,* and *kick* phonemically as /pɪk/, /tɪk/, and /kɪk/ and *derive* the correct phonetic representation as follows:

/pɪk/ ⟶ apply rule ⟶ [pʰɪk]
/tɪk/ ⟶ apply rule ⟶ [tʰɪk]
/kɪk/ ⟶ apply rule ⟶ [kʰɪk]

We can also represent *stick,* for example, as /stɪk/. The rule will not apply, since the voiceless stop /t/ does not occur at the beginning of a word and the phonetic form is thus identical with the phonemic, [stɪk].

A separate rule was not necessary for each word or for each voiceless stop. In fact, had we given individual rules for /p/, /t/, and /k/ we would have obscured a generalization about English—that the rule applies to a *class* of phonemes. This further illustrates why individual phonemes are better regarded as combinations of features than as indissoluble whole segments.

Notice that the "aspiration rule" adds a *nondistinctive* (that is, nonphonemic) feature to the specification of phonemes in certain phonemic environments. Such rules exist in every language. A similar rule in English adds the feature "nasalization" or [+nasal] to vowels when they occur before nasal consonants. While nasalization is a phonemic feature for consonants (since *bat* contrasts with *mat*, and *nip* with *dip*), it is nonphonemic or nondistinctive for vowels, as was discussed above. This rule adds a feature which is nondistinctive for a particular class of sounds to that class in particular contexts. It was stated above as:

**2** A vowel is nasalized when it occurs before a nasal consonant.

The nasalization rule is a very common one in languages of the world; it is probably a universal rule. Such a rule **assimilates** one segment to another; that is, it "copies" a feature of a sequential phoneme, making the two phonemes more similar. **Assimilation** rules are, for the most part, caused by articulatory or physiological processes.

The rule concerning the velarization of /l/ also adds a nonphonemic feature to the phoneme in certain contexts. It may be stated as:

**3** Velarize an /l/ when it occurs before a back vowel or when it occurs at the end of a word.

Such rules illustrate that their function in a grammar is to provide the phonetic information necessary for the pronunciation of utterances. One may illustrate the function of phonological rules in the following way:

*input* PHONEMIC (DICTIONARY) REPRESENTATION OF WORDS IN A SENTENCE

↓

Phonological Rules (P-Rules)

↓

*output* PHONETIC REPRESENTATION OF WORDS IN A SENTENCE

That is, the input to the P-Rules is the **phonemic representation**; the P-rules apply or operate on the phonemic strings and produce as output the **phonetic representation.**

This should not be interpreted as meaning that when we speak we actually apply one rule after another. What we do when we actually produce sounds is part of linguistic performance. What these rules show is what a speaker knows about the abstract and surface phonetic relationships. The rules are part of one's linguistic competence.

We have illustrated the nature of phonological rules (P-rules) by three English examples: (1) Aspiration rule; (2) Nasalization rule; (3) Velarization rule. By applying these rules to the *phonemic representation* of words in English, we can derive the *phonetic representation* of these same words. (NA means "not applicable," or "does not fit the specifications of the rule.")

| PHONEMIC REPRESENTATION | /pɪl/ | /spɪl/ | /pɪn/ | /spɪn/ |
|---|---|---|---|---|
| Rule 1—aspiration | pʰɪl | NA | pʰɪn | NA |
| Rule 2—nasalization | NA | NA | pʰɪ̃n | spɪ̃n |
| Rule 3—velarization | pʰɪɫ | spɪɫ | NA | NA |
| PHONETIC REPRESENTATION | [pʰɪɫ] | [spɪɫ] | [pʰɪ̃n] | [spɪ̃n] |

The examples illustrate that phonological rules may *add features* to phonemes, but they do more than this.

To form a regular plural in English one adds either a [z], [s], or [əz]. The particular sound added depends on the final phoneme of the noun. It is not necessary to learn or memorize all the sounds in each class as a list. There are regularities—"rules" —which determine the proper plural ending. That is, the addition of [s] to *cat*, and [z] to *dog*, and [əz] to *bus* is determined by the same rule as that which adds [s] to *cap, book, myth, cuff*, and which adds [z] to *cab, cad, dive, cow*, and which adds [əz] to *pause, bush, beach, judge*. A grammar which included lists of these sounds would not reveal the regularities in the language and would fail to model what a speaker knows about the plural formation.

The regular plural rule does not work for a word like *child*, which in the plural is *children*, or for *ox*, which becomes *oxen*, or for *sheep*, which is unchanged phonologically in the plural. *Child, ox*, and *sheep* are *exceptions* to the regular rule. One learns these exceptional plurals when learning the language. If the grammar represented each unexceptional or regular word in both its singular and plural forms—for example, *cat* /kaet/, *cats* /kæts/; *cap* /kæp/, *caps* /kæps/; and so on, it would imply that the plurals of *cat* and *cap* were as irregular as the plurals of *child* and *ox*. But this is not the case. If a new top appeared on the market called a *glick* /glɪk/, a young child who wanted two of them would ask for two *glicks* [glɪks] and not two *glicken* even if the child had never heard anyone use the plural form [of *glick*]. This is because he would know the regular rule to form plurals. A grammar that describes his knowledge (his internalized mental grammar) must then include the general rule.

If the plural ending is phonemically represented as /z/, the regular plural rules can be stated in a simple way:

4 a. Insert an [ə] before the plural ending when a regular noun ends in a sibilant (/s/, /z/, /š/, /ž/, /č/, or /ǰ/).
   b. Change the voiced /z/ to voiceless [s] if the regular noun ends in a voiceless sound.

Notice that it is not necessary to do anything to the /z/ if the noun ends in a nonsibilant voiced sound; its phonetic form is identical with its phonemic representation: /z/ is pronounced [z].

This phonological rule will derive the phonetic forms of plurals for all regular nouns:

| PHONEMIC REPRESENTATION | *bus* + plural /bʌs + z/ | *bat* + plural /bæt + z/ | *bag* + plural /bæg + z/ |
|---|---|---|---|
| | ↓ | | |
| Rule 4a | ə | NA ↓ | NA |
| Rule 4b | NA | s | NA |
| PHONETIC REPRESENTATION | [bʌsəz] | [bæts] | [bægz] |

As we formulated these rules, Rule 4a must be applied before Rule 4b. If we applied the two parts of the rule in reverse order we would derive incorrect phonetic forms:

PHONEMIC REPRESENTATION  /bʌs + z/

Rule 4b  ↓ s
Rule 4a  ə
PHONETIC REPRESENTATION  *[bʌsəs]

The "plural-formation" rule shows that, in addition to adding features to phonemes, *entire segments can be inserted* into a phonemic string; an [ə] is added by the first rule.

Phonological rules can also *change feature specifications*. In the previous chapter we pointed out that the phonetic form of the prefix meaning "not" is phonetically variant; it is [ɪn] before a vowel or an alveolar consonant, [ɪm] before a labial consonant, and [ɪŋ] before a velar, as illustrated in the following words:

| *in*operable | [ɪnapərəbəl] |
| *in*discrete | [ɪndəskrit] |
| *im*plausible | [ɪmpləzəbəl] |
| *in*conceivable | [ɪŋkənsivəbəl] |

Since in all these cases the same prefix is added, one would expect it to have the same phonemic representation. If it is represented phonemically as /ɪn-/, the phonetic forms are predictable by one rule:

5 Within a word, a nasal consonant assumes the same place of articulation as a following consonant.

The rule states the class of phonemes to which it applies (all nasal consonants) and where it is to be applied (before another consonant). Like the vowel nasalization rule, this is an *assimilation* rule; the nasal assimilates its place of articulation to agree with the articulation of the following consonant. When two consonants have the same place of articulation they are called **homorganic** consonants. We can call Rule 5 the "homorganic nasal" rule.

In the examples above, *inoperable* is composed of the prefix /ɪn-/ plus *operable*, which begins with a vowel. The rule cannot apply because it specifically mentions that it is only relevant if the nasal is followed by a consonant. Thus /ɪn-/ is phonetically [ɪn]. When /ɪn-/ is prefixed to *discrete*, since the /n/ and /d/ are already homorganic (that is, they are both [+alveolar]), the rule applies vacuously; it does not change the /n/, and the phonetic form of the prefix is [ɪn-]. The /ɪn-/ is changed to [ɪm-] before *plausible*, since /n/ is alveolar and /p/ is labial, and the /n/ a velar [ŋ] before the initial velar /k/ in *conceivable*. The phonetic representation of these words should also include the nasalization of the vowels that occurs before nasal consonants; this nasalization would be added by the nasalization rule given above as Rule 2.

In the previous chapter it was pointed out that the same "homorganic-nasal" rule occurs in Twi, and, in fact, this rule is found in many languages of the world. A rule such as this does not add a phonetic feature to a phoneme but *changes the feature specification* of that phoneme.

The spelling of *implausible* (or *impossible*) reflects the phonetic representation of these words, while the spelling of *incommunicable* (or *incompetent*) represents the phonemic representation.

# Applications for the Study of Modern Grammars

## "Syntactic Maturity" and Syntactic Appropriateness in Teaching Writing

JEAN MALMSTROM and CONSTANCE WEAVER

Is transformational grammar really a useful tool for teaching writing? In a search for ways of measuring good writing, the length of a "T-unit" (kind of sentence) and the number of words in "free modifiers" (part of a sentence) have been suggested as measures of the "syntactic maturity" a student writer shows. Since these measures can be translated into numbers, they can be used to write behavioral objectives; the goal will be to produce students who write longer T-units and use more free modifiers. Students will be writing longer and more complex sentences than they wrote before.

It seems to me that this excerpt raises some important questions by discussing the relationship between "syntactic maturity," clarity, and appropriateness. Are long sentences, with wordy "free modifiers," always clear and appropriate?

Perhaps true syntactic maturity consists of knowing when to use a simple sentence and when to use a complex one. Feedback from an audience you *want* to communicate with is one reliable teacher of this kind of syntactic maturity;

Stephen Judy's suggestions about connecting students with topics and audiences, in Part 1, should provide the right kind of feedback.

A final question to you as a student: would you prefer to see your textbooks rewritten in a more complex style, or in a simpler style?

Behind every piece of writing we can assume a narrator or persona, a mind reporting and/or commenting on an event or telling a story. In literary analysis, it is common to assume that the author of the work is never to be equated with the narrator of the work, regardless of apparent resemblances. For example, the first-person narrator of Ernest Hemingway's *A Farewell to Arms* resembles Hemingway in a number of ways, but it would be an oversimplification to say that he *is* Hemingway. He is a literary character, and the style of his narration—the style of the novel—is *his* style, not merely Hemingway's. Even in third-person narrations there is a distinction between author and narrator, since most authors are stylistically versatile, not limited to the style they use in any given work.

A narrator is characterized in part by his unique patterns of word structures and meanings and by his characteristic sentence patterns. In analyzing and comparing sentence patterns, we will make use of several criteria of "syntactic maturity," criteria that are particularly useful in describing and comparing first-person narratives and narrators. First, then, we will discuss two men's widely accepted measures—definitions, really—of syntactic maturity.

In 1965 Kellogg Hunt examined seventy-two 1000-word samples of writing from eighteen writers in each of four groups: fourth graders, eighth graders, twelfth graders, and adult professional writers for *The Atlantic* and *Harper's*. Hunt defined syntactic maturity simply as "the observed characteristics of writers in an older grade." [1] Statistical analysis of Hunt's data revealed that the best measure of syntactic maturity was the length of what Hunt called the "minimum terminable unit," or "T-unit" for short. [2]

A T-unit consists of one main clause plus whatever full or

---

[1] Kellogg Hunt, *Grammatical Structures Written at Three Grade Levels* (Urbana, Ill.: NCTE, 1965), p. 5.
[2] Hunt, *Grammatical Structures*, pp. 21, 23.

reduced clauses are embedded within it.[3] A sentence cannot be divided into two T-units if only one of the parts can stand alone as a grammatical sentence, with independent subject and predicate. For example, we cannot cut *I drove downtown and bought some art supplies* after the word *downtown*, because the latter part of the sentence has no surface subject. Although we might sometimes punctuate *and bought some art supplies* as a sentence, it is not a T-unit. Therefore the original sentence cannot be divided; it is one T-unit, with a compound predicate. The following sentences give further illustrations of how sentences, clauses, and T-units are related:

| | |
|---|---|
| 1 independent clause; 1 T-unit | I drove downtown |
| 1 independent clause, with compound predicate; 1 T-unit | I drove downtown and bought some art supplies |
| 2 clauses, 1 independent and 1 subordinate; 1 T-unit | I drove downtown and bought art supplies after I ate my breakfast |
| 2 independent clauses; 2 T-units | I drove downtown and I bought some art supplies |

According to Hunt's research, clause length is the second-best measure of syntactic maturity, the number of clauses per T-unit is the third-best measure, and sentence length is the fourth-best. Hunt's statistics on these four measures of syntactic maturity are as follows: [4]

| | 4TH | 8TH | 12TH | ADULT |
|---|---|---|---|---|
| No. of words per T-unit | 8.60 | 11.50 | 14.40 | 20.30 |
| No. of words per clause | 6.60 | 8.10 | 8.60 | 11.50 |
| No. of clauses per T-unit | 1.30 | 1.42 | 1.68 | 1.78 |
| No. of words per sentence | 13.50 | 15.90 | 16.90 | 24.70 |

Another useful measure of syntactic maturity is the percentage of words in what Francis Christensen calls **free modifiers**. Christensen explains that all words and constructions that stand before the subject nominal are free modifiers, with the exception of coordinate conjunctions like *and* and *but*. Every medial or final word or construction that is set off by commas or dashes or parentheses is a free modifier. Grammatically speaking, there

---

[3] Embedded clauses (adjectival, adverbial, and nominal) are traditionally called *subordinate* or *dependent* clauses. Hunt himself uses the term "subordinate."

[4] Hunt, *Grammatical Structures*, p. 56.

are three types of free modifiers: 1) movable adverbials; 2) absolutes; and 3) nonrestrictive adjectivalizations, either in their full relative clause form or, more often, reduced to appositives, participles, or other adjectival phrases or words. The following sentences illustrate these various categories:

> **yesterday** we went to shop at the new mall (movable adverbial)
>
> she fixed the rattlesnake meat for dinner, **because there was nothing else in the house** (movable adverbial)
>
> the boy suddenly appeared in the doorway, **his lips moving unintelligibly** (absolute)
>
> she could not see very well, **the light being out** (absolute)
>
> his best friend, **who was a lifeguard,** saved her (nonrestrictive adjectival clause)
>
> his best friend, **a lifeguard,** saved her (appositive)
>
> the woman, **yelling at us,** was some distance away (participial phrase)
>
> **upset by recent events,** the man stared uncomprehendingly at his son (adjectival phrase)
>
> the woman, **behind us now,** was still yelling (prepositional phrase functioning adjectivally)

Christensen analyzed fifty T-units in the essays of six writers for *Harper's*. On the average, thirty-two per cent of their total number of words occurred in free modifiers.[5] The two professional writers had a higher percentage of words in free modifiers than the two semiprofessionals, and the two semiprofessionals had a higher percentage than the two nonprofessionals.

Obviously Hunt's and Christensen's criteria for measuring syntactic maturity are interrelated, since the number and length of free modifiers affects the number of words per T-unit, clause, and sentence.

But it is important to realize that syntactically mature sentences as defined by these measures are not always as appropriate in context as sentences that are syntactically less mature. As an example, let us compare the two paragraphs below. The first is the original;[6] the second is a rewriting by a student, who was asked to change the style of the original without changing the basic meaning of the sentences. The contrasting parts are bold-faced:

[5] Francis Christensen, "The Problem of Defining a Mature Style," *English Journal*, 57 (April 1968), 577.

[6] Robert LaRue, "Mercy Killing," *Sage* (Spring 1967), 181–200.

*I*
*Original Version*

> Pollo's father, Felipe Calderón, ran a good
> business. **He was clever with his hands and made**
> **a decent living fixing broken toasters, lawn-**
> **mowers, and other small mechanical objects, and**
> 5    **sharpening all kinds of tools, from scissors to**
> **power saws.** The people of Santa Margarita
> brought their small mysteries of mechanical
> failure to Felipe for two reasons: he was a good
> mechanic, and he charged less for his work than
> 10   did Santa Margarita Feed & Hardware. **Goose**
> **Fortner, owner of the hardware, did not envy**
> **Felipe's business. There was little money in fix-it**
> **jobs anyway.** Goose always spoke of Felipe as
> "a good, honest Mex that does good work."
> 15   Then, winking a cheerless hound-dog's eye, he
> might add: "Just so long's he don't start selling
> feed. Them chiles'd ruin your stock!"

*II*
*Rewritten Version*

> Pollo's father, Felipe Calderón, ran a good
> business. **Being clever with his hands, he made a**
> **decent living fixing broken toasters and lawn-**
> **mowers and other small mechanical objects. He**
> 5    **also worked with sharpening all kinds of tools,**
> **from scissors to power saws. Because Felipe was**
> **a good mechanic and charged less for his**
> **work than did Santa Margarita Feed and**
> **Hardware, the people of Santa Margarita brought**
> 10   **their small mysteries of mechanical failure to**
> **him.** **Goose Fortner, the owner of the hardware,**
> **didn't envy Felipe's business since there was**
> **little money in fix-it jobs anywhere.** Goose always
> spoke of Felipe as "a good, honest Mex that does
> 15   good work." Then, winking a cheerless hound-
> dog's eye, he might add: "Just so long's he don't
> start selling feed. Them chiles'd ruin your stock!"

The bold-faced part of the student version has 21.8 words
per T-unit, on the average; this is slightly above the average
number of words per T-unit for the adult professional writers in
Hunt's study. Also the bold-faced part of the student version
has 49.4 per cent of its words in free modifiers, much more than
the average for the *Harper's* essays Christensen analyzed. Thus
by these criteria the student version is syntactically mature.

The bold-faced part of the original version has only 14.3 words per T-unit, about the same as Hunt's twelfth graders. And it has only 10.4 per cent of its words in free modifiers.

The main syntactic difference affecting these statistics involves adverbial clauses of reason. The student version has two such clauses: *Because Felipe was a good mechanic . . .* , and *since there was little money in fix-it jobs anyway.* Where the student version has a subordinate adverbial clause, the original version has two independent clauses:

> The people of Santa Margarita brought their
> small mysteries of mechanical failure to Felipe for
> two reasons: **he was a good mechanic, and he**
> **charged less for his work than did Santa**
> **Margarita Feed & Hardware.** [boldface ours]

In the other instance, the causal relation is again made explicit in the student version with the subordinator *since.* But in the original the causal relationship is merely implied, through the juxaposition of independent clauses. The first independent clause states a fact, and the second gives the cause:

> Goose Fortner, owner of the hardware, did not
> envy Felipe's business. There was little money
> in fix-it jobs anyway.

Since the original passage has independent clauses corresponding to the subordinate clauses of the rewritten version, the original version has shorter T-units and a much lower percentage of words in free modifiers. But this does not mean that the rewritten version is stylistically *better.* The original author created an omniscient narrator who apparently was not meant to be of interest in himself. The avoidance of adverbial clauses of reason in the original version helps to keep the narrator much less obtrusive than in the rewritten version, which does use adverbial clauses of reason.

This is one indication, then, that syntactically mature sentences are not always stylistically appropriate sentences. Neither are syntactically mature sentences necessarily syntactically clear; that is, the syntax of a syntactically mature sentence may be difficult to unravel. Let us look, for example, at one T-unit from William Faulkner's "The Bear." The free modifiers are bold-faced below:

> and, **his father and Uncle Buddy both gone now,**
> **one day without reason or any warning** the almost
> completely empty house in which his uncle and

Tennie's ancient and quarrelsome great-grand-
5    father **(who claimed to have seen Lafayette and
McCaslin said in another ten years would be
remembering God)** lived, cooked and slept in
one single room, burst into peaceful conflagration,
**a tranquil instantaneous sourceless unanimity**
10   of combustion, walls floors and roof: [7]

This T-unit is seventy-two words long, three and a half times
as long as the average for the adult professional writers in Hunt's
study. The free modifiers constitute almost sixty per cent of the
total number of words. This is nearly twice as high as the average for the *Harper's* essays that Christensen analyzed. Thus
according to these criteria, the T-unit is very mature syntactically. But on a first reading it is far from clear.

One explanation for the lack of clarity is that most of the
free modifiers occur in the middle of the sentence. This admittedly
is an extreme example, but it does suggest why today's readers
might find clearest the kind of syntactically mature sentence
that Christensen advocates, the **cumulative sentence,** in which
most of the free modifiers occur in final position. In examining
a thousand sentences in fiction, Christensen found that over
half the free modifiers were in final position.[8] And in analyzing
the *Harper's* essays referred to above, he found the same pattern: over half the free modifiers occurred in final position for
the two semiprofessional and the two professional writers.[9]

Thus, according to Christensen, syntactically mature writing is clear writing, and clear modern American prose seems to
have a high percentage of its free modifiers in final position.

But a further caution is needed: in fiction, at least, clear
writing is not necessarily good writing. Good writing suits the
style to the narrator, to the subject and purpose, to the audience.
Thus a *good* style is an *appropriate* style. As an example, let
us consider once again the lengthy T-unit above, from "The
Bear." This T-unit is hard to read because a high percentage
of its words occur in medial modifiers, and because these medial
modifiers are self-embedded adjectival clauses, one within another. The deepest embedding is the parenthetical adjectivalization *(who claimed to have seen Lafayette and McCaslin said in*

---

[7] William Faulkner, "The Bear," in *The Portable Faulkner* (New
York: The Viking Press, Inc., 1946), p. 337.

[8] Francis Christensen, "A Generative Rhetoric of the Sentence." In
*Notes Toward a New Rhetoric* (New York: Harper and Row, Inc., 1967),
p. 18.

[9] Christensen, "The Problem of Defining a Mature Style," p. 577.

*another ten years would be remembering God).* This adjectivalization modifies *great-grandfather,* which is the subject of another adjectivalization: *in which his uncle and Tennie's ancient and quarrelsome* **great-grandfather** *lived, cooked and slept in one single room.* And this latter adjectivalization modifies *house,* the main subject of the T-unit. T-units are difficult to read if, like this one, they contain one adjectival clause embedded into another.

But in context, this kind of construction is appropriate. Faulkner has used an interior monologue technique; the sentence structure suggests the way the protagonist's mind operates, not completing one thought before moving on to another but holding one memory in suspension while recalling something else, and holding *that* in suspension while recalling yet another detail from the past.

Thus stylistically appropriate sentence structures are not necessarily clear or syntactically mature. It is important to keep these facts in mind . . . in analyzing and comparing styles.

## Syntactic Ambiguity in the Poetic Dialect

JAMES C. STALKER

Perhaps analyzing "T-units" and "free modifiers" is more time-consuming than constructive; but connecting the surface structure of a poem with its underlying sentence structure is a worthwhile use of time, if you want your students to follow you into an understanding of the poem. Since poetry can communicate with students of all ages, talking about sentence structure with students can be a mind-opener.

We looked at dialects in Part 2. Here in Part 3 we have seen sentences described as having both underlying and surface structures; in the summary article for Part 3, I suggest that differences between dialects are mostly in surface structures, not in deep structures. Stalker here suggests that poetry is a kind of dialect; and his point, too, is that the differences between spoken dialects and the poetic dialect can be minimized by teaching students to look for the underlying meaning.

As literature teachers, we normally view the task of leading students to an understanding and appreciation of poetry as being synonymous with teaching them to analyze and understand the images and metaphors of poetry. If our students can comprehend the poet's figurative language, we reason, they will then be able to grasp the meaning of the poem. This insight will lead to appreciation of the poem, and perhaps to the essential point—that the poem states truths and observations applicable to the student as well as to the poet. Without a doubt, such an analytic approach to poetry is an accurate and essential one. To achieve understanding the student must grapple with the poet's original metaphors, his semantic structures, and come to terms with them. We sometimes find, however, that our valiant attempts to plumb the meaningful depths of poetry in the classroom seem to yield little comprehension in the student. He does not follow us into the meaningful depths, the meaning behind the meaning, because he does not even fully understand the surface meaning.

Why does he fall short? There are numerous answers—limited experience, lack of maturity, scanty vocabulary, native dialect radically divergent from the poet's dialect, complete disinclination to read anything other than comic books, preoccupation with men's magazines or other immediately relevant material, cultural belief that poetry is essentially "effeminate," or an inability to decipher the peculiar English that poetry frequently seems to be written in.

Although all are potentially valid stumbling blocks for the student, we will concentrate on the last reason—poetry is written in a peculiar form of English. In part the unusual flavor of poetry lies in the extensive metaphor and symbolism. But syntax, the structure of sentences, quite frequently adds a uniqueness all its own—one too frequently glossed over. In far too many poems, we assume that the metaphor is central and the syntax peripheral, with the natural corollary that teaching the students to understand metaphor will automatically unravel the syntactic tangles. For the experienced reader, a frontal assault on the metaphoric structure of the poem proves to be the most effective approach. Syntactic tangles do in fact unravel themselves, simply because the experienced reader performs a simultaneous metaphoric and syntactic analysis. The inexperienced reader, however, cannot be expected to perform at such a sophisticated level. At least during the initial learning stages, we must attempt to separate syntax and metaphor so that the student is aware that they can be separated and that both contribute to the poet's style and message. In practice, for many poems the peculiarity would vanish rather rapidly if the student read the poem aloud rather than silently. As well as learning that there is a rhythm to poetry that emphasizes some words and phrases over others, he would learn that the lineation of the poem sometimes suggests artificial and arbitrary syntactic breaks. When lines are read as if they were sentences or single phrasal units unconnected to the preceding or following lines, simple comprehension can drop considerably. For instance the first two lines of Wordsworth's "I Wandered Lonely as a Cloud" are perfectly clear if we read them as one sentence,

> I wandered lonely as a cloud that floats on high o'er vales and hills,

but are not so clear if we read them as two unrelated clauses,

> I wandered lonely as a cloud.
> That floats on high o'er vales and hills. . . ,

in which case confusion arises concerning the referent for *that*, which is normally an unpredictable word in English. The confusion for the student may be increased considerably if punctuation is unusual. Line four of this poem ends with a semicolon ("When all at once I saw a crowd,/A host, of golden daffodils;"), a sure sign that we have reached the end of one independent clause and are about to begin another, since in prose a semicolon conventionally indicates a major syntactic break. Lines 5 and 6 are then

> Beside the lake, beneath the trees,
> Fluttering and dancing in the breeze.

Clearly these lines constitute a nonsensical sentence fragment, if we read poetry by the punctuation rules we teach our students. Yet we know, and the student may figure out, that the semicolon in line 4 does not indicate a syntactic break, but rather a rhetorical break—an emphatic pause. Reading the poem orally can aid the student by providing an obvious intonation pattern which guides him to a natural reading of such syntax.

The syntax of "I Wandered Lonely as a Cloud" predominantly follows the usual patterns of English sentence structure. But a poet must occasionally manipulate the internal syntactic structure of lines and the syntactic structure that extends over two or more lines, because of the dictates of his rhythmic structure (metrical or free verse) and rhyme scheme. Often these manipulations are part of the tradition of poetry and simply require familiarity from the reader.[1] For the purposes of this discussion, we will classify such manipulations as part of the . . . dialect of poetry. Since they are inversions of one sort or another they are a basic source of difficulty for the student. In English, dependent structures usually follow the head or parent structures. Dependent structures that can occur before the parent structure are marked with particular lexical items (*because, since, when, if*) or structural features (*-ing*), and when these appear, the student is alerted that this is not the main part of the sentence. He must hold his complete analysis of the sentence, his full interpretation of the meaning, until he receives the parent structure. Poetic inversions are functionally analagous to normal dependent structure inversions. Skilled readers of poetry have learned to expect and accept inversion and to hold full semantic interpretation until an appropriate structural niche becomes available for the transposed constituent. In other words, they have attained a skill in processing the features of the . . . dialect of poetry. Through the centuries the amount and nature of inversion which the public and the poet allow varies, but some always seems allowable and necessary.

The student will need some initial guidance in coping with these inversions, but in the long range, they should offer only a minimum difficulty. A few exercises in reordering the syntax from poetic to prose order should harm neither the student nor the poem. The student should not be asked to interpret the poem in these exercises, only to shift syntactic structures around so that he produces an accurate prose version of the poetic line or lines. In the Wordsworth poem, from

> For oft, when on my couch I lie
> In vacant or in pensive mood,
> They flash upon that inward eye
> Which is the bliss of solitude
> (11. 19–22)

you would expect

> For when I lie on my couch in (a) vacant or (a) pensive mood, they oft(en) flash upon that inward eye which is the bliss of solitude,

or

[1] For a discussion of inversion as a feature of poetic dialect from a structuralist point of view, see Seymour Chatman, "Linguistics and Teaching Introductory Literature," *Language Learning* 7:3–10 (1955–56). Also anthologized in *Readings in Applied English Linguistics*, 2nd Edition, ed. Harold Allen, New York, 1964.

> For when I lie on my couch in (a) vacant or (a) pensive mood,
> which is the bliss of solitude, they oft(en) flash upon that
> inward eye.

From

> Thou by the Indian Ganges' side
> Shouldst rubies find; I by the tide
> Of Humber would complain. . . ,
>             "To His Coy Mistress"
>             Andrew Marvell
>             (11. 5–7)

you would expect

> Thou shouldst find rubies by the Indian Ganges' side;
> I would complain by the tide of Humber.

Just as you may find "I don't be goin' to no school" or "He's too
clever by half" somewhat incomprehensible, so the student is
likely to find the poetic versions of these sentences somewhat out
of his realm of experience and his inexperience may well fore-
stall any progress into interpreting and understanding the poem.
To understand the poetic dialect, he must first gain some insight
into and familiarity with its structure. . . .

We can assume that some ambiguity, syntactic and semantic,
arises quite naturally from the poet's attempt to extend the communicative processes of the language, and may, therefore be
simply accidental. However, the assumption that the poet controls
his language structures, therefore any ambiguity is a deliberate
and intentional component of the structure of the poem and must
be interpreted as such, promises a more fruitful analysis. In
essence, we must assume that all potentially meaningful ambiguities must be considered as we work toward an interpretation of
the poem. In those cases where we can clearly eliminate all but
one of the possible interpretations on semantic or syntactic
grounds, perhaps we can tentatively postulate that the poet may
have produced an unintentional ambiguity.

Let's consider some examples in detail. . . .

Emily Dickinson's "Apparently with no surprise" contains
an . . . example:

> Apparently with no surprise
> To any happy Flower
> The Frost beheads it at its play—
> In accidental power—
> The blond Assassin passes on—
> The Sun proceeds unmoved
> To measure off another Day
> For an approving God.

Line 4 can be read with either line 3 or line 5, as

> The frost in accidental power beheads it at its play,
> and the blond assassin moves on. . .

or as

> The frost beheads it at its play, and the blond assassin
> moves on in accidental power.

In this poem, we should read the lines both ways; we should accept "in accidental power" as part of both sentences simultaneously, so that we could paraphrase the lines as

> The frost in accidental power beheads it at its play,
> and the blond assassin moves on in accidental power.

    . . . [Ambiguities such as these] would seem to offer little trouble to someone reading the poem. They do not require creative interpretation to discover a suggested meaning; in fact, they do not obscure the meaning at all. However, just such syntactic manipulations are potential trouble spots for the inexperienced reader. The experienced reader either does not notice the ambiguity, because he digests it easily, or notices it and fleetingly recognizes it as a good (or bad) artistic device—one of the things poetry is made of. On the other hand, such a manipulation can easily confuse the inexperienced reader. He is not sure how to structure the syntax of the sentence, so he reads three disconnected lines rather than a sentence and in doing so loses the middle three lines of an eight line poem. As a result, he will never be able to "interpret" the poem.

    Perhaps of more interest and importance are those syntactic ambiguities which produce semantic ambiguities. For instance, in these lines from Dylan Thomas' "Fern Hill"

> And honoured among foxes and pheasants by the gay house
> Under the new made clouds and happy as the heart was long,
>     In the sun born over and over,
>         I ran my heedless ways. . .

we can read the lines as either

> I ran my heedless ways in the sun which was born over and over,

or as

> I who was born over and over in the sun ran my heedless ways,

or as

> I who was born over and over ran my heedless ways in the sun.

The first sentence is a mythic-poetic view of dawn, the speaker's view of the discontinuity of time in which only the daylight hours are important or alternatively, in which there is no night. The second sentence suggests that the speaker exists only from dawn to dusk and is born anew each day, or he has some special relationship with the sun which enables him to have many beginnings when the sun is shining. The third possibility makes no necessary connection between the speaker's continual rebirth and the sun. It says only that he ran in the sun, and thus limits the interpretative possibilities. If we notice this ambiguity at all, and we should, we must stop and consider its ramifications, or we will miss a statement vital to a complete understanding and interpretation of the poem. We may assume that one of the variant readings is preferable and discount the others; we can accept them all and assume that all are necessary for a full interpretation—a judgment to be made only in the context of the full poem, since other images and other ambiguities will parallel or counterpoint this interpretative crux.

Before we can begin our argument for or against any or all of the interpretative readings just suggested, we must realize that the syntactic structure allows for all three. . . . The semantic ambiguity arises directly from the syntactic ambiguity, and the student, or any reader, must be aware of this fact before he can adequately consider the semantic possibilities. . . .

The intent of these examples is to demonstrate that the interpretation of poetry is not simply a function of semantic analysis, that we cannot assume that once a student can analyze metaphor he is competent to deal with poetic discourse. Syntactic ambiguity adds at least two dimensions to poetry. First it can be used as a stylistic device to gain the compression and density which we expect to find in poetry. It can unify the poet's world view by interweaving the statements in his poem more tightly than we allow or expect in normal discourse, as we found in the Shakespearean and Dickinsonian examples. Syntactic ambiguity can also establish interpretative cruxes in a poem, a point where the poet wishes or allows several interpretations to be made by the reader. At these points, if we argue only about the poet's semantic intent, we ignore at least half of the available poetic data, the syntax which the poet offers us. The student who attains a level of syntactic acuity which aids him in seeing and analyzing such interpretative cruxes attains some of the poetic sophistication we strive to instill in him. When he attains it we have done well by him and ourselves. He has achieved an adequate competence in reading the syntax of that form of language which we have informally called the poetic dialect. With this competence, he should achieve an appreciation of the originality with which poets manipulate our language to communicate complex statements in a tightly controlled form, and hopefully begins to see how he too can manipulate his language to communicate more precisely and originally.

## Modern Grammars and Teaching

I think that, for teachers, modern grammars should usually be a means to an end, not an end in themselves. Study of these tools for describing language helps a teacher understand students' language, especially when their language differs from his; and students can use some of these tools to come to a similar understanding of language and its variation. Knowing some basic facts about language structure is especially useful in evaluating prescriptive approaches to language. Study of linguistic theories can be offered as an elective unit, for those who are interested. But few of your students will need or want to study modern grammars only to learn current linguistic theories.

### UNDERSTANDING LANGUAGE IN THE CLASSROOM

Reading scientific descriptions of language—such as the descriptions given in Part 3—should give teachers quite a bit of respect for any speaker of any language, including the students whom teachers work with. These students come into the classroom knowing a great deal about language. They know the phonemes of their language, and what sequences of phonemes are permissible. They know a huge number of the morphemes in their language, as evidenced by statements such as these:

1. Mommy, would you come outside and higher my bicycle seat?
2. So I said to myself, "Self, you did gooder than you knew."

3. This asparagu is too hard. (said as child pushes one piece of asparagus to the side of the plate)

These children—all under age seven—showed knowledge of the morpheme we spell *-er*, affixed to adjectives to form comparative adjectives—*low, lower; high, higher; good, gooder*. The child who said sentence 2 separated *myself* into the two morphemes *my* and *self*. The child who said sentence 3 demonstrated knowledge of the plural morpheme: *cat, cats; asparagu, asparagus*. Their supposed mistakes are actually evidence of their knowledge of the rules of English. Of course, they do lack some knowledge of the exceptions to these general rules: the regular form *gooder* is not used, being replaced by the irregular *better* (in the past, of course, there was a word *bet* whose comparative was *better*); though there is a verb *lower*, derived from the adjective *lower*, there is no verb *higher* derived from the adjective *higher;* and the /s/ sound in *asparagus* is not a plural in the same way that the /s/ sound in *beets* is a plural. A child of five may not have the gender of proper names fully straightened out:

4. Would you like to see my caterpillar? His name is Debbie.

But the same child is able to produce the sophisticated structure *Would you like to see my caterpillar,* involving substituting pronouns for nouns; inversion of subject and auxiliary verb; use of the conditional auxiliary verb; embedding of the sentence *you see my caterpillar* into the sentence *you would like it* (*it* is replaced with the sentence *you see my caterpillar*); and, of course, use of the English phonology for pronouncing the sentence.

Let us look, then, at some specific ways a teacher's respect for and understanding of students' abilities can be increased by studying modern grammars.

**Phonology: Underlying and Surface Levels**

The fact that there are underlying phonemes in a person's language is largely new information to teachers. This is important information; many teachers have been assuming that the surface of speech *is* speech, that a phoneme not superficially present in a word is not present at all. The implication is that the child forgot to include that phoneme, or never learned the complete form of the word, or does not have the phoneme in his understanding of language in general.

This mistake has led educational researchers like Bereiter (1966) to believe that children who speak a dialect with final consonants dropped before other consonants only partially control language, because, for example, they often drop the final /t/ and /s/ in "got" and "juice."

But a final consonant, like the /t/ in *got* and the /s/ in *juice,* can be present in the underlying form of the word but deleted by a phonological rule; in that case, the phoneme is present in the child's understanding of the word and of language in general.

The same phonological rule that deletes final consonants in the speech of these children operates—though with varying frequency—on the speech of all native speakers of American English.[1] American English has other rules that prevent underlying phonemes from appearing in the spoken (phonetic) representation of a sentence. Labov, in Part 2, explains how /r/ is dropped variably in New York speech, depending on the speaker's social group and on the situation as well as on the phonetic surroundings of the consonant.

So an ignorance of the existence of underlying levels of language distorts educators' understanding of small children's language, leading them to make claims like "these four-year-olds could make no statements of any kind." [2] But this same ignorance also distorts the understanding of older students' speech. Studies of oral reading by speakers of varying dialects have suggested that the absence of a final /s/ in contractions like "he's" and "she's" shows the lack of the verb "to be" in the reader's speech. Closer study shows other forms of "to be" present in the same speech—the /m/ on "I'm," for example (Labov, 1973, pp. 111–112). It turns out, in fact, that in the dialect being studied (one variety of Black English) there is a phonological rule dropping /s/ at the end of a word; the verb "is" is not absent from the language of any speaker Labov studied. In Part 2 of this book, Dale discusses similar phonological rules in Black English.

### Syntax: Underlying and Surface Levels

INFLECTIONS. As we just discussed, whole words are sometimes represented by one sound at the end of a contraction; so are many other morphemes in a speaker's syntax. These are *in-*

---

[1] William Labov, address given at the University of Texas at Austin, Spring, 1970.

[2] Quoted in William Labov, "The Logic of Nonstandard English," in *Language and Poverty,* ed. Frederick Williams (Chicago, Markham Publishing Co., 1970), p. 156.

*flections,* word endings like "-s," which means "plural, more than one." Researchers who have studied syntax but not phonology have often confused the kind of phonological variation we have just discussed with absence of one of these morphemes attached to the end of a word.

Of course, the morpheme may indeed be missing from that dialect. Lack of control of a morpheme is usually considered to be a fairly important matter, since syntax is the skeletal framework of meaning of a language. It is important, then, to listen carefully to students whose dialects have been labeled as not possessing some morpheme; do they show understanding of the morpheme used by other people? Do they express its meaning, one way or another, when they need to express it? If so, you can reevaluate the professional literature that says absence of this inflection in their dialect hinders communication.

TEACHING ABOUT SYNTAX. Teachers may want to teach some elementary facts about syntax to students older than ten or eleven. Then they can discuss variation in speech and listen and read for the styles their community sees as appropriate in varying situations. Perhaps they can then make informed choices about whether to adapt their own speech to community standards, and perhaps they will become better able to understand and accept other people's dialects.

Differences in bringing an underlying meaning or an underlying deep structure to the surface of speech cause most of the syntactic differences among dialects in American English. For instance, the underlying meaning is the same for both "It's not any paradise, with super lizards on it" and "It's not no paradise, with super lizards on it." But *no* is used in one dialect, *any* in another; and in other negative sentences, there are slight differences in the way these indefinite words (some, any, none) are used. This variation is created largely by differences in transformational rules, morphemes, and phonological rules, not by differences in the deep structure or underlying meaning of the sentence.

|  | DIALECT A | DIALECT B |
|---|---|---|
| *Underlying meaning:* | Negative—It is a paradise | Negative—It is a paradise |
| *Negative transformation:* | It is *not no* paradise | It is *not any* paradise |
| *Contraction transformation:* | *It's* not no paradise | *It's* not any paradise |

As we saw in Part 2, dialects share some rules; in each dialect, P-S rules are the same; the negative transformation inserts *not* before the indefinite *a* and substitutes another word (*no, any*) for that indefinite; and the contraction transformation makes *It is* into *It's*. The only difference is in the use of the morphemes *no* and *any;* and since these two words do not differ in meaning in these sentences, it might be said that they are two forms of the same morpheme (a *morpheme* is a unit of meaning), used by two differing dialects. Notice, too, that *no* can be used in Dialect B in the same position *no* is taking in Dialect A if *not* is not present in the same sentence—"He's no angel."

There is no reason why older students cannot study the contrast between underlying and surface levels of language, and every reason for their studying this contrast as a means to understanding language differences. Many people in our country are still in the sixteenth century as far as understanding language is concerned; some concepts from modern grammars could improve this situation. Of course, emotional reactions to language use will remain. But they will lessen in intensity and change their focus if an understanding of facts about language slowly becomes widespread.

No linguist would suggest that schools abandon standards for clear, effective rhetorical use of language, and abandon appreciation of appropriate, pleasing aesthetic use of language. But linguists would and do suggest that our general understanding of the structure of language rules could help us abandon our baseless, discriminatory views of dialect variation as "wrong" and "mistaken." Using these labels is *prescriptive,* not *descriptive.*

The information dramatized by Penfield in Part 1 is relevant here: language rules are learned in a special way, at a generally unconscious level, and after the age of twelve or thirteen they are very difficult to change. Lambert's brief article in Part 2 is also relevant; acquiring different language rules calls for identifying with the people who use that different language. Suppose a student feels forced to make a choice between his background and a speech community with a different background; will he have to renounce his own people and his previous identity in order to acquire the second dialect? Do we identify our speech with our own identities? I suggest that the answer to both of these questions is often yes. Do you resent ridicule of your own speech? Some investigation of your own feelings may help you imagine the position of students who are asked to change their language rules. The summary article in Part 2 suggests other approaches to this question.

## THE DETAILS OF LINGUISTIC THEORY

Do students need to know the details of modern grammars? Most (perhaps all) probably do not *need* to study detailed techniques of writing rules, arguments over the exact nature of transformational processes, and so on. But for those students who enjoy linguistics, teachers can offer reading in this area as an elective.

Transformational grammar does not improve writing;[3] thinking about sentence structure and manipulating sentence structure for whatever reason may help student writers develop flexibility in their writing style, but that goal is much lower in priority than others for most student writers. Most students (not to mention quite a few professional writers) need to write more clearly and with greater effect on their audiences. Malmstrom and Weaver mention clarity and appropriateness in evaluating the popular attention given to "syntactic maturity" as shown in long, complex sentences. Though Malmstrom and Weaver do not draw pointed conclusions (in the excerpt we have reprinted), I would suggest strongly that using effort and attention to count words and "T-units" is less fruitful than using the same effort in establishing a "talk group" in which students discuss one another's writing. Groups like this can write brief responses to pictures and wordless books, then talk about the pieces they've just written and set up long-term individual and group projects. For instance, students of many different ages like to design an imaginary country, as a group project. Young children can illustrate their writings, older students can read about utopias for comparison with their own creation. Reading what is written by these groups (and individual students) will be more interesting to many students than reading their usual texts—especially for reluctant readers. Rigg, in Part 4, describes using students' own compositions as reading material. And Judy, in Part 1, describes some ways to bring life to writing assignments. None of these approaches depends on students' knowledge of modern grammars.

[3] See J. Stephen Sherwin, *Four Problems in Teaching English: A Critique of Research* (Scranton, Pa.: International Textbook Co. for National Council of Teachers of English, 1969) for documentation of this claim other than the documentation supplied by Malmstrom and Weaver.

Reading does not require conscious knowledge of the details of language structure. If it did, how many of us would have been reading since age six or seven? Neither speaking nor talking (to use the distinction made in the summary article to Part 1) requires knowing the difference between deep and surface structures. It seems clear that teaching "language arts" does not have to include teaching the details of linguistic theory.

It is very important, however, for the general truths of linguistic theory to be taught to students of all ages, as we discussed in relation to prescriptive views of language. And it is important to the teacher to understand these general truths—and some of their details—in order to understand and guide students' use of their own language abilities.

# 4
# THE READING PROCESS

## Introduction

The psycholinguistic study of reading has been carried out with special intensity since about 1960, and during that time a great deal has been learned about the reading process. These discoveries call into question many of our current practices in teaching reading, and they suggest that a thorough understanding of language, its acquisition, and its variation is basic to an understanding of the reading process.

### FROM PARTS TO WHOLE, OR VICE VERSA?

Many of our current reading practices seem to direct the reader-to-be along a path that can be schematized, roughly, like this:

letters → words → sentences → meaning

Of course, most programs for teaching reading are more complex than this; but many such programs show an overall direction, or emphasis, that fits the pattern above. Students are thought to need mastery of "word attack skills," such as phonics generalizations, before they are exposed to whole sentences.

Bailey's article on phonics generalizations points out that "skills" such as these may not be efficient tools in the first place. With the aid of a computer, Bailey checked over five thousand words against some common phonics generalizations to see whether each word actually was pronounced the way these phonics "rules" would indicate. Out of forty-five phonics generalizations, only *six* "were found to be simple to understand and apply, to be applicable to large numbers of words, and to have few exceptions."

The information given in Part 1 about language acquisition, and the information in Part 3 about language structure, might suggest just the reverse pattern of emphasis in teaching children to read. As Jakobson points out in Part 1, the crucial difference between language and babbling is that language sounds are used to convey meaning—meaning is basic to language. As Bloom points out in Part 1, children control many of the basic grammatical relationships (sentence structures) even at the very early, two-word stage of acquiring language. By the time children are four or five years of age, they control all the major sentence structures of their language. The details of these sentence structures—described in Part 3—are complex indeed. Study of the grammar described in Part 3 should quickly convince us that children's linguistic abilities deserve respect. They understand sentence structure quite well by the time they begin to read; they create and understand hundreds of sentences each day (a conservative estimate).

It makes sense, then, to begin with meaningful sentences when we teach children to read. The sequence of emphasis children find most natural may be the reverse of the pattern previously mentioned:

meaning → sentences → words → letters

Once again, we are speaking of emphasis in a reading program; children should be oriented to look for meaning constantly, using their knowledge of sentence structure and of the topic to help make sense out of print. This does not rule out use of knowledge about the relationships between letters and sounds. But it does suggest that the role such knowledge plays has been overemphasized in many recent approaches to teaching reading.

Kenneth Goodman's article describes the psycholinguistic nature of the reading process, relating that process to readers' success in finding meaning and sentence structure in the material to be read. Miller's brief article then introduces the "language-experience" method of teaching reading, a method that guarantees familiarity of sentence-structure and vocabulary for beginning readers. Of course, as Kenneth Goodman's theory would suggest, readers who are past the beginning stage will probably profit from exposure to language somewhat more complex than their own—this suggestion is supported by the research in Part 1 indicating that children learn their native language from such exposure. But at the early stages of learning to read, and whenever a student of any age is finding available materials discouragingly difficult, the language-experience method can be used to establish the connection between spoken and written language and to build the reader's confidence in his ability to find meaning in the material he is asked to read. Yetta Goodman, in the section on applications at the end of Part 4, gives some specific suggestions for ways of using this teaching method.

## LANGUAGE VARIATION AND READING

Part 2 suggested that everyone speaks a dialect. Burke, here in Part 4, points out that written English does not represent any one of these dialects perfectly. Every reader relates graphic symbols to his own phonological system; the real question, however, is whether there are major differences between the syntax of written "Standard English" and the syntax of "nonstandard" dialects of American English—differences that might be responsible for the failure of many children who speak these dialects to learn to read. Several years ago, Kenneth Goodman published an article called "Dialect Barriers to Reading Comprehension" which suggested that dialect differences might indeed affect reading ability. Goodman and Buck, however, now believe that the earlier suggestion should be revised; dialect differences apparently are not responsible for problems in reading comprehension. Their article in Part 4 presents research evidence to support this new position. Baratz, on the other hand, continues to maintain that dialect differences are a problem, so much so that special readers should be written in "Black English." This position, of course, might be taken to imply that speakers of many other dialects should also have special readers. Sledd, in Part 2, points out (as we saw in Williamson's article, also in Part 2) that many black dialects are similar to southern white dialects; and he makes clear his disagreement with the idea that either black or white speakers need textbooks written in their native dialects.

Nonnative speakers of English, however, are a separate group from speakers with nonstandard features in their dialects. Nonnative speakers may have special problems in learning to read English, and Modiano discusses these problems. Rigg points out that the language-experience method of teaching reading will help solve some of these problems.

# Approaches to Reading

## Reading: A Psycholinguistic Guessing Game

KENNETH S. GOODMAN

Suppose a businessman visiting the West Coast calls a
lawyer on the East Coast and says, "I've got a contract
here but I don't understand a word of it." The lawyer says,
"Read it to me." After the businessman finishes reciting
the words in front of him, his lawyer explains what the
contract means.

Was the businessman really reading? Kenneth Goodman
would say that he was only *recoding* written language into
oral language, rather than *decoding* written language into
meaning. In order to decode the contract, to really read it, the
businessman would need some background information and
experience to bring to his inspection of the contract.

Goodman suggests that we have often asked students to
recode, rather than to decode; witness our emphasis on
oral reading in elementary grades. Part of our neglect of meaning
has been our attention to words rather than to sentences.
As we saw in Part 1, children use sentences—never isolated
words—almost from the beginning of speech. A sentence
is not just the sum of its words; "Power I because need I'd I

it the knew did" is a string of words, but it is not a sentence. By contrast, "I did it because I knew I'd need the power" [1] has meaning. We do not find that meaning, however, by adding together the meaning of the words. In fact, the meaning a word has depends on its context, as Lindberg and Smith discuss later in this section. Perhaps we should stop teaching children to look at words one at a time and start teaching them to look for an entire, meaningful sentence.

The article by Miller gives a brief overview of a theory of reading instruction that agrees with Goodman's theory of the reading process, and the concluding articles in this section —applying theory to teaching—are also compatible with Goodman's theory of the reading process.

As scientific understanding develops in any field of study, preexisting, naive, common sense notions must give way. Such outmoded beliefs clutter the literature dealing with the process of reading. They interfere with the application of modern scientific concepts of language and thought to research in reading. They confuse the attempts at application of such concepts to solution of problems involved in the teaching and learning of reading. The very fact that such naive beliefs are based on common sense explains their persistent and recurrent nature. To the casual and unsophisticated observer they appear to explain, even predict, a set of phenomena in reading. This paper will deal with one such key misconception and offer a more viable scientific alternative.

Simply stated, the common sense notion I seek here to refute is this:

"Reading is a precise process. It involves exact, detailed, sequential perception and identification of letters, words, spelling patterns and large language units."

In phonic-centered approaches to reading the preoccupation is with precise letter identification. In word-centered approaches, the focus is on word identifications. Known words are sight words, precisely named in any setting.

This is not to say that those who have worked diligently in the field of reading are not aware that reading is more than precise, sequential identification. But, the common sense notion, though not adequate, continues to permeate thinking about reading.

---

[1] This sentence was spoken by a New England farmer, questioned by a television reporter as to why he had built a generator.

Spache (*8*) presents a word version of this common sense view: "Thus, in its simplest form, reading may be considered a series of word perceptions."

The teacher's manual of the Lippincott *Basic Reading* (*6*) incorporates a letter by letter variant in the justification of its reading approach: "In short, following this program the child learns from the beginning to see words exactly as the most skillful readers see them . . . as whole images of complete words with all their letters."

In place of this misconception, I offer this: Reading is a selective process. It involves partial use of available minimal language cues selected from perceptual input on the basis of the reader's expectation. As this partial information is processed, tentative decisions are made to be confirmed, rejected, or refined as reading progresses.

More simply stated, reading is a psycholinguistic guessing game. It involves an interaction between thought and language. Efficient reading does not result from precise perception and identification of all elements, but from skill in selecting the fewest, most productive cues necessary to produce guesses which are right the first time. The ability to anticipate that which has not been seen, of course, is vital in reading, just as the ability to anticipate what has not yet been heard is vital in listening.

Consider this actual sample of a relatively proficient child reading orally. The reader is a fourth grade child reading the opening paragraphs of a story from a sixth grade basal reader (*5*).

"If it bothers you to think of it as baby sitting," my father said, "then don't think of it as baby sitting. Think of it as homework. Part of your education. You just happen to do your studying in the room where the baby brother is sleeping, that's all." He helped my mother with her coat, and then they were gone.

hoped © a
So education it was! I ~~opened the~~ dictionary and picked out a

s          PH—————————  He
word that sound~~ed~~ good. "Phil/oso/phi/cal!" ~~I~~ yelled. Might

what it means        1. Phizo 2. Phiso/soophical
as well study ~~word meanings first~~. "~~Philosophical~~: showing

his              1. fort  2. future
calmness and courage in ~~the~~ face of ill fortune." I mean I

3. futshion
really yelled it. I guess a fellow has to work off steam once in a while.

He has not seen the story before. It is, by intention, slightly difficult for him. The insights into his reading process come primarily from his errors, which I chose to call miscues in order to avoid value implications. His expected responses mask the process of their attainment, but his unexpected responses have been achieved through the same process, albeit less successfully applied. The ways that they deviate from the expected reveal this process.

In the common sense view that I am rejecting, all deviations must be treated as errors. Furthermore, it must be assumed in this view that an error either indicates that the reader does not know something or that he has been "careless" in the application of his knowledge.

For example, his substitution of *the* for *your* in the first paragraph of the sample must mean that he was careless, since he has already read *your* and *the* correctly in the very same sentence. The implication is that we must teach him to be more careful, that is to be more precise in identifying each word or letter.

But now let's take the view that I have suggested. What sort of information could have led to tentatively deciding on *the* in this situation and not rejecting or refining this decision? There obviously is no graphic relationship between *your* and *the*. It may be of course, that he picked up *the* in the periphery of his visual field. But, there is an important non-graphic relationship between *the* and *your*. They both have the same grammatical function: they are, in my terminology, noun markers. Either the reader anticipated a noun marker and supplied one paying no attention to graphic information or he used *your* as a grammatical signal ignoring its graphic shape. Since the tentative choice *the* disturbs neither the meaning nor the grammar of the passage, there is no reason to reject and correct it. This explanation appears to be confirmed by two similar miscues in the next paragraph. *A* and *his* are both substituted for *the*. Neither are corrected. Though the substitution of *his* changes the meaning, the peculiar idiom used in this dictionary definition, "in the face of ill fortune," apparently has little meaning to this reader anyway.

The conclusion this time is that he is using noun markers for grammatical, as well as graphic, information in reaching his tentative conclusions. All together in reading this ten page story, he made twenty noun marker substitutions, six omissions and two insertions. He corrected four of his substitutions and one omission. Similar miscues involved other function words (auxiliary verbs and prepositions, for example). These miscues appear to have little effect on the meaning of what he is reading. In spite of their frequency, their elimination would not substantially improve the child's reading. Insistence on more precise identification of each word might cause this reader to stop seeking grammatical information and use only graphic information.

The substitution of *hoped* for *opened* could again be regarded as careless or imprecise identification of letters. But, if we dig beyond this common sense explanation, we find (1) both are verbs and (2) the words have *key* graphic similarities. Further, there may be evidence of the reader's bilingual French-Canadian background here, as there is in subsequent miscues (*harms* for *arms*, *shuckled* for *chuckled*, *shoose* for *choose*, *shair* for *chair*). The correction of this miscue may involve an immediate rejection of the tentative choice made on the basis of a review of the graphic stimulus, or it may result from recognizing that it cannot lead to the rest of the sentence, "I hoped a dictionary . . ." does not make sense. (It isn't decodable.) In any case, the reader has demonstrated the process by which he constantly tests his guesses, or tentative choices, if you prefer.

*Sounds* is substituted for *sounded*, but the two differ in ending only. Common sense might lead to the conclusion that the child does not pay attention to word endings, slurs the ends or is otherwise careless. But, there is no consistent similar occurrence in other word endings. Actually, the child has substituted one inflectional ending for another. In doing so he has revealed (1) his ability to separate base and inflectional suffix, and (2) his use of inflectional endings as grammatical signals or markers. Again he has not corrected a miscue that is both grammatically and semantically acceptable.

*He* for *I* is a pronoun for pronoun substitution that results in a meaning change, though the antecedent is a bit vague, and the inconsistency of meaning is not easily apparent.

When we examine what the reader did with the sentence *"Might as well study word meanings first,"* we see how poorly the model of precise sequential identification fits the reading process. Essentially this reader has decoded graphic input for meaning and then encoded meaning in oral output with transformed grammar and changed vocabulary, but with the basic meaning retained. Perhaps as he encoded his output, he was already working at the list word which followed, but the tentative choice was good enough and was not corrected.

There are two examples, in this sample, of the reader working at unknown words. He reveals a fair picture of his strategies and abilities in these miscues, though in neither is he successful. In his several attempts at *philosophical*, his first attempt comes closest. Incidentally, he reveals here that he can use a phonic letter-sound strategy when he wants to. In subsequent attempts he moves away from this sounding out, trying other possibilities, as if trying to find something which at least will sound familiar. Interestingly, here he has a definition of sorts, but no context to work with. *Philosophical* occurs as a list word a number of times in the story. In subsequent attempts, the child tried *physica, physicacol, physical, philosovigul, phizzlesovigul, phizzo sorigul, philazophgul.* He appears to move in concentric circles around the phonic information he has, trying deviations and variations. His three unsuccessful attempts at *fortune* illustrate this same process. Both words are apparently unknown to the reader. He can never really identify a word he has not heard. In such cases, unless the context or contexts sufficiently delimit the word's meaning, the reader is not able to get meaning from the words. In some instances, of course, the reader may form a fairly accurate definition of the word, even if he never recognizes it (that is matches it with a known oral equivalent) or pronounces it correctly. This reader achieved that with the word *typical* which occurred many times in the story. Throughout his reading he said *topical.* When he finished reading, a check of his comprehension indicated that he knew quite well the meaning of the word. This phenomenon is familiar to any adult reader. Each of us has many well-defined words in our reading vocabulary which we either mispronounce or do not use orally.

I've used the example of this youngster's oral reading not because what he's done is typical of all readers or even of readers his age, but because his miscues suggest how he carries out the psycholinguistic guessing game in reading. The miscues of other readers show similarities and differences, but all point to a selective, tentative, anticipatory process quite unlike the process of precise, sequential identification commonly assumed.

Let's take a closer look now at the components the reader manipulates in this psycholinguistic guessing game.

At any point in time, of course, the reader has available to him and brings to his reading the sum total of his experience and his language and thought development. This self-evident fact needs to be stated because what appears to be intuitive in any guessing is actually the result of knowledge so well learned that the process of its application requires little conscious effort. Most language use has reached this automatic, intuitive level. Most of us are quite unable to describe the use we make of grammar in encoding and decoding speech, yet all language users demonstrate a high degree of skill and mastery over the syntax of language even in our humblest and most informal uses of speech.

Chomsky (*3*) has suggested this model of sentence production by speakers of a language:

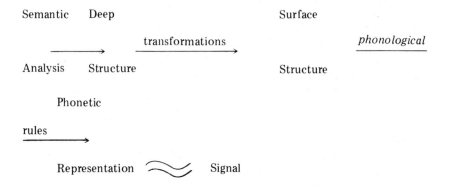

A model structure of the listener's sentence interpretation, according to Chomsky, is:

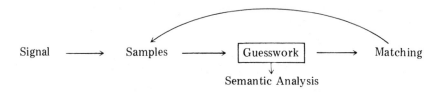

Thus in Chomsky's view encoding of speech reaches a more or less precise level and the signal which results is fully formed. But in decoding a sampling process aims at approximating the message and any matching or coded signal which results is a kind of by-product.

In oral reading, the reader must perform two tasks at the same time. He must produce an oral language equivalent of the graphic input which is the *signal* in reading, and he must also reconstruct the meaning of what he is reading. The matching in

Chomsky's interpretation model is largely what I prefer to call a recoding operation. The reader recodes the coded graphic input as phonological or oral output. Meaning is not normally involved to any extent. This recoding can even be learned by someone who doesn't speak the language at all, for example, the bar-mitzvah boy may learn to recode Hebrew script as chanted oral Hebrew with no ability to understand what he is chanting; but when the reader engages in semantic analysis to reconstruct the meaning of the writer, only then is he decoding.

In oral reading there are three logical possible arrangements of these two operations. The reader may recode graphic input as oral language and then decode it. He may recode and decode simultaneously. Or, he may decode first and then encode the meaning as oral output.

On the basis of my research to date, it appears that readers who have achieved some degree of proficiency decode directly from the graphic stimulus in a process similar to Chomsky's sampling model and then encode from the deep structure, as illustrated in Chomsky's model of sentence production. Their oral output is not directly related to the graphic stimulus and may involve transformation in vocabulary and syntax, even if meaning is retained. If their comprehension is inaccurate, they will encode this changed or incomplete meaning as oral output.

The common misconception is that graphic input is precisely and sequentially recoded as phonological input and then decoded bit by bit. Meaning is cumulative, built up a piece at a time in this view. This view appears to be supported by studies of visual perception that indicate that only a very narrow span of print on either side of the point of fixation is in sharp focus at any time. We might dub this the "end of the nose" view, since it assumes that input in reading is that which lies in sharp focus in a straight line from the end of the nose. Speed and efficiency are assumed to come from widening the span taken in on either side of the nose, moving the nose more rapidly or avoiding backward movements of the eyes and nose, which of course must cut down on efficiency.

This view cannot possibly explain the speed with which the average adult reads, or a myriad of other constantly occurring phenomena in reading. How can it explain, for example, a highly proficient adult reader reading and rereading a paper he's written and always missing the same misprints. Or how can it explain our fourth grader seeing "Study word meanings first" and saying, "Study what it means"?

No, the "end of the nose" view of reading will not work. The reader is not confined to information he receives from a half inch of print in clear focus. Studies, in fact, indicate that children with severe visual handicaps are able to learn to read as well as normal children. Readers utilize not one, but three kinds of information simultaneously. Certainly without graphic input there would be no reading. But, the reader uses syntactic and semantic information as well. He predicts and anticipates on the basis of this information, sampling from the print just enough to confirm his guess of what's coming, to cue more semantic and syntactic information. Redundancy and sequential constraints in language, which the reader reacts to, make this prediction possible. Even the blurred and shadowy images he picks up in the peripheral area of his visual field may help to trigger or confirm guesses.

Skill in reading involves not greater precision, but more accurate first guesses based on better sampling techniques, greater control over language structure, broadened experiences and increased conceptual development. As the child develops reading skill and speed, he uses increasingly fewer graphic cues. Silent reading can then become a more rapid and efficient process than oral reading, for two reasons: (1) the reader's attention is not divided between decoding and recoding or encoding as oral output, and (2) his speed is not restricted to the speed of speech production. Reading becomes a more efficient and rapid process than listening, in fact, since listening is normally limited to the speed of the speaker.

Recent studies with speeded up electronic recordings where distortion of pitch is avoided have demonstrated that listening can be made more rapid without impairing comprehension too.

Though the beginning reader obviously needs more graphic information in decoding and, therefore, needs to be more precise than skilled readers, evidence from a study of first graders by Goodman (*4*) indicates that they begin to sample and draw on syntactic and semantic information almost from the beginning, if they are reading material which is fully formed language.

Here are excerpts from two primer stories (*1*, *2*) as they were read by a first grade child at the same session. Ostensibly (and by intent of the authors) the first, from a second preprimer, should be much easier than the second, from a third preprimer. Yet she encountered problems to the point of total confusion with the first and was able to handle exactly the same elements in the second.

Note, for example, the confusion of *come* and *here* in "Ride

| *Ride In* | *Stop and Go* |
|---|---|

Run
~~Ride~~ in, Sue.
Run
~~Ride~~ in here.
Come here
~~Here~~ I ~~come~~. Jimmy.
Can Come
~~And~~ ~~here~~ I stop.

Jimmy said, "Come, here, Sue,
    too
Look at my ~~toy~~ (train.)

See it go.
    toy
Look at my lit/tle ~~train~~ go."
    toy
Sue said, "Stop the ~~train.~~
  Come
Stop it ~~here,~~ Jimmy."
    toy
Jimmy said, "I can stop the ~~train.~~
    toy
See the ~~train~~ stop."
    too.
Sue said, "Look at my ~~toy.~~
    toy.
It is in the ~~train.~~
    too
See my little red ~~toy,~~ Jimmy
    toy
It can ride in the ~~train.~~"
    toy
Jimmy said, "See the ~~train~~ go.
Look at it go."
Suzie    too
Sue said, "Look at my little red ~~toy.~~
    toy
See it go for a ~~train~~ ride."
Suzie    too
~~Sue~~ said, "My little red ~~toy~~!
  said  too
© Jimmy, my ~~toy~~ is not here.
    toy
It is not in the ~~train.~~
    toy
Stop the ~~train,~~ Jimmy.
    too
Stop it and look for my ~~toy.~~"

In." This represents a habitual association in evidence in early reading of this child. Both *come* and *here* as graphic shapes are likely to be identified as *come* or *here*. In "Stop and Go," the difficulty does not occur when the words are sequential. She also substitutes *can* for *and* in the first story, but encounters no problem with either later. *Stop* stops her completely in "Ride In," a difficulty that she doesn't seem to know she has when she reads "Stop and Go" a few minutes later. Similarly, she calls (ride) *run* in the first story, but gets it right in the latter one.

Though there are miscues in the second story, there is a very important difference. In the first story she seems to be playing a game of name the word. She is recoding graphic shapes as phonological ones. Each word is apparently a separate problem. But in "Stop and Go" what she says, including her miscues, in almost all instances makes sense and is grammatically acceptable. Notice that as *Sue* becomes better known she becomes *Suzie* to our now confident reader.

A semantic association exists between *train* and *toy*. Though the child makes the same substitution many times, nothing causes her to reject her guess. It works well each time. Having called (train) *toy*, she calls (toy) *too* (actually it's an airplane in the pictures), not once, but consistently throughout the story. That doesn't seem to make sense. That's what the researcher thought too, until the child spoke of a "little red *too*" later in retelling the story. "What's a 'little red *too*,'" asked the researcher. "An airplane," she replied calmly. So a train is *toy* and a plane is a *too*. Why not? But, notice that when *toy* occurred preceding *train*, she could attempt nothing for *train*. There appears to be a problem for many first graders when nouns are used as adjectives.

Common sense says go back and drill her on *come, here, can, stop, ride, and;* don't let her go to the next book which she is obviously not ready to read.

But the more advanced story, with its stronger syntax, more fully formed language and increased load of meaning makes it possible for the child to use her graphic cues more effectively and supplement them with semantic and syntactic information. Teaching for more precise perception with lists and phonics charts may actually impede this child's reading development. Please notice, before we leave the passage, the effect of immediate experience on anticipation. Every one of the paragraphs in the sample starts with "Jimmy said" or "Sue said." When the reader comes to a line starting *Jimmy*, she assumes that it will be followed by *said* and it is not until her expectation is contradicted by subsequent input that she regresses and corrects her miscue.

Since they must learn to play the psycholinguistic guessing game as they develop reading ability, effective methods and materials used by teachers who understand the rules of the game, must help them to select the most productive cues, to use their knowledge of language structure, to draw on their experiences and concepts. They must be helped to discriminate between more and less useful available information. Fortunately, this parallels the processes they have used in developing the ability to comprehend spoken language. George Miller (7) has suggested ". . . psycholinguists should try to formulate performance models that will incorporate . . . hypothetical information storage and information processing components that can simulate the actual behavior of language users."

I'd like to present now my model of this psycholinguistic guessing game we call reading English. Please understand that the steps do not necessarily take place in the sequential or stretched out form as they are shown here. [The model appears on page 383.]

1. The reader scans along a line of print from left to right and down the page, line by line.
2. He fixes at a point to permit eye focus. Some print will be central and in focus, some will be peripheral; perhaps his perceptual field is a flattened circle.
3. Now begins the selection process. He picks up graphic cues, guided by constraints set up through prior choices, his language knowledge, his cognitive styles, and strategies he has learned.
4. He forms a perceptual image using these cues and his anticipated cues. This image then is partly what he sees and partly what he expected to see.
5. Now he searches his memory for related syntactic, semantic, and phonological cues. This may lead to selection of more graphic cues and to reforming the perceptual image.
6. At this point, he makes a guess or tentative choice consistent with graphic cues. Semantic analysis leads to partial decoding as far as possible. This meaning is stored in short-term memory as he proceeds.
7. If no guess is possible, he checks the recalled perceptual input and tries again. If a guess is still not possible, he takes another look at the text to gather more graphic cues.
8. If he can make a decodable choice, he tests it for semantic and grammatical acceptability in the context developed by prior choices and decoding.
9. If the tentative choice is not acceptable semantically or syntactically, then he regresses, scanning from right to left along

the line and up the page to locate a point of semantic or syntactic inconsistency. When such a point is found, he starts over at that point. If no inconsistency can be identified, he reads on seeking some cue which will make it possible to reconcile the anomalous situation.

10. If the choice is acceptable, decoding is extended, meaning is assimilated with prior meaning, and prior meaning is accommodated, if necessary. Expectations are formed about input and meaning that lies ahead.

11. Then the cycle continues.

Throughout the process there is constant use of long- and short-term memory.

I offer no apologies for the complexity of this model. Its faults lie, not in its complexity, but in the fact that it is not yet complex enough to fully account for the complex phenomena in the actual behavior of readers. But such is man's destiny in his quest for knowledge. Simplistic folklore must give way to complexity as we come to know.

## REFERENCES

BETTS, EMMETT A. "Ride In," *Time to Play*, Second Preprimer, Betts Basic Readers (3rd ed.), Language Arts Series. New York: American Book, 1963.

BETTS, EMMETT A., and CAROLYN M. WELCH. "Stop and Go," *All In A Day*, Third Preprimer, Betts Basic Readers. New York: American Book, 1963.

CHOMSKY, NOAM. Lecture at Project Literacy, Cornell University, June 18, 1965.

GOODMAN, YETTA M. College of Education, Wayne State University, doctoral study of development of reading in first grade children.

HAYES, WILLIAM D. "My Brother is a Genius," *Adventures Now and Then*, Book 6, Betts Basic Readers (3rd ed.), edited by Emmett A. Betts and Carolyn M. Welch. New York: American Book, 1963, 246.

McCRACKEN, GLENN, and CHARLES C. WALCUTT. *Basic Reading*, teacher's edition for the preprimer and primer. Philadelphia: B. Lippincott, 1963, vii.

MILLER, GEORGE A. "Some Preliminaries to Psycholinguistics," *American Psychologist*, Vol. 20, No. 18, 1965.

SPACHE, GEORGE. *Reading In The Elementary School*. Boston: Allyn and Bacon, 1964, 12.

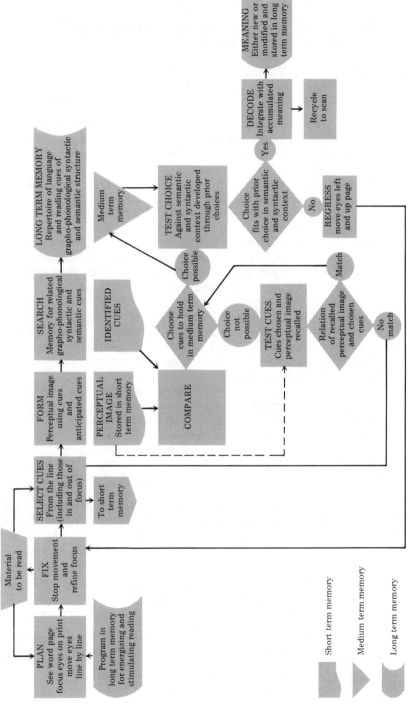

A Flow Chart of Goodman's Model of Reading

# The Utility of Phonic Generalizations in Grades One Through Six

MILDRED HART BAILEY

*Phonic* or *graphophonic* relationships are the rules that relate print to sound. If it were necessary to pronounce a word in order to understand it, phonic generalizations would be crucial to reading; as it is, however, many of us understand fully the meaning of *façade, impotent, epitome,* and many other words long before we find out how to pronounce them.

But programs designed to teach "phonics" have been popular in America off and on since Noah Webster's time. And this word gets thrown around quite a bit in both professional and public literature on reading. Examples of a "phonics" rule, however, are seldom seen. A few years ago, Theodore Clymer carried out a very important piece of research: He checked forty-five phonics generalizations against the words in several basal readers (readers designed for the early grades) to see whether or not those words actually were pronounced the way the rules said they should be pronounced. The percent of correctness, or utility, of these rules turned out to be extremely low.

Bailey has started with Clymer's work and has, with the aid of a computer, checked these generalizations against an enormous number of words used in basal readers for grades one through six. Her study seems to be very strong evidence against the policy of relying on phonics in our programs of reading instruction.

Phonic generalizations have long constituted a significant part of instruction in phonics. Many authors of textbooks in the teaching of reading recommend phonic generalizations as an important facet of the reading program, and basal reading series include phonic generalizations in the program of instruction. Despite such wide acceptance, little research on the utility of phonic generalizations had been reported until Theodore Clymer, in the January 1963 issue of *The Reading Teacher*,[1] reported the results of an investigation of the utility of forty-five phonic generalizations in the primary grades.

[1] Theodore Clymer, "The Utility of Phonic Generalizations in the Primary Grades," *Reading Teacher*, 16 (Jan. 1963), 252–258.

**384**

Clymer examined basal reading materials for the primary grades and selected the teachers' manuals of four basal series as the source of phonic generalizations to be investigated. Forty-five generalizations recommended in the manuals were identified for study. A list of some twenty-six hundred words was then assembled by Clymer through inclusion of all words introduced in the primary-level reading textbooks of the four previously identified basic reading series, plus the words from the Gates Reading Vocabulary for the Primary Grades. Webster's *New Collegiate Dictionary* was used as the authority in recording the phonetic respelling and syllabic division of the words. Clymer then checked the forty-five phonic generalizations against the composite word list to identify all words that conformed or were exceptions to each of the generalizations. A percentage of utility was computed for each generalization, and criteria were formulated by Clymer to determine a " 'reasonable' degree of application" for the generalizations. Only eighteen of the forty-five phonic generalizations met the criteria as set forth in the Clymer study.

The results of the above-described investigation proved disturbing to many people concerned with reading instruction. One question frequently posed was, "Would the results differ greatly if the forty-five phonic generalizations were applied to a vocabulary list for grades one through six, rather than just the primary grades?" In the belief that the answer to this question might possibly contribute toward an improved program of instruction in phonics, the following investigation was undertaken by the present writer. The purpose of the study was to investigate the utility of phonic generalizations in reading instruction through application of recommended generalizations to a list of words representative of words encountered in reading in grades one through six.

## PROCEDURE

Forty-five phonic generalizations, previously identified by Theodore Clymer in the above-described investigation, were selected for study. A list of words was collected from the entire vocabularies of all textbooks, grades one through six, of the following eight basal reading series:

EMMETT A. BETTS and CAROLYN M. WELCH, The Betts Basic Readers (New York: American Book Company, 1963).

GUY L. BOND and others, The Developmental Reading Series (Chicago: Lyons and Carnahan, 1962).

WILLIAM S. GRAY and others, The New Basic Readers (Chicago: Scott, Foresman, 1962).

PAUL McKEE and others, The Reading for Meaning Series (Boston: Houghton-Mifflin, 1963).

MABEL O'DONNEL, The Alice and Jerry Basic Reading Program (Evanston, Illinois: Harper and Row, 1963).

DAVID H. RUSSELL and others, The Ginn Basic Reading Program (Boston: Ginn and Company, 1961).

WILLIAM D. SHELDON and others, The Sheldon Basic Reading Series (Boston: Allyn and Bacon, 1963).

RUSSEL G. STAUFFER and others, The Winston Basic Readers (New York: Holt, Rinehart and Winston, 1960).

Certain limitations regarding inclusion of words were observed. For example, only words that appeared in two or more of the eight series were included, and place names, proper names, and foreign words were excluded. A composite list of 5,773 words resulted.

Computers were utilized for the identification of all words in the composite word list to which each of the forty-five phonic generalizations applied. Conformations and exceptions to each generalization were determined according to the 1961 edition of Webster's *New Collegiate Dictionary*, and percentage of utility was computed by dividing the total number of conformations identified by the total number of incidents investigated for each generalization. A summary of the findings pertaining to the utility of the forty-five phonic generalizations is presented in the table.

## CONCLUSIONS

A review of the literature failed to reveal either scientifically-evolved or widely-accepted criteria for judging the results of this study. Nevertheless, the following conclusions were drawn upon the basis of the evidence gained in the investigation:

1. Inclusion in the reading program of generalizations 1, 7, 12, 13, 15, 17, 18, and 34, all found to possess low percentage of utility, should be thoughtfully reconsidered by all persons concerned with reading instruction.

2. Since certain generalizations were found difficult to interpret and to apply, it is believed by the writer that children in the elementary grades would experience the same uncertainty. For this reason, generalizations 13, 16, 30, and 45 should be attended with caution.

3. Only generalizations 20, 22, 23, 28, 32, and 40 were found to be simple to understand and apply, to be applicable to large numbers of words, and to have few exceptions.[2]

## RECOMMENDATIONS

The findings of this study emphasize the need for the supplementation of future research to establish the value of phonic generalizations in reading in the elementary grades:

1. Research designed to establish scientifically-evolved criteria for judging the usefulness of phonic generalizations should be undertaken.

2. The ability of elementary school children to apply phonic generalizations in reading has not been considered in this or any previous investigation known to this writer. Future research, conducted through classroom experimentation, should contribute toward a better understanding of the usefulness of phonic generalizations to children.

3. In the present study, phonic generalizations were applied only to words collected from basal reading series. It is recommended that future research relative to the utility of phonic generalizations include vocabulary derived from the various subject-matter areas in the elementary school—such as science, social studies, and arithmetic. Vocabulary collected from children's trade books, magazines, and newspapers should also be included.

4. The necessity of utilizing the 1961 edition of Webster's *New Collegiate Dictionary*, rather than the more recent 1963 edition, is of significance to the present study. The schwa symbol, utilized in pronunciations of words in the 1963 edition of that dictionary, is incompatible with many phonic generalizations that are concerned with vowel sounds. Because the schwa symbol is also being employed in several widely-used children's dictionaries today, it is recommended that investigations be conducted to

---

[2] [Ed.'s note: See the summary article for Part 4 for further discussion of these rules.]

The Utility of Phonic Generalizations in Grades One Through Six

| Generalization | No. of Incidents | No. of Words Conforming | No. of Exceptions | Percent of Utility |
|---|---|---|---|---|
| 1. When there are two vowels side by side, the long sound of the first vowel is heard, and the second vowel is usually silent. | 1732 | 586 (leader) * | 1146 (breath) | 34 |
| 2. When a vowel is in the middle of a one-syllable word, the vowel is short. | 1021 | 730 | 291 | 71 |
| Middle letter | 430 | 335 (flank) | 95 (her) | 78 |
| One of the middle two letters in a word of four letters | 478 | 325 (glen) | 153 (long) | 68 |
| One vowel within a word of more than four letters | 113 | 70 (depth) | 43 (knight) | 62 |
| 3. If the only vowel letter is at the end of a word, the letter usually stands for a long sound. | 38 | 29 (go) | 9 (do) | 76 |
| 4. When there are two vowels, one of which is final e, the first vowel is long and the e is silent. | 578 | 330 (cradle) | 218 (judge) | 57 |
| 5. The r gives the preceding vowel a sound that is neither long nor short. | 1604 | 1378 (depart) | 226 (merit) | 86 |
| 6. The first vowel is usually long and the second silent in the digraphs ai, ea, oa, and ui. | 497 | 298 | 199 | 60 |
| ai | 121 | 87 (acclaim) | 34 (plaid) | 72 |
| ea | 259 | 143 (bean) | 116 (create) | 55 |
| oa | 66 | 63 (roam) | 3 (broad) | 95 |
| ui | 51 | 5 (pursuit) | 46 (biscuit) | 10 |
| 7. In the phonogram ie, the i is silent, and the e has a long sound. | 88 | 27 (grieve) | 61 (brier) | 31 |

* Words in parentheses are examples, either of words following the rule or of exceptions, depending on the column.

*The Utility of Phonic Generalizations in Grades One Through Six—Continued*

| GENERALIZATION | NO. OF INCIDENTS | NO. OF WORDS CONFORMING | NO. OF EXCEPTIONS | PERCENT OF UTILITY |
|---|---|---|---|---|
| 8. Words having double *e* usually have the long *e* sound. | 171 | 148 (exceed) | 23 (deer) | 87 |
| 9. When words end with silent *e*, the preceding *a* or *i* is long. | 674 | 340 (amaze) | 334 (give) | 50 |
| 10. In *ay*, the *y* is silent and gives *a* its long sound. | 50 | 44 (spray) | 6 (prayer) | 88 |
| 11. When the letter *i* is followed by the letters *gh*, the *i* usually stands for its long sound, and the *gh* is silent. | 35 | 25 (flight) | 10 (weight) | 71 |
| 12. When *a* follows *w* in a word, *it* usually has the sound *a* as in *was*. | 78 | 17 (wand) | 61 (sway) | 22 |
| 13. When *e* is followed by *w*, the vowel sound is the same as represented by *oo*. | 35 | 14 (shrewd) | 21 (stew) | 40 |
| 14. The two letters *ow* make the long *o* sound. | 111 | 61 (flow) | 50 (scowl) | 55 |
| 15. *W* is sometimes a vowel and follows the vowel digraph rule. | 180 | 60 (arrow) | 120 (drew) | 33 |
| 16. When *y* is the final letter in a word, it usually has a vowel sound. | 518 | 462 (lady) | 56 (key) | 89 |
| 17. When *y* is used as a vowel in words, it sometimes has the sound of long *i*. | 596 | 63 (ally) | 533 (silly) | 11 |
| 18. The letter *a* has the same sound (ô) when followed by *l*, *w*, and *u*. | 346 | 119 (raw) | 227 (laugh) | 34 |
| 19. When *a* is followed by *r* and final *e*, we expect to hear the sound heard in *care*. | 24 | 23 (flare) | 1 (are) | 96 |

*The Utility of Phonic Generalizations in Grades One Through Six—Continued*

| GENERALIZATION | NO. OF INCIDENTS | NO. OF WORDS CONFORMING | NO. OF EXCEPTIONS | PERCENT OF UTILITY |
|---|---|---|---|---|
| 20. When *c* and *h* are next to each other, they make only one sound. | 225 | 225 (charge) | 0 | 100 |
| 21. *Ch* is usually pronounced as it is in *kitchen, catch,* and *chair,* not like *sh.* | 225 | 196 (pitch) | 29 (chute) | 87 |
| 22. When *c* is followed by *e* or *i,* the sound of *s* is likely to be heard. | 284 | 260 (glance) | 24 (ancient) | 92 |
| 23. When the letter *c* is followed by *o* or *a,* the sound of *k* is likely to be heard. | 428 | 428 (canal) | 0 | 100 |
| 24. The letter *g* often has a sound similar to that of *j* in *jump* when it precedes the letter *i* or *e.* | 216 | 168 (genius) | 48 (eager) | 78 |
| 25. When *ght* is seen in a word, *gh* is silent. | 40 | 40 (tight) | 0 | 100 |
| 26. When a word begins *kn,* the *k* is silent. | 17 | 17 (knit) | 0 | 100 |
| 27. When a word begins with *wr,* the *w* is silent. | 17 | 17 (wrap) | 0 | 100 |
| 28. When two of the same consonants are side by side, only one is heard. | 826 | 809 (dollar) | 17 (accept) | 98 |
| 29. When a word ends in *ck,* it has the same last sound as in *look.* | 80 | 80 (neck) | 0 | 100 |
| 30. In most two-syllable words, the first syllable is accented. | 2345 | 1906 (bottom) | 439 (attire) | 81 |
| 31. If *a, in, re, ex, de,* or *be* is the first syllable in a word, it is usually unaccented. | 398 | 336 (reply) | 62 (extra) | 84 |

| GENERALIZATION | NO. OF INCIDENTS | NO. OF WORDS CONFORMING | NO. OF EXCEPTIONS | PERCENT OF UTILITY |
|---|---|---|---|---|
| 32. In most two-syllable words that end in a consonant followed by *y*, the first syllable is accented and the last is unaccented. | 195 | 190 (pony) | 5 (apply) | 97 |
| 33. One vowel letter in an accented syllable has its short sound. | 3031 | 1960 (banish) | 1071 (fortune) | 65 |
| 34. When *y* or *ey* is seen in the last syllable that is not accented, the long sound of *e* is heard. | 449 | 0 | 449 (ferry) | 0 |
| 35. When *ture* is the final syllable in a word, it is unaccented. | 22 | 21 (future) | 1 (mature) | 95 |
| 36. When *tion* is the final syllable in a word, it is unaccented. | 102 | 102 (notion) | 0 | 100 |
| 37. In many two- and three-syllable words, the final *e* lengthens the vowel in the last syllable. | 430 | 198 (costume) | 232 (welcome) | 46 |
| 38. If the first vowel sound in a word is followed by two consonants, the first syllable usually ends with the first of the two consonants. | 1689 | 1311 (dinner) | 378 (maple) | 78 |
| 39. If the first vowel sound in a word is followed by a single consonant, that consonant usually begins the second syllable. | 1283 | 638 (china) | 645 (shadow) | 50 |
| 40. If the last syllable of a word ends in *le*, the consonant preceding the *le* usually begins the last syllable. | 211 | 196 (gable) | 15 (crackle) | 93 |

391

The Utility of Phonic Generalizations in Grades One Through Six—Continued

| GENERALIZATION | NO. OF INCIDENTS | NO. OF WORDS CONFORMING | NO. OF EXCEPTIONS | PERCENT OF UTILITY |
|---|---|---|---|---|
| 41. When the first vowel element in a word is followed by *th*, *ch*, or *sh*, these symbols are not broken when the word is divided into syllables and may go with either the first or second syllable. | 74 | 74 (fashion) | 0 | 100 |
| 42. In a word of more than one syllable, the letter *v* usually goes with the preceding vowel to form a syllable. | 184 | 119 (river) | 65 (navy) | 65 |
| 43. When a word has only one vowel letter, the vowel sound is likely to be short. | 1105 | 759 (crib) | 346 (fall) | 69 |
| 44. When there is one *e* in a word that ends in a consonant, the *e* usually has a short sound. | 149 | 137 (held) | 12 (clerk) | 92 |
| 45. When the last syllable is the sound *r*, it is unaccented. | 761 | 601 (ever) | 160 (prefer) | 79 |

392

ascertain the possibilities of evolving new phonic generalizations that would utilize the schwa sound and symbol as presented by those dictionaries.

5. Regional pronunciations of words were not considered in the present study. Resulting utility of certain generalizations would have been considerably different had the pronunciation of words been considered upon the basis of pronunciations commonly used, for example in the Southern or Midwestern states. Therefore, it is recommended that future research be designed to consider the effect of regional pronunciations upon the usefulness of phonic generalizations.

Finally, this study does not conclusively establish the utility of phonic generalizations in reading for children in grades one through six. It is agreed with Burrows and Lourie [3] who, in reporting an investigation of the utility of the "when two vowels go walking" generalization, stated that "to know what not to teach when error is so apparent is one step forward, but only a short one."

## The Language-Experience Approach to Reading

WILMA H. MILLER

The "language-experience" theory of reading instruction, first developed by Roach Van Allen, can be the inspiration for a large number of successful methods for teaching reading, at many age levels. One teacher of my son started a continuing story on a large sheet of white paper tacked to a bulletin board; any child who wanted to add to the story simply wrote a few more sentences at the bottom of the writing already there. I saw children standing in front of this wildly plotted tale, writing, laughing at the newest developments, or rereading the whole thing and trying to think of an

[3] Alvina Treut Burrows and Zyra Lourie, "When 'Two Vowels Go Walking,'" *Reading Teacher*, 17 (Nov. 1963), 79–82.

appropriate (or inappropriate) twist in the story, every time
I came to the classroom. This story might be called a
communal language-experience product. It is a good example
of the way language-experience methods link creativity,
interest in the subject matter, and the relationship between
authorship and written language—as well as providing
familiar vocabulary and sentence structure to make beginning
reading as easy as possible.

The language-experience approach is considered by reading
specialists to be one of the main approaches to teaching beginning reading in the United States today. . . .

## BACKGROUND OF THE
## LANGUAGE-EXPERIENCE APPROACH

For a number of years, the experiences of first-grade children have formed the basis of some reading materials in beginning first-grade reading instructions. Every first-grade teacher
is familiar with the experience chart, a group-composed manuscript. However, the language-experience approach has been
refined and publicized in recent years by Dr. R. Van Allen, formerly Director of Curriculum Coordination of San Diego County,
California, but now of The University of Arizona. Dr. Allen apparently first noticed this approach being used with bilingual
Mexican-American children in a border area of Texas. Since these
children did not have the background of experiences to bring to
the interpretation of the basal readers, their teachers were using
dictated or child-written experience stories as the major basis of
their reading materials. The teachers of these bilingual children
also discovered that they were able to read their own language
patterns much more effectively than they could read the language
patterns found in the basal readers.
When Dr. Allen moved to San Diego County, he brought the
idea of a refined language-experience approach with him. The
approach was subjected to considerable experimentation in many
first grades in San Diego County. One major research study conducted there indicated that the language-experience approach,
the basal reader approach, and the individualized approach were
all excellent methods for teaching beginning reading. However,
the results further indicated that the language-experience ap-

proach and the individualized approach also developed a keen interest in learning to read on the part of the first-grade children.[1]

## DESCRIPTION OF THE
## LANGUAGE-EXPERIENCE APPROACH

The language-experience approach can be crystallized by the following statement which Dr. Allen uses in his materials:

> What I can think about, I can talk about.
> What I can say, I can write.
> What I can write, I can read.
> I can read what I write, and what other people can write for me to read.[2]

In kindergarten or in beginning first-grade, the children dictate many individual or group stories to their teacher who acts as a scribe. These stories capitalize on the in school or out of school experiences of the children and are recorded by the teacher using the language patterns of the children. The group-dictated experience charts are transcribed by the teacher on large chart paper. In using the group-composed experience charts, the teacher will read the chart to the class several times while emphasing left-to-right progression. She will also have the children read various words or sentences from the chart. The individually dictated experience stories are often typed by the teacher using a primary typewriter and given back to the child who dictated them.

Various art media are used to illustrate the individually dictated experience stories which are the unique feature of the language-experience approach. The children occasionally use a drawing or painting to motivate the telling of an experience story, but more often the dictated story is illustrated by the child who dictated it. The illustrated experience stories are later bound into a booklet for which the child has designed a gaily decorated cover. Each child then "reads" his booklet of experience stories at school and at home.

[1] Allen, R. Van, "Three Approaches to Teaching Reading," *Challenge and Experiment in Reading.* International Reading Association Conference Proceedings, Volume 7, 1962, 153–56.
[2] Department of Education, San Diego County. *An Inventory of Reading Attitude.* Monograph Number 4 of the Reading Study Project. San Diego: Superintendent of Schools, 1961.

By using both group-composed experience charts and individually dictated experience stories, the children in kindergarten or beginning first grade are able to conceptualize reading as "talk written down" and are able to learn a number of sight words in an informal manner.

As the children progress through first grade, they continue to use experience charts and stories as the major method of learning to read. They continue to dictate charts and stories to their teacher, but as they learn more and more words they can begin to write their own experience stories. Of course, in this beginning writing stage they still need considerable help from the teacher with the spelling of words, but the children are encouraged to spell the words in the experience stories as they think the words should be spelled. During the first grade, the children using the language-experience approach will read the experience stories that they themselves have composed as well as those of their classmates. The children will also read many stories from basal readers, but this reading is done on an individual basis for no ability grouping is found in the language-experience approach except for flexible short-term grouping. The children also will read many trade books in first grade.

There is no control of vocabulary in the language-experience approach for the child learns sight words found in his own experience stories or in the group-composed experience charts. Dr. Allen believes that the common service words will be learned by all children eventually since they are found in the dictated stories at some time during the early primary grades. Reading skills are taught in an incidental individual way in this approach, with phonics being taught on a "say it" to "see it" basis, the opposite of that found in the typical phonics program which emphasizes the "see it" to "say it" approach.

By the time the children have reached second grade, Dr. Allen assumes that they will be writing many experience stories with little help from the teacher. The children will be continuing to read their own experience booklets and the experience booklets of their classmates. They will continue to read stories from basal readers at their own reading level, whether it is the first grade, second grade, third grade, or perhaps the fourth grade levels. The second-grade children will also read trade books on their own reading level. The children will continue to learn the necessary reading skills on a basically individual basis.

The language-experience approach deemphasizes the use of experience booklets for reading material as the children approach the intermediate grades. It becomes mandatory at this level that the experience stories become supplementary instead of the basic reading materials.

## ADVANTAGES OF THE
## LANGUAGE-EXPERIENCE APPROACH

The language-experience approach has many unique features which make it very valuable. Perhaps one special advantage of this approach is that it enables children to conceptualize "reading is talk written down" during the early stages of reading instruction. This is a concept that many more mature readers do not seem to easily attain.

Another major advantage of this approach is that it insures that children have the background of experiences to bring to their reading since the experience charts and stories utilize their own experiences. This is a very important asset to the slow learning child or to the culturally [different] child.

The children can read their own language patterns very effectively, and the use of these more mature language patterns will not lead to the language regression that is sometimes the case when the basal readers are used in first grade. It has been found that older disabled readers, even those in junior high school, can easily read their own language patterns when given an opportunity to do so by a teacher who is using the language-experience approach as a remedial method with them. The approach also has a beneficial motivating effect to the disabled reader.

The language-experience approach can also be called an integrated language arts approach since it very effectively stresses the interrelationships among the four language arts of listening, speaking, reading, and writing. It particularly stresses the relationship between oral language and reading since the dictated experience charts and stories form the integral part of the approach at the early stages. It also stresses the relationship between reading and writing effectively since the child-written experience stories play an important part in the approach at its later stage.

The children's creativity is greatly enhanced when they are using this approach. The illustrations for the experience stories and the covers for the experience booklets give the children an opportunity to effectively explore various art media. The children who have used this approach usually are very adept at writing their own creative stories and often exceed children who were taught by other reading methods in creative writing ability.

Finally, the language-experience approach seems to develop a true interest in reading in the children who have used it. . . .

# Language Differences and Reading

**Juanito's Reading Problems:
Foreign Language Interference
and Reading Skill Acquisition**

NANCY MODIANO

Juanito does not just have a dialect with some nonstandard
features in it; he does not speak English. Modiano studies
his problems with reading.

Just as Juanito is very different from a speaker of Black
English, he is very different from a child who is fully
bilingual in English and Spanish. Spanish surnames have
nothing to do with bilinguality; their possessors can be
monolingual in English, monolingual in Spanish, or in full
control of one language with partial control over a second
language. Teachers have to be sensitive to the amount of
understanding between their bilingual students and themselves,
using other children as interpreters when necessary, or—
best of all—beginning to acquire the child's native language
themselves. Even a little use of the student's language
will go a long way toward establishing rapport with the child.
The student who is asked for some help in learning the language
can become the teacher for a while, instead of constantly

being cast as the passive observer. This may break the "soundless barrier," one teacher's term for the unwillingness of many migrant children to talk at all in school.

Saville, in Part 2, explains the influence Spanish or Navajo may have on the speech of children acquiring English as a second language. The implications of Penfield's article in Part 1 include some limitations on ability to speak a completely unaccented version of English; these are discussed in the summary article for Part 1. Rigg, here in Part 4, gives some methods for teaching ESL (English as a Second Language) students to read.

Juanito is a first or second grader. His mother tongue is Spanish, and his ability to understand and speak English is minimal.

There are approximately 5 million non-English speaking school-aged children in the United States, of whom at least 80 percent speak Spanish. The rest speak a great variety of languages, European tongues predominating; relatively small proportions are speakers of Amerind or Eskimo languages or Chinese (Pena, 1971).

As schools now operate, reading underlies almost all academic activities and, with the exception of a few bilingual programs, this means reading in English. Yet, how can one read in a language he can barely understand, let alone speak?

There are essentially two aspects of what is meant by "able to read." One concentrates on the skills necessary for the translation of the squiggly lines we call writing into meaningful utterances; these are the decoding skills. The other aspect, concerned with recreating the author's intent in the mind of the reader, is reading comprehension. Let us consider each aspect separately.

## FOREIGN LANGUAGE INTERFERENCE IN THE ACQUISITION OF DECODING SKILLS

Within the concern for the acquisition of decoding skills there are two major approaches. *The Great Debate* (Chall, 1967) rages between those who favor a "phonics" approach, stressing regularities and rules in sound-symbol correspondencies, and those who favor a more global, "sight-vocabulary" approach, which stresses the visual configuration of words and places a greater reliance upon their meanings.[1] Sometimes only the phonics approach is popularly identified with decoding skills, although advocates of both approaches see theirs as the key to unlocking meaning from writing. The debate rages hot between the two camps; the phonics group seems to have the upper hand just now. Actually both approaches are necessary for the decoding of written symbols, and few instructional programs so stress one as to ignore the other. Without judging the relative merits of either approach, let us look into the effects of foreign language interference on both.

The phonics approach assumes that the child can 1) hear the sounds of the language, 2) recognize each of the letters, and 3) learn to associate each sound with one or a combination of letters.

While most six-year-olds can, with enough time and patient instruction, learn to do each of the above in their mother tongue, they have considerable difficulty in doing any of them in a foreign language. First, all the teacher talk which we call instruction is largely unintelligible in a second language. Meaningful instruction can occur only at a primitive "grunt and point" level, with the child expected to react like a robot or a circus animal responding to the commands of its trainer.

Second, the child is incapable of distinguishing many of the sounds of the foreign language, especially those which do not involve minimal contrasts in his own. Thus, the Spanish speaker has difficulty in distinguishing the vowels in *ship* and *sheep;* the initial consonants appear to be easier for him to hear. The inability of second-language learners to hear many of the sounds of the new language has been recognized by linguists for a long time, but not by most reading teachers. For a particularly good review of recent developments in this field see Ervin-Tripp (1970), Greenberg (1968), and Hall and Robinson (1945). What reading teachers have recognized is something they call "listening ability," which they find relates directly to reading achievement (Cleland and Toussaint, 1963; Plessas, 1963).

Third, the child has difficulty in perceiving written symbols, especially individual letters. As reading is generally taught, the individual letters are presented in relation to words which include their sounds; for the child who cannot hear or understand the words, let alone attach meaning to them, this remains a meaningless, rote procedure. We have long known that an individual

[1] [Ed.'s note: The Goodman approach presented in this book is a third major point of view, in which sentence structure and meaning play a role more important than either phonics or word recognition.]

perceives and remembers only that which has meaning for him (Bartlett, 1932; Bruner, 1957, 1962; Fantz, 1961; Piaget, 1969; Smith and Dechant, 1961; and Vernon, 1937). Just as the child often has difficulty in distinguishing the words and their sounds, so he often cannot perceive differences in the shapes of the letters themselves. And if he does perceive them, he has difficulty remembering what he has seen (Mewhort, 1967; Mewhort, Merikle, and Bryden, 1969; Reicher, 1969; and Wheeler, 1970).

He encounters great difficulty in learning to read through the phonics approach. It is expected that he be able to hear all of the sounds of the second language as recognized by native speakers of that language, but he can hear only some of those sounds. It is expected that he be able to recognize the symbols with which the language is written, but often he cannot. Nor can he make many of the sound-symbol correspondencies native speakers are expected to learn. Moreover, he can understand only the most primitive of the teacher talk in which instruction is given.

Difficult as it may be for Juanito to learn decoding skills through the phonics approach, it is at least as difficult for him to learn using the sight-vocabulary approach. While there is no expectation that he be able to decipher a word through its individual letters, he is expected to recognize each word through its visual configuration and to attach an appropriate meaning to it (see Ervin, 1961; Loginova, 1962; and Van Krevelen, 1961). Although it has been shown that it is easier for a reader to recognize a word by its global configuration than by an analysis of its letters (Gray, 1956; Makita, 1963), Juanito still will have trouble in recognizing the word when he hears it, it is devoid of meaning, and he often cannot even perceive its shape, let alone attach meaning to it. Moreover, his teacher as with the phonics approach, will be able to communicate with him only at a rudimentary level.

Regardless of the method used to teach decoding skills, Juanito will have great difficulty in learning. In time, with enough urging, he may learn to perceive certain letters and words and, like a robot, to repeat them. More importantly, and independently of the reading lessons, he may begin to learn the new language. It is only when he knows enough of the second language to understand what he is "reading" that he can begin to really decode and to read.

The more he comes into contact with the second language, the more rapidly he is likely to learn it. Thus, those children who are the only non-English speakers in their classes are likely to learn the second language rapidly and are often able to catch up academically with their age-mates within a few years. Children living in heterogeneous neighborhoods where English is an important out-of-school language for them tend to learn it more rapidly than do those who live in ethnically homogeneous neighborhoods. Even the presence of radio and television in the home, when these broadcast only in the national language, is a stimulus for learning. But for those children who live completely isolated from the national language, mastery is a very lengthy process, often taking more than merely the elementary school years.

The longer it takes to learn the second language, the longer it takes to learn to read it. It is a very frustrating experience, one in which the children feel themselves to be stupid, incapable of remembering what on the surface appear to be simple details. Feelings of frustration and worthlessness serve only to further retard the learning of reading. In linguistically isolated communities, the most common response is to drop out of school after only a few years of attendance.

However, when children are taught to decode in their own language, they have less trouble in decoding a second one (Grieve and Taylor, 1952; Modiano, 1968; Orata, 1953). The more the two languages use the same sound-symbol correspondencies, the more this is likely to be true.

## FOREIGN LANGUAGE INTERFERENCE IN READING COMPREHENSION

Once Juanito has learned to decode in a foreign language, his troubles are not at an end. He still has to understand what it is he is decoding.[2] For native speakers, two major factors have been found to affect comprehension. Vocabulary accounts for about one-half of the variance; the second factor appears to be some type of verbal intelligence, which some researchers have linked to a knowledge of the structure of the language. There are additional factors, such as attitude, frustration level, and legibility, which also affect comprehension.

---

[2] [Ed.'s note: Modiano is using the term "decode" in a way different from that defined by K. Goodman earlier in Part 4; in Goodman's terminology, Modiano's *decode* would be *recode*. For Goodman, *decoding* is getting meaning; but Modiano's sentences here show that that is not the case in her use of this term.]

If knowledge of vocabulary, the first factor, accounts for about half of reading comprehension, the person who does not know the vocabulary is obviously at a serious disadvantage. This has long been recognized. In 1926 West published a study of Bengali speakers learning academic material in English; he concluded that knowledge of vocabulary was the single most important factor affecting reading comprehension. Since then other studies have further substantiated this point of view (Jan-Tausch 1962).

The second factor in reading comprehension has been described variously by different researchers. There are those who link it primarily with some aspect of logical reasoning (Anderson 1949; Davis, 1944, Hunt, 1952, 1957; and Jan-Tausch, 1962). Others have related it more directly to grammatical mastery. As long ago as 1917, Thorndike, in his pioneering study of reading comprehension, stated that reading comprehension is based on word and sentence meaning. Later Langsham (1941) and Hall and Robinson (1945) named the second factor the verbal factor; in further analyses Burt (1949) found that the verbal factor was composed primarily of words in context and words in isolation. Holmes (1954) has gone on to suggest that the second factor is composed of verbal intelligence and the understanding of verbal relationships. More recent empirical studies (Labov, 1970; Levin and Kaplan, 1970; O'Donnell, 1962; Sokhin, 1959; and Weber, 1970) have all shown that the reader depends upon grammatical clues to give meaning to the words and sentences he reads. Obviously, the person reading in a poorly mastered language, ignorant of the subtleties and nuances of its structure, is at a serious disadvantage. Stewart (1969) has gone so far as to suggest that it is the imperfect mastery of standard English grammar which lies at the heart of many of the reading problems of speakers of Afro-American English.

## FOREIGN LANGUAGE INTERFERENCE AND ATTITUDINAL FACTORS

Juanito has great difficulty in learning to read directly in English. Once he learns to decode, he continues to have great problems in understanding what it is he is reading until he learns to understand and speak the second language. He can hardly remain ignorant of how slow his progress is as compared to that of native speakers. In first grade he may have been given a first grade reader; in second and third grades he finds himself receiving lessons from the same book. Moreover, the book is likely to have a big *1* displayed prominently on its front and spine. Juanito knows he is not learning to read as quickly as he "should." He cannot do what his teacher asks of him. He feels frustrated. He is a failure.

That these feelings of frustration and failure directly affect the acquisition of reading skills and comprehension have long been recognized. Some have gone so far as to consider attitudinal factors the single most important element in reading achievement (Gregory, 1965; Groff, 1962; and Sopis, 1965–66). The inherent failure built into learning to read in a foreign language gives rise to negative feelings which serve only to further slow down and complicate the learning process. Moreover, they teach the child that, at best, reading is a disagreeable activity. The influence of the attitudinal factors is seen clearly in the bilingual programs which offer reading instruction first in the mother tongue, so that the frustrations of learning to read in a foreign language are eliminated. The child faces a task no more difficult than that of any other child learning to read in his own language.

The influence of attitudinal factors was illustrated clearly both in the Iloilo project (Orata, 1953) where school-inspired changes occurred much more frequently in the homes of children enrolled in the bilingual classes than in those of children enrolled in the all-English classes; and in Mexico (Modiano, 1968) where school enrollments in general, the enrollment of girls in particular, the reading achievement of the girls, and general levels of adult literacy were all higher in Indian schools offering bilingual education than in those offering instruction only in Spanish.

## SUMMARY

How does the use of a foreign language interfere with the acquisition of reading skills? In every way. First of all, the learner can understand only the most rudimentary type of instruction when his teacher speaks in a foreign language. His acquisition of the decoding skills is greatly hampered because he cannot hear many of the sounds and words of the foreign language; he cannot perceive the letters and visual configurations by which the words are represented; and he seldom can link the sounds and the symbols meaningfully. What he learns he learns by rote. The lack of vocabulary and nonmastery of grammatical structures greatly impede his comprehension of what he does read. All of this gives rise to strong feelings of frustration and often of failure, feelings which only serve to further impede the acquisition of reading skills and which tend to alienate the child from school.

## REFERENCES

ANDERSON, C. C. "A Factorial Analysis of Reading," *British Journal of Educational Psychology*, 19 (1949), 220–21.

BARTLETT, F. C. *Remembering*. (Cambridge, Massachusetts: University Press, 1932.)

BRUNER, JEROME. "On Perceptual Readiness," *Psychological Review*, 64 (1959), 123–52.

BRUNER, JEROME. "Social Psychology and Perception," *The Causes of Behavior*, J. F. Rosenblith and W. Allinsmith, Eds., 363–69. (Boston: Allyn and Bacon, 1962.)

BURT, C. "The Structure of the Mind," *British Journal of Educational Psychology*, 19 (1949), 176–79.

CHALL, JEANNE. *Learning to Read: The Great Debate*. (New York: McGraw-Hill, 1967.)

CLELAND, DONALD L., and TOUSSAINT, ISABELLA. "The Interrelationship of Reading, Listening, Arithmetic Computation, and Intelligence," *Reading Teacher*, 16 (1963), 252–60.

DAVIS, FREDERICK B. "Fundamental Factors of Comprehension in Reading," *Psychometrika*, 9 (1944), 185–97.

DAVIS, FREDERICK B. "The Teaching of Comprehension of Reading in the Secondary School," *Education*, 76 (1956), 541–44.

ERVIN, SUSAN M. "Learning and Recall in Bilinguals," *American Journal of Psychology*, 74 (1961), 446–51.

ERVIN-TRIPP, SUSAN. "Structure and Process in Language Acquisition," *Report of the 21st Annual Round Table Meeting on Linguistics and Language Studies*. (Washington, D.C.: Georgetown University Press, 1970), 313–44.

FANTZ, ROBERT L. "The Origin of Form Perception," *Scientific American*, 204:5 (1961), 66–72, 204.

GRAY, WILLIAM S. *The Teaching of Reading and Writing: An International Survey*. (Paris: UNESCO. Chicago: Scott, Foresman, 1956.)

GREENBERG, JOSEPH H. *Anthropological Linguistics: An Introduction*. (New York: Random House, 1968.)

GREGORY, ROBIN E. "Unsettledness, Maladjustment, and Reading Failure: A Village Study," *British Journal of Educational Psychology*, 35 (1965), 63–68.

GRIEVE, D. W., and TAYLOR, A. "Media of Instruction," *Gold Coast Education*, 1 (1952), 36–52.

GROFF, PATRICK J. "Children's Attitudes Toward Reading and Their Critical Reading Abilities in Four Content-Type Materials," *Journal of Education Research*, 55 (1962), 313–17.

GUDSHINSKY, SARAH C. *How to Learn an Unwritten Language*. (New York: Holt, Rinehart and Winston, 1967.)

HALL, W. E., and ROBINSON, F. P. "An Analytic Approach to the Study of Reading Skill," *Journal of Educational Psychology*, 36 (1945), 429–42.

HOLMES, JACK A. "Factors Underlying Major Reading Disabilities at the College Level," *Genetic Psychological Monographs*, 49 (1954), 3–95.

HUNT, LYMAN C., JR. "Can We Measure Specific Factors Associated with Reading Comprehension?" *Journal of Education Research*, 51 (1957), 161–72.

HUNT, LYMAN C., JR. "A Further Study of Certain Factors Associated with Reading Comprehension," unpublished doctoral dissertation, Syracuse University, 1952.

JAN-TAUSCH, JAMES. "Concrete Thinking as a Factor in Reading Comprehension," in J. Allen Figurel (Ed.), *Challenge and Experiment in Reading*, Proceedings of the International Reading Association, 7, 1962. (New York: Scholastic Magazines, 161–64.)

KEANE, GEORGE R. "The Measurement of Readability," *Encyclopedia of Educational Research* (4th ed.). (New York: Macmillan, 1969.)

LABOV, WILLIAM. "The Reading of the -ed Suffix," *Basic Studies on Reading*, H. Levin and J. P. Williams, Eds., 222–45. (New York: Basic Books, 1970.)

LANGRAM, R. T. "A Factorial Analysis of Reading Ability," *Journal of Experimental Education*, 10 (1941), 57–63.

LEVIN, HENRY, and KAPLAN, E. L. "Grammatical Structure and Reading," *Basic Studies on Reading*, H. Levin and J. P. Williams, Eds., 119–33. (New York: Basic Books, 1970.)

LOGINOVA, E. A. "Ovliyanii Interesa Na Zapominanie Novykh Slov Pri Izuchenii Inostrannogo Yazyka (On the Influence of Interest on Remembering New Words During the Study of a Foreign Language)," *Voprosy Psikhologgii*, 1 (1962), 61–64.

MAKITA, KIYOSHI. "The Rarity of Reading Disability in Japanese Children," *American Journal of Orthopsychiatric*, 38 (1968), 599–614.

MEWHORT, D. J. K. "Familiarity of Letter Sequences Response Uncertainty, and the Tachistoscope Recognition Requirement," *Canadian Journal of Psychology*, 21 (1967), 309–21.

MEWHORT, D. J. K.; MERIKLE, P. M.; and BRYDEN, M. P. "On the Transfer from Iconic to Short-term Memory," *Journal of Experimental Psychology*, 81 (1969), 89–95.

MODIANO, NANCY. "Bilingual Edducation for Children of Linguistic Minorities," *America Indigena*, 28 (1968), 405–14.

O'DONNELL, ROY. "Awareness of Grammatical Structure and Reading Comprehension," *High School Journal*, 45 (1962), 184–88.

ORATA, PEDRO T. "The Iloilo Experiment in Education through the Vernacular," *The Use of Vernacular Languages in Education.* (Paris: UNESCO, 1953), 123–31.

PENA, ALBAR. Personal Communication (1971).

PIAGET, JEAN. *The Mechanisms of Perception.* (New York: Basic Books, 1969.)

PLESSAS, GUS P. "Reading Abilities of High and Low Achievers," *Elementary School Journal,* 63 (1963), 223–26.

REICHER, G. M. "Perceptual Recognition as a Function of Meaningfulness of Stimulus Material," *Journal of Experimental Psychology,* 81 (1969), 275–81.

SMITH, HENRY E., and DECHANT, EMERALD V. *Psychology in Teaching Reading.* (Englewood Cliffs, N.J.: Prentice-Hall, 1961.)

SOKHIN, F. A. "A Farmirovanii Iazykovykh Obobschschenni v Protsesse Rechevogo Razvitiia (On the Formation of Language Generalization in the Process of Speech Development)," *Voprosy Psikhologgii,* 5 (1959), 112–23.

SOPIS, JOSEPHINE. "The Relationship of Self-Image as Reader to Reading Achievement," *Academic Therapy Quarterly,* 1 (1965–1966), 94–101, 113.

STEWART, WILLIAM A. "On the Use of Negro Dialect in the Teaching of Reading," *Teaching Black Children to Read,* Joan Baratz and Roger Shuy, Eds., 156–219. (Washington, D.C.: Center for Applied Linguistics, 1969.)

THORNDIKE, EDWARD L. "Reading as Reasoning, A Study of Mistakes in Paragraph Reading," *Journal of Educational Psychology,* 8 (1917), 323–32.

VAN KREVELEN, ALICE. "The Relationship Between Recall and Meaningfulness of Motive Related Words," *Journal of Genetic Psychology,* 65 (1961), 229–33.

VERNON, M. D. *Visual Perception.* (Cambridge, Massachusetts: University Press, 1937.)

WEBER, ROSE-MARIE. "First-Graders' Use of Grammatical Context in Reading," *Basic Studies on Reading,* H. Levin and J. P. Williams, Eds., 147–63. (New York: Basic Books, 1970.)

WEST, MICHAEL. *Bilingualism, with Special Reference to Bengal.* Occasional Reports, 13, Bureau of Education, India. (Calcutta: Government of India Central Publications Branch, 1926.)

WHEELER, D. D. "Processes in Word Recognition," *Cognitive Psychology,* 1 (1970), 59–85.

# Dialect Barriers to
# Reading Comprehension Revisited

KENNETH S. GOODMAN and
CATHERINE BUCK

Kenneth Goodman and Catherine Buck describe research
that modifies Goodman's previous position on the relationship
between "nonstandard" dialects and reading; in an earlier
article, "Dialect Barriers to Reading Comprehension," [1]
Goodman had suggested that "nonstandard" dialects might
interfere with reading. Notice that it is this earlier article
that Baratz, in the following selection, cites as support of her
position; that support is, of course, weakened now that
Goodman has revised his views.

Goodman and Buck examine miscues produced by
students reading aloud (a *miscue* is a difference between an
expected response and an observed response). Syntactic
miscues are judged as more important than pronunciation
differences between dialects, and Goodman and Buck
find relatively few syntactic miscues. Their position might
become even stronger if they closely examined the absence of
inflections—which they count as syntactic miscueing—to
see whether phonological processes might be responsible for
loss of some of these inflections. As we saw in Part 2,
endings like the /s/ or /z/ that represents the plural can be
deleted by a phonological rule that lops off final consonants. If
the inflection does appear in the speaker's spontaneous
speech part of the time, chances are good that it is part of the
speaker's syntax—only when the inflection is entirely absent
from natural speech can it definitely be considered to
be absent from the person's syntax. Even then, its absence
may represent loss of one allomorph of the inflectional
morpheme, not absence of the entire morpheme.

Much has been written in recent years on the possible influence of dialect differences on learning to read. A considerable
amount of the momentum for this interest comes from the in-
disputable fact that speakers of low status dialects of English
have much higher rates of reading failure than high status
dialect speakers. Analyses of contrasts between high and low

---

[1] *Elementary English,* 42 (December, 1965), 853–860.

status dialects suggest that the problem in reading acquisition *could* be due to mismatches between the dialect of the learner and that of the writer.

In fact, this writer hypothesized some years ago that there would be a direct relationship between the degree of dialect divergence and success in learning to read (Goodman, 1965). Because that article has been widely reprinted and the hypothesis widely quoted, it is doubly important that I report that evidence from several years of miscue research has convinced me that the hypothesis, at least as it applies to the range of dialects spoken by White and Black urban Americans, is untrue.

In the article cited above, I concluded that of several alternatives the approach most likely to solve the reading problems of speakers of low status dialects is the acceptance by teachers of the use in oral reading of the dialect of the learners.

The same data which causes me to abandon my own hypothesis causes me to believe even more strongly that the solution to reading problems of divergent speakers lies in changing the attitudes of teachers and writers of instructional programs toward the language of the learners.

## NEW HYPOTHESIS

I offer this new hypothesis:

The only special disadvantage which speakers of low-status dialects suffer in learning to read is one imposed by teachers and schools. Rejection of their dialects and educators' confusion of linguistic difference with linguistic deficiency interferes with the natural process by which reading is acquired and undermines the linguistic self-confidence of divergent speakers.

Simply speaking, the disadvantage of the divergent speaker, Black or White, comes from linguistic discrimination. Instruction based on rejection of linguistic difference is the core of the problem.

## THE EVIDENCE

For almost ten years my associates and I have been studying the reading process among urban kids in the Detroit area. The oral miscues of subjects reading a complete selection, which they haven't seen before and which is sometimes difficult for them, are analysed in order to get at the reading process. A miscue is any observed response (OR) which differs from the expected response (ER) to the text. Because of the location of the research project, somewhat more than half the subjects in our studies are Black.

Early in our research we became aware that the expected response in oral reading is not an exact single response but a range of responses which depends on variability among the subjects in their oral language. Dialect differences must certainly be considered in judging whether a particular response (OR) is within the expected range. But even within dialects, considerable variation must be expected. In our area, for example, the words *roof* and *root* have two common pronunciations. Both are to be expected. At one point we discovered that *with'm* was the most likely response to both printed phrases: *with them* and *with him* for all readers, all races, and all classes.

With our insights into the variability in ER's we became aware that all dialect difference that was purely phonological (a matter of pronunciation alone) was within the expected range for the readers being studied. What should one expect a reader to report orally in response to printed *help them* if he would in his everyday speech normally say, *he'p dem?* Clearly if he says in reading what he would say in speaking he is producing an expected response. In fact there might be more suspicion that a standardized pronunciation, unnatural to the speaker, might be a source of confusion. If he says *help,* is he aware that it's an alternate for his *he'p?*

We no longer even count as a miscue any OR that is simply a phonological variant in the reader's dialect of the printed word or phrase. What that means is that only miscues that involve inflection (mostly word endings), grammar or vocabulary will be found in our data.

Before leaving this matter of phonological dialect differences, I want to emphasize that teachers have tended to confuse attempts to change the speech of young learners with teaching them to read. This is, of course, not wholly the fault of teachers. The basal readers and other materials the teacher uses have frequently ignored all dialect difference. Exercises are provided in which *pin* and *pen,* for example, are treated as if they have contrasting vowel sounds. They do in some dialects, mine for one. But they don't in many others. Teaching pupils who do not use this difference in their dialects to hear and produce it (a more difficult task), can have no effect on their learning to read except to introduce discomfort, uncertainty, and lack of linguistic confidence.

Furthermore, spelling is standardized across dialects of English. *Almond* is the spelling regardless of which of the five or more common pronunciations your dialect uses (with /l/ or without, with initial vowel /æ/ or /a/ or /ə/). Phonics programs based on single acceptable pronunciations are simply ethnocentric. The author of the program rejects everything which varies from his own speech.

Urban kids who speak low-status dialects have a linguistic advantage over speakers of higher status dialects which can work for them in learning to read if teachers are aware of it. They build an ability to understand the dialects of others in their community. This acquisition of receptive control over other people's dialects is a simple matter of survival. If you don't understand what teachers, policemen, store clerks, TV announcers, and other high-status people are saying, you can be in big trouble. This does not mean that divergent speakers learn to talk like the teacher; that involves productive control. But it does mean that what they find in print is not as hard to deal with for them as we once thought. Sims demonstrated this in her study of inner-city Black English speakers (Sims, 1972).

Dialect-involved miscues represent a shift on the part of the reader to a surface representation which fits his own dialect rather than the writer's. Just as the sounds may shift, there may also be a shift involving a different rule for generating the surface structure from the deep structure—for example, the deletion of an -*ed* past tense morpheme because the reader's dialect doesn't require one. Or it may involve a dialect shift in choice of vocabulary, as when the reader prefers *headlights* to the writer's *headlamps*.

In a recently completed study of readers at low, average, and high proficiency levels in second, fourth, sixth, eighth, and tenth grades (Goodman and Burke, 1973) we found that no reader in our study is totally consistent in these dialect-based shifts. Readers who frequently eliminate -*ed* endings in their readings will sometimes produce them. This is consistent with the findings of recent urban socioeconomic dialect studies, including that of Shuy and his associates in the Detroit area (Wolfram, 1969).

These dialect studies show that dialect contrasts are not sharp and discrete among urban speakers, but show up more as a matter of preferences for certain alternatives.

In our research, dialect variations among the subjects are considerable between and within racial groups. Only a small number of subjects in the study, however, produce any notable percentage of miscues involving dialect. Furthermore, in every grade-proficiency group but four (10LA, 8L, 6L, 4A) [1] there are some subjects with no dialect miscues. Two groups (4H, 8H) have no subjects that produced dialect miscues. Only two subjects in the 2H, 10H, and 4A groups show dialect miscues.

All but one of the subjects with more than 10 percent dialect miscues are Black. But there are many Black subjects with few dialect miscues and others with none. And there are White subjects with dialect-involved miscues.

Seven subjects among the total of ninety-four in this research showed more than 20 percent dialect-involved miscues. All are Black. These are found in groups as follows:

2HA: 1—31%    6L: 2—30%, 21%
4A: 1—28%    8L: 1—25%
6A: 1—23%    10L: 1—28%

These can be seen to be well-distributed, except that none are in any high groups. Black speakers in the high proficiency groups tend to do little dialect shifting in their miscues.

Those subjects with high dialect involvement tend to be more consistent in oral reading in using certain features of a Black English dialect. No subject whose oral speech shows these features is entirely consistent in using them in oral reading, but these subjects come closest.

By far the most common kind of dialect shift involves changes in inflectional endings. Of even relatively frequent types of dialect-involved miscues, the first four involve inflectional suffixes, one involves irregular verb forms, one involves *be* forms, and the seventh involves confusion over base forms with *ed* suffix.

The dialect features which occur most commonly are:

1. Use of null form of past tense morpheme: look/looked, call/called, wreck/wrecked, love/loved, pound/pounded, help/helped/, use/used.

2. Use of null form of plural noun morpheme: thing/things, work/works, story/stories, prize/prizes.

3. Use of null form for third person singular verbs: look/looks, work/works, hide/hides.

---

[1] Groups of 5–6 subjects are designated by grade and level—for instance, 10LA means low average tenth graders, 6L are low sixth graders.

4. Use of null form for possessives: Freddie/Freddie's, Mr. Vine/Mr. Vine's, one/one's, it/its.

5. Regular present for past irregular forms: run/ran, have/had, keep/kept, do/did.

6. *Be* form substitution and deletion: was/were, is/are, we/we're, he be talking/he'd been talking.

7. Some readers tend to overcompensate for their tendency to delete *ed* with a resulting confusion over past tense forms. This produced: likeded/liked, helpeded/helped, stoppeded/stopped.

The dialect miscues listed above are much more common than more complex transformations of grammar or substitutions of preferred terms. In fact, these other kinds of dialect miscues, though they occur, must be considered rare.

Here are some examples of less common miscues with dialect involvement:

OR   It my little monkey here.
ER   Is my little monkey here?

OR   . . . out loud.
ER   . . . aloud.

OR   We got to tell.
ER   We've got to tell.

OR   A word what sounded good.
ER   A word that sounded good.

OR   His smiling muscle came
ER   His smiling muscle began to twitch again.

OR   He didn't have to worry
ER   He was not to worry

OR   hisself
ER   himself

OR   Classes left out.
ER   Classes let out.

Fortuitously, we chose one story for the study written by a British author which created dialect mismatch for all the subjects who read it and shed a light on the phenomenon of dialect shift from a different direction. *Poison*, a story by the British author Roald Dahl, provided many uncommon uses of language for Americans. It was read by 8H, 10LA, 10HA and 10H groups.

If the author himself had been the researcher listening to the retelling of his own story, he no doubt would have noted many examples to support the fact that the readers were speakers of a dialect other than his own. But Roald Dahl did not listen, American researchers did, and what they heard corresponded to their own system.

    1. OR                headlights
       ER   I switched off the headlamps of the car.
    2. OR         a minute
       ER   Stop. Wait a moment, Timer.
    3. OR              around
       ER   Look, could you come round at once?

These examples are produced not just by one reader, but by many and with dependability. Six of twenty-one readers substitute *lights* for *lamps*. Twelve say *minute* instead of *moment*. Fifteen prefer to say *around* instead of *round*. The phonological systems of the readers and the author, of course, differ far more radically than either their grammatical systems or their choices of lexical items for the same ideas.

The author tends to use certain adverbs without *-ly* that our American subjects add to fit the constraints of their dialects. His *quick* is read as *quickly* twelve times by our readers. (Do it quick.) *Quiet* (lying very quiet) is less of a problem but it is changed to *quietly* twice.

Old "usage" problems pop up in this story including the grammar book *lie-lay* bugaboo. Five times *lying* is changed to *laying*. *Laid* for *lay* occurs twice.

British idiom leads to some other difficulties:

This sentence, "It looked like a bad go of malaria," produces eight miscues. Only one directly involves *go* but four readers change the following word *of*. It becomes *from, on,* and *for* (twice). Two miscues involve *it*. One miscues on *malaria*.

"He rang off," a British alternate for hung up, produces four miscues. Two move to *ran off*.

Clearly, written English is not a single dialect and the possibility of producing dialect-involved miscues depends on the writer as well as the reader.

Shifts in dialect in oral reading are less likely to occur than might be predicted from the speech of the readers.

To get a comparison, we listened to the electronically recorded retelling of the story by each reader who produced *no* dialect-involved miscues.

The retellings of those subjects who make no dialect miscues while reading reveal several facts of great interest. Of the thirty in this group, twelve use a dialect other than the author's in recounting their own versions of the stories. These readers include the full range of grade and level from the 2H reader who describes the main character of a story by saying: "Freddie, he was thinking to be a scientist." to the 10L reader who, explained, "Then Peggy was hungry because she didn't get no food." And these readers are not all Black youngsters. A White 4H reader, who reads with no dialect miscues, explains to the researcher that the baby brother Andrew is very unusual because: "He said all them big words."

Unfortunately, the baby is not . . . "A baby just like ordinaries baby . . . who cries and says words that doesn't, you know, that ain't true. Like da-da."

And discovering this apparent deception, "Mr. Barnaberry asked him what was the idea." The numerous subjects with no dialect-involved miscues, particularly among those children ranked "high," does not mean that we have a group of White speakers who use standard English only. Some of the most interesting examples of bidialectalism in retelling come from proficient Black readers who show no dialect miscues in oral reading. They produce these examples of *embedded questions:*

1. They asked Harry did he really see it in the first place.
2. He called the doctor a few names and asked him was he calling him a liar.

*alternate verbal constructions:*

1. If I had wrote it, I'd have done it that way.
2. Andrew had bend over the crib.
3. He say it might be better to forget about birthdays.

and *double negatives:*

1. He said 'physiolical' and no baby never said that before.
2. He didn't do nothing right there.

From average readers come these examples:

1. Peggy was fighting with them and she surprise them and knock the coyote away from Chip and she start fighting with them.
2. So then the boy took out a dictionary and turned to the S's and start reading.

and from readers ranked *low* we find these:

1. Then one of the men said "Hold it! That wasn't no coyote."
2. He hurt hisself or something.
3. He ain't—he hasn't ever ate a sheep before.

## CONCLUSIONS

Shifts from the author's to the reader's dialect in oral reading occur among most of the readers in our study. They are never entirely consistent: the reader who tends not to produce -*ed* forms will produce some. Evidence of dialect in oral reading is less likely than in the subject's oral retelling; in fact, some readers with no dialect-involved miscues show frequent divergent dialect instances in retelling.

Less proficient readers show more dialect involvement, but we have no clear cause-effect evidence. Our study shows that Black speakers of low-status dialects can be proficient readers. It does not show that dialect difference or dialect rejection is *not* a cause of difficulty in learning to read. But the most important thing to understand about dialect is that dialect-involved miscues do not interfere with the reading process or the construction of meaning, since they move to the reader's own language.

Low-status urban speakers learn to understand dialects other than their own in the larger community—that is, they acquire receptive control over these dialects, though they may never change the way they speak.

The readers in our study appear to have receptive control of the dialect of the author, judging by their own dialect, and to process forms foreign to their own dialects as they read.

What, however, would be the result of teacher rejection of the dialect-related miscues? We have one example in the tendency of readers to insert /ed/ endings on all past tense forms: *sniffeded, drownded, askeded*. This is the result of teachers admonishing readers to "be sure and sound out the ends of words." The unnaturalness results from the reader attempting to produce forms inconsistent with his own dialect rules.

In fact, rejection or correction by the teacher of any dialect-based miscue moves the reader away from using his own linguistic competence to get to meaning toward a closer correspondence to the teacher's expected response to the text. Word for word accuracy, in a narrow sense, becomes the goal, rather than meaning.

We know that highly proficient readers produce few dialect-based miscues while reading with high comprehension. This has to be the result of increased receptive control over the high-status dialect.

But the appearance of greater accuracy is the result of proficient reading and not its cause. In encouraging divergent speakers to use their language competence, both receptive and productive, and accepting their dialect-based miscues, we minimize the effect of dialect differences. In rejecting their dialects we maximize the effect.

Rejection, then, and not dialect differences, is the problem educators must overcome to remove the school imposed disadvantage.

*(The data reported in this article come from a study, Kenneth S. Goodman and Carolyn Burke:* Theoretically Based Studies of Patterns of Miscues in Oral Reading Performance. *USOE Project 9-0375. Points of view or opinions do not necessarily represent official HEW position or policy.)*

**REFERENCES**

GOODMAN, K. S. "Dialect Barriers to Reading Comprehension," *Elementary English,* vol. 42, no. 8 (December, 1965).

GOODMAN, K. S., and C. L. BURKE. *Theoretically Based Studies of Patterns of Miscues in Oral Reading Performance,* USOE Project 9-0375 Technical Report, 1973.

SIMS, R. A. Psycholinguistic Description of Miscues Generated by Selected Young Readers During the Oral Reading of Text Material in Black Dialect and Standard English. Unpublished doctoral dissertation. Wayne State University, 1972.

WOLFRAM, W. A. *A Sociolinguistic Description of Detroit Negro Speech.* Washington, D.C.: Center for Applied Linguistics, 1969.

# Reading and Black Dialect: A Review of the Literature

JOAN C. BARATZ

The intent of using books written in "the vernacular" (dialect of low socioeconomic classes) is to give children who are just learning to read something written in a language they themselves use. Baratz is a very strong believer in this approach.

Goodman and Buck, in the previous article, disagree with Baratz's solution though not with her intent. I, too, have some reservations about the use of vernacular readers: first—as we discussed in Part 2—most linguists believe that dialect differences in the United States exist mostly at the superficial level, not in the underlying sentence structure; we are dealing not with different languages, but with different dialects. Second, a text written in "the vernacular" may be fine for one city, but not fully appropriate for another city. There may be differences in the "vernaculars" spoken in the two cities. The language-experience approach described elsewhere in Part 4 might do a better job of matching the child's reading material with his language than would vernacular readers.

One of the great virtues of Baratz's article is its critical approach to other research on reading and "nonstandard" dialects. Kinds of criticism are represented here—criticism of the choice of students, of methods, of conclusions. We do not have to remember every detail of this criticism, or agree with all of Baratz's suggestions, in order to learn a great deal from the article about the critical process.

Much has been written concerning the relationship between oral language skills and the acquisition of reading skills. It has been suggested by some that the failure of large numbers of black children to perform at or above national norms on reading achievement tests may be due, at least in part, to the fact that these children do not speak standard English (SE)—the language of instruction and the language of the text—when they first come to school (Baratz and Shuy, 1969). Although there is apparent agreement on the existence of Negro nonstandard English (NNE) and its possible role in reading retardation in black children, there remains a considerable difference of opinion among linguists who have been describing the dialect as to the amount of linguistic interference, the exact source of that interference, and even the amount of bidialectalism among NNE-speaking children. Venezky (1970), who has questioned the effectiveness of vernacular education, and Bailey (1970) have recommended that the problems of NNE-speaking children be dealt with by teaching them to speak SE before teaching them to read. In this way, presumably, there would be no linguistic conflict caused by SE beginning readers, since the NNE-speaking children would already know the language used in them. Wolfram (1970) and Stewart (1970) have questioned the assumption of Bailey and Venezky that children who speak only NNE can be taught SE in six months to a year. In addition, Baratz seriously questions whether the delaying of the teaching of reading to black children would not provoke as great a controversy as early reading instruction using dialect texts would. Earlier efforts to delay reading instruction until eight or nine (when the child's neurological system is further matured) met with considerable rejection by parents in middle-class communities who wanted their children to be taught reading when they entered first grade. Nonetheless, the teach-SE-first alternative deserves to be tested.

Labov (1967) attributes the poor reading performance of many black children to "the ignorance of SE rules" on the part of the black youngsters on the one hand and to "the ignorance of nonstandard English rules on the part of teachers and text-writers" on the other hand. In fact, he feels that "the great differences in the sets of homonyms" in NNE and SE may well result in "confusion in every reading assignment" (Melmed, 1970). For this reason, Labov sees the solution to teaching black NNE speakers to read as one of teacher education. That is, teachers must learn the rules of the dialect (especially as they relate to the phonology) so that they will not inadvertently penalize a child for a "reading error" which in fact is merely a NNE pronunciation.

Shuy (1969) takes the position that the best way to deal with the problems of NNE interference in learning to read SE is not only to teach the teachers about the phonology but also to construct special materials that would avoid those areas where there is potential syntactic interference with SE. The difficulty here, as Wolfram (1970) has pointed out, is that it is virtually impossible to write a text if one wishes to avoid all the potential points of syntactic interference. Indeed, the Shuy-Ginn (Project 360) approach (which one might call a "nonlinguistic" alternative in that it consciously attempts to avoid aspects of the child's linguistic competence) has no data to stand on, save the publisher's recommendation. And, given the past performance of such commercial materials, one cannot be optimistic. This "nonlinguistic" idea, however, deserves to be tested; only then—on the basis of, not prior to, results from such tests—should avoidance materials be promoted or rejected.

Baratz (1968) and Stewart (1967, 1969) have called for both teacher training and special materials for teaching NNE-speaking children to read. They have both suggested that, although phonological interference probably does occur, it is not likely to be the primary source of difficulty in reading. Concerning this problem, Stewart (1969) points out that:

> . . . if the differences [between SE and NNE phonology] are regular enough, which they often are, then the Negro dialect speaker may be able to set up his own sound-spelling correspondences between them—ones which will be different from those set up by a speaker of SE, but which will allow effective word identification nevertheless (pp. 177–78).

In fact, a phonics program can be constructed that makes the sound-spelling correspondence between SE orthography and NE phonology explicit for the child.

Baratz (1969a) has stressed the importance of interference on the syntactic level:

> Despite the obvious mismatch of the "teachers' and text writers'" phoneme system and that of the inner city child, the difficulties of the disadvantaged Negro child cannot be simplified solely to the pronunciation and phoneme differences that exist in the two systems. There is an even more serious problem facing the inner city child which concerns his unfamiliarity with the syntax of the classroom texts (p. 202).

Because of the mismatch between the child's syntactic system and that of the SE textbook, because of the psychological consequences of denying the existence and legitimacy of the child's linguistic system, and because of the success of vernacular teaching around the world, Baratz (1969b) has joined Stewart and others in calling for experimentation with reading instruction using texts that employ NNE syntax while preserving SE orthography.

These various discussions concerning the interference of NNE on the acquisition of standard English reading skills have spawned several studies attempting to determine whether there is in fact any interference from NNE on SE reading proficiency and, if so, the nature of that interference.

The first group of such studies was concerned with an analysis of the miscues of black children when reading SE (Goodman, 1968; Weber, 1969). The Goodman studies did not reveal much overt interference from NNE syntax, except when a fluent reader became engrossed in a story. Indeed, on the basis of his data concerning miscues involving dialect, Goodman hypothesized that:

> . . . as a reader with a deviant dialect gains proficiency [in reading], the number of dialect related miscues will increase.

The assumption here being that with added comfort and less emphasis of the individual symbols involved, an actual translation process will begin to emerge in which the dialect of the material is translated into the dialect of the reader (p. 43).

Thus Goodman confirmed a tendency which Stewart had noticed years earlier (Stewart, 1964). As useful as Goodman's studies have been in throwing light on the role of dialect differences in the oral performance connected with reading aloud, they leave largely unresolved a fundamental question of dialect interference in reading: Does it affect reading comprehension?

Weber (1969), too, did not find significant interference from NNE on children's reading miscues. However, the very nature of her design and selection of subjects may be responsible for this negative finding. She compared first grade white children from upstate New York with second grade and post-second grade black children from the District of Columbia on a typical first-grade reading passage. She eliminated any subject who made fewer than three, or more than eleven, reading miscues because she did not want "so many [errors] as to render the passage incoherent and thus stifle the young reader's ordinary use of contextual cues for proceeding through the passage, to say nothing of comprehending it." It is necessary, however, to understand that those linguists who were discussing the possible effect of NNE on the ability to read SE texts were concerned with precisely what Miss Weber rules out of consideration from her study, i.e., the effect of a SE text on a young black reader's potential use of ordinary cues (in this case, the grammar of NNE) for proceeding through a written passage, to say nothing of comprehending it! The very difficulty one encounters in locating black children at the first grade level to compare with white children in such tests serves further to underscore this point. In her study, Weber included only black children who seemed to be capable of reading the test passage. As a result, she had to use black children a year older than her white children in order to find a sufficient number of children who could cope with the passage at her criterion level. In fact, Weber's criteria virtually ruled out readers who might have exhibited dialect interference.

In a later study, which is in some respects similar to Weber's, Rystrom (1970) also asserted that the purpose of his research was "to determine the extent to which Negro dialect interferes with the acquisition of reading skills." Yet his entire study displayed an appalling ignorance concerning the very issue which he attempted to elucidate. He showed no evidence of having grasped the essential nature of the difference vs. deficit controversy—a failing which was pointed out by Goodman (1970) in his criticism of Rystrom's research. In addition, Rystrom's handling of NNE (or, rather, what he claimed to represent NNE) showed that he was most unclear as to the difference between phonology, morphology, and syntax—to say nothing of his confusion concerning the nature of dialect and dialect variation in the United States (another point discussed briefly by Goodman in his criticism). At no point did Rystrom actually examine the relationship between dialect differences and reading acquisition. What he did instead was to examine the effect of a hopelessly confused "dialect training course" in which, among other things, the copula form *is* was taught as an example of the "third person marker" (i.e., the drill for third person marking was "This *is* the way we wash our clothes"). Along the same line, one of the most serious products of Rystrom's linguistic naiveté was his apparent belief in a universal "linguistic" reader. Although the series he called "linguistic" was constructed so as to present a consistent sound-spelling correspondence, that correspondence was not consistent with the dialect of the children involved in his study, and therefore could hardly be considered as an appropriate "linguistic reader" for them. In summary, all Rystrom really demonstrated, if indeed he demonstrated anything at all, was the fact that black (and presumably NNE-speaking) first-grade children in rural Georgia do not achieve at the first-grade norm on the SAT—a fact which will come as something less than a revelation to reading specialists who have followed the literature on today's educational crisis.

In another recent dissertation, Melmed (1970) attempted to investigate the relationship between black English phonology and reading interference. He was concerned with examining both expressive and receptive competence in standard English phonology (especially in relation to points of difference from the phonology of black English) and the relationship this competence might have to reading proficiency. His interest in the comprehension of standard English was apparently motivated by the work of Claudia Mitchell (Kernan), who asserted in her dissertation, "It is the unhesitating opinion of this writer that, whatever difficulty some black English speakers exhibit in producing SE variants, there is not a corresponding difficulty in comprehending SE" (Mitchell, 1969). Yet Mitchell-Kernan was primarily concerned with SE/BE syntactic variation in her statement: whereas, Melmed was concerned in his thesis only with phonology. Nonetheless, since Mitchell-Kernan's statement was nothing more than "unhesitating opinion" (with no data on mutual intelligibility presented in her thesis beyond a few sentence repetition tests with older children—hardly a test of receptive competence), Melmed did attempt to gather some data concerning mutual intelligibility of SE/NNE phonological variation.

Melmed constructed tests of auditory discrimination, oral and silent reading comprehension, and speech production involving the five phonological differences which Labov (1967) identified as potential sources for interference between the phonologies of SE and NNE. Melmed found that black subjects did significantly poorer than white and other subjects (primarily Mexican-Americans) on the auditory discrimination and oral production tests but did not differ from disadvantaged whites and Mexican-Americans in SE reading competence.

Unfortunately, there is a major difficulty with Melmed's study. The sample studied was exceptional in that all the disadvantaged children—black, white, and Mexican-American—were already reading at or above grade level; thus it was not at all characteristic of the disadvantaged population in regard to reading performance. Melmed (personal communication, February 1971) had indicated that his sample was indeed an atypical third grade class. Thus, Melmed tested a group of disadvantaged children, who he admitted were extraordinary and who had learned to read, and he demonstrated that they had in fact learned to read.

Melmed, however, did call for more research concerning the relationship of syntactic interference and reading, since he only dealt with phonology and since Baratz and Stewart have been stressing that the major source of difficulty may well be with the syntax. Furthermore, Melmed, echoing many before him (Baratz and Baratz, 1968; Baratz and Shuy, 1969; Stewart, 1967, 1969, 1970), suggested that a project should be initiated to see if black children can learn to read if they are first taught in dialect syntax.

Davis, Gladney, and Leaverton (1969) several years ago began preparing materials to test the hypothesis that teaching children to read in the dialect would be helpful in terms of their ultimately learning to read standard English. Unfortunately, due to the small number of subjects, the sparseness of dialect content, and the methodology involved, it is impossible, from their study, to evaluate the effect of dialect readers on learning to read (Leaverton, 1971). Only one class, with thirty-five children, was used. The same teacher instructed the children for two years. This teacher was apparently very gifted, and there is no reason to believe that she could not have taught these children with any type of materials, especially if the Hawthorne Effect were considered. Indeed, the involvement of this teacher was so great that she gave extra after-school attention to some of the poorer-achieving students in the control group—obliging Leaverton to ask her also to give additional special attention to the experimental group. In addition, the subjects in this study were not assigned to the dialect reading group on the basis of their speech patterns, so it is not clear whether all the experimental subjects should have received the dialect materials.

In another study purporting to present data on dialect interference and reading, Fasold (1971), with help from Wolfram, Shuy, and Anisman, gave a NNE version of the Bible passage John 3:16 (For God so loved the world . . .) to six black NNE-speaking teenagers and asked them to read it twice—once as it stood and a second time supplying every seventh word which had been deleted. They found that the students hesitated or supplied the SE equivalent approximately 24 percent of the time. However, their data were very confused; they said, for example, that there were 34 chances for the six students to deal with the $\emptyset$ copula—yet, this comes out to 5⅗ chances per student! And their analysis of the seventh word cloze technique was not presented. In addition, they stated that their questions concerning whether the dialect version was preferred were not well understood. Nonetheless, these researchers concluded that the boys would prefer at least Biblical materials that were not written in NNE.

Baratz (1970b) in a study with 481 black first and second graders in the District of Columbia parochial schools discovered a significant correlation between learning to read and facility with SE. She gave the children a sentence repetition task involving SE and NNE and, on the basis of their performance, classified them as monodialectal in NNE or SE, or bidialectal. All students were also given the Lyons and Carnahan, New Developmental Reading Tests—Bond-Balow-Hoyt, Lower Primary Reading, Form L-II. A comparison of reading comprehension of the monodialectal NNE children in relation to the SE and bidialectal children revealed a significant difference (beyond .001) in favor of the SE group. These data suggest that monodialectal NNE speaking children are not learning to read with traditional materials as well as are SE speaking children.

In summary, a review of the data concerning dialect inter-ference and learning to read reveals that there are still no real tests of the alternatives discussed earlier, and the extant data are ambiguous at best and do not deal with using dialect as a process in reading instruction. There is, however, a noticeable backing away from testing the dialect-text alternative because of its con-troversy.

But what really are the issues involved in the backing away, since there was no data to discount the effectiveness of the dia-lect-text alternative? Although there is virtually complete agree-ment among the researchers that NNE does exist, there is also a strong feeling that the major difficulty with using dialect texts, and therefore the reason they should not be used, is that black parents and teachers reject these texts. It is, however, primarily the Johnny-come-latelys to the dialect research issue who are in-timidated by the rejection of the dialect by blacks. Indeed, if in the early 1960s deference to the rejection of discussions of NNE had been heeded by Dillard, Stewart, Johnson, and others, there would be no acceptance today of the existence of NNE and there-fore no discussion of its possible relationship to reading.

That blacks reject the dialect and dialect readers is a fact, a fact that has been documented in several places (Baratz, 1970 a and b; Stewart, 1970; and Wolfram, 1970). That that rejec-tion may be understood from an historical perspective is also clear. Nonetheless, that rejection must be met head on and dealt with in the same manner that the earlier objections to the mere mention of the existence of NNE were overcome—at least super-ficially.

It should be clear from the foregoing review, however, that there is still a crying need for adequate research on the question of dialect interference in the acquisition of reading skills. Con-sequently, the possibility that dialect readers might prove useful in the process of learning to read must be dealt with as an em-pirical question, involving their effect on children who otherwise are not learning to read. This possibility cannot be rejected by mere reason of the fact that some children who seem to speak the dialect have learned to read anyway, since there remain many, many more who speak the dialect and who have not learned to read by traditional methods. Nor can the possibility of using dialect readers as part of the process of beginning read-ing be rejected on the basis of the known negative attitudes of black parents, teachers, and community spokesmen to the peda-gogical use of the dialect in print. While it is true that they may say of NNE "That's just slave-talk" or "That ain't no real language" or "That's broken English" or "It's bad language" or "It'll hold the children back," such statements are just as much a manifestation of ignorance [and] misunderstanding as similar statements about any other form of human language would be. Such statements cannot be accepted by educators as the final answer on the matter, because the role of education is to inform others and to act on knowledge, rather than to perpetuate misunderstanding and act on mere folk beliefs. Thus, it is no less important for educators to stand up to black parents and spokesmen who say ignorant things about black language than it is to confront white parents and spokesmen who say ignorant things about black children.

The school use of dialect readers may not, in the early 1970s, be "an idea whose time has come," but, as Carrington (1971) has said in support of dialect readers for St. Lucia (but not yet for Jamaica), when the educational situation becomes desperate enough and the consumer-public frantic enough about the literacy problem, dialect readers will be an idea whose time has come.

## REFERENCES

BAILEY, BERYL LOFTMAN. "Some Arguments Against the Use of Dialect Readers in the Teaching of Initial Reading," *Florida FL Reporter*, 8:1–2 (Spring/Fall 1970), 8, 47.

BARATZ, JOAN C. "Beginning Readers for Speakers of Divergent Dialects," *Reading Goals for the Disadvantaged*, J. Allen Figurel, Ed. Newark, Delaware: International Reading Association, 1970a, 77–83.

BARATZ, JOAN C. "Linguistic and Cultural Factors in Teaching Reading to Ghetto Children," *Elementary English*, 46 (February 1969a), 199–203.

BARATZ, JOAN C. *Relationship of Negro Non-standard English Dialect Speech to Reading Achievement*, unpublished paper, Education Study Center, 1970b.

BARATZ, JOAN C. "Teaching Reading in an Urban Negro School System," *Teaching Black Children to Read*, Joan Baratz and Roger Shuy, Eds. (Washington, D.C.: Center for Applied Linguistics, 1969b), 92–115.

BARATZ, JOAN, and SHUY, ROGER, Eds. *Teaching Black Children to Read*. (Washington, D.C.: Center for Applied Linguistics, 1969b.)

BARATZ, STEPHEN S., and BARATZ, JOAN C. "Negro Ghetto Children and Urban Education: A Cultural Solution," *Bulletin of Minnesota*

*Council for Social Studies* (Fall 1968), 1–3. Reprinted in *Social Education*, 33 (1969), 401–04.

CARRINGTON, LAWRENCE D. *Language Culture and Education: A Symposium.* (Washington, D.C.: American Orthopsychiatric Association, March 1971.)

DAVIS, OLGA; GLADNEY, MILDRED R.; and LEAVERTON, LLOYD. Teachers Manual of *The Psycholinguistics Reading Series, A Bidialectal Approach.* Chicago: Board of Education, 1967.

FASOLD, RALPH W. *Report on the Use of a Dialect Bible Translation with YDI Teenagers,* unpublished paper, Center for Applied Linguistics, 1971.

FRAZIER, ALEXANDER, Ed. *New Directions in Elementary English.* (Champaign, Illinois: National Council of Teachers of English, 1967.)

GOODMAN, KENNETH. "Dialect Rejection and Reading: A Response," *Reading Research Quarterly,* 4 (1970), 600–03.

GOODMAN, KENNETH. *Study of Children's Behavior While Reading Orally.* Final Report Project S425, Contract #OE-6-10-136, 1968.

LABOV, WILLIAM. "Some Sources of Reading Problems for Negro Speakers of Nonstandard English," *New-Directions in Elementary English,* Alexander Frazier, Ed. (Champaign, Illinois: National Council of Teachers of English, 1967), 140–67.

LEAVERTON, LLOYD. "Dialect Readers—Rationale, Use and Value," International Reading Association Preconvention Institute VIII, Language Development and Reading, 1971.

MELMED, PAUL JAY. *Black English Phonology: The Question of Reading Interference,* unpublished doctoral dissertation, University of California, Berkeley, 1970.

MITCHELL, CLAUDIA. *Language Behavior in a Black Urban Community,* unpublished doctoral dissertation, University of California, Berkeley, 1969.

RYSTROM, RICHARD. "Dialect Training and Reading: A Further Look," *Reading Research Quarterly,* 4 (1970), 581–600.

SHUY, ROGER W. "A Linguistic Background for Developing Beginning Reading Materials for Black Children," *Teaching Black Children to Read,* Joan Baratz and Roger Shuy, Eds., 17–137. (Washington, D.C.: Center for Applied Linguistics, 1969.)

SHUY, ROGER W., Ed. *Social Dialects and Language Learning.* (Champaign, Illinois: National Council of Teachers of English, 1964.)

STEWART, WILLIAM A. "Current Issues in the Use of Negro Dialect in Beginning Reading Texts," *Florida FL Reporter,* 8:1–2 (Spring/ Fall 1970), 3–7, 46.

STEWART, WILLIAM A. *Language and Communication Problems in Southern Appalachia.* Washington, D.C.: Center for Applied Linguistics, 1967.

STEWART, WILLIAM A. "On the Use of Negro Dialect in the Teaching of Reading," *Teaching Black Children to Read,* Joan Baratz and

Roger Shuy, Eds., 156–219. Washington, D.C.: Center for Applied Linguistics, 1969.

STEWART, WILLIAM A. "Urban Negro Speech: Sociolinguistic Factors Affecting English Teaching," *Social Dialects and Language Learning*, Roger Shuy, Ed., 10–18. Champaign, Illinois: National Council of Teachers of English, 1964.

VENEZKY, RICHARD L. "Nonstandard Language and Reading," *Elementary English*, 47 (1970), 334–45.

WEBER, ROSE-MARIE. "Comparing the Oral Reading of Children Who Speak Different Varieties of English," unpublished paper, n.d.

WOLFRAM, WALT. "Sociolinguistic Alternatives in Teaching Reading to Nonstandard Speakers," *Reading Research Quarterly*, 6 (Fall 1970), 9–33; also reprinted in *Florida FL Reporter*, 8 (Spring/ Fall 1970), 16–23, 48.

# Applications for the Study of the Reading Process

## Reading for Speakers of English as a Second Language

PAT RIGG

Rigg applies the language-experience method of reading instruction (see Miller, in this section) to teaching students who are learning English as a second language and who have little or no ability to read in English. Among its other advantages, this method avoids the boredom of early reading primers as beginning texts in English for students who have come into this country at ages well over those for which early reading texts are usually designed.

In the article, note that the story one student dictated was recorded exactly as he said it, except that standard spelling was used regardless of the student's pronunciation. No one pronounces words "as they are written." English spelling is full of inconsistencies. Bailey's study of phonic generalizations, also in this section, confirms the difficulty of using these generalizations. So language-experience methods call for using standard spelling but following the student's sentence structure.

Modiano's article in this section also discusses reading for nonnative speakers of English.

In the U.S.A., national attention has recently focussed on immigrants from Indo-China, but immigration is certainly nothing new to this country. Almost every urban public school has at least one or two students whose first language is not English, and in some schools, over half the student body speaks English as a Second Language. One school in a southern suburb of Detroit, for example, has 70% Arab students. The western port cities, Los Angeles and San Francisco, have enormous populations of Japanese and Chinese speakers. In the southwest, the west coast, and in major urban centers throughout the United States, Spanish is the first language of a vast number of students. Medical schools and hospitals all over the U.S. train foreign-born interns, many of whom bring their families and settle permanently.

Often the individual school's resources are limited, and the individual classroom teacher who has a speaker of English as a Second Language (ESL) in her class has no one to turn to for help except perhaps the speech therapist or the reading specialist. Since speaking a language other than English is not a pathological condition, the ESL student does not really need the speech therapist; and if the student speaks almost no English, he cannot profit from any of the reading specialist's exercises which require a native knowledge of English, such as auditory discrimination of English speech sounds. Sometimes a teacher is fortunate enough to have a volunteer in the classroom, but if the volunteer has not been trained in teaching ESL, the responsibility for choosing the materials and techniques which will help the ESL student are still the teacher's. The teacher often has an added burden: she is held responsible by state or community guidelines for the student's performance on some standardized written test.

In this difficult but not uncommon situation, there are activities available to the teacher to increase the reading proficiency of the ESL speaker who already reads a little English, as well as to initiate reading in English for the ESL student who reads no English and who speaks very, very little English. The techniques can be used also by a volunteer or an aide, so that none of them require the teacher to give her undivided attention to that one student for an unreasonable length of time.

## HELPING THE CHILD WHO ALREADY
## READS ENGLISH

There are three basic methods to help improve the reading proficiency of an ESL speaker who already reads some in English. The single most helpful method is also the most difficult: leave him alone. Reading is not a three-person process; it involves only two people, the writer and the reader, at any one time. Any interruptions of the student's reading, particularly interruptions which "correct" or "help," only interfere with the student's reading, and such interruptions teach the student that reading is not something he can do alone, but that reading requires a teacher or teacher-like figure standing by to help him out. A student who has been trained to stop reading whenever he comes to something he doesn't know or cannot pronounce will very quickly learn to guess and go on reading if the person working with him consistently refuses to supply the answer. This is the most difficult method because it seemingly contradicts one's instincts and training—to help the student out. In reality, this method does help the student, and help him immensely. It shows him that he is capable of getting meaning from print on his own; that his teacher recognizes his ability; and it increases his ability to get meaning from print.

The second method of helping the ESL student improve his reading ability is to let him tell someone about what he has just read. This need not be the teacher; an aide or classmate can listen to his retelling. Any questions asked about the material read should be open-ended ones: Will you tell me about what you read? Then what happened? Why did he do that? These questions should focus on the meaning the student got from what he read; they should not require specific "right" answers. Consider a nonsense paragraph which begins, "The ermak was nalling his wank." Anyone can answer the following specific questions about that sentence with 100% correctness:

Who was nalling his wank?
What was the ermak doing?
What was the ermak nalling?

The answers are "correct" but still meaningless nonsense. It is much better to focus on meaning: what does the student think a story is about; why does he think so?

The third method of helping an ESL student increase his reading proficiency is to supply him with a wide variety of reading materials. These can include stories from basal readers or trade books, stories a classmate has written, articles, directions, etc. ESL speakers, like other people, get to be better readers when they read a variety of materials and when they read frequently. When the ESL student is encouraged to react directly to print, rather than through the teacher as intermediary, his reading improves. When he is asked to focus on the meaning of what he's read, his reading improves. When these two methods are used in conjunction with a wide offering of reading materials (and time to read them in), the student reads much more proficiently and reads with pleasure.

## HELPING THE BEGINNER

For the ESL speaker who is just beginning to read in English, the most productive method of helping him is the language experience approach. This technique is successful with adults as well as with children; with those who are literate in another language and those who are not. Basically, the language experience approach has the student dictate to someone, teacher or classmate, and then read back what he has dictated. This method has several advantages for the beginning reader of English: First, the ideas, vocabulary, and grammar of this reading material are the student's own; he doesn't need to grapple with unknown concepts, words, or sentence structure at the same time he is trying to learn to read English. Second, because what the student dictates makes sense to him, the reading material so dictated will have meaning for him, so he is not practicing reading ermak-like nonsense. Third, because what he reads is what he just said, the material will usually be quite interesting to him, just as the snapshots we most like to look at are those of ourselves.

How, exactly, does one get the student to dictate something? There are innumerable stimuli in daily class activities, everything from keeping an attendance chart to writing up a science experiment. Two especially useful sets of materials to stimulate creative story telling are pictures and wordless picture books. A file of pictures is both cheap and easy to build and to enlarge, since the pictures can be torn out of old magazines. With a file of pictures showing different people doing different things, the immigrant can select a picture he likes and can tell as much about the picture as he can and wants to, with the other person writing down what the immigrant says. Similarly, the immigrant can read a wordless picture book. Here is real-life example. A fifteen-year-old boy from the Soviet Union had been in the U.S.A. two months, attending a bilingual Hebrew-English private school when he received his first tutoring in English from a volunteer. He spoke very little English, very haltingly, and did not read much more English than the signs WALK, BOYS, GIRLS, OFFICE, etc. After a month of working with Isaac for half an hour three days a week, the volunteer brought in a copy of Alexander's *Bobo's Dream*, handed it to Isaac and asked him to read it. Isaac smiled when he saw there was no text, only pictures, and dictated the following story. This is the first of four paragraphs:

> A small boy going to school and his dog run for him. The boy coming in the store and buy for himself some lunch. It was not lunch; it was the bone. But come the big dog and took away his bone. The small dog start to cry. They run for the big dog. The boy said, "It's not your bone; give it back." It was a good dog and give back the bone.

The volunteer sat beside Isaac, so that he could see what she wrote as he dictated it, and he carefully paused when necessary so that she could finish writing a sentence. After he had finished dictating the story, Isaac read aloud what he had dictated. He told the volunteer that he liked the story and would like to do more. The next meeting, Isaac reread his version of *Bobo's Dream* and edited it, suggesting grammatical changes to the volunteer, who incorporated them. The second version, neatly typed by the volunteer, has been reread several times by Isaac, who has also lent it to another Soviet youngster in the school. With someone less proficient than Isaac, the same book and dictation can be used with this variation: when the student has finished dictating his story, he and the volunteer look at what she has written and she reads aloud. The student may chime in if he feels like it.

Another technique also involves reading aloud to the student. The teacher, or aide, or another student and the ESL speaker look at the same book while the aide reads the book aloud, lowering her volume when the student chimes in and raising it when the student falters. A variation of this is to tape-record stories, and give the student a chance to hear the story as he reads it. If one of the ESL speaker's classmates tapes the story, the teacher can simply place both story and tape at the listening post. The student should have an opportunity to tape his language experience stories, so that his classmates can read and hear his stories at the listening post.

There are many other opportunities available in the classroom to use what the student can already say as initial reading materials for him. Songs, for example, are easy to read after they have been learned orally. The sorts of directions used in treasure hunts, shared with a classmate, can be read as the teams look for the hidden treasure, following the directions on one note to a place where another note with further directions is hidden. Excerpts of conversation, either real or invented to fit a picture, can be written in cartoon style. After the ESL speaker has decided what the people in the cartoon are saying, it can be written in the balloons. Younger students especially like this form.

All of the approaches suggested here are based on the assumption that reading is a process of getting meaning from print, and this process is a language process. Reading is not a set of auditory or visual skills, nor is it word recognition ability. The new speaker of English may or may not already read; if he is to learn to read in English, he needs materials which communicate meaning to him. No amount of auditory discrimination drills with the speech therapist, no amount of phonics exercises with the reading specialist can assist his reading in English, because this sort of skill-oriented approach does not provide print that communicates meaning to the student. The single most important criterion of any materials or techniques for teaching speakers of other languages to read in English is this: does it communicate meaning to them? If it does, use it. If it doesn't, don't.

## REFERENCE

ALEXANDER, MARTHA. *Bobo's Dream*. New York: Dial, 1970.

# Teaching Vocabulary as an Introduction to New Material: Is it Worthwhile?

MARGARET LINDBERG and LAURA A. SMITH

> While my eight-year-old son David was getting ready for bed, I was skimming the comic book he had chosen for me to read to him. One of the words used in the story was "annihilate." When David came into the room, I asked him what *annihilate* meant; he had no idea. Then we read the story, "Batman vs. the Beast Bomb." This beast had strapped explosives to his belly; when Batman finally grabbed him, the beast flicked a switch that would set off the explosives if he touched the ground. Batman is holding the beast bomb off the ground; but Batman begins to wilt. "Don't let him touch the ground, Batman!" Robin yells. "If you do he'll annihilate the city!"
>
> "What does *annihilate* mean, David?"
>
> *"Destroy."*
>
> The meaning of *annihilate* was clear from the context. Lindberg and Smith encourage teachers to let students read material containing words they may not be able to define out of context. After all, Lindberg and Smith point out, there are several kinds of vocabulary; some vocabulary carries the plot, some gives dispensable details of setting and characterization.
>
> Lindberg and Smith want to see students become independent readers, readers who do not feel that they need a teacher and a dictionary in order to get meaning and pleasure out of reading.

The pre-teaching of vocabulary is still an extremely popular method for helping students deal with difficult and unfamiliar materials. Yet even when the vocabulary taught is presented selectively and in sentence context, its value as a reading aid is questionable (Hasselriis, 1972).

Reading is not word centered, but meaning centered. And meaning is conveyed through ideas and experiences embodied in whole language, not by individual words alone. What does "bus" mean? You cannot be sure until you see the word used in context:

THE NICEST PEOPLE BUS THEIR DISHES [sign in cafeteria]

**436**

BUS STOP [sign on sidewalk]
BUS VOTE STALLED IN COMMITTEE [headline]

With so many possible meanings of a simple word like "bus," how are we to adequately understand the author's meaning for any word unless that word is left in the total language context of the story in which it belongs? What meaning-gathering strategies will we be able to use when we meet that word in another context, with other meanings, if we must depend on outside assistance each time we encounter unfamiliar language?

There are a number of ways meaning can be developed as one reads. Context can supply understanding even if a word is not familiar. . . . Many words need not be read at all. Important information is usually repeated in various ways and at various times throughout the text so that the reader has many opportunities to build meaning.

The word "vocabulary" has tended to be a catch-all for several quite distinct kinds of language, each of which may require different meaning-processing strategies. At least two kinds of "vocabulary" are represented by the following excerpt from a Russian short story found in a familiar reading text.

> Late one winter's night, when the bitter wind and snow beat against the saloon, the regular customers started their familiar mockery and teasing of the fearful Ivan. Ivan's weak protests only fed their taunts, and they jeered cruelly when a young Cossack lieutenant flung a horrid challenge at the frightened victim, Ivan.
>
> *"You're chicken, Ivan, you'll walk all around the cemetery in this cold—but you dare not cross the cemetery."*
>
> Ivan murmured, "The cemetery is nothing to cross, Lieutenant. It is nothing but earth, like all the other earth."
>
> The lieutenant cried, "A challenge, then! *If you will dare to cross the cemetery tonight, Ivan, I'll give you five rubles—five gold rubles!"*
>
> Perhaps it was all the vodka he had drunk. Perhaps it was the glittering temptation of the five gold rubles. No one ever knew why. Ivan, moistening his lips, said suddenly, *"Yes, Lieutenant, I'll cross the cemetery!"* [L. A. Ross, 1968]

In order to understand the gist of the story, the reader needs to focus on what might be called *plot-carrying vocabulary:* language essential to understanding the story line (see italicized information above). Plot-carrying information is usually presented in relatively simple, straightforward language. The plot-carrying vocabulary in the above excerpt clearly tells us of Ivan's fears and the circumstances which persuade him to change his mind.

*Descriptive vocabulary,* however, is part of an author's style and involves language used to convey metaphor, subtlety, flavor or mood (see underlinings above). Such language is far less essential to the plot of the story. Rather, it adds richness to the spare story line. Descriptive vocabulary is usually highly redundant. A reader can omit far more of it and still build meaning. For example, any or all of the following—"fearful," "weak," "frightened"—effectively indicate Ivan's character.

A reader can encounter plot-carrying and descriptive vocabulary in many kinds of reading material of varying degrees of difficulty. Comic books and popular fiction as well as works of recognized literary quality contain their share. The following excerpt from a popular collection of children's ghost stories provides an additional example.

> *Waldo Dexter found the book in* the most prosaic of places *—a second-hand shop.* Not even a good second-hand shop. Just a dingy hole in the wall on Canal street, east of Broadway, a region as commonplace as Manhattan has to offer.
>
> It was a shop devoted chiefly to second-hand luggage and old clothes of the most depressing appearance. *Mr. Dexter entered it in the first place only because a high wind had blown away his hat,* whisking it in a series of eccentric leaps out of sight into a dark alley well supplied with puddles. [Arthur, 1972]

The plot-carrying vocabulary tells the reader where Waldo Dexter went and why, even if the reader is not sure exactly how the wind has disposed of Waldo's hat. He also has a number of opportunities to get the feel of the second-hand shop: "the most prosaic of places"; "a dingy hole in the wall"; "depressing in appearance." However, to many residents of Manhattan, just the reference "on Canal street, east of Broadway" is sufficient to evoke the character of the shop.

*Concept-carrying vocabulary,* language representing a structure of complex ideas, is most frequently found in mathematics, science, and social studies materials. Literary essays often have their share of this kind of language. Concepts such as "industrial revolution," "Victorian Era," or "transformational grammar," would be examples.

Concept-carrying vocabulary is not developed through a plot, yet is crucial to understanding the text. In conceptually sparse material, the reader may be able to build essential concepts through explanation and redundancy in the text. Neither technique can adequately communicate a concept that is totally unfamiliar. Unfortunately, most content area materials are densely packed with unfamiliar conceptual information.

The following excerpt is taken from a recent and highly significant work in the field of reading. The paragraph is reasonably representative of the entire article.

> At a rough level of approximation, each feature may be regarded as a bit of information (that is, it reduces uncertainty by a half), with N features or bits of information eliminating all the uncertainty among $2^N$ equiprobable alternatives (rather less information is required if the distribution is not equiprobable). The uncertainty among 26 alternatives of the letter domain is 4.7 bits if each letter is regarded as equiprobable, and 4.03 bits if the distributional redundancy of English is considered. [Smith and Holmes, 1973]

Although this article is written for the reading specialist, a great deal of prior conceptual information is probably necessary for most of us to make much sense of it. Pre-teaching this vocabulary, assuming one could separate out the concepts, would not be of much help. With materials containing a large proportion of concept-carrying vocabulary, no amount of vocabulary instruction will make the information comprehensible to someone who does not already have the relevant conceptual background.

If we were motivated enough to attempt this article, we would probably put it aside for a while, do a lot more background reading, talk with experts, attend classes, etc., and then try again. But as teachers, how often do we give our students such options? Can we assume they are better at dealing with unfamiliar conceptual information than we?

When we do attempt to use conceptually dense material with students, we need to build a bridge of concrete experiences from the students to the text so that they already understand the concepts before they encounter them in print. A chapter on the industrial revolution might first require student exposure to films, trips to a factory, diagrams of preindustrial machines, etc., and discussions of the significant concept-carrying vocabulary in relation to these simulated and real-life experiences. An important body of recent research is clearly demonstrating the limitations of print as a means of acquiring new knowledge (Smith, 1975). Our teaching practices must accommodate such information.

Both teachers and students should realize that strategies for dealing with language will vary not only with the kinds of vocabulary the reader encounters, but also with the purposes for which one reads and the depth of reading required. Plot-carrying, concept-carrying and descriptive vocabulary, then, will become more or less important (will have different "weight") as the reading situation changes.

For example, the Russian short story could be used in different ways with students of widely varying reading abilities. To encourage risk-taking among reluctant readers, the teacher might first have them read for plot and predict the story outcome. One of the authors has seen the Russian story successfully used for that purpose in a "remedial" classroom. . . . A follow-up lesson might teach strategies for building meaning from the descriptive vocabulary which each student can read. The more sophisticated readers might concentrate on whether the use of metaphoric language such as "fed their taunts," and "flung a horrid challenge" is clichéd or enhances the story.

Much of the content of literature deals with experiences that are universally familiar, but the presentation is unique to a specific author in a specific time and place. Students do not need to be pre-taught particular vocabulary words. They do, however, need to be equipped with flexible meaning-gathering strategies for dealing with unfamiliar language.

In general readers need to know that if the ideas carried by the unfamiliar vocabulary are significant, they will be repeated at other times and expressed in other ways throughout the text. Such knowledge allows the reader to read selectively. He can continue to process for meaning without losing the thread of the story by engaging in vain attempts to "read" every word. The customers' reactions to Ivan reoccur in such language as "mockery and teasing," "taunts," "jeered cruelly," etc. In contrast, the "eccentric leaps" of Waldo's hat are not important to the story and the idea is not picked up again.

Readers also need to know that if none of what they are reading makes sense as they progress through the text, they should not waste their time "barking at print." The objective in reading is not to say the words correctly but to understand the ideas. When they are not getting meaning, readers will need to use a variety of non-print resources and/or less complex materials before attempting to deal with the original text. This strategy can be initiated by the teacher or the reader.

We do not believe that language taken out of context—

whether it be in lists of isolated words or in vocabulary definitions presented prior to the reading of a story—produces able readers. Nor do we believe that anyone can learn to read without reading to learn something. Initial reading materials need to say something meaningful to children. As long as there is a distinction made between "learning to read" and "reading to learn," we will continue to produce readers who cannot read, i.e. get meaning from print. And secondary teachers will continue to encounter students who "can't read the text."

It is extremely important that as teachers we clearly define our purposes for selecting and using specific materials. We need to clarify the focus of our instruction and the kinds of reading requirements we place on our students. We often expect readers to process complex language while understanding unfamiliar content (action, setting, significant historical information, etc.) in the same lesson.

If our focus is to be content, the stylistic problems need to be minimized and means other than print must be used to build the background students require. If our focus is on style, the content needs to be familiar. If our purpose is to develop strategies for reading particular kinds of material, the content and the style should both be familiar. Materials selected and/or written with specific tasks in mind will enable students to concentrate on what is being taught.

Above all, students need to spend time actually reading. Like adults, they will do more reading if they are interested and the reading task is not overwhelming. The greater the variety of materials available, the greater the possibility that each student's taste, interests and ability can be accommodated.

## BIBLIOGRAPHY

ARTHUR, ROBERT. "Mr. Dexter's Dragon." *Ghosts and More Ghosts.* New York: Random House, Inc., 1963, p. 188.

HASSELRIIS, PETER. "Reading in Literature: Student Involvement Is Just the Beginning." In J. L. Laffey (ed.) *Reading in the Content Areas.* Newark, Delaware: IRA, 1972.

ROSS, L. A. "Cemetery Path." In L. Trout and M. Flanigan (eds.) *At Your Own Risk.* New York: Holt, Rinehart and Winston, Inc., 1968, pp. 86–87.

SMITH, FRANK, and HOLMES, DEBORAH LOTT. "The Independence of Letter, Word, and Meaning Identification in Reading," in Frank Smith (ed.) *Psycholinguistics and Reading.* New York: Holt, Rinehart and Winston, Inc., 1973, pp. 54–55.

SMITH, FRANK. *Comprehension and Learning.* New York: Holt, Rinehart and Winston, Inc., 1975.

## Reading Comprehension:
## A Redundant Phrase

YETTA GOODMAN

Yetta Goodman speaks against focusing on skills—too many of our students are victims of "overskill." She gives some alternatives to the emphasis on skills. Her suggestions agree fully with the suggestions in Part 1, which emphasize creativity, context, and communication as essential parts of the natural language-acquisition process.

Reading is a language process. The purpose of language is communication. Comprehension must be involved for reading to be taking place. There is *no* reading without comprehension. Programs or instructional approaches which do not focus on comprehension may interfere with the development of proficient reading.

All readers from the beginning of learning to read make use of the graphophonic system (the relationship of sounds and letters), the syntactic or grammatical system and the semantic or meaning system of language. (Clay 1967 and Goodman, 1971) They do this intuitively by virtue of being users of a language.

At any point that readers overuse any one of the language systems to the exclusion of others, there seems to be a breakdown in the reading process.

Usually, when readers overuse any one system, it is the graphophonic system. This is characterized by children omitting words which are unfamiliar to them, making four or more attempts to sound out a word while reading orally or producing a look alike substitute which makes little sense such as reading: *He was riding on a house* for *He was riding on a horse.* This overuse of phonics analysis to the exclusion of making sense is due in part to an over emphasis on phonics and other word attack skills in early reading instruction. If such an over emphasis continues to be the focus of reading instruction for a number of years it is not uncommon to find readers in special programs and classes for reluctant or disabled readers suffering from *OVERSKILL.*

Unfortunately the concern with test scores also reinforces the focus on isolated, abstract units of language. Developers of standardized tests lack the sophistication of evaluating comprehension in reading. Tests often focus on letter and word recognition. The paragraphs used in standardized tests for comprehension usually focus on knowledge or content unrelated to the lives of readers. We must find other means of evaluating reading proficiency and not permit standardized test items to decide the focus of reading instruction. (Goodman and Burke, 1971)

"Skills" fragment and isolate language into highly abstract units. Learning abstract units is a more complex task for young readers than learning to handle the same unit embedded in a familiar language context. Language in its whole and natural state is greater than the sum of its parts. Sounds change depending on linguistic environment such as the word *can* in the sentence:

*Can you put it in the trash can?*

Words change sounds as well as grammatical function depending on linguistic environment such as the word *police* in the sentences:

*I will call the police* and
*The police car will be coming soon*

Sentences change meaning from one language context to the other. For example consider the following:

Mary whispered to her husband as she furtively pointed to the bride's ring. *"Look at the size of that stone!"*

*"Look at the size of that stone."* The highway construction foreman shouted loudly to all the men as he surveyed the huge boulder that the avalanche had placed in the path of his construction project.

Children learn to select the appropriate cues to minimize any confusion in oral language because: 1) of all the cues which exist in an oral language environment 2) the oral language setting is familiar to the children and they know the limits or constraints of what will or will not be discussed in that environment and 3) children know that they, themselves must understand or comprehend the message being communicated. The test of whether understanding has occurred is not dependent on a red check on a paper or a disappointed look on a teacher's face.

Written language can provide the same kinds of cues if reading instruction helps focus on meaning and thus keeps all the cueing systems in proper relationship.

If children know from the beginning of their reading that reading is similar to listening then they can use their language sense to predict, to reread and correct or to continue reading and search for additional cues if their predictions don't work out.

An emphasis on isolated skills makes readers believe that each letter, each word, period and comma in written language is equally significant to every other letter, word or detail. In language learning it is important to differentiate the significant from the insignificant. Readers in difficulty often exhibit an inability to treat language phenomena in a variable way. Rather than try an appropriate substitute like *pony* for *horse* or *house* for *home* which proficient readers tend to do, less proficient readers will either omit the word or keep after the word, trying again and again unproductively to sound it out. Such readers sometimes believe that the only way to learn a word is to be given that word by the teacher. Such children will say "I haven't had that word yet" or "We didn't learn that yet." These children tend not to trust their own sense of language and fall further and further behind as they continue to process each word and each letter as if each carries as much information as any other. Such students will even stop at proper nouns which would be difficult if not impossible for adult readers and try to sound them out. This takes so much energy that the reader will be discouraged at the end of a sentence containing one such name. (How did you handle the name Aleksandr Solzhenitsyn when you saw it for the first time? I bet you didn't reach for your Russian-English dictionary.)

Even, however when readers focus on graphic information there are times the human ability to produce language seems to emerge.

When focused on letter-sound correspondence or provided with minimal language context beginning readers are known to confuse words which are similar in configuration or letter shape. Sometimes they even begin to reverse some letter-sound sequences producing *on* for *no*, *spot* for *stop* and *was* for *saw*. When these phenomena are examined in the reading of a whole story and evaluated in terms of what language phenomena are involved in producing such miscues a complex picture emerges.

In context *was* is substituted for *saw* occasionally but rarely if ever is *saw* substituted for *was*. In addition, the *was* for *saw* substitutions occur in subject-verb-object sentences like:

> *Text:* I saw a monkey
> *Reader:* I was a monkey.

However, when *was* is a verb marker or when *was* is in a subject-verb-adjective sentence such as *I was happy* a different set of constraints is involved and the same type of miscues are not produced. Also, if one considers that these sentences are embedded in long stories where both semantic and syntactic constraints operate, then it becomes easier to understand why certain miscues do not occur in contextual material to the same degree as they occur in isolated word lists or unrelated sentences.

Another such reader confusion may add to the understanding of how grammar is involved in many miscues which were usually considered simple graphic confusions. Early readers often confuse *said* with *and*. Both words occur frequently at similar pivotal points in sentences. When readers make such miscues their oral intonation is usually produced appropriately.

> *Text:* "I will call Father," said Mother.
> *Reader:* I will call Father and Mother.
> *Text:* Mary and John and Sally do not go to school yet.
> *Reader:* "Mary and John," said Sally. "Do not go to school yet."

It is significant that the readers who produced miscues like the ones cited above did not make the same kind of miscues when they were provided with a story including similar sentences but with a more involved plot which clarified who was speaking and what was happening. The more information readers have about what they are reading the easier it is to understand.

## IF NOT SKILLS WHAT THEN

We must treat written language as *language* and help readers do the same. Looking back at the points made earlier about oral language constraints in relation to comprehension, we can use similar written language experiences to plan reading instruction.

*1. Provide the readers with a rich environment of written language so that there are abundant language cues available for reading.* Saturate the classroom with a variety of written language such as books, magazines, comics, newspapers, recipes, directions for making things, charts, signs, books that are authored by the children, notes written by children, teachers and parents, letters from pen-pals or other important people. A good part of the reading period should be spent in silent, independent uninterrupted reading. Children should learn how to select their own reading materials and not rely on teacher selection. Learning to swim is done by swimming in lakes, pools, rivers and oceans. Learning to drive is done by driving on mountain roads, highways, rural-one lane roads and busy city streets. Learning to read can only happen if the reader has many experiences reading all kinds of written language.

In addition to doing a lot of reading, children should be read to a great deal. With tape recorders and listening posts available children have the opportunity to listen to all kinds of stories. Teachers should also read to children and rediscover the lost art of storytelling. Children exposed to a variety of linguistic styles and context through their ears are more likely to be able to predict such structures when they appear in their own reading.

*2. The content of the written language is familiar to the children and they know the limits or constraints of what will or will not be appropriate in that environment.*

When charts, labels and directions are written for the classroom, children should be involved in the process. Children could help develop charts listing the rules and regulations for classroom management. This should be written by the teacher in front of the children. When a decision is reached, the children can dictate the appropriate sentences so the written form is similar to their own language structures. These can be reread frequently when appropriate to decide who is going to do what, or where different students will be. At the end of a work period these can be reread for purposes of evaluation and to plan the subsequent activities.

When fish tanks, animal cages or plants are going to be part of the classroom, the children should be involved in actively building the necessary structures and dictating or writing signs, rules for their care, etc. These should also become reading materials for the children on future days to show visitors what has been done or to re-examine or re-discuss the experiences to examine what is happening to the animals or plants. Once a week the children can write a short newsletter about their week's experiences, read the paper to each other and then take them home to read to their parents.

When students show a special enjoyment for certain kinds of written material, they should be encouraged to write their own stories using similar patterns. Songs and rhymes are good subjects for such experiences. Writing supports and enhances reading.

When children are to read social studies, science, math or other content area materials, the teacher must know the children are familiar with the content or provide the children with many non-reading concrete experiences with the particular concepts to be presented in the material prior to their reading. Meanings change depending on the content or field being discussed. For example, *Let's look at the problem* means widely different things depending on whether you are reading about classroom behavior, mathematics or English literature. *Is that a set?* will have varied meanings and answers depending on whether the written material is concerned with mathematics, dentistry, furniture or jewelry.

*3. Children know that they themselves must understand or comprehend the message.* Reading is a receptive process. It goes on inside a reader's head. We all know when we are understanding what we are reading. We must help children develop their own sense of "Am I understanding?" Too many children are willing to read for the teacher looking up frequently for a smile or a nod to know that everything is o.k. We must help readers rely more on knowing that *they* comprehend. They must know that reading is for themselves or they will never become readers.

Since reading is receptive it is important to help students realize that it is not necessary to know the pronunciation or to be able to pronounce every word as one reads. All readers have many words in their reading vocabulary which they have never heard or spoken and are unsure of their pronunciation. Readers should be encouraged to continue reading even when they come to unknown words and phrases and not to rely on the teacher or another student for the oral pronunciation. Teachers should help students realize that if they continue reading through to the end of the material, they may be able to understand the meaning of an unfamiliar word, phrase or sentence even if they cannot pronounce it. *Understanding is the most important aspect of reading, far more important than learning to pronounce words.* Students need to be encouraged to guess at meanings. The greater the context and the closer the content is to the experiences of the reader the more appropriate a reader's guess will be. Reading involves this kind of risk taking all the time.

Readers are able to provide meanings for many concepts such as *transom, typical, live, experiment, chemistry* and *fawn* even though they were unable to pronounce such words appropriately as they read them orally. (Goodman and Burke, 1973) On the other hand, there are students who can pronounce such words appropriately but they do not necessarily understand the concepts.

Reading instruction should help students focus on comprehension by using open ended discussion questions about the material that is being read rather than focusing students' attention on minutia. If readers' opinions, interpretations or points or view are treated with respect they will want to discuss what they've read with others. Questions such as Did you like _____? (a main character) Why or why not? Would you like to have such a person as a friend? What was the problem in this story? Did you agree with the way the author solved the problem? What other ways could it have been solved? Why do you think the author wanted to write this story? What was the author's bias or point of view in writing this? Do you agree?

These types of questions can help students realize that reading is for themselves not just an assignment to prepare for a teacher which has a specified right answer.

If we keep in mind that reading does not exist without comprehension then we can drop the word comprehension from the phrase reading comprehension. The two word phrase is unnecessary and redundant. Therefore, let's focus all of our instructional efforts on *reading*.

## REFERENCES

CLAY, MARIE M. The Reading Behavior of Five Year Old Children. A Research Report. *New Zealand Journal of Educational Studies* Vol. 2. May, 1961, pp. 11–31.

GOODMAN, KENNETH, and CAROLYN BURKE. Theoretically Based *Studies of Patterns of Oral Reading Performance,* U.S. Dept. of Health, Education, and Welfare, Project No. 9-0175, April, 1973.

GOODMAN, YETTA M. *Longitudinal Study of Children's Oral Reading Behavior,* U.S. Dept. of Health, Education, and Welfare, Project No. 9-E-062, September, 1971.

GOODMAN, YETTA, and CAROLYN BURKE. *Reading Miscue Inventory,* Macmillan, 1971.

# Leeway in Matching Books and Children

DANIEL N. FADER and ELTON B. McNEIL

The Maxey Boys' Training School was filled with students whose vocabulary and previous performance in school was not such as to suggest that they would ever become people who enjoyed books. This brief report of one Maxey student's encounter with a demanding book is representative of the success of Fader's widely known "hooked on books" program.[1] This report provides an illustration of the validity of Lindberg and Smith's views about vocabulary and reading.

On a Friday morning, an English teacher watched one of his poorest readers choose Hawthorne's novel from the rack. Knowing how difficult the boy would find the book, and fearing that he would be discouraged by the experience, the teacher suggested that perhaps he had mistaken *The Scarlet Letter* for something else. "Ain't this the one about a whore?" asked the boy. "And don't that big 'A' stand for whore?" When the teacher had to admit that this description was more or less correct, the boy had heard enough. If it was a book about a whore, it was a book for him.

Three days later, on Monday, the same boy came to his English teacher with *The Scarlet Letter* in hand and two sheets of notebook paper. On those two sheets, front and back, were all the words—and their definitions—the boy hadn't known in the first eleven pages of the book. He had clearly spent the weekend with Hawthorne and the dictionary, and he was looking for praise —which he got, lavishly. His English teacher was amazed; the two sheets of notebook paper represented at least six hours of work. According to the teacher, this was a boy who may not have spent six hours reading since he was nine years old, and had no apparent idea of how to use a dictionary when he came to the Maxey School. Motivated by Hawthorne's whore, he fought his way through the entire book. He produced no more lists but he kept at the book (between other novels) for months; during that time, and long after, his conversations with his English teacher

---

[1] See Daniel N. Fader and Elton B. McNeil, *Hooked on Books: Program and Proof* (New York: Berkley, 1968).

were full of his view of what was happening to Hester Prynne. Proceeding as slowly as he did through the story of her life, she took on dimensions of reality for him which authors dream of imparting to their readers and teachers despair of conveying to their students. His valediction on Hawthorne's heroine may not have been couched in the author's own phrases, but it conveyed an understanding of the book that no one could improve upon: "That woman," he announced as he returned the book, "she weren't no whore."

One implication of this boy's experience is especially interesting. Hawthorne's vocabulary is difficult for *college* students. I have taught *The Scarlet Letter* to freshmen and sophomores at two universities where more than half the students come from the top 10 percent of their high school class. I have invariably followed the first reading assignment of the introductory chapter with a ten-minute written quiz asking for definitions of ten words chosen from the first three pages of that chapter. Each time, I caution the students to "read the introductory chapter *carefully*." Every student is allowed to use his textbook and any notes he may have prepared. Only the dictionary is forbidden. Full credit is given for the barest suggestion of knowledge, *e.g.*, *bark:* some kind of boat; *truculency:* meanness; and even *prolix:* says a lot. But no matter how ominously I emphasized the word "carefully" in the assignment, and no matter how undemanding my standards of definition, no more than one-fifth of the students in any of the classes managed to define as many as five of the ten words.

My ringing, rhetorical, unfair question as I return the quizzes at the next meeting of those unfortunate classes is always, "How can you claim to have *read* anything when you don't even know what the words mean?" The question is unfair because I know perfectly well that they could read with great understanding without knowing what all the words mean. The quiz is merely one method of forcing a slower and more careful reading practice upon students convinced that fast reading is the best reading.

But what has this to do with a juvenile delinquent struggling through *The Scarlet Letter?* Just this: Semiliterate readers do not need semiliterate books. The simplistic language of much of the life-leeched literature inflicted upon the average schoolchild is not justifiable from any standpoint. Bright, average, dull—however one classifies the child—he is immeasurably better off with books that are too difficult for him than books that are too simple. But this generalization involves a whole theory of education. All I want to emphasize here is what teachers have observed at the Maxey, Garnet-Patterson and Northwestern schools and what I have experienced as a teacher of students of a considerably different type—"reading" is a peculiarly personal interaction between a reader and a book, an interaction differing in each case as widely as readers may differ from each other in breadth of experience and quality of mind. But *in no case* does this interaction demand an understanding of every word by the reader. In fact, the threshold of understanding—of meaningful interaction —is surprisingly low, and even in many complex books can be pleasurably crossed by many simple readers.

## Teaching with the Reading Process

Our first suggestion about teaching with the reading process deals with the total language system of the reader; articles in Parts 1 and 3 explain that language system. The second major suggestion we can make about reading relates reading to "nonstandard" dialects. Part 2 directly concerns language variation of this type, and Part 3 has given the descriptive tools for understanding language variation in detail.

**SUGGESTION I:** A reader uses his total language system to get meaning from written language.

*Central Article:* Kenneth Goodman, "Reading: A Psycholinguistic Guessing Game"

*Supporting Evidence in Other Articles:*

Bailey: "Phonic generalizations" apply to such a small percentage of written language that reading would be impossible if it relied only on phonics.

Jakobson, McNeill, Bloom (Part 1): Even at the earliest stages of acquiring language, children appear to use sound systems, sentence structures, and meaning all at once. By the time they are in the telegraphic stage it can be said flatly that all their communicative utterances use the whole system of language rules. It would be strange indeed were they suddenly unable to use syntactic and semantic information in using language to read.

## Implications for Teaching

"I'M READING, AREN'T I?" When my six-year-old son first started reading orally, he produced "sentences" consisting of words spelled like those on the page, but lacking meaning. I stopped him at the end of a page. "David, what does this mean?" David looked indignant. "I'm reading, aren't I?"

Students should learn that reading uses the total language system, not just the relationships between print and sound. In the following example, we see what happens when the graphophonic system—relationships between print and sound—is over-emphasized in the reading program:

> *Text:* The boy ran through the forest.
> *Student 1:* The boy ran though the first.
> *Student 2:* The boy ran through the trees.

Student 1 paid attention to the graphophonic system at the expense of meaning (the semantic system) and sentence structure (the syntactic system). Student 2 emphasized the semantic system and syntactic system. Which is the better reader?

It might be objected that Student 1 was abusing, not using, the graphophonic system—and that objection is at first plausible; it appears that Student 1 failed to "sound out" the letter *r* in *through* and the *e* in *forest,* and his "sounding-out" of the *o* in forest was incorrect.

But consider the great inconsistency of the rules for "sounding" out letters—the phonics generalizations that Bailey studied. For one thing, as Bailey noted, phonics generalizations ignore dialect differences. Suppose Student 1 had an *r*-dropping dialect, as do speakers in the urban centers on the East Coast, throughout the South and much of the Southwest, and in the Northeast. For these speakers, the letter *r* is silent in an enormous number of words; why not in this one? As for the *e* in *forest,* silent *e*'s appear at the end of a huge number of words, and in words such as *reader* and *system* the letter *e* in the last syllable—the position of the *e* in *forest*—might reasonably appear to be silent (with the *d* and *t* followed by a syllabic *r* and *m,* respectively). As for the *o* in *forest,* consider the following words: *gone, bone, done, lot, women,* and *hoot* all contain the letter *o*—but they are pronounced with six different vowels. Student 1 was not failing to use the graphophonic system; that system was failing to be of use to him.

Yet he tried to use it exclusively, ignoring the other two language systems at his disposal. Teachers can help remedy this problem by directing students' attention toward meaning and toward the sentence as a whole. One way of doing this is to emphasize communication between the author and the reader, communication like that in oral language between speaker and listener.

A close look at the forty-five phonics generalizations studied by Bailey raises many questions about their utility, questions that Bailey's brief article did not treat—though her conclusion was that most of these generalizations were inappropriate. For instance, many of the generalizations have to do with where syllables begin and end. Many more have to do with the placement of stress—on the first syllable rather than the second, and so on; some of the generalizations depend on previous generalizations—"if stress is on the first syllable," when the placement of stress was ordained by a previous phonics "rule." How often do we need to know where syllables begin and end, in order to read? How often do we need to know where stress is placed, in order to read a word? And how many of us—adult, proficient readers—can hold previous phonics generalizations in mind in order to apply other such generalizations?

And finally, it should be pointed out that some of these generalizations have a high percentage of utility—they hold true for most words—but their statements are trivial. Number 24, for example, states that when two identical consonants are side by side, the sound of only one consonant is heard. This fact is probably obvious even to beginning readers; even if it is not, once stated it becomes so—phonics generalizations such as this can hardly be considered mainstays of a program that teaches reading.

The basic assumption that readers have to process each word through knowledge of its sound is behind all phonics generalizations. Though we do not yet know precisely what role sound plays in learning to read, sound certainly cannot be essential; if it were, deaf children would never learn to read, and we would be unable to read dead languages whose sound systems are not known. All of us read and understand words whose stress placement or pronunciation we do not know; *desultory* and *epitome* are common in reading vocabularies whether or not their pronunciation is known. In using the entire system of language—syntactic, semantic, and graphophonic cues—a reader does well to rely on the first two cue systems more heavily than on the third; but our teaching methods have only begun to recognize this fact and to stop directing all the beginning reader's attention toward the least reliable of the three cue systems available for making sense out of written language.

RELATE READING TO COMMUNICATION. Describe reading in terms of communication with an author. Finding the author's meaning should be kept firmly in the foreground as the major goal of reading. Perhaps the best way to do this is to rely heavily on silent reading, from the very beginning. Exercises in silent reading should outnumber exercises in oral reading. Teachers can post various kinds of instructions on large sheets of paper around the classroom, thus providing practice in reading while eliminating misunderstandings that may follow from directions given orally. One enjoyable silent-reading exercise for a wide age range of students is illustrating the stories written by classmates; the story must be silently read and understood before the student can decide what illustrations are appropriate. Another silent-reading exercise that children enjoy at ages ranging from six to twelve is a treasure hunt, with clues written in sentence form.

The question teachers and future teachers most often ask about silent reading is, "How can I tell how well the child is reading?" One answer is, "By asking the child questions that lead him to tell you what he has gotten out of the reading." Perhaps he can retell a story he has read, or tell you his understanding of written directions he has read. It should be made clear to children that adults use reading to get meaning; as adults, most of their own reading will be silent. Hardly anyone makes his living reading aloud.

ORAL READING. When you do decide to have children read orally, have each student look at the entire sentence he is to read before saying anything. If he cannot make sense out of the sentence, perhaps he should look at the paragraph it is in; the more information he has to work with, the easier it will be to make sense out of any particular sentence. While oral reading is going on, do not interrupt with trivial corrections; if you must interrupt a student because his miscues show that meaning is not being sought, say something like, "Does the rest of the story fit with what you just said?" or "Do you see what the author is saying to you?"

If the student is looking at the sentence "The dog chewed up the newspaper," and he begins with "The dog chewed the . . . ," do not interrupt to point out the word *up* between *chewed* and *the* in the text; left alone, the student may finish the sentence with

". . . newspaper up." He has simply moved *up* to the end of the sentence, a stylistic change that does not change the meaning of the sentence:

> *Text:* The dog chewed up the newspaper.
> *Student:* The dog chewed the newspaper up.

As we saw in Part 3, sentences have both a surface level and an underlying level. The student who moves *up* to the end of the sentence is making a change in the surface level of the sentence, not in the underlying relationships between the words of the sentence.

Before the concept of underlying versus surface levels was available to teachers, they often felt that the absence of a word from the spoken sentence meant that the student had failed to perceive that word. But we now recognize that just the opposite may be true; a completely exact, parrotlike oral rendition of a sentence may indicate *lack* of comprehension, while some changes in the sentence may indicate decoding, or comprehension, of the sentence; the student decoded the sentence into its underlying meaning and then encoded that meaning into a surface-structure slightly different from that appearing in the book.

Two final points can be made about the secondary role phonics and oral reading should take in reading instruction. First, students in "remedial" reading classes have usually had phonics, more than any other kind of instruction, for years. Obviously, this instruction has not worked. Bailey's work is relevant here, helping us understand why phonics generalizations are entirely insufficient as the sole base for reading. Yet we continue to drill "remedial" students in this area of their failure, putting students through their paces in their weakest area year after year. What effect would continual emphasis on your weakest area have on you?

Secondly, we have assumed that students come to school without experience with written language. There may be some families in which this is the case—families who do not own a television set, walk in a town, drive a car. We might expect rural families and ghetto families to fit this description. But those stereotypes are usually not accurate.

Students of all ages, rural, ghetto, or otherwise, do bring to school experience with print. One child at age nine showed clearly the effects of her previous experience with print: in writing secret messages for a spook house, she produced the following warnings:

Be war!
Death!
Dracula will bite you!
Frankenstein will smush you!

Note that *Frankenstein* is spelled correctly. Now look at a sentence the same child wrote as part of a story about Angela, a young girl who owned all the stuffed animals in her town.

Angela had dogs, lions, tigers, cats, birds, mice, deers, hipophippoatamuses, etc.

Why did this child, who correctly spelled a word whose spelling cannot be directly related to pronunciation, become hopelessly lost in the spelling of *hippopotamuses,* a word whose pronunciation *is* closely related to its spelling? With a disgusted "etc." she gave up on further listing of stuffed animals. The answer is that this child has watched horror and monster movies on television, and so has seen in print *Godzilla, Frankenstein,* and *Dracula.* Likewise, I doubt that we could find a teenage boy in a remedial reading class who could not read *Chrysler Imperial* and many other brand names. These students have had and are having experience with printed language every day.

SYNTACTIC AND SEMANTIC INFORMATION. Besides experience with print, a student brings an enormous knowledge of language to school. Part 3 indicated the areas of syntactic knowledge and described a few of the syntactic processes controlled by speakers of all languages and dialects. Part 1 showed the extremely early age at which speakers gain control of syntactic structures, and emphasized the place of whole language as meaningful communication in the life of a child. Slobin lists the varied syntactic structures that children from all cultures in the world use at the two-word stage of language acquisition. Bloom criticizes "pivot-open" grammar as unable to describe the many syntactic structures children are using at the same two-word stage; and some children begin this two-word stage at age fifteen months.

By the age of six, all children are very accomplished linguists. Why do we suddenly deprive them of a match between their truly huge syntactic knowledge and the syntactic structures in print? Our attempts to make reading easier by shortening sentences often make reading harder. Kenneth Goodman's article gives an excellent example of the child's greater ease with reading complete sentences, in comparing "Ride In" and "Stop and Go." Another example is, "Then she cooked the cake in the oven," read aloud to me as "Then she baked the cake in the oven." I have no doubt that the author used the more general term "cook" thinking it would be easier for the reader than "bake." The child, however, understood what was being said and used the normal word to fit the meaning.

Perhaps the major role of Kenneth Goodman's article in this section is to provide evidence that children use syntactic and semantic systems to read well. In syntax: why would a reader substitute a noun for a noun, a verb for a verb, and so on through the word classes, unless he was using syntactic and semantic knowledge?

In semantics, Kenneth Goodman brings up the fact that readers use their entire previous experience to interpret what they see. Lindberg and Smith discuss the role of students' background experience in reading. Though many vocabulary terms can and should be learned from context, some require previous experience, and a teacher has to prepare for these.

INTEREST, ENTERTAINMENT, AND LITERATURE. The topics of vocabulary and background bring up the question of interest in the material being read. Interests are extremely important in reading. Study of children's literature comes into play here: thorough knowledge of children's literature allows selection of tempting books for students of all ages. These books must connect with the readers' background in some way in order to be appealing. As Lindberg and Smith and Fader point out, however, the student need not know every word that appears in the book in order to be interested in its plot.

In order to learn what sort of literature may appeal to their students, teachers need to spend time in discussion groups of students, listening to them talk about their interests and their problems. Such talk is important to students' success, not just an entertaining waste of time; "talking" as opposed to "speaking" is discussed in the summary article for Part 1. This talking serves a particular purpose in relation to reading; it tells teachers what sort of books, magazines, or newspapers to make available to each student. A "nonreader" may turn himself into a reader by getting much-needed practice while reading to entertain himself or to follow up some interest in print. "Nonreaders" may never have been real nonreaders, in fact; they may have simply been uninterested in the material they were given to read.

**SUGGESTION II:** Language variation in dialects of American English probably is not great enough to interfere significantly with students' understanding of material written in "standard" English.

*Central Article:* Kenneth Goodman and Catherine Buck, "Dialect Barriers to Reading Comprehension Revisited"

*Supporting Evidence in Other Articles:*

Bailey: All readers are reading language different from that they speak. The spelling of English is so inconsistent that none of us reads "what is on the page."

Troike (Part 1): Children whose dialects contain "nonstandard" linguistic features have receptive as well as productive language abilities; they are usually able to comprehend "standard" dialectal features even if not producing them.

Dale, Williamson (Part 2): Speakers of Black English differ in a few language features from the dialects of others, but most of these are phonological differences which do not directly relate to meaning changes. Southern whites have several of the dialect features attributed to Black English, yet no one considers their dialects as interfering with reading.

## Implications for Teaching

This is a controversial area, and our information is not so complete as to be definitive. The issues are laid out in detail by Goodman and Buck and by Baratz. Most researchers probably would agree that children who differ in vocabulary and background experiences from those in reading primers will benefit from beginning with their own dictated material, i.e., with the language-experience method of teaching reading. There are numerous recent texts on applying language-experience methods to teaching students of many different backgrounds.

Two points should be carefully noted: most of the material on "nonstandard" dialects fails to make clear that these are not separate systems from "standard" dialects. As we stressed in Part 2 and again in Part 3, dialects overlap, being characterized only by the marginal features that are different from other dialects. Second, the marginal differences in rules that do exist should always be organized into phonological and syntactic differences, with syntax including morpheme differences. Phonological differences are not directly related to meaning. Of course, a number of phonological differences can pile up to make a dialect difficult to understand; but this difficulty usually disappears with exposure to the dialect, as discussed in the summary article for Part 2. Even syntactic differences may not significantly interfere with meaning. The syntactic differences among American dialects are usually few in number, and they can be explained to speakers of the dialects involved far more readily than they can be stamped out in their users' speech. Besides the difficulty of eliminating differing features, the psychological considerations discussed in Part 2 make this sort of eradication undesirable.

Finally, it must be admitted that our research on "nonstandard" dialects (those with some nonstandard features) has built upon itself, taking initial speculations as fact when more recent views better explain dialect phenomena. Students may be able to do a better job of describing the dialects in their own communities (as suggested in the summary article for Part 2) than can some text written for another community. Older students' studies, like those recommended in the summary article for Part 2, can be saved and verified by succeeding classes; and a large body of confirming information could even make these observations publishable in the community or state-wide press.

# Appendix

Phonemes (defined by Laird and by Fromkin and Rodman in Part 3) are usually enclosed in slashes, in contrast to phonetic segments (also defined by these writers in Part 3), which are enclosed in square brackets. Fromkin and Rodman use slashes both for phonemes and for "broad transcriptions," in which International Phonetic Alphabet (IPA) symbols are used but phonetic information is not given in exhaustive detail. Since there are disagreements among scholars as to the appropriate choice of symbols to represent the phonemes of American English, I have—unless otherwise noted—used the "broad transcription" notation in the editorial apparatus of this book. Both IPA symbols and the Trager-Smith phonemic alphabet (used in several articles reprinted in this book) are given here.

Phrase-structure rules used by Liles (Part 3) are also listed.

## PHONETIC AND PHONEMIC SYMBOLS

*Consonants*

| MANNER OF ARTICULATION | IPA SYMBOL | TRAGER-SMITH SYMBOL | EXAMPLE |
|---|---|---|---|
| Stops | [p] | /p/ | *p*at |
| | [b] | /b/ | *b*at |
| | [t] | /t/ | *t*ap |
| | [d] | /d/ | *d*ip |
| | [k] | /k/ | *k*it |
| | [g] | /g/ | *g*et |
| Nasals | [n] | /n/ | *n*et |
| | [m] | /m/ | *m*et |
| | [ŋ] | /ŋ/ | ra*ng* |
| Affricates | [tʃ] | /č/ | *ch*oke |
| | [dʒ] | /ǰ/ | *j*oke |
| Fricatives | [f] | /f/ | *f*it |
| | [v] | /v/ | *v*et |
| | [θ] | /θ/ | *th*in |
| | [ð] | /ð/ | *th*en |
| | [s] | /s/ | *s*it |
| | [z] | /z/ | *z*ip |
| | [ʃ] | /š/ | fi*ss*ion |
| | [ʒ] | /ž/ | vi*s*ion |
| Liquids | [l] | /l/ | *l*imb |
| | [r] | /r/ | *r*im |
| Glides | [j] | /y/ | *y*et |
| | [w] | /w/ | *w*et |
| | [h] | /h/ | *h*ate |

For a complete discussion of phonetic and phonemic alphabets, see chapters fifteen through seventeen, nineteen, and twenty in *An Introduction to Descriptive Linguistics* (New York: Holt, Rinehart and Winston, Inc., 1961), Revised Edition, by Henry A. Gleason.

*Vowels and Diphthongs*

| IPA<br>SYMBOL | TRAGER-SMITH<br>SYMBOL | EXAMPLE |
|---|---|---|
| [i] | /iy/ | b*ee*t |
| [ɪ] | /i/ | b*i*t |
| [e] | /ey/ | b*ai*t |
| [ɛ] | /e/ | b*e*t |
| [æ] | /æ/ | b*a*t |
| [ɨ] | /ɨ/ | p*i*tted |
| [ə] | /ə/ | b*u*t |
| [a] | /ah/ | h*a*lf<br>(in some eastern<br>dialects) |
| [u] | /uw/ | b*oo*t |
| [U] | /u/ | p*u*t |
| [o] | /o/ | h*o*tel |
| [ɔ] | /ɔ/ | b*ou*ght |
| [ɑ] | /ɑ/ | b*o*ttle |
| [ai] | /ay/ | f*i*ght |
| [au] | /aw/ | c*ow* |
| [ɔi] | /oy/ | b*oy* |

# PHRASE-STRUCTURE RULES USED BY LILES (PART 3)

P1: S → (SM) Nuc [1]

P2: Nuc → NP + VP

P3: VP → Aux + MV (manner) (place) (time) (reason)

P4: Aux → tense (M) (have + en) (be + ing)

P5: Tense → $\left\{ \begin{array}{l} \text{present} \\ \text{past} \end{array} \right\}$

P6: MV → $\left\{ \begin{array}{l} \text{be} \left\{ \begin{array}{l} \text{NP} \\ \text{AP} \\ \text{Place} \end{array} \right\} \\ \text{V (NP)} \end{array} \right\}$

P7: NP → (Det) N (Pl)

P8: AP → (Intens) Adj

---

[1] [Ed.'s note: *Nuc = nucleus; SM = sentence modifier; M = modal; AP = adjective phrase;* and *Intens = intensifier.*]